Theories of
Comparative Politics

SECOND EDITION

THEORIES OF COMPARATIVE POLITICS

The Search for a Paradigm Reconsidered

RONALD H. CHILCOTE

University of California, Riverside

WESTVIEW PRESS
Boulder • San Francisco • Oxford

Copyright © 1981, 1994 by Westview Press, Inc.

Published in 1994 in the United States of America by Westview Press, Inc., 5500 Central Avenue, Boulder, Colorado 80301-2877, and in the United Kingdom by Westview Press, 36 Lonsdale Road, Summertown, Oxford OX2 7EW

Library of Congress Cataloging-in-Publication Data
Chilcote, Ronald H.
   Theories of comparative politics : the search for a paradigm
reconsidered / Ronald H. Chilcote.—2nd ed.
      p.   cm.
   Includes bibliographical references (p.   ) and index.
   ISBN 0-8133-1016-4.—ISBN 0-8133-1017-2 (pbk.)
   1. Comparative government.   I. Title.
JF51.C44   1994
320.3—dc20   94-5751
                                                                                          CIP

Printed and bound in the United States of America

The paper used in this publication meets the requirements
of the American National Standard for Permanence of Paper
for Printed Library Materials Z39.48-1984.

10   9   8   7   6   5   4   3   2   1

To the professional colleagues who search for alternatives and take the risk of attempting to implement them

To the students who shaped this book, its content and direction, and from whom I have learned

Contents

PART 1   INTRODUCTION

PART 2   IDEOLOGY AND EPISTEMOLOGY

PART 3   THEORETICAL DIRECTIONS

Tables and Figures

Preface to the Second Edition

This revision of my critical survey of comparative politics was undertaken with some reluctance. In 1980, after many years of thinking through and writing the original manuscript, I was asked by one publisher to cut its length in half; another, prompted by an indignant reviewer, recommended eliminating all criticism of the field; finally, Lynne Rienner, then of Westview Press, overcame her concerns about length and graduate-level audience and moved forward with publication. After it appeared, some of my departmental colleagues initially rejected it as irresponsible in its criticism of political science, but they soon retreated with the appearance of reviews: The book was described in the *American Political Science Review* as "a very carefully written book ... an excellent overview of the development of comparative analysis over the last few decades as a systematic and comprehensive field of inquiry" and in *Journal of Politics* as "one of the most careful, provocative books in the field of political science, one that will be widely read and cited." The many years devoted to writing the original version were rewarded with the generous comments of academics and graduate students, especially those preparing for their doctoral exams, who made use of it. It was difficult returning to such an enterprise years after publication because my research had taken a turn toward more specific concerns; furthermore, my tendency is to look ahead rather than return to the past. When my publisher suggested that I undertake revision, I debated the possibility for a couple of years. During my visits to other universities, colleagues often insisted that the book not be revised even if it was partially outdated; thus, I have attempted to retain much of the original edition but to refine and update its content. At a recent conference, a distinguished colleague who used it as a text in a course suggested that an overview chapter be written to deal with changes in the field that have occurred during the decade since the first edition appeared. That suggestion has been partially incorporated into the new initial chapter along with other changes that should provide detail, referencing, and updating of issues and debates that give the book special relevance for the 1990s.

My agreement to prepare a new edition was conditioned on the writing of another book, a sequel that would carry the reader into the ideas that promise to dominate our attention in the decade ahead and into the next century. The sequel, *Comparative Political Economy* (forthcoming), builds on the proposition set forth in the final chapter of this book: that the study of politics and economics has evolved usefully into political economy. It was my desire ten years ago to write such a book, but I also needed to explore new ideas in a proliferating literature, and eventually I settled on five themes that dominate the current literature on political economy and should absorb our attention well into the 1990s: theories of transition, class, state, imperialism, and democracy.

Thus, this revised edition has involved a revisit with the central problem of searching for a paradigm to guide us in comparative political inquiry. That task includes an introductory chapter that assesses my framework and views that appeared when the book was originally published. I provide a retrospective self-criticism of my perspectives of the field a decade ago. I review my organization and content, the emphasis on theoretical trends, and the state of the discipline and comparative politics. For example, I acknowledge the emerging literature of the past decade on a politics of gender, feminism, and women; I do likewise with the rise of ecological and other social movements and popular groups that have influenced comparative politics everywhere. Ten years ago public choice and rational choice became theoretical concerns in the political science literature. Formal models, including rational Marxist choice and individual choice theories, have since made an impact.

At the same time, in order to balance new with old writing and to keep this revision within manageable length, I have eliminated much of the biographical material on Karl Marx and Max Weber in Chapter 4, reduced drastically the synthesis of ideas and writings drawn from David Easton and Gabriel Almond in Chapter 5, and cut substantial portions of Chapter 6 on culture theory. The reader is encouraged to return to the first edition to find the excised material because of its importance in understanding these historical trends in comparative politics.

When the book began to take shape about fifteen years ago, I was committed to a clarification and an understanding of concepts and theory. The traditional focus on system, culture, and development was incorporated, yet those terms were utilized less as central orienting concepts than as central thrusts around which the literature of the field tended to cluster. I added the literature of elites and masses, with attention to theories of class and class struggle. As intended in its original conception, the first edition moved toward an understanding of the whole rather than a microscopic examination of the parts, a holistic orientation related to my desire that the comparative study of politics be integrated with the study of societal phenomena other than politics. I was also interested in economic matters, as emphasized in the final chapter on political economy. Thus the book built upon theoretical foundations and attempted to relate the problems and actions of contemporary society. The enterprise also added a new dimension often neglected in the study of politics: the early thought that shaped the study of nineteenth- and twentieth-century politics.

The final phase of this undertaking has involved the updating of the first edition, the reorganizing of the introductory overview chapter, considerable revision of the chapters in the second part, the deletion of some referencing no longer of historical importance, and the enhancing of the text with some relevant ideas and

PART ONE

Introduction

1

Comparative Inquiry

This initial chapter briefly examines comparative politics as a field in the study of politics and political science. I look at issues of theory in comparative inquiry, I describe the evolution of the field in five theoretical directions, and I identify the objectives of this book.

In addition, I have included two appendixes that relate to this chapter; both appear at the end of the book. The first attempts to clarify the terms employed in the mainstream of comparative politics, since the terminology of the field generally is used loosely and inconsistently in the literature. The other surveys the general literature of comparative politics.

Issues of Theory and Comparative Inquiry

The study of comparative politics has evoked much confusion for student and scholar alike. A variety of terms is used loosely and interchangeably in the comparative study of politics. *Comparative government,* for example, usually refers to the study of institutions and functions of countries or nation-states in Europe, with attention to their executives, legislatures, and judiciaries, as well as such supplementary organizations as political parties and pressure groups. *Comparative politics,* in contrast, studies a broader range of political activity, including governments and their institutions as well as other forms of organizations not directly related to national government—for example, tribes, communities, associations, unions.

Political science and comparative politics relate both to theory and to method. *Theory* refers to sets of systematically related generalizations, and *method* is a procedure or process that involves the techniques and tools utilized in inquiry and for examining, testing, and evaluating theory. *Methodology* consists of methods, procedures, working concepts, rules, and the like used for testing theory and guiding inquiry, and the search for solutions to problems of the real world. Methodology is a particular way of viewing, organizing, and giving shape to inquiry.

Confusion arises over these terms because the comparative study of government often refers to the study of foreign governments, and comparative politics is utilized in the search for comparisons in the study of all forms of political activity—governmental as well as nongovernmental. Thus, the comparative politics specialist tends to view comparative politics as the study of everything political. Any lesser conception of comparative politics would obscure criteria for the selection and exclusion of what the field might study.

One might also explore the relationship of politics and comparative politics to other fields, as I do in Chapter 3. I note that both theory and method owe a great deal to the "classical" political philosophers Aristotle and Plato, Machiavelli and Montesquieu, and Hegel, Marx, and Mill. Comparative politics is also indebted to the early twentieth-century contributions of Woodrow Wilson, James Bryce, and Carl Friedrich, whose attention was directed toward the formal study of government and state. I also show that work in related fields has shaped comparative political inquiry, notably the work of A. R. Radcliffe-Brown and Bronislaw Malinowski in anthropology, Gaetano Mosca, Vilfredo Pareto, Max Weber, and Emile Durkheim in sociology and political sociology, and John M. Keynes, Karl Marx, and V. I. Lenin in economics and political economy. Finally I suggest that attention should be directed toward political economy.

The movement toward the study of all political phenomena and the need to draw upon the theories and methods of other disciplines gave to comparative politics an all-encompassing orientation. The Second World War heightened interest among scholars in the study of foreign systems, especially systems in Europe and Asia. The decline of empires after the war and the turmoil of independence in the Third World influenced scholars to turn their attention from the established to the new nations. The consequences for comparative politics were substantial. According to Braibanti (1968), there was an acceleration of research on the new nations, prompted by research technology and the funding by and interests of foundations and government, which exacted from scholars the knowledge needed to guide programs in foreign aid. Additionally, a fragmentation of case materials was the result of problems related to method in the gathering of data, to research terminology that has not been standardized, and to the rapid proliferation of new nations in which research conditions are uncertain and the cumulation of knowledge is uneven. There was also an expansion of the sphere of politics so as to allow the examination of politics as a total system, on the one hand, and as an analysis of individual behavior, on the other. Finally, there was a tendency toward model building, including highly imperfect and transitory devices, and classificatory schemes easily divorced from reality and undermined by unreliable and tentative data.

Given these trends, still another problem faces the students of comparative politics, that of value-free investigation. For the study of political behavior, many political scientists emphasize attention to explicit assumptions and to systematic, quantitative, and cumulative investigation. Investigators assume the role of objective social scientists, separating themselves from the role of active citizens. Despite the pretensions of such political scientists, however, there is now a widespread understanding that values enter into all investigations of politics. Christian Bay (1965), for example, argued that work that pretends to be neutral is actually imbued with real value biases and indeed is both conservative and antipolitical. These concerns are supported in other assessments as well (McCoy and Playford 1967; Myrdal 1969). Searing (1970) delved into the problem and concluded that value judgments enter six stages of research but do not necessarily bias consequences. In the first two stages, problem selection and concept formation, value decisions are significant but do not always bias research. The intrusion of value judgments into the stages of data selection, interpretation, and theory construction can result in bias. Searing admitted too that value choices represent a problem for the last stage, verification.

The above stages suggest a systematic method of procedure for social science investigation. That method may be construed as emulating the work of the natural scientists, who look for regularities in the abstractions that they select from the nonhuman world. Thus, social science might simply borrow the theories and rules of natural science to study the human world. But a stress on regularity will certainly obscure any recognition of irregularity. Values, beliefs, and personal interests might intrude upon the scientific enterprise, and in the end little understanding will be gained. Such has been the concern of many people interested in comparative politics.

All these problems relate to the search for theory and method in comparative politics. The reader may be interested in background reading and understanding in this search for theory and method, so I turn briefly to a summary of some of the major work that has influenced comparative politics.

Past Influences

More than a century ago Edward A. Freeman (1873) optimistically manifested his belief that comparative politics offered promise for the discovery of universal laws through global investigation. Often it is maintained that we have established no basic universal laws or principles, although well into the past there were social scientists who were conscious of theoretical and methodological problems.

Two people who wrote about such problems were Max Weber in *The Methodology of the Social Sciences* (1949) and Emile Durkheim in *The Rules of Sociological Method* (1938). Weber focused on the meaning of value judgment and neutrality in sociology and economics, examined the implications of objectivity in social science, and examined the methodological views of scholars of his time. Durkheim attempted to describe and define the method used in the study of social facts; at the same time he acknowledged that among his predecessors, Herbert Spencer had devoted no attention to the problem of method, and John Stuart Mill had dealt with the question at great length, but only by synthesizing what Auguste Comte had set forth in his earlier work. Durkheim suggested rules for the observation of social facts, for classifying social types, for explaining social facts, and for establishing sociological proofs. Durkheim believed that his method separated social science and especially sociology from philosophy, as well as from positivistic, evolutionary, and idealistic orientations that had pervaded social science through successive periods.

Unlike Weber and Durkheim, Karl Marx did not prepare a manual on theory and method, but those concerns are apparent throughout his writings. Marx was a comparative analyst who focused on the monarchies of Europe but also extended his discussions elsewhere, most notably Asia. Marx would probably explain contemporary social science understandings of society in equilibrium as the consequence of actions of a ruling class. That class enforces rules and norms that legitimize the relations of production, which arise from particular means and forces of production. Those means and forces may become outmoded as change and equilibrium become dialectical parts of a single process. I shall elaborate later (Chapter 4) on the contributions of Marx and demonstrate that his theory and methodology tend to run counter to the dominant tendencies of the contemporary literature of comparative politics.

Theoretical and methodological problems of comparative politics were of concern to Maurice Duverger (1964), who offered an introduction that is useful to the reader. First, he explored the idea of social science, tracing the historical development of the social sciences. Second, he described and discussed the techniques of observation, relating to written documents, and statistics as well as questionnaire methods and interviews. Third, he examined the use of theory and hypotheses as well as classifications and conceptualization in research. Supplementing Duverger but delving into the ramifications of inquiry is work by Frohock (1967), who examined the implications and issues of theory and the scientific method. Scientific method was assessed in terms of the search for paradigms, and the work of Max Weber was introduced as one basis for contemporary social science.

Other writers have concentrated on methods that are helpful in comparative inquiry. For example, Howard Scarrow (1969) offered a brief introduction to the methods of comparative analysis, and Holt and Turner (1970) and Przeworski and Teune (1970) explored more deeply the subject of political inquiry. Galtung (1967) also looked critically at theory and method.

Outline of This Study

I have established the need for a new overview of comparative politics and have examined some general issues of theory and comparative inquiry. At the end of this book, Appendix 1 offers definitions that facilitate a clarity and an understanding of the terminology of political science and comparative politics; I also identify some prominent methods and techniques for comparative political inquiry. Appendix 2 traces the evolution of ideas that have influenced comparative inquiry since 1980, identifies the basic introductory literature of the field, and refers to recent important comparative works that make use of a macro theoretical approach in their attention to one or more national political systems or countries.

Since 1953 the major theoretical trends in the comparative field have tended to cluster into five general areas: state theories, culture theories, developmental theories, class theories, and theories of political economy. Each of these areas is the focus of a chapter in this book; the concluding chapter serves not only to show the importance of political economy to political science and comparative politics but also to introduce an extensive analysis and critical literature review that appears in my forthcoming sequel, *Comparative Political Economy*. It is instructive to identify briefly the major contributions that shaped and allowed each area to become a central thrust in the field of comparative politics.

State and Systems Theories

The impact of the systems literature on comparative politics first became evident during the early 1950s. Three writers are representative of trends in systems theory, and all three utilized the political system as a macro unit in comparative analysis. David Easton in *The Political System* (1953) and other works set forth the concept of the political system together with its inputs and outputs, demands and supports, and feedback. The basis of his conceptualization of system is contained in a well-known essay published in 1957. Gabriel Almond was influenced by the functionalist anthropologists Bronislaw Malinowski and A. R. Radcliffe-Brown as well as by the sociologists Max Weber and Talcott Parsons. Almond was also influenced by work on group theory, such as that of David Truman. Almond first offered a simplistic classification of political systems in *Journal of Politics* in 1956; he included systems in non-Western and newly independent nations. He then set forth categories of structure and function, relating them to all systems in the introduction to *Politics of the Developing Areas*. Later he related his conception of system to culture and development. Finally, Karl Deutsch in *Nerves of Government* drew heavily upon the cybernetic theory of Norbert Wiener in postulating a systemic model of politics.

Almond and other comparativists convincingly argued in the late 1950s that the notion of the state had long been obscured by a multitude of conceptualizations and should be replaced by the political system, which was adaptable to scientific inquiry in the emerging age of computers. Easton undertook to construct the parameters and concepts of a political system, though he recognized that political science owed its existence to the traditional emphasis on the state. These two political scientists insisted well into the 1980s on the importance of political system as the core of political study.

Mainstream attention to the state was not ignored altogether, however, as the emergence of military regimes in Argentina, Brazil, and elsewhere in Latin America during the 1960s and 1970s prompted a retrospective interpretation of state corporatism as it had emerged earlier in Europe, in particular in Spain and Portugal. This led to new understandings of corporatism elsewhere and a contrasting between traditional and societal corporatism, as in the work of Philippe Schmitter and Howard Wiarda. The persistence of dictatorship was interpreted along lines of the bureaucratic authoritarian model of Guillermo O'Donnell, who looked primarily to Argentina for his example. Alternative work also appeared with the publication of Ralph Miliband's *The State in Capitalist Society* (1969) and Nicos Poulantzas's *State, Power, Socialism* (1978), and political sociologists Peter Evans, Theda Skocpol, and others argued for more attention to the question of the state in their *Bringing the State Back In* (1985), signifying that despite the objections of Almond and Easton, the comparative mainstream had come full circle and re-stored a focus on the state to its important place in the study of politics. These studies tended to shift from a focus on the national political system to state and government and their role and impact on capitalist development. Mainstream political scientists emphasized bureaucracy and policy implementation in adapt-ing to the terminology of state, and although economic issues were recognized in their analysis, they generally cast their perspectives in a traditional institutional framework in which executive, legislative, and judicial actions are dominant within the state, and political party, interest group, and individual actions prevail in the civil society.

Culture Theories

The cultural thrust in comparative politics, conspicuously prominent during the 1960s, emanated from traditional work on culture in anthropology, socialization and small group studies in sociology, and personality studies in psychology. The concept of political culture was related to nations or national cultures. In this sense political culture represented a sort of recasting of the older notions of na-tional character. Political culture related to systems as well. Political culture con-sisted of beliefs, symbols, and values that define situations in which political ac-tion occurs. Types of political culture characterized systems; for example, parochial, subject, and participant political cultures. These types of political cul-tures reflected the psychological and subjective orientations of people toward their national system. The pioneer comparative effort to construct a theory of po-litical culture was Gabriel Almond and Sidney Verba's *Civic Culture*, which was based on a survey of the attitude of citizens toward their nation in the United States, Great Britain, Germany, France, Italy, and Mexico. Inherent in this study was the proposition, set forth earlier in the work of Almond, that the ideal politi-cal or civic culture could be found in an Anglo-American model of politics. Lucian Pye and Sidney Verba elaborated on the theory and brought together es-says by prominent specialists in the field in *Political Culture and Political Develop-ment*. Although there have been efforts to relate political culture to the politics of specific nations—such as Pye's *Politics, Personality, and Nation Building: Burma's Search for Identity*—generally the literature has been divided into two subareas: political socialization and communications. Edited volumes by James S.

Coleman, *Education and Political Development,* and by Pye, *Communications and Political Development,* reflect the work in these areas.

During the 1970s political scientists moved from general studies of political culture to more specific inquiry on political socialization and the shaping of political attitudes through such agencies as family, school, and work place. They also emphasized the study of public opinion, the role of mass media, and communications in general as reflections of the general political culture. During the 1980s the emphasis shifted to studies of individual choice, with attention to political parties, public opinion, and electoral politics. Attention to rational and individual choice permeated the non-Marxist efforts of Ronald Inglehart in analysis of the survey data of the Eurobarometer collection on Western Europe, while a Marxist perspective was associated with the empirical and quantitative efforts of Adam Przeworski.

Although the concept political culture was often criticized for abstract idealizations, it was not only recycled in later literature but also became part of the discourse of intellectuals everywhere. Michael Thompson, Richard Ellis, and Aaron Wildavsky in *Cultural Theory* (1990) did very well in recounting the contributions of major thinkers from Montesquieu and Comte to Durkheim, Marx, and Weber in arguing that cultures are plural, not singular, and presenting a multivaried conception of political culture and its implications.

Because cultural characteristics tend to reflect the conservation of values, attitudes, and norms, political cultural studies inevitably emphasized stability and patterns of continuity in political life. Research questioning this approach and concerned more with the prospects for societal change, however, could utilize the approach to study how power holders maintain control or how indigenous peoples oppose outside penetration—for example, the cultural resistance of Africans in Mozambique or Angola to the commercialization and colonization schemes of the Portuguese during the colonial period. The notion of culture also was incorporated into the idea of the new man or person, the selfless and sacrificing individual who was willing to work for the betterment of socialist society. Cultural influences were of importance in the role of family and capitalism; an example was the analysis by Eli Zaretsky in *Capitalism, Family, and Social Life* (1986).

Developmental Theories

The concern with development was prompted by the emergence of many new states in the Third World. Almond and others in *Politics of the Developing Areas* directed attention to backward areas that promised to develop, and he found it necessary to tie his ideas about the nature of the political system and about political culture to development. The result was a journal article in *World Politics* in 1965 and a book with G. Bingham Powell, *Comparative Politics: A Developmental Approach.* In that work Almond more consciously began to work out a model of concepts and stages that would characterize development. The volume commissioned by the Social Science Research Council's (SSRC's) Committee on Comparative Politics (1963 to present) also place an emphasis upon comparative developmental theory.

The mainstream literature on development actually falls into at least five categories. The first, represented by Almond and others, attempts to utilize traditional notions of democracy and political development and to recast them into more sophisticated, sometimes abstract, terminology. A stage theory of development is depicted in A.F.K. Organski's *The Stages of Political Development,* a work modeled after that of the economist Walt Rostow. These conceptions of political development, however, rest heavily upon the Anglo-American experiences in politics. Studies in the second category focus on conceptions of nation building. These studies attempt to combine old notions of nationalism, those of Hans Kohn for example, with new interpretations of development. Karl Deutsch's *Nationalism and Social Communication* is an excellent example of this combination, and Rupert Emerson's *From Empire to Nation* and Kalman Silvert's *Expectant Peoples: Nationalism and Development* are examples of works that apply to nationalism and development, respectively, to the areas of Africa and Latin America.

Modernization is the focus of a third category of studies on development. Examples of this type of literature include Marion J. Levy's *Modernization and the Structure of Societies,* an ambitious effort to apply structural-functionalism to a theory of modernization, and David Apter's *The Politics of Modernization,* a provocative attempt at model building. A fourth category comprises studies of change, a prominent example being Samuel P. Huntington's *Political Order in Changing Societies.* The fifth category includes works critical of ethnocentric theories of development, such as those mentioned above.

Criticism of these approaches emphasized their ethnocentrism and failure to address the lack of development in backward nations; instead the theories concentrated on solutions through the diffusion of capitalism and technology from the advanced to the less developed nations. Theorists focused on the Third World in order to work out a theory of underdevelopment. The idea that the diffusion of capitalism promotes underdevelopment and not development in many parts of the world was embodied in André Gunder Frank's *Capitalism and Underdevelopment in Latin America* (1967), Walter Rodney's *How Europe Underdeveloped Africa* (1972), and Malcolm Caldwell's *The Wealth of Some Nations* (1979). Theotônio dos Santos worked out the idea of the "new dependency" to explain the traditional relationship of nations in these areas to the advanced capitalist countries, especially the United States; this form of dependency was especially characteristic of the multinational firms in the period after the Second World War. A variation of this theme appeared in Ruy Mauro Marini's notion of "subimperialism," a situation in which some Third World countries could serve as intermediaries for imperialist nations in the exploitation of other countries. Finally, Fernando Henrique Cardoso advocated the idea of associated dependent development, whereby some capitalist growth was possible in dependent countries. These ideas appeared as radical alternatives to the North American literature on development, but they eventually became absorbed into the mainstream of political science, despite the objections of Almond, Huntington, and some other comparativists who responded to criticism that had largely discredited their earlier theories.

Class Theories

Sometime during the mid-1960s, the SSRC's Committee on Comparative Politics decided to direct attention to studies of elites. During the 1950s Floyd Hunter and C. Wright Mills had concerned themselves with questions of power and who rules, but their work was attacked by Robert A. Dahl and others who relied on a pluralistic conception of politics. Weaknesses in a generation of community studies by political sociologists were exposed, and U.S. political scientists turned to the new field of urban politics. Comparative political scientists, however, tended not to be distracted altogether by the pluralist-elitist debates of the early 1960s. The rise of charismatic figures such as Fidel Castro and Kwame Nkrumah dramatized the need to study political leaders of the Third World. Then too, the failure of the parliamentary institutions to provide stability in the nations of Asia, Africa, and Latin America prompted the study of elites. Elite theory, however, moved in several directions, somewhat influenced by the earlier work of Marx, Mosca, and Pareto. In the tradition of C. Wright Mills and G. William Domhoff, some theorists focused on power structure alone, ignoring mass behavior. Other theorists pursued study along the lines of stratification analysis, outlined by sociologists, and Marxists turned to questions of class struggle and an analysis of a ruling bourgeois class and a proletariat.

Comparativists moved in at least two directions. One tendency looked at masses in many nations, examples being Alex Inkeles and David Smith in *Becoming Modern* (1974) and Sidney Verba, Norman Nie, and Jae-on Kim in *Participation and Political Equality* (1978). Both endeavors emphasized the role of the individual rather than the elite, the former study being especially interested in how the relationship of the individual to the means of production determines his or her consciousness and the latter study delving into the extent to which a participant population is representative of a whole population. Another tendency turned to questions of class struggle and an analysis of particular social classes in an effort to formulate theory.

Theories of class stemmed from a number of traditions, including the attention to circulation of elites, evident in Vilfredo Pareto's *Sociological Writings* (1966); the idea of a governing class in Gaetano Mosca's *The Ruling Class* (1939); and the concern with ruling class in various works of Marx. Among significant efforts to build on a Marxist approach were studies by Nicos Poulantzas in *Political Power and Social Classes* (1973), who emphasized the expanding role of the "new petty bourgeoisie" or service sector, and Erik Olin Wright in *Class, Crisis and the State* (1980) and *Classes* (1985), who called this group the "new middle class." Among the criticisms of this literature were the attention on power structure behavior; emphasis on stratification studies without examination of the economic, especially capitalist, basis of class; and undue stress on working class as agency in changing conditions of capitalism and socialism when in fact other popular forces (ecological, feminist, pacifist, and so on) had emerged to push for reforms and changes.

Political Economy Theories

Political economy was a particular concern of nineteenth-century thinkers Adam Smith and David Ricardo as well as Marx who criticized them. Evolving from their debates were bourgeois and radical theories with concepts like state, class, and ideology used to analyze politics and like mode, relations, forces, and means of production to comprehend economics. The classical writers of political economy employed all these concepts in their writings, and their successors drew upon them in the evolving phases of theoretical development from classical liberalism, utopian socialism, neoclassicalism, and Keynesianism and post-Keynesianism, to neo-Marxism.

The emphasis on political economy at the end of Chapter 9 suggests a division of labor between international and comparative political economy, with attention to theories of imperialism, dependency and underdevelopment, state, and class. This distinction is suggested as a means of sorting out how political science might be organized around the focus of political economy. The sequel to this volume, however, will stress comparative political economy, embracing all these and other themes, on the assumption that comparative politics assimilates all major questions of politics and the study of politics cannot be isolated from social and economic questions.

*   *   *

The critical examination of these areas of theory is a principal concern of this book. The curious reader, however, may wish to examine the more general references to the field. Thus the "Survey of the General Literature of Comparative Politics Since 1980" classifies materials into general overviews, cross-national studies, comparative series, and area and configurative studies (see Appendix 2). The remainder of the volume delves more deeply into the field. Ideological tendencies are noted in an exposure of the contradictions in politics and the profession as well as the profession's ties to government and business. Chapter 3 focuses on the search for a paradigm in comparative analysis and probes into the historical roots and fundamental premises of positivist and historicist thought that have dominated the field. Chapter 4 turns to the life, thought, and writing of both Karl Marx and Max Weber, two precursors of contemporary theorists whose influence has been substantial. Chapters 5, 6, 7, and 8 deal with the theoretical areas noted above—systemic, cultural, developmental, and class theories. A critical synthesis of the trends in each of these areas is combined with an attempt to identify paradigmatic influences and conflicting understandings and explanations of politics.

The central chapters synthesize trends and assess the literature of comparative politics, and each chapter carefully distinguishes dichotomies of paradigmatic influences. Chapter 5 identifies two major strands of systems theory in its abstract and neutral form: the organic framework of David Easton and the structural-functional approach of Gabriel Almond. Although it may be argued that these approaches are outmoded today, I believe they remain influential within political science. It is abundantly clear, however, that attention to the state—to its forms, policies, and impact on society—has dominated the attention of comparativists, not only in the early years of the field but in recent years. During the 1960s and 1970s both mainstream and alternative theories of the state challenged the systems theories, and by the 1980s these theories were dominant. Chapter 6 originally emphasized the now discredited early mainstream theory of political culture, but in its revised form incorporates self-criticisms of the notion of civic culture and demonstrates that cultural theory, in both mainstream and alternative approaches, remains ever influential. Chapter 7 retains the original dichotomy between mainstream and alternative theories of development and underdevelopment, but now shows how capitalist development and concerns with modernization, nationalism, and democracy can be juxtaposed to socialist development and perspectives of underdevelopment, dependency, and imperialism. It also shows how comparative politics has returned to the once discredited theories of development and modernization and how alternative theories have been assimilated into the mainstream of the field. Chapter 8 examines the group as an interest seeking a share of power and recognition, on one hand, and social class as a struggling force within capitalist society, on the other. It also extends the original concern with various theories of class, but identifies certain theoretical endeavors since about 1980. The final chapter argues for the reconstitution of comparative politics within a framework of political economy. To aid the student, most literature referred to in the text is listed, with annotation, at the end of each chapter, although several well-known sources are merely in the text and identified by author, book title, and date of publication.

Into the 1990s:
Assessment of Old and New Directions

The themes of this revised edition incorporate the general framework of the original published a decade ago. The concluding section of this chapter examines these themes as a means of demonstrating that I then accurately portrayed from where comparative politics had evolved and where it was headed and of advancing the proposition that continuity rather than substantial change reflected the evolution of comparative political theory.

My characterization of the field in 1980 generally followed the lines of inquiry pursued by the Committee on Comparative Politics under the aegis of the SSRC and its chairman, Gabriel Almond. Their interests evolved from a focus on political system to political culture to political development to elites and masses. I traced this history of the field and suggested that these themes appropriately con-

stituted four interrelated subfields in comparative politics. I suggested alternatives to the mainstream paradigm of thinking that had become embedded in political science and comparative politics; my intent was to encourage students to
consider a variety of interpretations, approaches, methods, and analyses and to
build their own frames of reference through constructive and critical examination
of the field. My emphasis on a foundation of theory was clearly appropriate, as attested in the scholarship of many young academics who combined theory with a
case study of one or more situations in their doctoral dissertations and published
monographs. Consequently, the level of scholarship has advanced considerably,
and our understanding of comparative politics has been enhanced less by general
grand theorizing and superficial frameworks than by in-depth case studies based
on theory and empirical inquiry. These studies usually have involved field work,
archival investigation, and in-depth interviewing. Further, a number of important historically grounded but interpretive comparative studies have appeared, in
the tradition of Barrington Moore's *Social Origins of Dictatorship and Democracy*
(1966) and Theda Skocpol's *States and Social Revolutions* (1979). A small group of
scholars carries on with this tradition today, their work drawn from syntheses of
scholarly monographs. Finally, there has also been a proliferation of European
studies based on public opinion survey data; for example, Ronald Inglehart and
Russell Dalton in their work have analyzed information available through data
banks such as the Eurobarometer surveys.

When I completed my manuscript in 1980, I was satisfied with a comprehensive
survey and synthesis on comparative politics, written with respect for the contributions of the past but infused with a critical overview of successes and failures.
The review of basic terminology at the outset (now Appendix 2) was intended to
clarify the meaning of mainstream concepts. The focus on the politics and ideological roots of political science and comparative politics was but a reflection of
much of the dissatisfaction with the field and was designed to stimulate alternative thinking. I believed (and still believe) that neither an end of ideology nor a
postindustrial revolution could accurately characterize the contemporary setting.
The sketch of the origins and evolution of comparative politics attempted to contrast varying lines of inquiry and understanding. The comparison of the theories
and ideas of two early thinkers, Marx and Weber, demonstrated similarities and
differences in their approaches and methods as well as argued for the need to return to their primary writings rather than rely on interpretative secondary works.
Their contributions to contemporary social science were substantial and significant, though my attention to their work was not intended to slight other useful
precursor or contemporary thinkers.

My focus on theories of the political system was a recognition of the powerful
influences of these theories on political science and comparative politics since the
1950s, whereas my attention to theories of the state attempted to give historical
context and to demonstrate that the roots of the discipline were traceable not only
to Aristotle and Plato but also to Montesquieu, Machiavelli, Hegel, Marx, and a
host of other thinkers who directed attention to the state. This focus among

mainstream and radical political scientists during the 1980s has further legitimized our continuing interest in this theme. My critical review of political culture
theories exposed the superficiality and limitations of most general studies and
was a reflection of the decline in such theories about 1980. Although I anticipated
that empirical work on socialization and public opinion would continue to be influential, I anticipated neither the revival of interest in political culture nor the
widespread reference to this theme by both mainstream and progressive scholars.
My juxtaposition of mainstream developmental approaches such as modernization with prevailing opposing approaches focused on underdevelopment, dependency, and imperialism partially anticipated the amalgamation of many of the
progressive ideas into the mainstream of the field, but it did not account for a re-
cycling and regeneration of interest in theories of modernization. There were also
many new developmental theories introduced during the 1980s that I have incorporated in this revised edition. My attention to theories of class was justified by a
plethora of studies on class during the late 1970s and early 1980s, and indeed interest continues today in this theme. However, the decline of the state-dominated
and command economy societies in Eastern Europe and the former Soviet Union
has been accompanied by a retreat from class as a concept and a return to interest
groups and institutional forces that have traditionally captivated the thinking of
North American political scientists and their interest in pluralism and social
democracy. The present text argues that comparative inquiry must analyze both
class and institutional forces.

The first edition terminated with a plea for a focus on political economy as the
core of comparative inquiry, and this edition continues with that emphasis. It is
also apparent that comparative political scientists need to direct attention to
themes that emerged in the 1980s that now are incorporated in the book: the gender question, feminism, and women's studies; the role of ecological and environmental groups, pacifists, and greens; questions of choice (public, rational, and rational Marxist); questions of democracy as related both to capitalism and
socialism; the role of capitalism in development and the rise and decline of the
United States in the international political economy. The decade of the 1980s also
reminded us of the influence of Antonio Gramsci in political science and the
study of comparative politics.

In sum, comparative politics is not a settled field, and old and new ideas continue to impact on its evolution. This diversity not only permits controversy and
debate but also keeps open a rich dialogue on issues and permits both scholar and
student to delve into previously unexplored questions or to challenge and recon-
sider established assumptions about a rapidly changing and evolving world.

References

Bay, Christian. 1965. "Politics and Pseudopolitics." *American Political Science Review* LIX
(March), 39–51. Argues that political behavior work fails to make clear its real value
biases, that it is not neutral, but that instead it is conservative and antipolitical.

Braibanti, Ralph. 1968. "Comparative Political Analytics Reconsidered." *Journal of Politics* 30 (February), 25–65. A review of trends in comparative politics up to 1966 with attention to four major problems: the relationship of configurative analysis to comparability; the relation between functional and institutional analysis; the relation of new political systems to established ones and the reliance upon scientific method; and the rapid and uneven expansion of comparative political analysis.

Durkheim, Emile. 1938. *The Rules of Sociological Method.* Translated by Sarah A. Solovay and John H. Mueller and edited by George E.G. Catlin. Chicago: University of Chicago Press. An effort to move beyond such predecessors as Comte, Spencer, and Mill by setting forth a manual on method. The author distinguishes his methods from natural science as well as from philosophy.

Duverger, Maurice. 1964. *An Introduction to the Social Sciences with Special Reference to Their Methods.* Translated by Malcolm Anderson. New York: Frederick A. Praeger. An introductory section on the nature of social science is followed by a section on techniques of observation and another section on systematic analysis, including discussion on the comparative method.

Freeman, Edward A. 1873. *Comparative Politics.* London: Macmillan. Offers the promise of discovering universal laws through global and longitudinal comparisons.

Frohock, Fred M. 1967. *The Nature of Political Inquiry.* Homewood, Illinois: Dorsey Press. Focuses on topics relating to theory, function, and causality in social science, science and social analysis, facts and values, and political inquiry.

Galtung, Johan. 1967. *Theory and Methods of Social Research.* New York: Columbia University Press. Examination of strengths and weaknesses in social science methodology. Attempts to integrate "widely scattered approaches in data collection, data processing, data analysis, and theory formation."

Holt, Robert T., and John E. Turner (eds.). 1970. *The Methodology of Comparative Research.* New York: Free Press. Essays on methodology by Holt and Turner, Holt and Richardson, Riggs, La Palombara, Apter, Frey, and others.

McCoy, Charles A., and John Playford (eds.). 1967. *Apolitical Politics: A Critique of Behaviorism.* New York: Thomas Y. Crowell. Previously published essays are brought together to focus on the conservative implications and bias of behavioral studies, on the behaviorist perception that mass democracy and mass movements may be unmanageable and chaotic, and on the antipolitical orientation of the behaviorists. Included are essays by Bay, Kim, Schwartz, Petras, Gitlin, Bachrach, Baratz, and others.

Myrdal, Gunnar. 1969. *Objectivity in Social Science.* New York: Pantheon Books. A critical look at values, beliefs, and opinions and a recognition that these are opportunistically injected into theory and research.

Przeworski, Adam, and Henry Teune. 1970. *The Logic of Comparative Social Inquiry.* New York: Wiley-Interscience. Concerned with the methodology of comparative inquiry, this volume is divided into two parts: theory and measurement. There are no case studies, only illustrative country citations. Topics include explanations in social science, research design, levels of system analysis, cross-national theory, conceptualization.

Scarrow, Howard A. 1969. *Comparative Political Analysis: An Introduction.* New York: Harper and Row Publishers. Brief introduction to methodological aspects of comparative political analysis. Examines description through classification, typologies, rankings, and surveys; sociological perspectives; problems of explanation; problems of evidence; explanatory modes; and descriptive focus and explanatory factors.

Searing, Donald D. 1970. "Values in Empirical Research: A Behaviorist Response." *Midwest Journal of Political Science* 14 (February), 71–104. Attempts to distinguish between value bias and value choices and their effect upon six stages of research, from problem selection to verification. Argues that value-free research is impossible but that rigorous attention to methodology can eliminate bias, even though the value choices may have significant consequences for research and application of research results to political life.

Weber, Max. 1949. *The Methodology of the Social Sciences.* Translated and edited by Edward A. Shils and Henry A. Finch. New York: Free Press. Essays by Weber written between 1903 and 1917 that attempt to clarify problems of theory and methodology encountered in actual research.

PART TWO

Ideology and Epistemology

2

Ideology and Issues of Comparative Politics

A new revolution is under way in American political science. … Its battle cries are relevance and action. Its objects of criticism are the disciplines, the professions, and the universities.

—David Easton, presidential address to the
American Political Science Association, September 1969

The dissenting view draws no great number of adherents in the American political science profession. But many of us are aware that some of our students, including many of the brightest, are exploring it independent of our tutelage.

—Charles E. Lindblom, presidential address to the
American Political Science Association, September 1981

Historically, scholars and students of comparative politics have expressed dissatisfaction with the field, the discipline, and the profession. One hears or reads about the malaise that pervades political science and comparative politics. The discipline, it is argued, is notorious for its conservatism and has been avoided by activists concerned with policy changes. Further, the flaws of the discipline are intimately related to the U.S. political system, which it seeks ethnocentrically to describe. Illusions of democracy in the United States were shaken not only by events in Vietnam but by the Watergate crisis, which exposed weaknesses in the political system and brought down the Nixon presidency, and by the Iran-Contra scandal, which revealed corruption and the practices of a "hidden government." U.S. military interventions in the Dominican Republic in 1965, in Grenada in 1983, and in Panama in 1989 were but manifestations of the gunboat diplomacy of the past century and constituted an effort to restore an image of U.S. supremacy throughout the world. All these developments implied that ideology and politics were very much alive in American life and raised many issues for debate.

Some of the questions often asked revolve around the implications of the familiar situation in which the teacher-scholar assumes an advisory role to the government and contributes to the shaping of policy, to the propagation of that policy, to the decisions determining the allocation of research funds for studies that buttress that policy, and so forth. In the United States especially, students and scholars examined the relationship of university research and other activities to government agencies, especially the Central Intelligence Agency (CIA), the Federal Bureau of Investigation (FBI), the Pentagon, and the State Department. The significance of the industrial-military complex was made clear in the late 1950s. During the 1960s the universities and the private foundations were being implicated at a time when many comparative political scientists were professing the myth of a science neutral in its values.

In his retrospective account, Todd Gitlin in *The Sixties: Years of Hope, Days of Rage* reminded us that "invisible from the outside, there were questions, endless questions, running debates that took their point from the divine premise that everything was possible and therefore it was important to think, because ideas have consequences" (1987: 7). In another view of the 1960s, James Miller in *Democracy Is in the Streets* wrote "of passionate debate, during sit-ins, in marches, at violent confrontations—at times when people, discovering discontents and ideas and desires in common, sensed, often for the first time and sometimes in the teeth of danger, that together they could change the world" (1987: 317).

American social science has been characterized as liberal and practical with shallow historical vision and technological confidence: "It is modeled on the natural rather than the historical sciences and imbedded in the classical ideology of liberal individualism" (Ross 1991: xiii). These values can be related to "the national ideology of American exceptionalism, the idea that America occupies an exceptional place in history, based on her republican government and economic opportunity." Within this context, political scientists focused on Western historical experience, but "their categories of analysis and prescriptions, like the topics themselves, followed their inherited tradition, with its antimajoritarian conception of liberty, its desire to expand elite governance, and its focus on institutional analysis. A political science constructed on the self-interested motive of liberal, interest-group politics still lay in the future" (Ross 1991: 298).

John Gunnell appropriately argued that the real history of American political science begins with its founders, such as John Burgess, who "were racists and imperialists, and that many of the others who were most instrumental in shaping the discipline were simply, in themselves, not very interesting." Gunnell mentioned an interview in which Gabriel Almond told of Charles Merriam's insistence that Almond delete parts of his dissertation dealing with wealth and power in politics because of references to the Rockefellers, who were benefactors of the Social Science Research Council and the University of Chicago (Gunnell et al. 1990: 36).

Almond reminded us that during the 1960s Robert Dahl and Heinz Eulau could affirm that a new political science and scientific approach had become established in the discipline, but by the 1980s the discipline itself was split among political through mass education, mass production, and mass consumption; and a diminishing of ethnic, linguistic, regional, and religious loyalties along with a marginalization of total ideologies. In variants of this thought, Amitai Etzioni spoke of "the postmodern era," George Lichtheim of "the postbourgeois society," Herman Kahn of "posteconomic society," Murray Bookchin of "the postscarcity society," Kenneth Boulding of "postcivilized society." Empirical applications of "postmaterialism" are in the work of Ronald Inglehart, who extended his analysis to the search for "postbourgeois man." Many of these ideas have been criticized as idealistic or as manifestations in defense of the capitalist order.

In line with the argument that ideology is indeed a crucial concern in the comparative study of politics is the rebuttal that the study of politics is a science. This notion is rooted in the industrialization and technicalization of a society characterized by bureaucracy, specialization, and division of labor. These trends also have affected the university and education itself, because knowledge has been viewed by the Left as a commodity, something detached from those who produced it and something that can be sold in the market. The consequence is alienation as the intellect becomes detached from the self and as fact is distinguished from value. The specialist in society and in the university ignores the whole process of learning, and cumulative knowledge becomes the assembly line of the modern university. The transformation of politics into a science was premised on the success of the natural sciences (Somit and Tanenhaus 1967: 110–117). Political science evolved as a "behavioral science," neutral in character and acceptable to both natural and social scientists seeking to find some unit of measurement, whether it be money for the economist or the vote for the political scientist.

A critical assessment of the ideology of political science most certainly must take into account the thesis, posited by Thomas Kuhn (1970), that scientists inevitably adopt a structure of beliefs, values, and myths about the objectivity of their work. Guiding the scientists' thought is a paradigm or a basic ordering notion about the fundamental character of reality. In their search for a scientific paradigm, political scientists often skirt important substantive questions as they quantify and attempt to remove the personal biases of the observer, their scientific inquiry focuses upon the routine and repetitive processes of government, and their techniques and methodology reveal a tendency to manipulate reality for the sake of efficiency. That reality is based on the assumption that the nature of American society is correct and good, that an alternative arrangement is unrealistic. Such an assumption conditions the conceptualization—of a "civic culture," seen in Anglo-American society, and of pluralism, represented by the U.S. democratic process—underlying an understanding of the prevailing ideology in American political science.

This ideology might be characterized as constituting the beliefs that the United States is good, that progress is inherent in the evolution of U.S. institutions, and that political relations with other nations are to protect and extend freedom and to ensure economic prosperity on a mutual basis. This progress is premised on the functioning of a free market in which firms compete for profits and workers compete for wages. The market is dominated by large, competing corporations, marginally regulated by government, which efficiently produce according to consumer demand the best-quality goods and services and the highest standard of living for the general population. The basis of individual freedom is the right to own private property, civility is the basic standard of morality, and disrespect for authority threatens this order. Thus the United States had to defend itself from the penetration of outside forces such as international communism, which created a worldwide conflict between good and evil. As the wealthiest and most powerful country on earth, the United States had to manifest its civilizing traditions among the peoples of the world, especially those in the underdeveloped countries.

This ideology probably is held by a majority of people in the United States today, yet its fundamental premises have been challenged on many fronts. During the U.S. involvement in Indochina, racial discrimination against Afro-Americans, Chicanos, Puerto Ricans, and other minority groups at home was linked with war, imperialism, and exploitation abroad. Inequality for women in the work place was conspicuous where wages for women were lower than those for men working similar jobs, and in the universities women held only a small percentage of the available academic positions. The evidence, in fact, was alarming: of 37 political science departments sponsoring doctoral programs in the United States, only 4 percent (11 of 249) of full professors were women, 10 percent were associate professors, and 25 percent were assistant professors (*PS: Political Science and Politics,* March 1990: 82–86).

The realities of society have awakened some political scientists to an awareness of the mythological underpinnings and the ideological premises that buttress academia. Students are exposed to the ideological mystique that pervades the relationship of political science to university professors, government officials, business interests, and the military. During the 1960s several radical political scientists contributed to this awakening. Todd Gitlin (1965) examined local pluralism in characterizing an ideology of political science, implying that power is distributed among a variety of groups and institutions so that no one can dominate the others. This ideology of local pluralism, with historical roots in North America after the Second World War, was premised on the belief that there are no power elites, that power is widely distributed in communities, that power is observable and may be investigated in case studies of decisions by formal political bodies, and that the power system allows for change. James Petras (1965) referred to ideological schools: one espoused stability and maintenance in the name of equilibrium and balance, premised on limited commitment and participation so that consensus dominates political action and conflict remains minimal; another school emphasized group interactions of society but viewed politics as a balance of various forces contending for power and making of decisions; a third school envisaged the role of the autonomous politician as the political broker, mediator, or statesman in the resolution of issues; and a fourth school focused on political parties as organizers that make the political system accountable to the electorate

TABLE 2.1
Perceptions of Political Science

Myth	*Reality*
Ideologies are no longer relevant.	Traditional and new ideologies are pervasive.
Political science is neutral in its values.	American political science is based on an ideological foundation and is dependent on dominant institutions.
Politics is based on pluralism, equilibrium, bargaining, and consensus.	The dominant Anglo-American model fails to question the real meaning of capitalism and power politics.

the U.S. debacle in Vietnam, the impression being that the discipline was avoided by activists concerned with policy changes. Yet intellectuals, constrained by their academic institutions, dependent on private and public foundations for funding their research, and conditioned more to conform than to rebel, were no longer the "public intellectuals" that Gramsci believed were essential to shaping decisions in everyday life. The decline of the public intellectual in North America was delineated by Russell Jacoby in *The Last Intellectuals* (1987).

Governments are able to manipulate information and events and cover up illegal activities with relative ease. A few examples illustrate the difficulty in exposing these practices. First, nearly fifty years after the event, historian Jon Wiener was able to reveal that Talcott Parsons, perhaps the most influential American sociologist of the twentieth century, while associated with Harvard University also worked with U.S. Army intelligence officers to smuggle Nazi collaborators into the United States as Soviet studies experts. Parsons had advocated a value-free social science, but his tie to Nazi collaborators was further evidence to the claim of critics that in reality his work "masked a commitment to the status quo and to cold war ideology" (Wiener 1989: 306). Diamond (1992) presented more elaborate evidence of collaboration of universities, Harvard and Yale in particular, with U.S. intelligence agencies.

Second, manipulative power and illicit dealings of government were evidenced during July 1970 when Nixon aide Thomas Huston sent a memo to the president that was endorsed by FBI director J. Edgar Hoover and other intelligence officials. The plan, which ultimately was not implemented, was aimed at the activities of the New Left. The Huston plan was endorsed by Nixon on July 14; it included electronic surveillance of individuals and groups, covert opening of mail, surreptitious entries and burglaries to gain information on leftist groups, and recruitment of campus informants (Colodny and Gettlin 1991).

Third, after more than a decade of questioning, Gary Sick (1991), a former official of the National Security Council, was able to overcome his own skepticism about the "October Surprise" and show how the Reagan-Bush presidential campaign team in 1980 ensured its election by penetrating national security and dealing with Iran so that American hostages would not be liberated until the day

Reagan took office as president. The account exposed Israel's connection and covert arms transfers that later resulted in supplies for the Contra forces in Central America (see, for example, Cohen and Mitchell 1989). Once Reagan was in office, he served as "a monarchy of the people, incarnate in him, the twice-selected and popularly chosen leader, who delegated his authority, though never officially, to a few loyal servants in whom he had absolute confidence" (Graubard 1992: 35). Ultimately, this arrogance led to exposure of Iran-Contra and illegal efforts to undermine the Sandinista revolution in Nicaragua. This pattern of administration was to carry on into the presidency of George Bush: "The Reagan White House was morally corrupt; those who were close to Reagan knew him to be ideologically simplistic and intellectually barren, particularly in the area of foreign policy. ... Bush, a silent Vice President in the tradition of Richard Nixon under Dwight Eisenhower, expected to succeed him as his anointed heir" (6).

Fourth, the Reagan and Bush administrations appeared to confront the serious problem of drugs, yet were hampered in practice by policies that enhanced rather than contained the problem, as demonstrated in the major research on the topic. CIA operations in Afghanistan during the 1980s, for example, "transformed southern Asia from a self-contained opium zone into a major supplier of heroin for the world market" (McCoy 1991: 441). Support of the Contras in Central America "coincided with a major expansion in the Caribbean cocaine trade" (484). In addition, direct intervention into the Andes and into Panama did not have any impact on the U.S. drug problem because foreign policy impeded resolution of the problem: "Adopting a pragmatic policy of accepting any effective ally in the struggle against communism, the CIA has, over the past forty years, extended the imprimatur of its protection to a number of the world's leading drug lords. Indeed, if we review the history of postwar drug traffic, we can see a repeated coincidence between CIA covert action assets and major drug dealers" (491).

Finally, there was CIA failure to predict the likely consequences of the Soviet collapse: "an egregious example of its cold war mindset—its fiercely ideological cast and its belief in the value of stability over change" (Raskin 1992: 776). This thinking led to a Pentagon working paper, "Defense Planning Guidance: 1994–1999," and a plan that showed "the United States would preside over a Pax Americana and 'discourage' advanced industrial nations from 'challenging our leadership,' as well as deter 'potential competitors from even aspiring to a larger or global role'" (777).

Noam Chomsky (1969) once referred to the failure of the social scientists to counterbalance government policies and actions with an emphasis on traditional values of democracy. Instead social scientists surrender their independent judgments, neglect teaching, and distort scholarship. The primary causes of this phenomenon are access to money and influence, an almost universally shared ideology, and professionalization. The social scientists have become a technical intelligentsia interested in stability and order. In the late 1960s students and faculty in political science at the University of California, Berkeley, initiated a discussion about the discipline. They argued that political investigators often tended to camouflage their partisan allegiances and contempt for human beings by professing themselves to be discoverers of truth, unchanging forces of history, or masters of objective laws of science. "The political experimenter is part of the experimental system and his work is value-laden in terms of the system. If his methodology fails to take this into account his efforts may become irrelevant at best, or destructive at worst" (Berkeley Students and Faculty 1969?: 10). Such views were articulated in the professional associations, which confronted challenges from within their ranks during the late 1960s and early 1970s.

In political science, the challenge evolved both within and outside the mainstream of ideas and practices. For example, dissidents in political science argued that the discipline had become conservative in stance and devoid of activists. Its professional organization, the American Political Science Association, sidestepped two resolutions at its annual meetings in 1967. One called for the dismissal of its executive director and its treasurer-counsel because of their involvement in a CIA-financed front organization. The other resolution called upon universities to withhold membership lists of campus groups from the House Un-American Activities Committee. The failure of the association to act on these two resolutions prompted the formation of a splinter group called the Caucus for a New Political Science. The association had never held a contested election for president, and the caucus challenged this traditional practice in the ensuing years. The caucus also challenged a constitutional provision that disavowed organizational interest in the political issues of the day.

Alan Wolfe (1969), a caucus leader, delved into the structure, procedures, and cliques of the association. He found that few members attended the annual business meetings and that the nominating procedures tended to "take politics out of political science and place it into the hands of a gentlemanly club." He noted that nine of the ten-member nominating committee had received their doctorates from the top ten political science departments. He observed that the election process of the association resembled that of "either the state of Alabama or the Soviet Union, depending upon one's field of interest." He concluded that there was almost no way to become an established political scientist without accepting the association:

> Without the association, there is no career; with it, only an absence of intelligence or an excess of integrity stand in the way. This conclusion makes the question of who governs the association important. If little choice and democracy are present, then the rules of careerism and proper scholarship are established by a small, unrepresentative elite of political scientists, to which all others are responsive. Abstract principles like value neutrality and proper scholarship can then be seen not as eternal truths but as devices by which some try to maintain their position in the profession at the expense of others. [Wolfe 1969: 357]

Elsewhere Wolfe (1970) analyzed the professional mystique of political science. The demand for professional behavior, he argued, was a demand for conservative politics and for political conformity. The practices of political science were defended in the name of professionalism. These practices included the acceptance of an unrepresentative elite, which militated against democracy within the profession; the preservation of only prevailing points of view, particularly political as well as methodological views; the affiliation of political scientists with institutions that supported U.S. policy, namely, the State and Defense departments; and the systematic exclusion of research writing with a political bias in favor of "scientific" or "scholarly" writing.

The experiences of political science were not unlike those of other disciplines that were beset by dissident movements. In sociology, for example, a radical caucus emerged at the Boston convention of the American Sociological Association in 1968, and radical splinter groups such as the Sociology Liberation Movement and the Union of Radical Sociologists were formed at the San Francisco meeting in 1969 (Nicolaus 1969). The Union of Radical Sociologists soon launched a new journal, *Insurgent Sociologist* (later renamed *Critical Sociology*), as an alternative to the professional sociological journals. Then radical texts soon appeared (see Colfax and Roach 1971 and D. Horowitz 1971). Among the well-known sociologists who joined the movement, Alvin Gouldner (1970) noted the growing importance of radical sociology and its exposure of the central contradictions of modern sociology, especially in the United States. He saw sociology as the "market researcher for the welfare state," and he acknowledged that academic "objectivity" fosters the sociologists' accommodation to the way things are. Gouldner demonstrated that the historical roots of sociology are found in the bourgeois reaction to the Enlightenment and the French Revolution. That reaction was evident in the sociological positivism of Saint-Simon and Comte, who viewed progress as slowly evolutionary and inevitable. Just as Comte understood positivism as a restraint upon the revolutionary spirit, so too did subsequent study of society call for a detached scientific method that sought apolitical alternatives to the political conflicts of society.

Social unrest in the 1960s also led to divisions in the field of economics. A young generation of radicals challenged the orthodox economists who, in defense of capitalism, guided the world's most advanced economy over traditional hurdles of inflation, unemployment, and uneven growth (Lifschultz 1974). As these problems persisted, public confidence in economists eroded. Divisions arose within the American Economic Association as a splinter group formed the Union of Radical Political Economics and launched a journal, *Review of Radical Political Economics*. Later they published a popular weekly, *Dollars and Sense*, and a group of radical economists in and around San Francisco combined with small collectives around the world in the irregular publication of a journal, *Kapitalistate*. Radical economics texts became popular in university courses (Mermelstein 1970 and Sherman 1972), and radical economists attacked orthodox economists for their defense of the capitalist system. They tended to adopt a Marxist alternative to the orthodox position, and their criticisms focused on the dominant characteristic of capitalism in the contemporary world. Specifically, they argued that the development of the advanced capitalist countries was based on the subjugation and exploitation of the backward countries. Trade, investment, and aid served as the foundation for relations between these two types of countries, resulting in development for one and underdevelopment for the other. The dependence of the backward nations upon the advanced nations was the inevitable consequence of the global capitalist system, and development could occur in the backward areas only if the existing pattern of relations was broken (Sweezy 1970).

Radical dissent in other disciplines was evident. In anthropology, Marvin Harris (1968) attempted to trace the rise of anthropological theory from the discipline's beginnings as a science of history in the nineteenth century to later ahistorical tendencies. The epistemological, philosophical, and methodological differences that had long divided anthropologists were brought forward into a struggle between radical and orthodox anthropologists in the late 1960s. From about 1967 a radical caucus began to prod anthropologists to concern themselves with human problems rather than with the documenting of customs of "primitive" peoples for use by colonial powers. They challenged the manipulative procedures of the American Anthropological Association in an effort to establish democratic voting procedures. They established a Committee on Ethics to investigate the activities of social scientists in Thailand (Wolf and Jorgensen 1970), and they proposed resolutions opposing the participation of anthropologists in counterinsurgency research. Countertextbooks with a Marxist thrust were introduced to students in the classroom (Hymes 1969, for example).

The struggle to counter mainstream interpretations of society emerged in other disciplines as well. Divisions were clearly portrayed at the 1969 and 1970 conventions of the American Historical Association (Radosh 1970 and Weinstein 1970). Leftist concerns focused on the apolitical *American Historical Review* and on tensions between professionalism and social involvement in the problems of the day. In 1968 the annual meeting of the Modern Language Association of America was confronted with the demands of radical scholars (see Ohmann 1969 for details). Noam Chomsky, the linguist and radical who had brought about a revolution in linguistics, began to tie his ideas on language to politics. The impact of his writing was to influence other scholarly fields, including psychology, philosophy, and biology. Attention by scholars like Chomsky to the war in Indochina, as well as later to U.S. intervention in Central America and the Caribbean, and to the dominant influence of multinational firms on world affairs was to shake the foundations of the scientific community as well. Questions about the relevance of science and about the relationship of science and society were introduced to the meetings of the National Academy of Sciences in the late 1960s (Spiro 1969), and radical journals such as *Science for the People* were widely circulated to the scientific community.

These intrusions into the professional academic disciplines were extended into the associations of the area specialists. Black discontent, which surfaced at the Los Angeles meetings of the African Studies Association, exploded at the Montreal meetings a year later as black American and African scholars brought matters to a halt by insisting that there be racial parity on the association's board of directors. The Africa Research Group began to disseminate its findings on the ties of the profession to the U.S. intelligence community (Chilcote and Legassick 1971). From its inception the Latin American Studies Association was wracked by the dissent of radicals concerned with the exploitation of Latin America. Political resolutions opposing U.S. imperialism and supporting developments in Cuba were approved in the association's business meetings, although the failure to implement those resolutions culminated in the founding of an alternative journal, *Latin American Perspectives* (Chilcote 1973). Publications of the North American Congress on Latin America provided useful information. The Committee of Concerned Asian Scholars directed attention against the U.S. military efforts in Asia with its publication, *The Bulletin of Concerned Asian Scholars,* and the Pacific Studies Center was established to research and report on developments in that part of the world through a bimonthly publication, *Pacific Research and World Empire Telegram.*

Scholarship, Ethics, and the Establishment

Intellect has also become an instrument of national purpose, a component of the military-industrial complex.

**—Clark Kerr, former president of the University of California,
quoted in Berkeley Students and Faculty (1969?)**

It is usually assumed that the university is neutral with respect to the major questions of society and that the university is primarily devoted to teaching and research in the service of society. In an age of technology and science, the university takes these patterns of society for granted, works within them, and serves to affirm them. At the same time the university depends on society for support, and it caters to those needs that society seeks to promote by providing university support. Given this mutual relationship between the university and society, knowledge becomes a commodity, something detached from those who produce it and something that can be sold in the marketplace—for instance, knowledge may be requisite for the holding of a particular job. Thus, the student learns to exercise intellect in a detached way rather than to use intellect in a dialogue between self and the outside world. This is similar to the way in which some social scientists tend to distinguish between fact and value, the assumption being that in a professional capacity one works without values and emotions. Reflecting the society around it, then, the university becomes a bureaucratic industry, oriented toward specialization and division of labor. The traditional ideal of the academic as learned first and specialized second has been turned upside down, and many of today's academics tend to be specialized and restricted to limited tasks. As such, the academic does not need to be concerned with the whole, nor with what the final product looks like. Indeed, as Clark Kerr suggested, intellectual endeavor has become a component of the modern military and industrial complex.

The relationship of the university to the society at large was called into question by certain developments. The U.S. defeat in Indochina, the Watergate scandals, and surveillance by intelligence agencies over the everyday affairs of thousands of U.S. citizens prompted questions about the organization and purpose of society (Berman and Halperin 1975) and likewise about the organization and purpose of the university. Political science was similarly affected, as mentioned previously, because its professional association was confronted with the revelation that its executive director and its treasurer-counsel had been officials of an active conduit foundation of the CIA.

This revelation led to the formation of a committee on professional standards, responsibilities, and conduct. In its report to the association, this committee blandly concluded that ethical problems in the profession are peripheral and insignificant (American Political Science Association, Committee 1969). The committee found that political scientists are "men of property"—affluent researchers who must balance conflicting institutional commitments between university and government. Further, scholars must be wary of research in foreign countries, especially research conducted under the auspices of other institutions. Also scholars may wittingly or unwittingly condition their findings on the assumed values of their financial sponsors, thereby sacrificing objectivity. Some people interpreted the report as invoking objectivity, detached scholarship, and methodological rigor in order to escape the commitments of action and responsibility. Students at Berkeley summed up their feelings, "We get the disquieting feeling that to become professional political scientists, we must strip ourselves of human feeling and abstain from political involvement. If that is so, it constitutes an ethical problem of the greatest magnitude. Yet most of our professors do not see it as a problem at all. And that is an ethical disaster" (Berkeley Students and Faculty 1969?: 21).

From within the academic community, Keith Griffin decried the bureaucratization of knowledge:

> Scholarship is no longer a vocation; it is a profession. And with the growth of professionalism has come formal job markets: advertising, job descriptions, legal requirements intended to prevent gender and ethnic discrimination, administrative review of appointments. ... Professional associations and associated professional journals have been established, and with this has emerged a pecking order of journals and publishers. Faculty promotions, periodic assessments and tenure decisions have become routinized and bureaucratized, assisted by citation indexes and external reviews. All this has added to the pressures to conform, to stick to the mainstream, to plough a narrow furrow. [Griffin 1991: 3]

Griffin noted that the pressure to publish in quantity in "good" journals obscures critical thinking: "Quality, note, is measured by proxy: not by reading and evaluating what scholars have to say, but by observing where they say it" (5). All this discourages deep thought, inhibits originality, and results in academics not becoming thinkers because they rely on funded research to sustain the knowledge industry: "Research in the social sciences has become globalised, or is in the process of becoming so" (6). Consequently, "The criteria ... have the effect ... of screening out eccentrics, radicals and critics of the establishment. The shift from thinking to research has further strengthened the mainstream and helped it silence heretical voices: big grants have replaced big ideas. Academic controversy is largely a storm in a teacup; genuine intellectual storms occur elsewhere" (6).

This indictment was underscored by a report on learning in political science. John C. Wahlke and a task force of scholars called for "the development of students' general intellectual abilities—curiosity, powers of critical analysis, aesthetic appreciation, and creativity—thus equipping them 'to master complexity,' 'to undertake independent work and [to attain] critical sophistication,' objectives we would easily support" (1991: 48). Efforts to stimulate creativity and thinking, however, were undermined from the Right in attacks on professors for imposing "politically correct" perspectives on their students. For example, the former editor of the right-wing *Dartmouth Review,* Dinesh D'Souza, alleged a sinister leftist conspiracy on university campuses. *Nation* editor George Black, however, noted that politically correct students were in fact very conservative. Whereas a generation ago students were suspicious of university authority, today "worried by the unholy trilogy of racism, sexism, and homophobia [they] are likely to take their cue from a litigious society and seek redress in the university tribunal and the official code of conduct" (*Los Angeles Times,* May 13, 1991; see Berman 1992 for a review of the debate).

The magnitude of the ethical problems facing political scientists, especially in comparative political inquiry, can be better understood by briefly summarizing some of the revelations of the past two decades, namely, those relating to a scholar's relationship, first, to government (including the military and intelligence agencies) and, second, to the corporate world (including private foundations).

Social Science and Government

Political scientists are concerned with policy, and their research may shape the formation of policy. Thus, the acceptance of funds from government agencies has ethical implications. Sponsoring public institutions do not always guarantee complete freedom to researchers to publish their findings without censorship or interference, and such restrictions or classification of information usually is imposed by defense and intelligence agencies. Perhaps the most blatant attempt to undertake clandestine research was Project Camelot (I. L. Horowitz 1967).

Project Camelot was conceived late in 1963 by U.S. army officers associated with the Army Research Office of the Department of Defense. They were concerned about insurgency movements around the world and desired to find ways of coping with such movements. Latin America was the first area selected for concentrated study, and under the aegis of the American University in Washington, D.C., a four-to-six-million-dollar contract over three to four years was arranged with the Social Operations Research Organization. Efforts to establish the project in Chile were exposed in 1965, in the Chilean leftist press and Congress, prompting opposition to the project by the U.S. Department of State and intervention by President Lyndon B. Johnson to stop the project altogether. The repercussions for U.S. citizens undertaking research outside their own country were substantial. Such research was suspect, and many Third World countries attempted to establish guidelines and controls. The exposure and criticism of Project Camelot raised questions in the United States as well. The State Department viewed the Pentagon as intruding upon the State Department's authority in the area of foreign affairs, and congressional skeptics were fearful that foreign alliances might be shaken. Academic social scientists questioned the links between the Pentagon and U.S. universities. Not only did the unfavorable publicity leave a residue of distrust for U.S. social scientists all over Latin America, but the connections between U.S. universities and defense and national security projects constituted gross violations of the principle of nonintervention in the internal affairs of other countries.

Dissent over Project Camelot was a prelude to protests during the late 1960s by students and faculty members about Defense Department–sponsored foreign affairs research. Some of that research was carried out in federally contracted research centers at the University of Wisconsin, George Washington University, American University, Columbia University, Penn State, the University of Washington, Johns Hopkins University, and Massachusetts Institute of Technology (MIT); other research was conducted at military-sponsored institutions such as the Rand Corporation, the Institute for Defense Analysis, and the Hudson Institute. After complaints from social scientists in Japan and Sweden, it also became apparent that the Pentagon was sponsoring research in universities in those and other countries. Eighteen institutions in Japan, for example, held $170 million in U.S. defense contracts as of 1967, and $300 million was allocated to twenty-nine institutions in Sweden (U.S. Senate 1968, part 1: 20–24). In Latin America, the U.S. Army sponsored twenty-six projects in Argentina, Brazil, Chile, Peru, Uruguay, and Venezuela—all countries where the Pentagon maintained close ties with the domestic military. Given such disclosures, it was not out of order for one U.S. senator to question the usefulness of an $84,000 "Pax Americana" study by the Douglas Aircraft Corporation, which concluded that "While the United States is not an imperialistic nation, she exhibits many of the characteristics of past imperiums and in fact has acquired imperial responsibilities" (U.S. Senate 1968, part 2: 32).

Limited resources had resulted in many universities becoming dependent on the federal government for research funds. In return, the universities made available their "technical intellectual resources." In 1968 the Pentagon handed out some $40 million for nonmilitary studies in the social sciences alone. Some 250 colleges and universities were participating in such projects in that year, despite growing suspicions about government intrusions into the academic world. Under the Pentagon's Project Themis, 42 institutions in thirty-one states were provided with long-term financing to develop fifty new research centers in areas not then being supported; a total of 173 schools submitted 483 proposals for the minimum annual funding of $200,000 per project. Typical of the Pentagon-sponsored projects was Quantitative Political Science, which for $590,000 drew its information from the *New York Times Index* and the *International Yearbook*. According to the Pentagon, this project related characteristics of nations to the occurrence of riots and revolutions and participation in external wars. Another project under the direction of a political scientist focused on "Comparative Research on Behavioral Change" and was funded at $4 million over five years (Rabb 1968).

The revelation of such projects prompted antiwar students and faculty to oppose contractual agreements between their universities and the Department of Defense. Their tactics shifted from teach-ins to strikes and occupations of administration buildings on the campuses. Because of the persistent disintegration of its university-based research system, the Pentagon offered to stop classified contracts for basic research, but the offer was of little avail. Princeton University and the University of Chicago severed some defense ties, and the University of California, Berkeley, MIT, and other institutions began reducing secret military research.

Ties between U.S. universities and the CIA were even more insidious. It was not uncommon, for instance, for university administrators to suggest that faculty on sabbatical leave in foreign countries cooperate with CIA agents. Military research carried out at the University of Michigan may have helped the CIA and the Pentagon, together with the Bolivian military, capture and assassinate Ché Guevara in Bolivia during 1967 (Sugarman 1968). Guevara, hero of the Cuban revolution, was apparently the victim of infrared photography, which can measure the human body temperature and was thereby able to trace Guevara's movements, speed, and campsites and even able to identify the number of persons with him.

Especially shocking to the academic world was the revelation that the CIA had subsidized the National Students Association (NSA) with about $4 million from 1952 until 1967 and that about three-fourths of the NSA's top officers from 1956 to 1962 were recruited as CIA agents (*Los Angeles Times*, February 26, 1967). Millions of dollars of CIA funds were filtered into other youth organizations as well as into academic, research, journalistic, legal, and labor organizations in the United States and abroad. Among them were the Foreign Policy Research Institute of the University of Pennsylvania, the National Education Association, the Institute of Public Administration, the American Newspaper Guild, the International Confederation of Free Trade Unions, and Operations and Policy Research. The last institution was headed by the executive directors of the American Political Science Association, as alluded to earlier (*New York Times*, February 19, 1967). Additionally, the CIA established conduit foundations through which money could be filtered to the academic community—for example, to the Pan American Foundation, connected with the University of Miami in Florida, the International Marketing Institute, which held seminars at the Harvard Business School, and the American Society of African Culture.

Finally, there were the CIA efforts to penetrate, even to direct the thinking of, various cultural organizations. (For a synthesis of CIA involvement in the cultural life of the United States, see Wills 1976.) The secret subsidization of *Encounter* magazine was well publicized, and there were secret fundings of Henry Kissinger's journal, *Confluence*. In *Give Us This Day,* Howard Hunt published an account of the Bay of Pigs operation, which he patronized with CIA money. William Buckley's semiautobiographical novel, *Saving the Queen,* revealed his CIA activities. CIA and other government agency subsidies through New York and Washington publishers permitted the publication of hundreds of other books favorable to U.S. policies and actions. Such subsidies did not reach Philip Agee, a former agent, who vividly described his day-to-day adventures in Ecuador, Mexico, and Uruguay in his best-selling *Inside the Company,* a book the CIA was successful in temporarily banning from publication in the United States. In addition to Agee's work, personal accounts by several former CIA agents appeared, revealing the subversive activity of U.S. intelligence agencies in the internal affairs of other nations. These accounts included *The CIA and the Cult of Intelligence* by Victor Marchetti and John Marks, a revelation of secrets learned during fourteen years with the CIA; *Decent Interval* by Frank Snepp, an exposé of the period leading up to the fall of Saigon; and *In Search of Enemies* by John Stockwell, who unveiled his role as director of CIA operations during the Angolan civil war of the mid-1970s. (See Ransome 1980 for a review of these and other works critical of the U.S. intelligence establishment.)

Obviously the CIA intrusion into academic and cultural life affected political science. So too did the activities of the FBI. The recruitment by these agencies of student and faculty operatives to report on activities abroad and at home undermined work in comparative politics; indeed it jeopardized whatever integrity remained within the field. The linking of the intelligence activities abroad with those at home was evidenced by Howard Hunt's ability to move freely among counterrevolutionary Cuban exiles, Nixon's White House advisers, and the Watergate burglars and by the fact that FBI agents worked hand in hand with Mexican customs officials to check on U.S. scholars flying to Cuba via Mexico City. The FBI also harassed academics in the United States, one conspicuous case being that of Peter Bohmer, a radical economics professor who was run out of San Diego, a victim of FBI-promoted terrorism (Viorst 1976). One of Bohmer's chief antagonists was Howard Godfrey, a San Diego fireman and FBI agent who, with agency support, helped organize the Secret Army Organization (SAO) and served as its San Diego County coordinator. The SAO was a small vigilante group that terrorized persons who protested the Vietnam War, and it was organized partially to combat demonstrations at the 1972 Republican National Convention, once planned to be held in San Diego. Godfrey was known to have been in contact with Donald Segretti, the former White House employee of Watergate and "dirty tricks" fame (full details can be found in an eight-part series by Patrick Dillon, *San Diego Union,* January 11–18, 1976).

Such activities spurred Congress to investigate the consequences of intelligence activities at home and abroad. Two reports were published in 1976 (U.S. Senate 1976 and U.S. House 1976). The House investigation revealed that although in 1967 President Johnson had ordered that no federal agency provide any covert financial assistance or support to the nation's educational or private voluntary organizations, testimony in late 1975 revealed that the CIA still had ongoing contracts with some universities, some of which involved classified work. The Senate study reported that three-fourths of the CIA covert actions had never been approved or reviewed outside the agency. The agency also had sidestepped the presidential ban against CIA ties to universities by establishing direct links with individual academics, several hundred of whom were providing leads, arranging contracts, and producing books. Many of these academics were political scientists, and many were involved in research on foreign countries.

An example of a research center with policy influence in the scholarly community is the Rand Corporation of Santa Monica, California, dubbed "the first federally funded policy-planning outfit to inspire the term 'think tank,'" according to Sara Diamond and Richard Hatch (1991: 39). As these authors noted, Rand was founded in 1946 as a project of the U.S. Air Force and Douglas Aircraft. With its $90 million annual budget, it operates three federally funded research and development centers: Project Air Force, the U.S. Army Arroyo Center, and the National Defense Research Institute. It once supported such strategic geniuses as Albert Wohlstetter, who advocated a "delicate balance of terror" doctrine in the nuclear arms race between the United States and the Soviet Union; and it once employed Daniel Ellsberg, who released the Pentagon Papers that showed government deception about the U.S. role in Vietnam. Rand economists were involved in depriving Sandinista Nicaragua of much-needed international credit by pushing U.S. policymakers to pressure European governments to reduce export credit subsidies. Diamond and Hatch noted that had "solidarity activists better understood the sources and methods of the economic warfare waged against Nicaragua, we might have more effectively challenged the propaganda theme that the Sandinistas were responsible for the country's economic plight" (41). Likewise, Rand proposed as early as 1984 that the United States manipulate Soviet access to high-technology oil-drilling equipment through embargo of sales and other means. On Ethiopia, Rand proposed U.S. military and economic aid to the Marxist regime as a means of splitting it from the Soviet Union, a position that deviated from the view of typical right-wing activists: "in Rand's position papers, the most cynical brand of cold-blooded pragmatism outrules predictable right-wing ideological preferences" (41). Rand operates in cooperation with the Pentagon, the CIA, and private industry. Its personnel have included Brent Scowcroft, a confidant of former president Bush, Brian Jenkins, a counterinsurgency specialist, and a host of other well-known persons who have influenced U.S. policy abroad.

With the dismantling of the Soviet Union and Eastern Europe and the winding down of the Cold War, U.S. strategists continued as late as March 1992 to push for a plan that would ensure that no rivals emerge to challenge U.S. hegemony over the international scene. They argued for a benevolent leadership by a single superpower and insisted in the plan document that the United States "must sufficiently account for the interests of the advanced industrial nations to discourage them from challenging our leadership or seeking to overturn the established political and economic order" (*New York Times*, March 8, 1992). Such official arrogance extended from government to university, as in the case of the National Security Education Act of 1991, which according to David MacMichael gave "the directors of the national security system a solid foothold on university campuses and a significant amount of control over their programs of international affairs, language and area studies, and of the students enrolled in them. ... Justified in the name of a very broad and dubious post–cold war definition of national security, this intrusion raises serious questions for the integrity and independence of the university system" (1992: 780). MacMichael referred to the CIA penetration of the Rochester Institute of Technology that led to the resignation of its president and chief administrative assistant.

Government intrusion into university life also was illustrated in the unification of Germany under the guise of a free market economy and democracy, when in fact it involved what one observer called a process of "colonization" in which the East German "right to freedom of speech and opinion and the presumption of innocence until proven guilty have been negated by the mass firings of entire university faculties and members of the civil service for 'pressured' political beliefs or membership in legal parties—without any individual examination, presentation of evidence, or opportunity of defense. Even daycare workers and kindergarten teachers are being dismissed as being ideologically unfit to care for small children" (Dorothy Rosenberg, "The Colonization of East Germany," *Monthly Review* 43 [September 1991]: 41).

In his examination of the crisis of authoritarianism and appeal for analyzing events during the 1980s that threw into question the legitimacy of all authoritarian regimes, Lucian Pye attributed the changes to modernization and hailed the "vindication of modernization theory." As evidence he pointed to the flows of international trade, finance, and communications; the impact of science and technology; and the emergence of a middle class and a technically educated population that resulted in "new centers of power leading to drastically altered attitudes about the nature of authority" (Pye 1990: 9). However, modernization theory sometimes led to unfortunate outcomes. For example, in 1988 North American scholarship influenced theorists in the Chinese Academy of Social Science and in some of China's top universities to promulgate a theory of "new authoritarianism"; it drew upon the analysis of Samuel Huntington and members of the SSRC Committee on Comparative Politics who in the 1960s had emphasized the significance of institutionalizing government authority in order to ensure development. This thesis, inherent in Huntington's *Political Order in Changing Societies* (1968), may have bolstered hard-liners in implementing their crackdown and massacre of protesting students in Tiananmen Square during June 1989.

Social Science and the Multinationals

During the late 1960s radicals also directed attention to the corporations. They argued that academics work only for the administration and trustees of research and development corporations called universities. The decisions of these university corporations are made by their directors, who serve the nation's business corporations, banks, bureaucracy, and military. A public entity like the University of California is governed by members of the Hearst, Chandler, Simon, and other influential families, for example, while a private institution like Harvard University is run on a self-perpetuating basis (when a member of the governing board dies or resigns, his successor is chosen by seven members of that board). Harvard executives serve on the Council for Foreign Relations, and academics like Henry Kissinger shape foreign policy and promote links with the intelligence community (Africa Research Group 1970?).

It was further argued that the corporate ties of university to business serve the needs of the capitalist world and, in particular, U.S. capitalism at home and abroad. Universities and factories alike produce goods and services packaged to contain a U.S. view of the world. Thus, according to Ivan Illich (1969), a basic need will be defined as owning a car while expensive remedies to relieve the traffic jams in our cities are being promoted, or as using the schools to get children out of their parents' hair or off the street, even though the children's schooling will seem endless and they will need incentives to endure the ordeal. Illich used these examples to explain underdevelopment as "the surrender of social consciousness to pre-packaged solutions." Underdevelopment is the consequence of rising levels of aspirations brought about through the intensive marketing of "patent" products. Education really is "the awakening awareness of new levels of human potential and the use of one's creative powers to foster life" (Illich 1969: 22).

University research is also dependent on private foundations. The annual income of the Ford Foundation exceeds that of the world's largest bank, and the assets of the Ford Foundation exceed those of the Rockefeller Foundation fourfold. As nonprofit, charitable foundations they serve as "the base of the network of organizations through which the nerve centers of wealth impress their will on Washington" (D. Horowitz 1969 (1): 47). This network consists of research and policy organizations that are financed and staffed jointly by the foundations and the corporate community. Among these organizations is the Council on Foreign Relations and its prestigious quarterly, *Foreign Affairs*. The council has spawned such foreign affairs specialists as McGeorge Bundy and Henry Kissinger. The organizational complex also includes the Brookings Institution, the National Bureau of Economic Research, the Foreign Policy Association, and the Twentieth Century Fund—all of which finance academics and assimilate their findings into foreign policies and actions.

Foundation-sponsored research into foreign areas has, of course, been questioned by the host countries, as have the multinational corporations with which the foundations are allied. As a consequence, the motives, objectives, and conduct

Jacoby, Russell. 1987. *The Last Intellectuals: American Culture in the Age of Academe.* New York: Basic Books. Analysis of ideological shifts among leftist intellectuals and their ties to universities such that there no longer are "public intellectuals" willing to criticize society.

Kesselman, Mark. 1982. "Socialist Pedagogy." *New Political Science* (Summer), 113–136. Explains the weaknesses in Marxist political science as related to the hegemony of capitalism and the lack of a large working-class–based socialist party.

Kuhn, Thomas S. 1970. *The Structure of Scientific Revolutions.* 2d ed. Chicago: University of Chicago Press. From 2, 2 of *International Encyclopedia of Unified Science.* A scientist's historical perspectives about the struggle among scientists to formulate and work within dominant paradigms. Ideology becomes a part of each scientist's ordering notions about the character of reality.

LaPalombara, Joseph. 1966. "Decline of Ideology: A Dissent and an Interpretation." *American Political Science Review* 40 (March), 5–16. A critique of the behaviorist unquestioning belief in science and an effort to challenge advocates of the end-of-ideology thesis.

Lifshultz, Lawrence S. 1974. "Could Karl Marx Teach Economics in America?" *Ramparts* 12 (April), 27–30 ff. An account of radical efforts to challenge the American Economic Association as well as neoclassical economics in U.S. universities.

McChesney, Robert W. 1989. "The Political Economy of the Mass Media: An Interview with Edward S. Herman." *Monthly Review* 40 (January), 35–45. Herman, coauthor (with Noam Chomsky) of *Manufacturing Consent: The Political Economy of the Mass Media* (1988), argues that the U.S. media frame issues and news to serve the needs of those ruling society. Sets forth a propaganda model of five filters to demonstrate how the U.S. media dominate concentrated ownership among a small number of large corporations; advertising; sourcing; right-wing pressure; and anticommunism.

McCoy, Alfred. 1991. *The Politics of Heroin: CIA Complicity in the Global Drug Trade.* New York: Harper and Row, Lawrence Hill Books. A revision of a book originally published in 1972. Shows the links between the CIA and crime syndicates, including the Mafia, and how the drug trade was tied to espionage and U.S. policy objectives. Scholarly and carefully researched. Concludes that "America's heroin plague is of its own making" (23). The book exposes CIA ties to the drug traffic and to arms shipments from Asia to Libya to the Contras in Central America. Also exposes the drug sources in Afghanistan, Pakistan, and Iran.

MacDougall, A. Kent. 1988 and 1990. "Boring from Within the Bourgeois Press." Parts 1 and 2, 1988, in *Monthly Review* 40 (November), 13–24, and 40 (December), 10–24. See also "Boring Within the Bourgeois Press: A Postscript." *Monthly Review* 41 (January 1990), 15–27. A memoir of a radical journalist who wrote for the *Wall Street Journal* and the *Los Angeles Times* and who claims he used his writing to popularize radical views.

MacMichael, David. 1992. "Spooks on Campus." *The Nation* 254 (June 8), 780. Analysis of the devastating implications for college campuses of the National Security Education Act of 1991.

Mannheim, Karl. 1936. *Ideology and Utopia: An Introduction to the Sociology of Knowledge.* Translated by Louis Wirth and Edward Shils. New York: Harcourt, Brace, and World. Significant effort to expand upon Marx's conception of ideology as false consciousness and to relate ideology to the problem of formulating a science of politics.

Mepham, John. 1979. "The Theory of Ideology in *Capital*." In John Mepham and David-Hillel Ruben (eds.), *Issues in Marxist Philosophy,* vol. 3: *Epistemology, Science, Ideology,*

24–173. Sussex, England: Harvester Press. Argues that Marx's understanding of ideology was much clearer in *Capital* than in his earlier work. A rebuttal by Steve Butters and Kathryn Russell is offered.

Mermelstein, David. 1970. *Economics and Mainstream Radical Critiques.* New York: Random House. Presents radical alternatives to traditional economics.

Mills, C. Wright. 1962. *The Marxists.* New York: Dell Publishing. Argues that there can be no adequate social science without Marxism.

Mullins, Willard A. 1972. "On the Concept of Ideology in Political Science." *American Political Science Review* 66 (June), 498–510. Synthesis of various interpretations of ideology and an attempt to conceptualize ideology as well as to relate ideology to science.

Nicolaus, Martin. 1969. "The Professional Organization of Sociology: A View from Below." *Antioch Review* 29 (Fall), 375–387. Identifies the historical and contemporary foundations for conservative thinking in sociology, then relates these foundations to the workings of the American Sociological Association.

Ohmann, Richard. 1969. "An Informal and Perhaps Unreliable Account of the Modern Language Association of America." *Antioch Review* 29 (Fall), 329–347. Summary critique as well as discussion of the radical perspectives of the Modern Language Association of America.

Ollman, Bertell. 1978. "On Teaching Marxism and Building the Movement." *New Political Science* 1 (Spring-Summer), 7–12. Emphasizes how bourgeois ideology interferes with learning alternative modes of thinking, especially Marxism.

Petras, James. 1965. "Ideology and United States Political Scientists." *Science and Society* 29 (Spring), 192–216. Identifies four ideological schools of political science as a basis for criticism of contemporary bourgeois studies of U.S. politics.

Pye, Lucian. 1990. "Political Science and the Crisis of Authoritarianism." *American Political Science Review* 84 (March), 3–19. Sees modernization as an explanation for the expanding world economy alongside democratic trends and progress.

Rabb, Charles. 1968. "Military 'Software.'" *Nation* 207 (July 22), 46–48. Critical analysis of Pentagon-sponsored research in the social sciences.

Radosh, Ronald. 1970. "The Bare-Knuckled Historian." *The Nation* 210 (February 2), 108–110. An analysis of radical dissent within the American Historical Association.

Ransome, Harry Howe. 1980. "Being Intelligent About Secret Intelligence Agencies." *American Political Science Review* 74 (March), 141–148. A review of twenty-four accounts of U.S. intelligence activities, including memoirs of former agents and government reports.

Raskin, Marcus. 1992. "Let's Terminate the CIA." *The Nation* 254 (June 8), 776–784. A proposal for dismantling the CIA in the post–Cold War epoch based on an analysis of its past activities. The proposal is followed by comments from Gore Vidal, Gary Stern and Morton H. Halperin, and others.

Ross, Dorothy. 1991. *The Origins of American Social Science.* Cambridge: Cambridge University Press. Traces the origins of American social science during the period 1865 to 1929 with the intention to "historicize" American social science. This history shows that American social science has worked with models embodying the values of the national ideology of American exceptionalism, which has led to scientism with its prediction and control of the historical world and orientation to abstraction and quantitative methods.

Sherman, Howard. 1972. *Radical Political Economy: Capitalism and Socialism from a Marxist-Humanist Perspective.* New York: Basic Books. A radical synthesis of capitalism and socialism.

_____. 1987. *Foundations of Radical Political Economy*. Armonk, New York: M. E. Sharpe. Examines the bases of political economy, capitalism, statism, socialism, and communism.

Sick, Gary. 1991. *October Surprise: America's Hostages in Iran and the Election of Ronald Reagan*. New York: Times Books, Random House. A former official of the National Security Council overcomes his own skepticism of the "October Surprise" and reveals the results of his investigation showing how the Reagan-Bush campaign team in 1980 penetrated national security and dealt with Iran so that American hostages would not be liberated until the day Reagan took office as president. The account exposes Israel's connection and covert arms transfers that later resulted in supplies for the Contra forces in Central America.

Somit, Albert, and Joseph Tanenhaus. 1967. *The Development of American Political Science*. Boston: Allyn and Bacon. Traces divergent tendencies in the field of political science from its origins in the late nineteenth century when the German university served as the model for contemporary efforts to formulate a science of politics.

Spiro, Thomas. 1969. "Science and the Relevance of Relevance." *Antioch Review* 29 (Fall), 387–403. Review of radical dissent within the community of scientists.

Sternberg, David. 1981. *How to Complete and Survive a Doctoral Dissertation*. New York: St. Martin's Press. Useful guidelines for graduate students and their dissertation tasks.

Sugarman, Albert G. 1968. "Michigan, Ché and the CIA." *New Republic* 159 (November 9), 9–10. Analysis of how military research at the University of Michigan led to the capture and death of Ché Guevara in Bolivia.

Surkin, Marvin. 1969. "Sense and Nonsense in Politics." *PS* 2 (Fall), 573–581. Critical examination of the ideological underpinnings of contemporary political science.

Sweezy, Paul M. 1970. "Toward a Critique of Economics." *Monthly Review* 2 (Spring), 1–8, and as Warner Modular Publication Reprint 43, 1973. Sharply distinguishes between marginalist and Marxist economics, while favoring the latter.

Trilateral Commission. 1975–1978. *Task Force Reports, 1–7; The Crisis of Democracy* by Michael J. Crozier, Samuel P. Huntington, and Joji Watanuki; and *Task Force Reports, 9–14*. New York: New York University Press. The policy reports of scholars and policymakers from Japan, North America, and Western Europe.

Unger, Roberto Mangabeira. 1975. *Knowledge and Politics*. New York: Free Press. An important statement and critique of knowledge, the theory of knowledge, political theory, the disciplines of knowledge, dominant systems of ideas, and the practice of partial and total criticism.

U.S., Congress, House of Representatives. 1976. *The Select Committee's Investigative Record*. Reprinted in *Village Voice* 21 (February 16), 70–92. Suppressed report of the Pike Committee on covert intelligence operations in the United States and abroad.

U.S., Congress, Senate. 1968. *Defense Department Sponsored Foreign Affairs Research*. Washington, D.C.: Committee on Foreign Relations. Parts 1 and 2, May. Investigation into the dominance of Pentagon-sponsored research in North American and foreign universities.

_____. 1976. *Foreign and Military Intelligence*. Final Report of the Select Committee to Study Governmental Operations. Washington, D.C.

Viorst, Milton. 1976. "FBI Mayhem." *New York Review of Books* 23 (March 18), 21–28. Analysis of FBI repression of economics professor, Peter Bohmer, and support of right-wing terrorist activities in San Diego.

Wahlke, John C. 1991. "Liberal Learning and the Political Science Major: A Report to the Profession." *PS: Political Science and Politics* (March), 48–60. A task report on political science as an academic major, with concrete recommendations for undergraduate education.

Weinstein, James. 1970. "Can a Historian Be a Socialist Revolutionary?" *Socialist Revolution* 1 (May-June), 97–106. Analysis of Marxist criticism within the discipline of history.

Wiener, Jon. 1989. "Bringing Nazi Sympathizers to the U.S." *The Nation* (March 6), 289 ff. Shows evidence that sociologist Talcott Parsons worked with U.S. intelligence officers to smuggle Nazi collaborators into the United States after the Second World War.

Wills, Garry. 1976. "The CIA from Beginning to End." *New York Review of Books* 22 (January 22), 23–33. Overview and analysis of the CIA's intrusion upon the cultural life of the United States.

Wolf, Eric R., and Joseph G. Jorgensen. 1970. "Anthropology on the Warpath in Thailand." *New York Review of Books* 15 (November 19), 26 ff. A discussion of documents implicating U.S. social scientists in counterinsurgency activities in Thailand.

Wolfe, Alan. 1969. "Practicing the Pluralism We Preach: Internal Processes in the American Political Science Association." *Antioch Review* 20 (Fall), 352–373. Exposé of the structure, procedures, and ruling clique of the American Political Science Association by a leader of the radical Caucus for a New Political Science.

———. 1970. "The Professional Mystique." In Marvin Surkin and Alan Wolfe (eds.), *An End to Political Science*, 288–309. New York: Basic Books. States that there is a bias in the methods and means by which professional social scientists seek understandings of reality and argues that without change in the rigidity with which academic professionals study politics, all other reforms will be meaningless.

3

Politics and the Science of Politics in Comparative Inquiry

Inquiry into the nature of politics seeks to incorporate methods of science. This is not simply a contemporary phenomenon but one that dates well before the nineteenth century. In this chapter attention is focused on the search to formulate, and the struggle to maintain, a paradigm in the field of comparative politics. First, three approaches that have dominated the field during the past century are examined: the traditional, behavioral, and postbehavioral approaches. Next, the historical roots and the fundamental premises of the paradigmatic search are looked at. On the one hand, positivist thought and the legacy of thinking and conceptualization that have shaped the movement to establish a mainstream paradigm are examined. In this regard the early positivists, the early political sociologists, and the early behaviorists are identified and briefly discussed. On the other hand, historicist thought, influential in the movement to seek an alternative paradigm, is examined, and the early historicists as well as the later historicist trends are identified. Finally, the characteristics of these dominant paradigms in comparative politics are contrasted and compared.

The Search for Paradigms (Synthesizing the Field of Comparative Analysis)

Contemporary students of politics generally distinguish among three approaches in their search for a science of politics. These are the traditional, behavioral, and postbehavioral approaches. All three approaches, which are discussed below, have been used in the study of comparative politics (see Table 3.1).

TABLE 3.1
Three Approaches to Comparative Politics: Some Characteristics

Traditional Approach	Behavioral Approach	Postbehavioral Approach
Interrelates fact and value; speculative	Separates fact from value	Fact and value tied to action and relevancy
Prescriptive and normative	Nonprescriptive, objective, and empirical	Humanistically and problem-oriented; normative
Qualitative	Quantitative; usually based on survey data	Qualitative and quantitative
Concerned with irregularities and regularities	Concerned with uniformities and regularities	Concerned with regularities and irregularities
Configurative and non-comparative; focuses on individual countries	Comparative; focuses on several countries	Comparative; focuses on several countries and is interdisciplinary
Ethnocentric; focuses especially on Western European "democracies"	Ethnocentric; especially concerned with Anglo-American model	Especially Third World–oriented
Descriptive, parochial, and static	Abstract, ideologically conservative, and static	Theoretical, radical, and change-oriented
Focuses on formal (constitutional and governmental) structure	Focuses on formal and informal (group) structures and functions	Focuses on class and group relations and conflict
Historical or ahistorical	Ahistorical	Holistic, historical, and macro-oriented theory

Three Approaches

The *traditional approach* historically interrelated fact and value in the study of comparative politics. During the early twentieth century, however, its orientation shifted to the study of the institutions of individual countries. As such, the traditional approach became noncomparative, descriptive, parochial, and static (Macridis 1955). The traditional approach focused analysis on the structure of the state, elections, and political parties. It tended to describe political institutions without attempting to compare them, other than to identify types, such as parliamentary in contrast to presidential institutions. Often traditional studies centered on the evolution of certain formal institutions, tracing, for example, the origin of the British parliamentary system to the Magna Carta. Then, too, there was concern with legal forms and prescriptions; the study of the various branches of government, for instance, referred to constitutional and legal provisions. Traditional studies usually limited their examination to West European institutions, especially the so-called representative democracies of Great Britain, France, Germany, and Switzerland. This parochialism combined with attention to such questions as sovereignty and the nature of constitutions accounted for the essentially static character of the traditional approach.

The *behavioral approach* was a reaction to the speculation of theory that offered explication, inference, and judgments based on norms or authoritative rules and standards as well as to the Western ethnocentrism, formalism, and description characteristic of the contemporary traditional approach. A 1944 report of the American Political Science Association criticized the field of comparative politics as narrow in its descriptive analysis of foreign institutions and advocated a mixture of methods and designs to achieve a "total" science of social engineering. Another report a decade later called for systematic empirical research, including the elaboration of classificatory schemes, conceptualization at various levels of abstraction, hypothesizing, and testing of hypotheses by empirical data (Macridis and Cox 1953). These reports were to serve as the basis for the behavioral approach to the study of politics that accompanied most of the research in the rapidly expanding field of comparative politics during the 1950s and 1960s.

The tendency of behavioral research in politics has been toward the construction of logically consistent models from which "truth" is deductively derived. Images of empirical reality undermine the pure theory of formal models of politics, and behaviorists usually seek some mixture of experience and theory, while striving to mold the study of politics with a rigorously scientific discipline modeled on the methods of the natural sciences.

In an effort to differentiate between the behavioral and the traditional modes of inquiry, the major tenets of the "behavioral credo" have been identified. These tenets include (1) *regularities* or uniformities in political behavior, which can be expressed in generalizations or theory; (2) *verification* or the testing of the validity of such generalizations or theory; (3) *techniques* for seeking and interpreting data; (4) *quantification* and measurement in the recording of data; (5) *values* as distinguished between propositions relating to ethical evaluation and those relating to empirical explanation; (6) *systematization* of research; (7) *pure science*, or the seeking of understanding and explanation of behavior before utilization of knowledge for solution of societal problems; and (8) *integration* of political research with that of other social sciences (Easton 1965: 7).

In the challenge to the traditional approach, political scientists referred to their alternative as the behavioral revolution. During the 1960s, however, there was a great deal of dissatisfaction with research and teaching that were oriented toward making the study of politics into a more rigorously scientific discipline. This dissatisfaction evolved into what one major proponent of the behavioral revolution called the *postbehavioral revolution*. Future-oriented toward "relevancy" and "action," the credo of postbehaviorism consisted of a number of tenets. First, substance precedes technique so that urgent problems of society become more important than the tools of investigation. Second, behaviorism itself is ideologically conservative and limited to abstraction rather than to the reality of the times in crisis. Third, science cannot be evaluatively neutral, fact cannot be separated from value, and value premises must be related to knowledge. Fourth, intellectuals must bear the responsibility of their society, defend human values of civilization, and not become mere technicians isolated and protected from the issues and problems that envelop their work. Fifth, the intellectual must put knowledge to work and engage in reshaping society, and sixth, the intellectual must enter the struggles of the day and participate in the politicalization of the professions and academic institutions (Easton 1969).

The confrontation and shifting emphases of the above approaches, as well as the "revolutionary" replacement of one approach by another as political science has evolved through time, make clear the struggle of social science to seek a paradigm. Thomas Kuhn's use of paradigm has interested political scientists. His notion of paradigm relates to "research firmly based upon one or more past scientific achievements, achievements that some particular scientific community acknowledges for a time as supplying the foundation for its further practice" (Kuhn 1970: 10). Those achievements become paradigmatic—examples of actual scientific practice. These examples "include law, theory, application, and instrumentation together—[providing] models from which spring particular coherent traditions of scientific research." A paradigm is a scientific community's perspective of the world, its set of beliefs and commitments—conceptual, theoretical, methodological, instrumental. The paradigm guides a scientific community's selection of problems, evaluation of data, and advocacy of theory.

Identification of Paradigms

In discerning the nature of a paradigm, Kuhn acknowledged the difficulty of discovering rules that guide scientific traditions. The concepts, laws, and theories of science are found historically in prior experience, not in the abstract, and they become the basis of scientific learning and initiation into one's profession. They thus shape and condition one's orientations. The paradigm to which one subscribes, however, guides research by direct modeling and abstracted rules. Paradigms establish the limits of what is possible, the boundaries of acceptable inquiry. A successful paradigm then enables a scientific community to maintain criteria for the selection of problems to be used for finding solutions. Scientists working with a successful paradigm, however, might be unable to perceive possibilities beyond their own assumptions. They may be unable to keep adherents from shifting their attention to competing modes of scientific activity. A new scientific revolution may ensue through a number of phases through which science tends to pass.

First, there is the *preparadigmatic phase* in which no single theoretical approach or school predominates in the scientific community, although a number of such approaches or schools are in competition with each other. Second, there is the *paradigmatic phase*, in which the scientific community adheres to a dominant paradigm. Third, there is the *crisis phase*. The dominant paradigm is subject to challenge and revision, and new paradigms may evolve and old ones may be revived, giving rise to debate and competition among a variety of perspectives. Fourth, there is the *phase of scientific revolution,* which occurs when the scientific community shifts to significantly different paradigms.

The traditional, behavioral, and postbehavioral approaches described earlier do not precisely fit Kuhn's definition and discussion of paradigms, and they will continue to be identified simply as varying approaches to comparative politics. Within these approaches, however, the struggle to find a dominant paradigm is evident. Since Kuhn's work on the use of paradigms, the behaviorists have alluded to themselves as "normal scientists," in recognition of the fact that they accept and work with a dominant theory approved by the scientific community. But, argued Wolin (1968), no such scientific revolution has occurred, and no new and dominant theory such as the one described by Kuhn has been erected. In fact, Wolin insisted, no dominant theoretical paradigm of normal political scientists yet exists. He acknowledged, however, that even though there is no extraordinary theory such as the one Newton produced, there is a framework of guiding assumptions—"the ideological paradigm reflective of the same political community"—that applies to political science (Wolin 1969: 1064).

Beardsley (1974) essentially agreed with Wolin that neither in the past nor in the present has a paradigm along the lines identified by Kuhn been established for political science, although Beardsley believed that political science can and should establish one in the future. He disagreed with David Truman's assumption that since the 1880s political science has envinced something similar to a paradigm. And he described as ambiguous Gabriel Almond's identification of an unscientific paradigm that established itself in the eighteenth and nineteenth centuries. Both Truman and Almond saw political science acquiring a new paradigm, however. Truman's paradigm is associated with a renewal of interest in the political system, in political theory, and in science. Almond's "scientific" paradigm is tied to a statistical approach, specification of variables and the assumptions of probability, and the system.

Today many political scientists emphasize the methodological pluralism of the field (Johari 1987) as well as the shift from a configurative approach that describes an array of variables in a single-country political system to a comparative approach that focuses on a single variable across several systems. There also is recognition of a shift from understanding to explanation. Dalton asserted that comparativists "came close to creating a Kuhnian paradigm of a behavioral approach" (1989: 15), although he acknowledged that the revolution in comparative politics never materialized. Mayer (1989), however, noted that a majority of studies in the field fail to live up to new directions and that the revolution in comparative politics has stalled.

Some political scientists such as David Ricci (1977) elaborated on the relevance of paradigm and scientific revolutions, and these ideas were influential in rethinking comparative politics. Kuhn himself acquired a significant place in the history of social science (Barnes 1987), yet there also was a fundamental reassessment, including some self-criticism by Kuhn himself. In his reassessment, Kuhn acknowledged that in his work the term *paradigm* was allowed to expand and embrace all shared group commitments in the disciplinary matrix, the result being "confusion" (1977: 319). A crude Hegelian dialectical approach rather than the Kuhnian conception of paradigm was suggested in Bronfenbrenner's overview (1971).

Clearly, historical approaches are important to debates and understandings and reveal a variety of approaches (Dryzek and Leonard 1988). For example, Charles Merriam once envisaged the history of political science as evolving through four stages (deductive, up until the midnineteenth century; historical and comparative, during the second half of the nineteenth century; observing with measurement, early in the twentieth century; and psychological analysis, since 1925). Most histories have been either negative in their appraisal or have failed to understand progress in the discipline. Gunnell (1983), for instance, showed how political theory has been marginalized, and Ricci (1984) gave an especially negative accounting.

Four scientific revolutions in the study of politics were identified by Rogowski (1978). During the 1930s and 1940s the formal-legal assumptions of the past century were replaced by attention to studies of psychology and coercion; during the 1950s behaviorism was in effect; during the 1960s the Parsonian social model, with its related theory of political culture and system, dominated; and in the 1970s there was a shift, in the Kuhnian sense, toward theories of rational choice in such areas as conflict and strategy, coalitions, participation and influence, institutions, collective choice, and constitutional choice and legitimacy. Rogowski was particularly interested in theories of rational choice, which by the early 1990s had become popular in the United States. Analysis of rational behavior and emphasis on individual choice in politics may justify the existence of a positive science of politics, as in the work of Anthony Downs. Formal modeling, it is hoped, may help in the search for a deductively powerful and conceptually rich paradigm, along with solutions for basic technical and methodological problems that hamper cross-cultural comparative research (Almond 1988 in his historical overview of rational choice in social science).

Sometimes formal modeling is linked hypothetically and not very creatively in an effort to predict international activity. Santos argued against a single global model of scientific rationality that he traced to the scientific revolution of the sixteenth century; he advocated a "postmodern science" in which knowledge becomes common sense and serves to enhance our relationship with the world: "Common sense collapses cause and intention. It rests on a world view based on action and on the principle of individual creativity and responsibility" (1992: 44). According to Reich, corporate life is part of "a global web," soon there will be no national economies, and every nation must cope with the forces of the global economy. Policy should invest in people and their education to prepare them well enough to participate in the world economy. He argued for a third position, between nationalism and cosmopolitanism, in which the citizens of each nation assume responsibility for "a positive economic nationalism" not only to enhance "the capacities of their countrymen for full and productive lives, but who also work with other nations to ensure these improvements do not come at others' expense" (1991: 311).

Historical Roots and Fundamental Premises of the Paradigmatic Search

Two modes of thought provide the foundation of comparative political analysis. One, historicism, grew out of German academic debate late in the nineteenth century. It was embraced by Hegel, Marx, and others. Sometimes referred to as perspectivism, subjectivism, relativism, and instrumentalism, historicism dealt with history. The German sociologist Karl Mannheim considered historicism as an extraordinary intellectual force that epitomized "world views" and permeated everyday thinking. A second mode of thought, positivism, served as a reaction to historicism. David Hume was the chief precursor of positivism, which grew out of classical British empiricism and apparently was the basis of positivism in contemporary political science. Partially influenced by Henri Saint-Simon who stressed science, knowledge, and technology, Auguste Comte elaborated some principles of positivism, despite having been molded in the historicist tradition. These and other thinkers provided some of the principles of positivism, which today emphasize empirical science—with concepts, laws, and theories that reflect occurrences in the real world. Knowledge is based on objectivity and on observations of real experience. The assumptions underlying these two modes of thought relate to dominant paradigms in comparative politics (see Figure 3.1).

Positivist Thought: The Legacy of Thinkers and Concepts in the Movement to Establish a Mainstream Paradigm

A reconstruction of positivist thought suggests the following tendencies. First, scientific principles are based on sensory experience and thus are independent of time, place, and even circumstance, although they may be revised according to subsequent experience. Such principles are the foundation of the empirical sciences, which stress laws, concepts, and theories that differ from metaphysical accounts of the world as well as from nonempirical endeavors in logic and pure mathematics. Second, generalizations about the external world are meaningful only if they are constructed from or tested by the raw material of experience. Knowledge based on experience is objective. One cannot know what one cannot see, touch, or hear.

FIGURE 3.1
Theoretical and conceptual roots of dominant paradigms in comparative politics

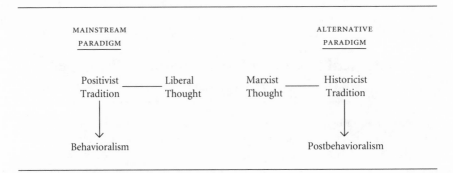

Positivists (including some early positivists who had been historicists) criticize the early historicists for theorizing about broadly conceived questions, for utilizing data to illustrate rather than to test their theories, and for failing to tie theory to data. The historicists, it is argued, postulated overly ambitious theories of history rather than engaging in any meticulous empirical testing of hypotheses and formulations of concepts. Historicism thus was vulnerable because of its emphasis on universal history, in particular because of its predictions of an imminent universality of democracy. Historicism often stressed evolutionary theory, unilinear and deterministic in scope.

The positivist reaction to historicism, especially that which emanated from German academia and influenced U.S. political scientists at the turn of the twentieth century, moved the study of politics toward abstract, formal legal, and configurative studies and toward evolutionary theory (Eckstein 1963: 9–16). At the same time a school of political sociologists, broadly ranged in their theory and dedicated to formulating a science of politics, emerged from their European experience. These early political sociologists in turn influenced contemporary social science thinkers to use the behavioral approach in comparative inquiry. The theoretical and conceptual contributions of these three schools constitute what we shall call the mainstream paradigm in comparative politics today. Let us examine each school of thinkers and then identify the legacy of the liberal and positivist concepts upon which this paradigm is based.

The Early Positivists

The roots of positivist thought, especially as it influences the study of politics today, are found in the works of three thinkers. David Hume is considered to be the precursor to positivist thought and its conception of science. Hume reasoned in his *Treatise of Human Nature* (1739–1740) that knowledge based on experience is objective and that statements are factually meaningful only if verified through empirical observation. Writing about obedience and authority, Hume believed that usually it is best to accept the authority of those who actually govern, as long as the existing rulers are not oppressive. Government should be stable, power depends on obedience, and social order based on inequality may be useful and acceptable.

Auguste Comte, who together with Saint-Simon was a founder of sociology, was concerned with establishing a new science of society, and Comte conceived of a system based on three stages of philosophical thought: theological, metaphysical, and positive. In the third stage one could observe and understand facts with empirical certainty. Sociology, he believed, was the most advanced and complicated of the many sciences. In his *Cours de philosophie positive* (1830–1842), he stressed that progress is dependent on the consolidation of authoritarian *order*, and that progress emanates from stages of evolution.

Herbert Spencer, a philosopher of evolutionism, was influenced by the Darwinian theory of natural selection. In his works *Social Statics* (1851) and *The Man Versus the State* (1854), he differed with Comte's notion of authoritarianism by advocating that the state should play a minimum role in society, and the state should not be allowed to intervene in private enterprise. Through evolution, he believed, *equilibrium* would result in a perfect society.

These three thinkers and their ideas stimulated a reaction to historicism. Whereas historicist studies tended to combine thought with data, the emphasis on abstract political analysis resulted in a separation of content and form from political thought. This accounted for the frequent isolation of political thought from the study of political institutions in the curriculum of political science, a development mentioned in the initial chapter that profoundly influenced the study of comparative political institutions—constitutions and structure of government. A stress on the hard facts found in formal legal documents and an adherence to a purported neutral empiricism often led to superficial and mechanistic interpretations of politics. Political analysis also tended to become configurative (focused on a particular country) and not comparative. This trend was not only a consequence of the formal legal attention to government but was also a response to the influence of and attention to nationalism, as well as a reaction to broad speculative theory. Evolutionism in politics focused in a detailed fashion on the rise of the state in its primitive form and on its evolution through stages to more complex forms.

The Early Political Sociologists

A number of thinkers were deeply interested in constructing a science of political and social life, thinkers who were influenced by positivism but were not limited to the study of formal distinctions among types of governments. Instead they constructed broad theories of politics and incorporated a wide range of data into their analyses. They were interested in questions of power and rule, and their contributions were especially significant for sociology and comparative politics.

Gaetano Mosca, a Sicilian political theorist and practitioner, was one of the first to distinguish between elites and masses and to build a science of politics based on that formulation. Specifically, Mosca was concerned with the political or ruling class, defined as the people who directly participate in government or influence it. His conception of the ruling class, elaborated in *Elementi de scienza política* (1896), is more limited than that of Marx, who was concerned with an economic class of property owners and employers who ruled politically. Thus, Mosca's ruling class is a *political class* that represents the interests of important and influential *groups*, especially in parliamentary democracies. Mosca's detailed examination of this political class reveals its divisions as well as the lower strata of civil servants, managers, and intellectuals. Participation is dependent on *competition* among the segments of the political class. The political class, however, undergoes changes in composition through the recruitment of members from the lower strata and through the incorporation of new social groups. This phenomenon is known as the *circulation of elites.*

Vilfredo Pareto, an Italian aristocrat and liberal, also elaborated on the circulation of elites in *Cours d'économie politique* (1896–1897) and other works, but Pareto distinguished more sharply and systematically than did Mosca between the rulers and the ruled in every society. He referred to governing elites and nongoverning elites, arguing that correlations could be found in the degree of political and social influence and position in the hierarchy of wealth of any and all societies. Pareto conceived of society as a system of interdependent forces moving together in *equilibrium.*

Roberto Michels, a German sociologist and a naturalized Italian, was influenced by the ideas of both Mosca and Pareto. Although he criticized classical theory, which viewed governments as divided among democracy, aristocracy, and tyranny, Michels argued that in fact governments are always led by the few. Democracy and a large bureaucracy engendered by the complexity of an advancing society are incompatible, a thesis he attempted to demonstrate in *Political Parties* (1915). In this regard Michels differed with his predecessors over the assumption that competitive struggle within the political class would allow access to political power. He demonstrated the impossibility, in his view, of ending the division between the rulers and the ruled within complex society. He agreed with the Marxist interpretation of history, that history consists of a series of class struggles, tying that conception to his own doctrine that class struggle would culminate in the creation of new oligarchies.

Max Weber, a German liberal and political sociologist, wrote prolifically on many methodological and theoretical subjects. He was concerned with whether the German bourgeoisie could assume the leadership of the nation. In *The Protestant Ethic and the Spirit of Capitalism* (1920), he examined implications of motivation and drives of the entrepreneurial individual in capitalist economies. In his work on economic and social history, he analyzed the evolution of Western civilization in terms of a developing rationality brought about through the impact of capitalism and technology and science, as well as the gradual specialization of the bureaucracy. Weber also referred to ideal types or conceptual formulations, which describe and classify phenomena that approximate empirical probability. His attention to the question of authority was premised on ideal types—traditional, charismatic, and legal authority. An unequal distribution of powers and therefore opportunity, he believed, became a basis for class, but he also focused on groups and status. In summary, his concern with the stages of development and the rationalization of social activity, his focus on the groups that compete for power, and his perception of the ideal types of authority served as one of the intellectual foundations of contemporary social science and contributed substantially to the mainstream paradigm of contemporary politics.

During the early twentieth century comparative politics at first reacted against the broad sweep of propositions inherent in the work of the early sociologists. The ideas of Mosca, Pareto, and Weber in particular were common to comparative political inquiry and were incorporated into political science theory. At the same time, the early sociologists influenced the study of parties and pressure groups. This attention to informal rather than formal legal political institutions was tied to conceptions of pluralism, especially as related to beliefs about political competition and distribution of power among semiautonomous groups and interests in society. This tendency was carried on later in the writings of Arthur F. Bentley and David Truman.

Then too there was an effort, as demonstrated in James Bryce's *Modern Democracies* (1921) or Carl Friedrich's *Constitutional Government and Democracy* (1941), to combine theory and data through a synthesis of configurative studies in comparative works. Such works tended, at least implicitly, to envisage a comparison of political systems and to analyze data within structural and functional categories. Friedrich referred frequently to Mosca, Pareto, Michels, and Weber, and his work is an early example of the systemic and structural-functional analysis that explicitly came to dominate comparative inquiry toward the middle of the century.

In summary, then, the early sociologists were interested in formulating a science of politics. They constructed broad theories and sought data through empirical inquiry. They were inclined to examine informal institutions and processes and not become entrapped by legal-formal and configurative studies. They were influenced by evolutionary theory and viewed societies as progressing through successive stages of development. They also emphasized the division of labor and specificity of institutions as societies reached advanced stages. They were particularly concerned with refuting a Marxist conception of the ruling class by showing a continual circulation of elites, which in turn precluded the existence in most societies of a stable and closed ruling class. They attempted to demonstrate that classlessness was impossible given the hierarchical structure of most societies.

The Early Behaviorists

After the Second World War, comparative politics rapidly expanded to the study of the non-Western world as old empires collapsed and new nations were created. There was also a gradual awareness that comparative political inquiry no longer adhered to the assumption of an inevitable representative democracy in the development of nations. Totalitarianism in Germany and Italy, authoritarianism in most of the socialist nations, and a highly differentiated Third World shattered the traditional conception of representative democracy. The enlargement of the field into areas and aspects of politics previously little studied was accompanied by a recognition that the study of politics should become more scientific. Consequently, new concepts, methods, and rigorous testing procedures became commonplace in the attempt to systematize the study of political behavior into a science.

The evolution of political science as a behavioral science was related to the discipline's incorporation of quantitative procedures for the testing of theory. Comparative politics was especially influenced by sociology and cultural anthropology. In comparative politics there was a movement toward two levels of analysis. The first level consisted of the introduction of broad frameworks of analysis, somewhat in the tradition of the early political sociologists. Talcott Parsons, for example, in *The Social System* (1951) attempted to build a systematic theory of action. Explicitly acknowledging the influence of Pareto and Weber upon his work, Parsons elaborated on his structural-functional level of analysis and alluded to the functional prerequisites of social systems. Later, he identified five sets of pattern variables: affectivity versus affective neutrality; self-orientation versus collective orientation; universalism versus particularism; achievement versus ascription; and specificity versus diffuseness. Finally, he described the characteristics of systems of human action: they are profoundly influenced by physical, chemical, and biological properties; they are boundary-maintaining systems; and they are related to culture and shared symbolic patterns. Parsons was thus attempting to introduce a broad framework, showing the interrelationship of all social phenomena. At the same time, he was setting forth new categories that permitted analysis at a second, narrower level, where political phenomena would be subject to rigorous qualitative analysis.

Parsons's work contributed substantially to the growth of behaviorism in comparative political analysis. His attention to systems stimulated David Easton to formulate a systemic theory of politics based on stability and equilibrium. Parsons's elaboration of structural-functional categories influenced not only fellow sociologists, such as Marion Levy and Robert Merton, but also Gabriel Almond, one of the major figures in comparative politics. Parsons's identification of pattern variables moved Almond and later Sidney Verba to the study of political culture, and Parsons's concern with a theory of action and his concern for change in society provoked Almond and others to relate their concerns with system and culture to the study of development. Broad frameworks for the study of political behavior on a narrower categorical level, however, did not stimulate interest in the study of elites and in questions of power and class. These concerns of the early sociologists were often obscured by the early behavioral writings. Instead the study of elites became the endeavor of those political scientists and sociologists who focused on power in the local community. Floyd Hunter in *Community Power Structure* (1953) and C. Wright Mills in *The Power Elite* (1956) were prominent in such study.

Historicist Thought: Past and Present in the Movement to Establish an Alternative Paradigm

Historicists take exception to positivist thought by arguing that data based on sensations are not acquired in unbiased situations. The mind is active, not passive, and it selects and shapes experience according to prior awareness. One cannot determine if the source of experience corresponds to the perspective of the objective world. Furthermore, historicists argue that there are a variety of views, not a single view, of the objective world. Distinctive perspectives of the world are found from one epoch or culture to another. Truth is relative to the world view characteristic of the epoch or culture to which one belongs. Thus, world views are temporal and relative, not absolute.

With these premises of historicism in mind, we turn to an assessment of the impact of historicism on social science and the study of politics. Historicism questioned the positivistic belief in the progressive character of scientific development. Science, it is argued, must be understood in terms of history. Thomas Kuhn, to whom reference was made earlier, exemplifies the antipositivist position of contemporary historians of science. He argued that the scientific community is governed by a prevailing paradigm and that the paradigm represents the historical perspectives of the scientific community. The paradigm guides and determines the selection of problems, data, and theory—until another paradigm takes its place. This process represents what Kuhn called the "scientific revolution." Within this context the positivist and historicist movements have been involved in the search for a paradigm, and behaviorism and postbehaviorism are the latest manifestations of this hundred-year-old struggle. Liberalism and positivism clearly have reigned in the study of politics, but the antipositivist historicist tradition and the effort to establish an alternative paradigm remain ever challenging. We turn now to a brief look at some of the early historicists, then to the political sociologists who carried on in the historicist tradition, and finally to those contemporary writers who contribute to postbehaviorism.

The Early Historicists

The roots of historicist thought, especially as it influences the radical study of politics today, are found in the works of several German thinkers. Georg Hegel, a German philosopher and nationalist, was concerned with a conception of the authoritarian state. In his approach in *The Science of Logic* (1812–1816), he searched for reality and for truth. His thought embraced the experience of many generations and civilizations, both past and present, and his search for truth involved a process of stages. From this process emanated Hegel's conception of dialectics and his triad of thesis, antithesis, and synthesis. New levels of understanding were reached in synthesis.

Hegel distinguished three powers within the state and tried to fit them into his dialectical scheme. One power was to determine the universal will (legislative power), another to settle particular matters in conformity with the universal will (executive power), and a third to will with ultimate decision (sovereign power). Sovereign power symbolizes the unity of the state, and it relates to the other two powers as synthesis relates to thesis and antithesis. Here his conception of state is unclear and different from that of Marx, who characterized Hegel's thought as idealist and as a defense of the Prussian state. So too is Hegel's conception of social classes. He saw society as divided into three classes: the agricultural class, those who work or derive income from the land; the business class, all who work in commerce or industry; and the universal class of magistrates and civil servants. Unlike Marx, Hegel failed to distinguish landowners from peasants or employers from the employed; nor did he distinguish merchants from industrialists, or owners of property from workers who have nothing other than their labor to sell.

Karl Marx and Frederick Engels were German thinkers who took a special interest in the distinct roles of different classes in the process of production and in their relations to the state. From previous philosophy Marx and Engels retained a materialist conception of the world and dialectic thought, and they fused the two into a world outlook that posed a struggle for emancipation of the working class and a transformation of society. In the preface to his *Contribution to the Critique of Political Economy* (1859), Marx stated that "relations of production correspond to a definite stage of the development of the material forces of production. The totality of these relations of production constitutes the economic structure of society—the real foundation on which legal and political superstructures arise and to which definite forms of social consciousness correspond." Relations and forces of production are tied to class and class conflict. One's class depends on ownership of property and the type of property owned. The proletarian owns his or her labor, which can be sold to others. The slave does not own his or her labor, and the serf is obliged to work for the lord at some periods. The capitalist, in contrast, owns the means of production, which allows the appropriation of a large portion of other people's work. Thus, these classes are unequal and an exploitation of class by class is evident. Therefore, the history of all societies has witnessed class struggle. Society divided by class requires a state or an organized hierarchy to govern. This state serves the interests of or can become an instrument of class rule. Thus, if a society becomes classless, the state will disappear. Since these ideas are discussed in a subsequent chapter, let us now focus briefly on some trends that carry the historicist tradition to the postbehaviorism of today.

Later Historicist Influences and Trends

Another German thinker, the sociologist Karl Mannheim, was deeply committed to historicism. He believed that all thought is socially determined and historically variable, as is evident in his *Ideology and Utopia* (1929) and in his conceptions of "particular" and "total" ideologies. All thinking, including scientific inquiry, relates to a particular perspective and to each thinker's epoch and culture. This perspective provides an individual with beliefs and values as well as with concepts for the interpretation of experience. Ideology evolves from perspective. Ideology comprises beliefs and assumptions about the world that are accepted but not fully verified. Additionally, one's outlook is bound by inherited knowledge and beliefs as well as by social position. Mannheim's approach differed considerably from the efforts of positivist sociologists to seek models in the natural sciences, to formulate empirical generalization into systems, and to place an overriding concern on rigor, quantifications, statistics, and so on.

A contemporary current, labeled the "new historicism," offers support for the belief that historical investigation and interpretation should reject past understanding on the basis of present values, the purpose being to understand particular authors and ideas in terms of the context in which they experienced and wrote about politics (Gunnell 1989).

The competing efforts of the positivists and historicists in sociology were similar to those that emerged in political science, especially in the study of U.S. politics. In this regard Samuel Huntington (1974) identified three competing models of U.S. politics, but he distorted this use of models by calling them paradigms. The first, related to progressive theory, stressed class conflict and the significance of economic interests in history. This model was reflected in the works of Charles Beard, Frederick Jackson Turner, and others in the early twentieth century. The reaction to this historical approach was set in motion by an emphasis on a pluralist model in connection with the emergence of the new discipline of political science in the late nineteenth century. Political scientists at that time were influenced by the systematic study of politics and government in German universities. The pluralist character of U.S. politics was seen in the role of multiple groups and interests in the shaping of public life.

The progressive model, advocated by historians, and the pluralist model, held in esteem by political scientists, were dominant until the Second World War. Thereafter, a consensus interpretation of U.S. politics, with de Tocqueville as prophet, established itself in the writings of Louis Hartz, Daniel Bell, Seymour Martin Lipset, and others. The consensus interpretation influenced many historians who abandoned the progressive interpretation, in which sociologists promoted an "end to ideology" and models of equilibrium. Political scientists related the earlier pluralist analysis, evident first in Arthur Bentley and later in David Truman and Robert Dahl, to the consensus interpretation. The pluralist and consensus interpretation fits neatly into positivist notions about science, behaviorism, and empirical inquiry.

The belief in the end of classical ideologies led to a plethora of interpretations about the future of society. Daniel Bell in *The End of Ideology* (1960) argued that nineteenth-century ideologies such as liberalism and socialism no longer have relevance in contemporary society. This theme was extended by Theodore Lowi in *End of Liberalism* (1979), which offers a detailed critique of liberalism, its strengths and weaknesses. Bell elaborated in *The Coming of Post-Industrial Society* (1976) by suggesting that the conflicts and tensions of capitalism and socialism are being transcended by new patterns of life. This advocacy of postformulations of society was carried on by Fredric Jameson in his critique of "postmodernism," by Alain Touraine in his view of "postsocialism," and by Ernesto Laclau and Chantal Mouffe in their positing of a "post-Marxism." Most of this thinking was characterized as "utopian" by Boris Frankel in his excellent critical overview *The Post-Industrial Utopians* (1987). The notion of postliberalism was developed by Samuel Bowles and Herbert Gintis in their *Democracy and Capitalism* (1986). They criticized contemporary liberal and Marxist political theory and sought space for a radical democratic synthesis in which representative democracy can be applied to the economic sphere to ensure a more equal distribution of income and resources. Capitalism and democracy are incompatible, they argued, and the welfare state does not give citizens the power to participate in the economy. In the face of the changing international situation, Johari (1987) in his treatment of theoretical trends in comparative politics argued that intellectual trends are evolving toward space between "postliberalism" and "scientific socialism."

The postbehavioral attempt to link the past historicist and progressive interpretations to an antipositivist view of U.S. politics is evident in the writings of several political scientists. The revolt against positivism relied on the position of Kuhn and attacked the deductive explanation of the positivist conception of science and social science. For example, John Gunnell argued that political science derives its conception of science and empirical inquiry from a restricted segment of the literature dealing with the philosophy of science, namely that of logical empiricism. Logical empiricism assumes a tie between the meaning and the verification of a statement; statements that cannot be verified are meaningless. Political scientists have derived from logical empiricism a basis of explanation known as the deductive model. According to this model the logic of social science must be compatible with the logic of natural science. However, faith in the unity of science is offset by the absence of an argument supporting the logical equivalence of the social and natural sciences. Notwithstanding references to the "scientific method," "scientific rules," and "scientific credo" in the prestigious theoretical literature of political science, political scientists seldom interpret the meaning of science beyond formal and empty statements relating to "generalization" or "proposition" or the like. Gunnell thus challenged the advocates of behaviorism who believe that within the philosophy of science there is a consensus favoring a positivist conception of scientific inquiry.

Summary Comparison of Dominant Paradigms in Comparative Politics

The movement toward the formulation of a mainstream paradigm has been traced from its positivist tradition, especially the logical empiricism that captivated many positivist thinkers of the late nineteenth century and the behaviorists of the midtwentieth century. In part, this paradigm evolved as a reaction to the noncomparative, descriptive, parochial, and static character of the traditional approach, which focused on formal and legal aspects of government. The mainstream paradigm also incorporates a critique of traditional political thought, including Marxism, that interrelates fact and value in comparative analysis. Finally, the paradigm, despite the nonideological nature of inquiry which it advocates, in fact assimilates some liberal premises—for example, the separation of religion from government. Secularism in politics was accompanied by the liberal notion, in the tradition of John Locke and later of John Stuart Mill, that every person has the right to hold and profess an opinion, as long as the opinion is not seditious. A positive belief in the liberty of conscience was seen as a law of nature. These premises were to reinforce the pluralist and consensus interpretation of U.S. politics in the twentieth century. (For background on the liberal and pluralist positions, see Pennock 1990.)

Capitalist society shapes the mainstream paradigm, according to Jeffrey Lustig, who argued that contemporary times are dominated by collectives rather than individuals: "These collectives are organized, however, in line with the requirements of a capitalist society, according to individualist principles. ... [E]xclusivist and control-oriented forms of wealth-holding are preserved within an organized world." He characterized organization information and institutional positions as private commodities "hoarded, fenced off, and exchanged for profit, as people attempt to preserve privacy within association, and to assert control over elements of cooperation" (Lustig 1982: 246). Thus, in the United States, constitutional rights depend in large measure on one's attachment to private and secondary associations, which tend to annex the power of an increasingly dominant state as a means of assisting people in their private endeavors; as such, "the nation approaches the European corporativism of the twenties" (247). In Lustig's view, the corporate liberalism that emerges in American political thinking necessitates choice between different forms of associations in the search for liberty and union.

The mainstream paradigm is reinforced by a process of modernization that breaks down authoritarianism everywhere, according to Lucian Pye: "what is different is that the forces of modernization have made it harder for political will power to mobilize and dominate a society. ... The emergence of a middle class and the growth of a technically educated population create new centers of power, leading to drastically altered attitudes about the nature of authority" (1990: 9).

TABLE 3.2
Comparison of Dominant Paradigms in Comparative Politics

Characteristics	Mainstream Paradigm	Alternative Paradigm
Thrust	Ahistorical Micro or macro Compartmentalized Disciplinary boundaries	Holistic Macro Unified Interdisciplinary
Unit of analysis	System, in equilibrium, stable	State, in conflict
Structure	Groups, interaction and civic culture	Classes, struggle between bourgeoisie and proletariat
Authority	Order decentralized with authority narrowly based within specialized units	Order centralized with scope of authority broad and general
Rulers	Diffused, dispersed among many centers, pluralist competition in decision making	Concentrated and unified in a dominant position of authority and decision making
Development	Evolutionary, unilinear, materialistic, progressive, and capitalist	Revolutionary, multilinear, materialistic, humanistic, and socialist in attention to needs of all people

Nevertheless, political scientists are in disarray: "the current confusion arises from the determination of political scientists to employ both scientific and humanistic approaches without a consensus as to where the emphasis should lie" (1990: 4).

The movement toward the formulation of an alternative paradigm has been traced from its historicist origins and antipositivist reactions to the postbehaviorism of the midtwentieth century. Historicism takes the position that science can only be understood in terms of history, and the alternative paradigm draws its historicist assumptions from Marxist thought. Although Michael Harrington in his *Twilight of Capitalism* (1974) argued that a Marxist paradigm was firmly established (especially in the socialist world), it is clear that in comparative politics and political science in general such a paradigm has not embedded itself. Instead, Marxists continue to challenge the dominant ideas of the discipline in their search for a new paradigm.

A comparison of the characteristics of the mainstream and alternative paradigms is given in Table 3.2. Six general characteristics distinguish these paradigms in their interpretation of the most advanced, especially the capitalist, societies. First, the mainstream paradigm tends to be ahistorical in interpretation and analysis, a consequence of its micro orientation, its compartmentalized view of society, its rationalist orientation, and its focus on problems delimited by disciplinary boundaries. In contrast, the alternative paradigm is holistic in interpretation and analysis. Its macro perspective views society as unified and nonrationalist in behavior, and its analysis is interdisciplinary. Second, whereas the mainstream paradigm focuses on stable systems whose elements are in equilibrium, the alternative paradigm relates politics to a conception of the state in concert with a hierarchy of constituencies in conflict with the masses of society. Third, the mainstream paradigm envisages an ideal civic culture of participation and interaction among diverse groups that compete for power and influence in decision making. In contrast, the alternative paradigm offers a class analysis of society. Classes and the conflict between them are defined by their relationship to the mode and forces of production.

Fourth, both paradigms relate to authority, with the mainstream stressing decentralized order in an increasingly specialized society and the alternative emphasizing centralized authority with a broad and general base. Fifth, the mainstream paradigm views rulers as diffused and rationally dispersed among many centers of power or as representative of broad segments of population, and the alternative paradigm sees rulers as dominant, concentrated socially, and unified in political and economic interests. Finally, the mainstream paradigm defines development as evolutionary, generally unilinear, materialistic, and progressive. In contrast, the alternative paradigm understands development to be revolutionary and multilinear and attentive to the basic needs of all people. Subsequent chapters will delineate and elaborate on these general characteristics.

References

Almond, Gabriel. 1988. "Rational-Choice Theory and the Social Sciences." In Gabriel Almond, *A Discipline Divided: Schools and Sects in Political Science*, 117–137. Newbury Park: Sage Publications. A useful historical overview of rational-choice theory and its significance to political science.

Barnes, Barry. 1987. "Thomas Kuhn." In Quentin Skinner (ed.), *Return of Grand Theory in the Human Science*, 85–100. Cambridge: Cambridge University Press. A brief biographical sketch of this historian of science.

Beardsley, Philip. 1974. "Political Science: The Case of the Missing Paradigm." *Political Theory* 2 (February), 46–61. Argues that it is doubtful that political science has had a paradigm in past and present, but believes it possible that political science can acquire a paradigm and desirable that it do so.

Bronfenbrenner, Martin. 1971. "The 'Structure of Revolutions' in Economic Thought." *History of Political Economy* 3 (Spring), 136–151. Argues in favor of a "crude Hegelian dialectic" approach rather than the Kuhnian view of paradigm as a means of dealing with economic history. Criticizes economics as insufficiently innovative and scientific in the Kuhnian view. Examines possible revolutions in economics, none of which compares to the Copernican, Newtonian, and Darwinian revolutions in astronomy, physics, and biology: the laissez-faire revolution associated with Hume and Smith; the classical school led by Ricardo and Mill; the neoclassical school under Marshall; and the welfarism in the Keynesian school.

Dalton, Russell J. 1989. "Comparative Politics of the Industrial Democracies: From the Golden Age to Island Hopping." Paper subsequently published in William Crotty (ed.), *Political Science: Looking Toward the Future*. Evanston, Illinois: Northwestern University

Press, 1991. An overview of the field of comparative politics in industrial democracies, with emphasis on behavioral methods and advances and a recognition of a diversity of approaches.

Dryzek, John S., and Stephen T. Leonard. 1988. "History and Discipline in Political Science." *American Political Science Review* 82 (December), 1245–1260. The authors affirm that histories of the discipline are important to debates and understandings in political science. Further, there are pluralities of historical accounts in line with the diversity of approaches.

Easton, David. 1965. *A Framework for Political Analysis*. Englewood Cliffs, New Jersey: Prentice-Hall. Includes an elaboration of the "behavioral credo" and a framework for comparative analysis of political systems.

———. 1969. "The New Revolution in Political Science." *American Political Science Review* 63 (December), 1051–1061. Presidential address to the American Political Science Association; focuses on approaches to the field with attention to the "postbehavioral revolution."

Eckstein, Harry. 1963. "A Perspective on Comparative Politics, Past and Present." In Eckstein and David Apter (eds.), *Comparative Politics, A Reader*, 3–32. New York: Free Press of Glencoe. Comprehensive, yet concise overview of the field.

Gunnell, John G. 1969. "Deduction, Explanation, and Social Scientific Inquiry." *American Political Science Review* 63 (December), 1233–1246. Antipositivist critique of the deductive model that serves behavioral research.

———. [1989]. "The Historiography of American Political Science." Albany. Manuscript. See also his "Political Theory: The Evolution of a Sub-Field." In Ada W. Finifter (ed.), *Political Science: The State of the Discipline*. Washington D.C.: American Political Science Association, 1983. A review of histories of American political science with the aim of showing this theme has become a research specialty in the field.

Huntington, Samuel P. 1974. "Paradigms of American Politics: Beyond the One, the Two, and the Many." *Political Science Quarterly* 89 (March), 1–26. Focuses on three tendencies in U.S. politics: progressive theory, pluralism, and consensus.

Johari, J. C. 1987. *Comparative Political Theory: New Dimensions, Basic Concepts and Major Trends*. New Delhi: Sterling. Presents comparative political theory as both empirical and normative, liberal and Marxist, Western and non-Western. Reviews the major trends, identified as liberalism, behaviorism, postbehaviorism, existentialism, new leftism. Focuses on essential concepts such as law, rights, liberty, equality, property, justice, revolution, political legitimacy, political alienation, and power.

Kuhn, Thomas S. 1970. *The Structure of Scientific Revolutions*. 2d ed. Chicago: University of Chicago Press. From 2, 2 of *International Encyclopedia of Unified Science*. Argues that the theory and practice of science are found historically in prior experience and become established as paradigms.

———. 1977. "Second Thoughts on Paradigms." In Thomas S. Kuhn, *The Essential Tension: Selected Studies in Scientific Tradition and Change*, 293–318. Chicago: University of Chicago Press. Originally in his essay in Frederick Suppe (ed.), *The Structure of Scientific Theories*. Urbana: University of Illinois Press, 1974. Self-criticism of his earlier work, *The Structure of Scientific Revolutions*.

Lustig, R. Jeffrey. 1982. *Corporate Liberalism: The Origins of Modern Political Theory, 1890–1920*. Berkeley: University of California Press. An argument that a corporate liberalism has emerged in American political thinking that comes close to the European corporatism of the 1920s.

Macridis, Roy C. 1955. *The Study of Comparative Government*. Studies in Political Science (21). New York: Random House. A critique of the traditional approach to comparative government and an outline of a new scheme for comparative analysis, based on deliberations by political scientists during 1953–1954.

Macridis, Roy C., and Richard Cox. 1953. "Research in Comparative Politics." *American Political Science Review* 47 (September), 641–675. A report embodying the deliberations and findings of the Social Science Research Council Interuniversity Research Seminar on Comparative Politics. Supportive of a behavioral thrust in comparative politics, although Macridis was not a behaviorist.

Mayer, Lawrence C. 1989. *Redefining Comparative Politics: Promise Versus Performance*. Newbury Park: Sage Publications. An appraisal of the field of comparative politics with attention to traditional and new comparative politics; epistemology and comparative method; development and dependency; industrial democracies; parties and political behavior; culture and personality; and autocracies.

Pennock, J. Roland. 1990. "Liberalism Under Attack." *Political Science Teacher* 3 (Winter), 1, 6–10. See also an accompanying article, "The 'L-Word': A Short History of Liberalism," 1–6. Useful historical reviews of how liberalism originated and evolved in political theory and political science.

Popper, Karl R. 1957. *The Poverty of Historicism*. London: Routledge and Kegan Paul. A positivist argument against historicism, both Marxist and non-Marxist. Offers first a synthesis of the anti- and pro-naturalistic doctrines of historicism, then criticizes both.

Pye, Lucian W. 1990. "Political Science and the Crisis of Authoritarianism." *American Political Science Review* 84 (March), 3–19. Sees the world in a crisis of authoritarianism—that is, challenge to authoritarian regimes—and anticipates emergence of a variety of postauthoritarian regimes that will not necessarily be democratic. Believes political science must provide intellectual leadership in the changing scenario.

Reich, Robert B. 1991. *The Work of Nations: Preparing Ourselves for Twenty-First–Century Capitalism*. New York: Alfred A. Knopf. Argues that the large corporations are part of international or multinational "enterprise webs" and that although the United States trains its elites well, it must provide better education to all in order to mitigate the ever widening gap in real income between rich and poor and to ensure competitiveness in the international order.

Ricci, David. 1977. "Reading Thomas Kuhn in the Post-Behavioral Era." *Western Political Quarterly* 30 (March), 7–34. Elaborate discussion of the relevance for contemporary political science of Kuhn's notion of paradigm and scientific revolution. Shows the relevance of Popper's understanding of science to behaviorism.

———. 1984. *The Tragedy of Political Science: Politics, Scholarship, and Democracy*. New Haven: Yale University Press. Argues that contemporary political science is sterile and irrelevant to contemporary times. The discipline has shifted from emphasis on great thinkers to reliance on prominent universities: "large numbers of American citizens have come to learn about public life from a particular aggregation of academic specialists rather than, as in the past, from a tradition based upon the works of great men in many walks of life" (x).

Rogowski, Ronald. 1978. "Rationalist Theories of Politics: A Midterm Report." *World Politics* 30 (January), 296–322. A review of four major books on theories of rational choice, which leads the author to the conclusion that a "fourth great scientific revolution" is under way in the study of politics.

Santos, Boaventura de Sousa. 1992. "Discourse on the Sciences." *Review* 15 (Winter), 9–47. Argues that the distinction between natural and social sciences is beginning to seem meaningless and that social science will serve as the catalyst to synthesize both of them, assuming the rejection of empirical or logical positivism and mechanistic idealism or materialism and the return to the humanities (12).

Wolin, Sheldon S. 1968. "Paradigms and Political Theories." In P. King and B. C. Parekh (eds.), *Politics and Experience: Essays Presented to Michael Oakeshott*, 125–152. Cambridge: Cambridge University Press.

———. 1969. "Political Theory as a Vocation." *American Political Science Review* 63 (December), 1062–1082. Although acknowledging that a framework of assumptions dominates contemporary political science, Wolin argues that no dominant theoretical paradigm of normal political scientists yet exists.

4

Marx and Weber
as Precursors

Advances in knowledge are facilitated by the existence of a base of ideas upon which new theory can be built. Karl Marx and Max Weber presented the study of politics with two such bases, each with its set of assumptions and understandings. Contemporary students of comparative politics can benefit by a close examination of their theories and insights, for the extent of the influence of past thinkers is not always fully understood. Our purpose is to focus on the thought of Marx and Weber in an effort to search for the roots of a paradigm of comparative politics. The reader should be cognizant, however, that exclusive attention to Marx and Weber ignores a wide range of other thinkers whose ideas might be helpful in the paradigmatic search.

Marx and Weber are two of the early major thinkers whose ideas have substantially influenced social science. The work of Max Weber seems to have enjoyed the widest influence among North American students of comparative politics. Weber made little attempt to synthesize his ideas into a tight and comprehensive theory, but as a whole his writings reveal a line of thought that has been fully assimilated into the contemporary social sciences. Talcott Parsons has been largely responsible for this assimilation of Weberian theory into contemporary thought (and at times for distortion of the theory), and Parsons has refined many of Weber's general propositions into a set of statements that have been employed in a wide range of comparative investigations.

Many lines of thinking that divide contemporary social scientists, especially sociologists, are myths, according to Anthony Giddens (1976), and he urged a rethinking of the foundations of contemporary thought. The 1890 to 1920 generation of thinkers, led by Durkheim and Weber, substantially influenced today's social science, but criticism of them by partisans of socialism and conservativism obscured the contributions of the early generation of nineteenth-century thinkers, especially Comte and Spencer as well as Marx. Comte gave social science its positivist origins, and Weber adapted positivist notions to his liberal social theory. Such connections of thought as well as schisms must be held in perspective by critics of positivism and contemporary social science.

The interpretations of Comte and Saint-Simon provided the French intellectual tradition, upon which Durkheim based much of his work. Durkheim's early works were also concerned with the ideas of contemporary German thinkers, especially those who were influenced by Darwin's theory of biological evolution and who directed attention to organic analogies through comparisons of organs of the body to parts of society. In this sense, Durkheim set forth the foundations of systemic theory, which has influenced contemporary social science and especially sociology. A trilogy of thinkers—Durkheim, Weber, and Marx—absorbed the attention of Giddens (1971) in his synthesis of their thought. Although we agree that an understanding of Durkheim as a precursor is useful in a critical assessment of the mainstream of today's social science, our attention will primarily be devoted to Marx and Weber and their influence upon the struggle to establish a dominant paradigm.

With its positivist roots intact, the mainstream paradigm continues to prevail in U.S. social science, and its pervasive impact already has been identified in an earlier chapter. Although the thought of Comte and probably of Saint-Simon, among others, serves as a basis for this paradigm, Weber's work reinforces and preserves the positivist thrust. In contrast, the historicist influences upon an alternative paradigm, notably the idea of dialectics in the thought of Hegel and Marx, have resulted in another way of thinking about the contemporary world. Apparently this tradition of dialectical social science remains embedded today in German thought. Debate in Germany centers around distinctions between positivist and dialectical considerations.

The work of Karl Marx also represents a body of propositions that facilitates comparative analysis. Unlike Weber, Marx worked progressively toward a comprehensive work grounded in the accumulated insights of his previous writings and empirical investigation. Engels was responsible for much elucidation and refinement of Marxist theory. There are obvious differences between Weber and Marx, especially in their theoretical assumptions and the direction of their investigations. Marx, especially in his later work, consciously worked toward an all-inclusive explanation of human history and social transformation. Weber, in contrast, worked consciously at a critique of Marxism and the elaboration of an alternative perspective.

Whether Marx or Weber intended that their works should serve as the starting point for future investigations need not concern us here. Whether it does justice to their intentions or not, their works have come to serve the paradigms of thought and inquiry of comparative analysis.

This chapter begins with a summary of the life and works of Marx and Weber. Then these two thinkers are examined in comparative perspective, and finally, their influence upon comparative politics is traced and their thought and ideas are looked at in relation to theories of state and system, culture, development, class, and political economy. Recognition of similarities and differences in the ideas of these two precursors helps in delineating and contrasting lines of inquiry in contemporary comparative politics.

Karl Marx

The philosophical foundations of Marx's thought are rooted in the traditional German preoccupation with idealism and history. In the second decade of the nineteenth century these two dominant trends came together in the philosophical system of Georg Hegel. Hegel's conception of cyclical historical change allowed Marx, in his own way, to elaborate a revolutionary theory of society.

In 1818, Hegel presented an inaugural lecture in philosophy at the University of Berlin. Deeply troubled by the recurrent violence of European history, Hegel undertook to construct a philosophical system that would at once explain the source of the social upheaval that attends human development and reveal the future of civilization. The device by which he advanced his interpretation of civilization and its history was the dialectic, which traces its origin to the ancient Greeks, but to which Hegel added a new twist.

In Hegel's system, mind and spirit are declared the moving forces of history, and civilization is carried continually to a higher attainment through their interaction. The dialectic consists of three elements: thesis, antithesis, and synthesis. For Hegel, each stage of history is characterized by a dominant viewpoint or idea, which represents the thesis. Through its elaboration, the thesis produces its own contradictions or oppositions, which formulate themselves into a contrary viewpoint or idea, the antithesis. The antithesis represents the negation, or the contradiction, of the existing viewpoint or thesis. The violent clash of thesis and antithesis yields a synthesis or a new viewpoint for civilization. The synthesis is not a combination of the better elements of the thesis and the antithesis, but an entirely new phenomenon of human thought. Once extant, the synthesis itself becomes the thesis in a new stage of history and the dialectic is set in motion again. The clash between thesis and antithesis manifests itself in history as war or rebellion, from which it follows that the progress of man is accompanied by inescapable, but ultimately beneficial, violence. For Hegel, the dialectic was an eternal movement toward the perfection of mind and spirit, whose culminating point he perceived to be the modern state. His system, therefore, logically settled upon the Prussian autocracy as the highest achievement of the German spirit and mind.

Hegel's philosophy of history found an immediate acceptance among German intellectuals, who responded from the standpoint of traditional mysticism and frustrated nationalism. (At that time in history, Germany did not exist as a nation-state but was divided into numerous independent kingdoms and municipalities. German liberals had anticipated German unification at the close of the Napoleonic wars, but the Congress of Vienna failed to bring the unification about in 1815.) The Hegelian admiration of the Prussian state, it should be noted, ignored completely the reactionary police tyranny upon which it reposed.

In the same year that Hegel presented his first lecture at Berlin, Karl Marx was born in Trier, in the Rhine province of Prussian Germany. His father, a prosperous and highly educated lawyer, desired his son to pursue a career in law, and accordingly Marx began the study of jurisprudence at the University of Bonn in 1835. He continued his legal studies in 1836 at the University of Berlin, where Hegel had been a professor until his death in 1831. As a youth, Marx valued art and poetry over other endeavors, but between 1836 and 1838 he replaced his idealistic romanticism, first with intense investigations of philosophy generally and then with a complete immersion in the Hegelian system. During this period, Marx became an atheist and concluded that the Hegelian system would itself do better without the notion of God (Garaudy 1967). Under the influence of a new circle of intellectual companions, Marx substituted a specialization in philosophy for jurisprudence and began preparation to assume a lectureship at the University of Bonn upon completion of his doctorate from the University of Jena. (These and other biographical details are in Riazanov 1973.)

In 1841 Marx received his doctorate in philosophy, but both he and Otto Bauer were refused the appointments they anticipated at the University of Bonn as a consequence of their radical views. Marx turned to journalism when it became evident that he would not be permitted an academic career. By 1843, however, Prussian censorship caused Marx to emigrate to Paris, where he assumed the position of coeditor of the political journal *Jahrbücher*. In Paris, Marx became acquainted with French socialism (whose leading figure was Pierre Joseph Proudhon) and English political economy (to which he was introduced by an article submitted to his journal by Frederick Engels). During this stay in Paris, Marx wrote the *Economic and Philosophical Manuscripts of 1844*, which were not discovered until after his death and were first published in 1932. In that work, Marx developed his thesis on alienation in capitalist society. More important for the development of his thought, Marx formed what became a lifelong friendship with Engels about this time.

Between 1846 and 1849 Marx was involved consecutively in organizing German workers in Brussels, stimulating the League of Justice in London to reorganize as the League of Communists, writing the *Communist Manifesto* for the league, and editing a prorevolutionary journal in Prussia during the revolutions of 1849. Having already established a unique system of thought, during these years Marx acquired his practical political experience, which he subsequently drew upon in organizational activities in England. About 1850, with the failure of the Revolution of 1848 in France a historical fact, Marx retired to London where he resided for the remainder of his life.

The thrust of Marx's works during the London period reflects a more mature analysis and a concern with producing a synthesis of his life's work. For example, as an application of scientific socialist analysis, the *Eighteenth Brumaire of Louis Bonaparte* (1851–1852) was Marx's most serious attempt to explain a specific historical event in terms of material forces and class conflict. The notable product of Marx's last years was *Capital*, the first volume of which was published in 1867, with the remaining volumes published under the editorship of Engels from notes and drafts after Marx's death in 1883. In this work, Marx undertook to empirically validate the system of thought embodied in the *Communist Manifesto* and other writings of the late 1840s.

Two other works from this period are notable. As a concise statement on communist programmatic orientations, the "Critique of the Gotha Program" (1875) was an important statement by Marx on political practice. Finally, *Grundrisse*, consisting of seven notebooks drafted during 1857 and 1858, was intended by Marx to represent his first scientific and theoretical elaboration of communism and be an outline of his full project. *Grundrisse* was not published in the German original until 1939 and not in English until 1973.

After Marx took up residence in London, there were few if any changes in his thinking. His efforts were directed toward elaborating and documenting his system and making it the dominant mode of thought within working-class organizations. In this latter sphere, the efforts of Engels count as much as those of Marx. Aside from the important works of this period, both Marx and Engels engaged in violent polemics against leaders of the European labor movements who did not subscribe to a Marxist line. The concern of Marx and Engels was to prevent the proletarian movement from falling into the hands of ideologically suspect opportunists. In reviewing the body of literature that dates from this time, it is necessary to separate the expedient polemics from the seriously theoretical.

In summarizing this discussion of Marx, let us first outline the major periods and works of his life and thought and then focus on some of his principal ideas.

Early Works: 1840–1845

This is Marx's "ideological" period, including his doctoral dissertation, *Economic and Philosophical Manuscripts of 1844*, and *The Holy Family*. In this period Marx broke with Kant, contended with Hegel's idealism, and modified Feuerbach's materialism.

Works of the Break: 1845 and 1846

As representative works of this period, *The German Ideology* and *Theses on Feuerbach* signify Marx's break with "ideological philosophy" as well as his development of a "new theoretical consciousness" embracing conceptualization of dialectical and historical materialism. Marx himself located his break in *The German Ideology*.

Transitional Works: 1846–1857

The transition from "ideological" to "scientific" works was represented by such works as the *Communist Manifesto, Eighteenth Brumaire,* and *The Poverty of Philosophy*.

Mature Works: 1857–1883

These include in particular *Capital* but also *Grundrisse.*

The outline relies especially upon the periods suggested by the French Marxist scholar Althusser (1970: 31–39), who marked the break in Marx's works at 1845. He was concerned with Marx's critique of Hegel and Feuerbach, while the Italian Marxist scholar Colletti (1972) identified the break at 1843. Nicolaus (1973) demonstrated the significance and the scientific nature of Marx's mature works, while at the same time making clear the continuity in thought that pervades the early as well as the later writings.

The concept of *alienation* is of considerable significance in Marx's writings. The Young Hegelians gave an idealistic conception to Hegel's metaphysical use of the term. Influenced especially by Feuerbach's humanism, Marx turned against idealism and gave a concrete meaning to the term by rooting it in the labor process and thereby establishing a basis for a humanistic critique of capitalist society. According to Marx, labor and its product assume an existence separate from the individual once private property and the division of labor develop. This separation results in alienation for the worker. Marx's elaboration of this idea in the 1844 manuscripts was followed shortly by his criticism of Feuerbach, set down in eleven theses.

The manuscripts provide an initial framework for a critique of capitalism. It is argued by some that they are an early draft of *Capital,* that the explicit discussion of alienation that appears in Marx's early works is implicitly rooted in his later works. Erich Fromm, for example, asserted the continuity in thought between the young and the mature Marx and demonstrated the importance of alienation as a concept in Marx's late as well as his early writings (Fromm 1961). Fromm's position also opposes the view and analysis of Althusser, who carefully distinguished between Marx's early and late writings and emphasized his mature "scientific" work.

Some early themes, such as alienation, are not dealt with directly in *Capital* but appear in *Grundrisse* where they are clarified (Nicolaus 1973: 50–51). Writers such as David McLellan (1973) placed *Grundrisse* at the center of Marx's thought, and they stressed the linkage with the alienation theory of 1844 to show the humanistic aspects of Marxist theory and to project a utopian vision of the individual and society. Such a vision deviates from the interpretation of Engels and other early writers, who argued that Marx gave socialism its scientific foundation while eliminating its utopianism. Clearly Marx was concerned in his mature writings with the discovery of economic laws. Thus *Grundrisse,* indeed the full range of Marx's work, brings humanistic aspects and a vision of society beyond capitalism together with a scientific theory that exposes the workings of a capitalist political economy.

Also deserving of elaboration is Marx's theory of history or *historical materialism.* In setting forth his theory Marx repudiated the metaphysical and ideological abstractions of the German philosophers. His conception of historical materialism is alluded to in the 1844 manuscripts and elaborated in *The German Ideology.* Marx understood alienation as a historical and social phenomenon related to the emergence of private property and the division of labor. He attacked the philosophy but retained the *dialectic* of Hegel's writings. He criticized Feuerbach's philosophical materialism as ahistorical and passive. He argued that human consciousness is conditioned by the dialectical interplay between the subject, or the individual in society, and the object, or the material world in which one lives. Thus history is a process of continuous creation, satisfaction, and re-creation of human needs. A summary of Marx's perspective of history, drawn from *The German Ideology,* follows.

The initial premise of history is that people must be able to live in order to shape history. This involves the production of means, such as tools, land, and machinery, to satisfy the basic needs of food, shelter, clothing, and the like. Satisfaction of these primary needs leads to new needs. By the procreation of life, families develop both natural and social relationships. Social relationships involve the cooperation of several individuals. It follows that a certain *mode of cooperation* or relation is always combined with a certain *mode of production.* The mode of production is the totality of the relations of production and the *productive forces* of the members of society. The forces of production comprise the productive capacity of a society and the machinery, level of technology, and size and skill of the working population. In these primary historical relationships people possess a *consciousness* of sensuous environment and of relationships with other persons and things. Consciousness comes into contradiction with the forces of production, which results in a *division of labor.* The division of labor provokes an unequal distribution of labor and its products in the form of property, so that wife and children may become slaves of the husband in the family, or the family may become the slave of some alien entity, which takes the form of the state. The division of labor determines social classes of rulers and masses.

The struggles of history in illusory form are those among democracy, aristocracy, and monarchy, but in real form they are the struggles of the different classes. And these struggles extend from individual and family, to community and nation, and ultimately to the whole world. Under capitalism, one class lives by owning, and the other class lives by working. The interests of those who own the means of production and of those who work for them are opposed. The owners defend their property; the workers defend humanity. Thus conflict exists between the two classes. Class struggle disappears with the absolution of private property and the implementation of a communistic regulation of production, which in turn destroys the alien relation between people and what they produce—this results in exchanges and production under their own control.

This summary and the preceding discussion have been concerned with concepts such as alienation, historical materialism, dialectic, mode of production, productive forces, relations of production, consciousness, division of labor, and class structure and struggle (see Bottomore 1983 for elaboration of these and other concepts). As will be demonstrated in ensuing chapters, these concepts are essential in understanding the efforts of Marxist and other scholars to establish an alternative paradigm in comparative politics.

Max Weber

In 1864 Marx finished the first volume of *Capital* and participated in the founding of the First International. That was also the year Max Weber was born in Frankfurt in western Germany. The son of a civil servant and an erstwhile politician, Weber grew up under the influence of the narrow intellectual circle in which his father moved. Historians held sway in the group, and art and literature were neglected. The outcome was that Weber remained something of a philistine throughout his life.

Weber entered the University of Heidelberg in 1882, electing to study economics, philosophy, and Roman law. In 1883, the year Marx died in London, Weber served briefly in the military on the eastern marches of the new Prussian Empire, returning to his studies later at the University of Berlin. Unlike the impact it had on the young Marx nearly a half century earlier, Weber's study at Berlin does not seem to have had any special influence on the development of his thought. His intellectual crises came later in life. By 1885 Weber had moved to the University of Göttingen where, in 1889, he completed his doctoral dissertation on medieval trading companies.

From 1889 to 1891 Weber served in a minor legal post in Berlin, while composing a thesis in order to qualify for university teaching. He subsequently received an appointment in 1892 to the University of Berlin law school, where he lectured until receiving a full professorship in economics at the University of Freiburg im Breisgau in 1894. In 1896 Weber was elected to a chair in economics at the University of Heidelberg, thus having attained the status of full professor in the space of four teaching years. The distinction he received as a scholar, however, did not prove sufficient compensation for his failure to achieve success in active politics. Weber openly detested the responsibilities of university lecturing. During these early years he pursued a separate career alongside his university post, serving as a consultant to several public and private organizations. In connection with these duties, he examined a wide range of subjects, including the German stock exchange and the East Prussian agrarian question. The results of these studies, along with his university lectures, reveal the formative phase of his thinking, and are a prelude to the subjects and techniques that distinguish his later works.

In 1897 Weber suffered a nervous breakdown, and eventually he found it necessary to suspend his university duties. Between 1899 and 1904 he found a partial remedy to his illness in traveling, and during that time he toured much of Europe. By 1903 he was sufficiently recovered to join Werner Sombart and Edgar Jaffe as a coeditor of the *Archiv für Sozialwissenschaft und Sozialpolitik*. This facilitated his reaffiliation with the academic community and the beginning of a new period of productivity. About this time, he was offered a new university appointment, but in the end he felt compelled to decline for reasons of health. In reality, a family inheritance allowed him to live the life of a private scholar, thus sparing him the "drudgery" of university life.

In 1904, after a short visit to the United States, Weber undertook to write his most widely known work, *The Protestant Ethic and the Spirit of Capitalism*. In this study Weber sought to demonstrate that the tenets of Protestantism concerning the notion of predestination transformed themselves over time into a class pathos of the bourgeoisie (Weber 1958b: 160–176). His intention was to prove that the Reformation of the sixteenth century was necessary (along with a number of other social and economic considerations) for the subsequent development of modern capitalism. In this vein, he attempted to explain the special behavior of the entrepreneur by referring to the possibilities of the socioeconomic environment and to the motivating influence of the Protestant ethic as infused into the secular sphere of life.

During this same period, Weber published an essay on methodology in which he outlined the use of "ideal types." The ideal type is an artificial construct the social scientist can use to conceptualize analytical categories with utility for historical understanding (Weber 1962: 32–33). Weber's most famous ideal types are those that pertain to authority: traditional authority, charismatic authority, and legal-rational authority. These are not presumed to exist in history in the "pure form" portrayed in the ideal type, Weber asserted, but they provide typical features of different systems of authority visible in history. The scholar can, therefore, assess the relative proximity or divergence of a system of authority found in history to the three types and, on the basis of the theoretical propositions implicit for each ideal type, assess the impact of that system of authority upon the subject civilization.

In the following years Weber worked on a comparative study of the great world religions in an effort to substantiate his contention in *The Protestant Ethic* that religion is crucial in one's explanation of the alternative paths along which the major civilizations have developed. During this study, Weber became certain that the division between church and state that developed gradually within European civilization was central to the explanation of modern rationalism. It was in the course of these investigations that Weber declared himself preeminently a "sociologist," and he set for himself for the remainder of his life the task of developing this nascent discipline. Oddly enough, however, he remained largely ignorant of the findings of his greatest contemporary, the French sociologist Emile Durkheim.

In 1918 Weber returned to academia in a specially created chair of sociology at the University of Vienna. In 1919 he was appointed professor of sociology at Munich and began the writing of a comparative study of sociology that was to serve as the core of the new discipline and the starting point for later elaborations of the field. Weber died in 1920 with only a portion of that work completed. It was published in German two years later. Only fragments of the final attempt at a synthesis of his thought have been translated into English. Weber was only 56 when he died of influenza, and had he lived longer he might have succeeded in pulling the diverse strands of his writings into a coherent whole. But since this did not happen, the modern student of Weber's sociology is confronted with a vast body of literature that contains contradictions and ambiguities.

In summary, we identify the major periods and works of Weber's life, then turn to a brief discussion of some of his principal ideas.

Early Works: 1889–1897

During this period Weber wrote a doctoral dissertation, "A Contribution to the History of Medieval Business Organizations," a technical work dealing with legal aspects of the medieval trading enterprise. His second work (1889), "Roman Agrarian History and Its Significance for Public and Private Law," presented a detailed analysis of Roman land tenure. From 1894 to 1897 he published articles on the operation of the stock exchange and its relationship to capital financing; he argued that the stock exchange did not operate solely for speculation but also facilitated planning for the businessman. These early writings reflect the thrust of Weber's later work, notably the concern with an analysis of European capitalism. Giddens acknowledged that this concern brought Weber "into direct relation with the areas in which Marxist thought was concentrated" (1971: 124) but stated that his views were developed not only in the context of a confrontation with Marxism but within the intellectual milieu of his time.

Works on Religion and Secularity: 1903–1920

Weber was not productive during the years of his illness from 1897 until about 1903 when he became a journal editor. Two long articles published in 1904 and 1905 constituted his *Protestant Ethic and the Spirit of Capitalism*. In this examination of the relationship of Protestant beliefs and disciplines to modern capitalism, Weber contended with Engels's premise that Protestantism is an ideological reflection of the changes that accompanied the early development of capitalism. In subsequent works Weber also delved into the comparative study of religion in other parts of the world, including China, India, and ancient Palestine. His attention to religious beliefs led him to focus on the degree of rationalism in many forms of economic activity. At the same time he advocated the rejection of a materialist as well as an idealistic interpretation of history.

Works on Political Sociology and Methodology

English translations of Weber's original writings in German have tended to draw from portions rather than the complete works. For example, most of his relevant work on the social sciences has been extracted from *Wirtschaft und Gesellschaft*, a series of incomplete studies that was edited and published posthumously. Bendix (1960) provided a guide that clarifies the relationship between the original and the translated versions of Weber's work.

Portions of *Wirtschaft und Gesellschaft* are found in a number of modern editions of Weber's work (especially Weber 1947, 1958a, and 1967). In addition, the reader should examine Weber's *Basic Concepts in Sociology* (1962), a fragmentary effort at conceptualization, and *The Methodology of the Social Sciences* (1949), which comprises Weber's most important essays on the topic.

Weber came to his view of history by way of Heinrich Rickert and Theodor Mommsen, who influenced him both personally and academically, and in response to the intellectual atmosphere of his childhood. From the historian, Rickert, he accepted the proposition that the "sensible" world with which social science contends is infinite, and hence no knowledge of it can be complete. In contradistinction to the natural sciences, then, social science cannot proceed systematically to the discovery of universal axioms. History cannot, in this view, supply social science with general laws. From Mommsen's history of Rome, Weber extracted the basis of his historical technique. Mommsen employed the terminology of the nineteenth-century partisan political struggle to construct a narrative of Roman history that would be at once comprehensible to his contemporaries (while recognizing that the concepts denoted orientations not in existence for the time period under study). Given Weber's notion of the relativity of values in history, he approved of Mommsen's approach and used it as the jumping-off point for his own treatment of history. Drawing upon conceptualizations grounded in his own age, Weber built a matrix of analytical categories by means of which a comparative analysis of history could be undertaken. This approach aims at understanding history through the process of comparing the past to the present.

Congruent with the specializations of his education, Weber began refining his comparative historical perspective by concentrating upon political and economic phenomena. By this selection, he arrived at a preoccupation with capitalist behavior, rational systems of social authority, and the manipulation of power through the institution of bureaucracy. In adopting these topics as guidelines for the study of history, he did not aim at revealing them to be teleological outgrowths of antecedents to be found in earlier civilizations. For Weber, history was valuable for its heuristic properties: history reveals the principles of cause and effect for the particular subjects under study, but history is incapable of producing laws of causation. Moreover, the principles of causation that history can teach us are complex, and composed of the counterconditioning of a multiplicity of variables.

Weber believed that one cannot deduce from history what is not there and that history contains no universal laws, much less single-factor laws such as the economic explanation of development (Aron 1964). What the study of history does permit is the identification of probabilities. From this standpoint, the researcher searches for variables that militate in this or that direction—variables that increase the likelihood that history will unfold in a given direction. Weber's historical methodology seeks for the "necessary" conditions of a given path of historical development, and it abandons the notion that the "sufficient" conditions can be pinpointed. When applied to an extended period of time, this methodological outlook attempts to demonstrate that at each successive stage of a civilization, an array of variables will combine to render a particular future course of development more or less likely. With this treatment of history, the scholar can affirm the hypothesis that a certain variable (say, religion) was critical in the subsequent course of events, by conceiving the civilization without that variable and constructing a hypothetical alternative history based on logical deduction. If the alternative that is most probable in history leads to developments markedly different from those that in fact occurred, the scholar is justified in theorizing about the importance of the variable that has been isolated for the society in question. Such is the methodological basis for Weber's causal imputations.

Weber was not directly enmeshed in the tradition of positivism that had influenced his French contemporary, Emile Durkheim, that is, to build his ideas on Comte and those before him. Weber rejected the Comtian notion that the sciences are ordered into some logical hierarchy. However, he frequently has been identified with positivist and liberal social science (Roth 1965). Indeed there are aspects of Weberian thought that provoke some critics to associate him with contemporary positivist social science, upon which he has exerted a considerable influence. On the one hand, Weber was readily assimilated into structural functionalism. On the other, pieces of his work have been torn out of context and adapted to the narrow ahistorical forms of many social scientists in the United States.

One area of criticism relates to Weber's attention to objectivity and empirical science, to values in inquiry, to ideal type constructs, and to rationalization, which has come to dominate economic life in the Western world. Weber's use of sociology was oriented to a separation of empirical and normative tendencies and an acknowledgment of sociology as an empirical science; to a distinction between sociology and history; and to an empirical investigation that would use qualitative tools to find facts and information about contemporary phenomena (Roth 1969).

Weber argued, for example, that *objectivity* must not be sacrificed in social science inquiry, that intuition must not be substituted for causal analysis. Although value judgments may intrude upon scientific discussion, they cannot be validated through scientific inquiry. Weber was not apolitical in everyday life, however. He held a highly articulate view of politics, and he took positions on political issues of his day (Bendix and Roth 1971).

Weber's understanding of objectivity and values led him to compare ideal types and facts. He did so by the construction of an *ideal type* in a heuristic way. The ideal type construction was the means for explicitly relating a historical event to its real causes. He even went so far as to argue that all specifically Marxian laws and developmental constructs—insofar as they are theoretically sound—are ideal types. Clearly Weber was not a Marxist, and he held doubts about the prospects for democratic socialism in Germany, but he also hesitated to reject many of Marx's ideas out of hand. For example, he was very much concerned with the dialectical view, and thus there was an ambivalence in his desire to be as scientific as possible. Schneider (1971) has elaborated on this ambivalence in his work.

Weber's obsession with science became wrapped up in his ideas of *rationality*. Essentially his essays on Protestantism and the rise of capitalism in the West challenged Marxist interpretations of history. Efficiency, professionalization, and bureaucratization were all characteristics that Weber saw in the rationalization process (Ritzer 1975).

Influenced by Weber, some contemporary social scientists have unwittingly confused their interpretations of Weber's work. One example is Talcott Parsons, whose early writing focused on Weber. In their critique, Cohen, Hazelrigg, and Pope (1975) stated, for example, that it is assumed that Parsons has offered a faithful interpretation. Yet Parsons, by building on the strengths of Weber and enhancing his views by allusions to the heritage of Weberian ideas, has confused readers as the direction of his own theoretical perspectives has changed from a voluntaristic theory of action in his early writings to structural functionalism and evolutionism in his later works. This confusion is a consequence of Parsons's emphasis on some aspects of Weber's theory in a manner different from that of Weber; his assertion of interpretations rejected by Weber; his equation of concepts, resulting in distortion of Weber's meaning; and his generalization of aspects of Weber's work in contradiction of a particular characterization.

Marx and Weber in Perspective

In many respects, the writings of Karl Marx are a logical outgrowth of the period in which he lived. The course of European thought during his lifetime was subject to a variety of currents, and it was from this very diversity that Marx was able to build his own system. What he approved of in the works of his predecessors and contemporaries, he incorporated; what he disapproved of, he rejected. From German philosophy he adopted the dialectic, but he stigmatized the metaphysical formulations in which Hegel had first cast it. From France Marx first learned about socialism, but after doing so he destroyed its previous proponents polemically for their utopian and escapist mentalities. From the English political economists Marx gleaned a composite picture of the abuses inherent in the capitalist mode of accumulation and production, and he rejected any notion that mere reforms might ameliorate the abuses. But Marx passed beyond simply abstracting facts from others; he brought a new insight to bear on the pressing questions of his age.

Marx sought to impose a coherence on knowledge by forcing it into the confines of a single, all-inclusive theory of history. In the development of this theory, Marx may be observed to pass moral judgment on his own civilization, which can be paraphrased as follows. Capitalist society, with its abuses and exploitation, has played out its hand in history and contributed to the progress of man by elevating human productivity to a new plane. The very success of the capitalists has now rendered them superfluous, and the workers themselves will overthrow the state and take over the management of production for the benefit of society as a whole and not for the benefit of a select few.

The political implication of this prophecy was that the class conflict is inevitable and, in the final analysis, beneficial. Marx's emphasis on action stemmed from his rejection of the romanticism of his youth. At the same time, European thought in the midnineteenth century was, for all the advances of the Enlightenment, still heavily romanticized. Consequently, Marx was seldom at a loss for a strain of thought to criticize for its fanciful reasoning or utopian undertones. Against such intellectualism, Marx distinguished his theories by a rigorous system and produced historical materialism as the basis of "scientific socialism." The political unrest of the late 1840s and the intellectual ferment that preceded it for a generation confronted Marx with a course of events that seemed to substantiate his insights. And the capitalism of his day was not inaccurately revealed in its excess and exploitation in the writings of Marx, as even his critics will attest. It can be seen, therefore, that the socioeconomic milieu in which Marx lived was extremely conducive to his genius developing in the directions it did.

But by the time Max Weber was a young man, the Europe of Marx no longer existed. The entire array of political, technological, and economic conditions of the Continent was changed. From the Franco-Prussian War of 1870 until the outbreak of the First World War, the major European states were at peace internally and externally (exclusive of colonial struggles). The internal setting of the more developed European states seemed to present a refutation to the Marxist prophecy of revolutionary change. In this context, Weber, as the student par excellence of the unfolding rationalism of capitalist society, appears to many as a counterpoint to Marx (Bendex and Roth 1971).

It must be remembered, however, that a number of Marxist writings were not published until after Weber's death, nor was it Marx himself who was controversial so much as the political activists who claimed to be Marxists. It was against the Social Democratic Party (SPD) of the German Empire, then, that Weber took most direct exception. Weber held the leadership of the SPD to be politically unskilled and unable to wield power effectively should they chance to acquire it. On the more theoretical side of the issue, Weber took the Marxist notion of class consciousness (upon which the SPD attempted to build its electoral strength) to be a gross error, and he stigmatized the explanation of history found in dialectical materialism as simplistic and unscientific. Throughout all of this his references to Marx are never direct, and the depth of his investigation into the other aspects of Marxism is not notable.

A fundamental difference between the orientations of Marx and Weber that helps reveal the nature of their thought is that Marx concerned himself with discovering the patterns of uniformities that underlie every period of history. Weber, for his part, viewed European capitalism as the culmination of European history considered as a single civilization. In this sense, every period in European history is important for its uniqueness (which in turn provides insight into the uniqueness of capitalist civilization) rather than for its regularity (which causes difficulty when trying to explain the difference of other civilizations, e.g., Chinese culture). Both systems of historical conceptualization, however, have gained utility in the comparative study of government and politics.

On behalf of the curious reader we now delve into some of the critical literature that compares and contrasts the thought of Marx and Weber. First, we attempt to establish the setting of contemporary social science into which their ideas have been cast. Then we summarize some major distinctions between their thinkings.

It has been argued (Tiryakian 1975) that the thought of Weber rather than that of Marx most appropriately relates to an interpretation of U.S. society. This is so because Weber visited and knew more about the United States. Further, his Protestant background and his insights into Puritan culture and the Protestant ethic facilitate the "fit" of his thinking with a conception of U.S. society. Weber's view of liberalism often is associated with his impact on U.S. social science. Richard Ashcraft argued that Marx and Weber have profoundly influenced divergent tendencies. "Their common agreement on the characterization of liberalism as bourgeois ideology concealed differences of historical interpretation, conflicting conceptions of methodology, and opposing views of the social structure" (1972: 131). Some of the differences he cited relate to views on economic causes, ideology, and class.

The significance of comparing the thought of Marx and Weber has been emphasized by Carl Mayer, who stated that prior to Weber's illness at the turn of the century he was not much influenced by Marx nor did he attempt any critical analysis of Marx until the later years of his life. Mayer noted substantial differences between their understanding of system and ideology, social action, dialectic, evolution, and science, and he concluded that in the thought of Marx and Weber "there is agreement in many essential details, but there is a fundamental difference in regard to the decisive methodological positions with which we are confronted in the social sciences (Mayer 1975: 714–715). He attributed these differences ultimately to his belief that Marx methodologically was a Hegelian, and Weber a Kantian. Curiously, such a dichotomy of philosophy continues to permeate German academic life today.

Günther Roth believed that the thought of Marx and Weber is not as incompatible as many critics suggest. For example, Irving Zeitlin (1968) focused on Weberian thought as an elaboration of Marxism, and George Lichtheim supported the view that "the whole of Weber's sociology of religion fits *without difficulty* into the Marxian scheme" (1961: 385). No doubt the German academic milieu was profoundly influenced by Marx at the turn of the century, and often it is assumed that Weber too was so influenced. One of Weber's contemporaries, Ernst Troeltsch, who had compared the holistic and dynamic character of the dialectic with the piecemeal and static character of positivism, interpreted Weber's work as profoundly Marxian and argued that it may even have transcended the Marxian dialectic: "Marx, in particular, seems to have made a deep and lasting impression" (Troeltsch, quoted in Bendix and Roth 1971: 230). Early in his career Talcott Parsons wrote that Weber's *Protestant Ethic* was a "refutation of the Marxist thesis"

(1929: 40), and Roth documented that Weber opposed Marxism, but he examined alleged Marxist influences upon Weber's early work and concluded that "Weber never had a Marxist phase." Even though Weber accepted the heuristic usefulness of historical materialism, he considered it unscientific, assumed it not to be linked to socialism, and condemned determinism in Marxism (Bendix and Roth 1971: 240). A different perspective suggested that Weber's view of historical materialism was distorted by the translation and interpretation of Talcott Parsons. Although Weber showed the relationship of the Protestant ethic to capitalism, he did not altogether negate historical materialism based on economic considerations (Löwy 1989).

Giddens (1971) and Atkinson (1972) outlined the major differences between Marx and Weber. Weber, for example, argued that revolution need not be necessary for the advancement of the working class; indeed the interests of the bourgeoisie, within capitalism, might involve an improvement in the political and economic conditions of the working class. Weber also acknowledged the importance of class conflicts in history but placed emphasis on the conflict among status groups and within other interests, such as those of political parties. Further, Weber, unlike Marx, separated factual from normative statements: "It is Weber's conviction that historical development cannot be interpreted in terms of a rational scheme which expresses what is normatively valid" (Giddens 1971: 195).

Colletti (1972) critiqued Weber's use of the ideal type as "a purely abstract and *conventional* 'model.'" Weber's scientific concept became "a utopia," he argued, and theoretical generalization could not contend with reality. Marx, in contrast, offered a history of economic thought, examining in particular the historical dynamics of the mode of production of bourgeois society. Colletti attempted to awaken the reader to some misinterpretations of Marx's work. First, there is the orthodox view of some Marxists that Marxism is a science, not an ideology, and it makes only objective and impartial judgments of fact. Colletti argued that such a "view clearly allows no room for a link between *science* and *class* consciousness, between science and ideology" (1972: 230). Another distortion is the view of some Marxists that political economy is essential. But, argued Colletti, all of Marx's major works focus on political economy: "For Marx, political economy is born with the extension and generalization of commodity production. It is born with capitalism and dies with it" (232).

Many differences and some similarities in the thought of Marx and Weber have been identified. Table 4.1 summarizes in a schematic way some of the major ideas that flow through their works.

Paradigmatic Influences on Comparative Politics

In examining the influence of Marxian and Weberian thought upon each subfield, we do not mean to imply a degree of categorical distinctiveness that in practice may be illusory. The subfields of state, culture, development, and class cluster

TABLE 4.1
Synthesis of the Thought of Marx and Weber: An Inventory of Ideas

Concept Idea	Marx	Weber
View of history	Holistic, historical, and materialistic. Based on mode of production.	Fragmentary and ahistorical. No knowledge of the world can be complete.
Reality	Reality is the objective of science.	Reality is unattainable because investigator and scope of inquiry are limited.
Theory (praxis)	Theory and practice combined in thought and action.	Theory is the foundation of inquiry. Application of knowledge to inquiry is marginal.
Social science knowledge	Liberated from ideology, social scientific knowledge exposes exploitation of one class over another.	Social science explains through empirical findings.
Politics	Social scientist is political, and should mix investigation with political activity.	Social scientist is apolitical and objective.
Values	Values mixed with knowledge and facts. Values have material bases.	Values separated from facts that are a basis for inquiry. Empirical science cannot provide binding norms.
Laws	History predicated on common laws related to differing modes of production, productive forces, and relations of production and economic development.	History has no common laws. History cannot generate general laws for social science.
Capitalism	Promotes exploitation of worker, resulting in alienation. Capitalism is wasteful, inefficient, and irrational.	Promotes development through rationalization, efficiency, and stability.
Dialectic	Contradictions of capitalism bring about its demise.	Capitalism transcends its contradictions through rational planning.
Society	Ultimately socialist, then communist, as means of production pass from private control to public control and to hands of workers' committee for managing affairs of bourgeoisie.	Ultimately secular and rationally bureaucratic in industrial capitalism. Competition. The highest good viewed in a nationalist context.
State	Disappears with emergence of classless society.	Strengthens with industrial capitalism, imperialist expansions, and rationalization of bureaucratic order.

(continues)

TABLE 4.1 (*cont.*)

Concept Idea	Marx	Weber
Action	Reflection of objective material conditions determined by production of individuals.	Actors reflect on subjective meaning of what they do or refrain from doing.
Industrial freedom	Possible under socialism, but limited under capitalism where choices are determined by class position. Freedom with elimination of alienation.	Possible under capitalism, as long as people can choose among alternative life styles.
Heuristic device (construct or categories)	Mode of production as material basis of society.	Ideal types in comparison with real situations.
Method	Dialectic.	Ideal typification.
Power	Dominating interests.	Competing and diffused interests.
Authority	Illegitimate through state or ruling class.	Legitimate domination through traditional, charismatic, and rational forms.
Imperialism	Historical phenomenon necessitated by capitalism and later characterized by Lenin as the highest stage of capitalism.	Expansive foreign policies of governments.

around theories and do indeed overlap, but we shall discuss each separately. Political economy also is relevant to the thinking of both men but will be discussed in a later chapter. Table 4.2 may also help the reader identify the essential concepts in the thought of Marx and Weber that are distinguishable among the four subfields.

State Theory

Contemporary politics has been considerably influenced by theories of state and system. The contributions of the anthropologists A. R. Radcliffe-Brown and Bronislaw Malinowski stimulated inquiry about system, especially its functional and structural characteristics. The sociologist Talcott Parsons drew upon their work as well as that of Weber in a formulation of system. In political science David Easton abstracted a theory of political system, with its inputs of demands and supports and outputs of decisions and policies. Influenced by Easton as well as by Parsons and Weber, Gabriel Almond combined their various approaches so that the applicability of systems theory to comparative politics might become more apparent. Almond explicitly substituted a conception of system for the more elusive term *state*. Neither Marx nor Weber directed attention explicitly to system, but both concerned themselves with the state, especially under capitalism. Thus, we turn to a discussion of their respective conceptions of the state.

TABLE 4.2

Essential Concepts in the Thought of Marx and Weber That Are Applicable
to Four Subfields of Comparative Politics

Theoretical Thrust	Marx	Weber
State	Monolithic capitalist state and ruling class (the economic class that rules politically through the state). Superstructure (ideology) and structural base (reality). Changes in the substructure of material forces, relations of production, and modes of production result in conflict and transformation of the superstructure.	Pluralist state of physical force and legitimized domination that promotes competition and distribution of power. Rationality, functional differentiation, and specialization, resulting in order, harmony, and efficiency.
Culture	Dominant authority is hierarchical and related to state and ruling class. Beliefs and symbols of culture conceived as part of the superstructure of ideology and false consciousness. Exploitation and illegitimate authority are parameters of ruling class dominance.	Dominant authority based on beliefs and symbols in relation to ideal types: traditional, charismatic, and rational. Routinization of rational authority reflects increasing socialization. Individualism plus voluntarism (obedience) and legitimate control are parameters of liberty.
Development	Historical materialism and the dialectic method. Theory grounded in the facts of historical reality, not in idealist and illusory conceptions. Development relates to human needs, and human consciousness is based on the dialectical interplay of human beings with the material world: its productive forces and modes of production. Focus on capitalist development.	Rationalization and ideal typology method. Theory grounded in clarification. Systematization of ideas and their impact on society. Emphasis on requisites of development. Focus on capitalist development.
Class	Bourgeoisie and proletariat as opposing classes under capitalism. Industrial capitalists and landowners conflict with wage laborers but fragmentation found in each of these big classes. Power concentrated in the dominant classes that control means of production.	Class and status groups seen as ideal types that affect dispersion of power and interests in the community. Mobility of individuals within status groups and status groups within classes based on initiative, achievement, and talent. Class fragmentation rather than solidarity viewed as consequence of religious beliefs, ethnic loyalties, and nationalism.

Marx offered an important conception of the state and its ruling class. All history, he believed, was the struggle of classes. Through time and struggle, society has become increasingly more simplified as antagonisms divide people into two hostile classes, the bourgeoisie and the proletariat. The first elements of the bourgeoisie sprang from the merchant class in towns that had been established in feudal times. Manufacturing quickly replaced the earlier form of production of the closed guilds, and as manufacturing was stimulated by the demands of new markets, a manufacturing bourgeoisie pushed aside the guild masters. With the further expansion of the markets and the invention of machinery, modern industry began to take the place of early manufacturing. A modern bourgeoisie emerged along with the establishment of modern industry and world markets, and it became essential that this bourgeoisie assure not only its economic dominance but also its political control over the modern state. As a consequence, "The executive of the modern state is but a committee for managing the common affairs of the whole bourgeoisie" (Marx 1974a: 69).

In his understanding of state, Marx was influenced by Hegel, but their conceptions differed nevertheless. The state was essential in Hegel's philosophy. He considered the state to be separate from civil society, that is, a society with government and laws, yet the state moderates and resolves the conflicts that emerge within civil society. After Hegel's death, his followers diverged in their interpretations of the state. The Left, or Young Hegelians, criticized his idea of state, and Marx took a radical position as early as 1843, arguing that the state is a creation of the civil society; the state perpetuates a hierarchical class structure and thus protects the interests of the ruling class. Although the interests of the ruling class may promote clashes with the state from time to time, the relationship between the ruling class and the state must not be obscured by such conflict; ultimately both the state and the ruling class should be abolished.

In Marx's view the class that rules economically, that is, owns and controls the means of production, also rules politically. Under capitalism the state is the agency that maintains the property relations of the wealthy minority, and the consequence is the oppression of one class by another. Thus the state does not represent all the people, rich and poor. The state does not stand above class as long as classes exist; it is always on the side of the rulers.

In drawing the relationship of the state to the ruling class, Marx offered a perspective of society. Differentiation exists within society between its superstructure and its structural base, sometimes referred to as the substructure or infrastructure. The base comprises productive forces and the social relations of production built upon them; that is, productive forces and the control and ownership of the means of production determine the divisions of labor that separate some members of society from other members. The legal and political superstructure consists of low or high levels of conceptions that the people have about the world. Such conceptions are dependent upon the base. They also are ideologies, resulting in false consciousness. The role of science, said Marx, is to expose those ideologies that are preserved in the interest of the dominant class. Only a revolution against those classes can rid the system of such ideologies. In the preface to his *Contribution to the Critique of Political Economy,* Marx summarized the following position as the essence of his thought.

> In the social production of their existence, men inevitably enter into definite relations, which are independent of their will, namely relations of production appropriate to a given stage in the development of their material forces of production. The totality of these relations of production constitutes the economic structure of society, the real foundation, on which arises a legal and political superstructure and to which correspond definite forms of social consciousness. The mode of production of material life conditions the general process of social, political, and intellectual life. It is not the consciousness of men that determines their existence, but their social existence that determines their consciousness. At a certain stage of development, the material productive forces of society come into conflict with the existing relations of production. ... From forms of development of the productive forces these relations turn into their fetters. Then begins an era of social revolution. The changes in the economic foundation lead sooner or later to the transformation of the whole immense superstructure. In studying such transformations it is always necessary to distinguish between the material transformation of the economic conditions of production, which can be determined with the precision of natural science, and the legal, political, religious, artistic or philosophic—in short, ideological forms in which men become conscious of this conflict and fight it out. ... No social order is ever destroyed before all the productive forces for which it is sufficient have been developed, and new superior relations of production never replace older ones before the material conditions for their existence have matured within the framework of the old society. ... In broad outline, the Asiatic, ancient, feudal, and modern bourgeois modes of production may be designated as epochs marking progress in the economic development of society. [Marx 1975: 425–426]

In summary, the essential elements of Marx's thinking that may be relevant to a critical discussion of state theory are ruling class, superstructure and structural base, reality and ideology, material forces and relations of production, as well as modes of production that have characterized epochs of history. The state exists alongside the ruling class and manages its affairs. The structural base is found in the material forces and relations of production—the mode of production or the real foundation that determines division in labor and class. The superstructure consists of the legal and political conceptions or theories that envision society as it should be, not as it is; they are ideals, abstracted from concrete historical phenomena, but such ideals perpetuate the false ideologies about the world in which people live.

Weber certainly was familiar with the Marxian use of superstructure and structural base as well as with the connotation of ideology. Weber, however, did "not accept Marx's assertion that social existence determines consciousness" (Mayer 1975: 706). Instead he examined the differences between the ideal and the real, an approach Mayer called "dualist." This willingness to focus on the ideal as well as on the real undoubtedly inspired Parsons and many other systems theorists to suggest abstractions and schemes that today pervade much of the comparative politics literature.

Weber was interested in general theory of society, and his use of the "ideal" type proved useful in such theory. He believed that the investigator could place himself subjectively into an actor's place and thereby interpret actions and motives. Weber also was concerned with the "interests" of individuals as linked with what Parsons has referred to as "systems of meanings" (Parsons, in Weber 1968: xxiii). It is not clear, though, that Weber stood as a systems theorist: "He explicitly repudiated the desire to set up a 'system' of scientific theory, and never completed a systematic work" (Parsons, in Weber 1947: 3). But Parsons insisted that there are important systematic elements in Weber's thought. For example, Weber believed that capitalism was essential to the modern world. Further, he identified Protestantism as an ingredient in the capitalist worldwide enterprise of market, money, property, and profit. Protestantism characterizes what Parsons inferred was Weber's modern Western system. Two aspects of the Protestant orientation help us understand Weber's conception of system. One is rationality; the drive of Protestantism is "for rational mastery over the world." The other is "functional differentiation and specialization of roles," a Protestant orientation promoted by valuing individualism in the "process of active mastery over the world" (Parsons, in Weber 1947: 80–81).

Weber also referred to the "ideal and material interests" in which all people are engaged. His observation implied a multiplicity of interests and many competing forces, and authority was based on "legitimate order" (Bendix 1960). All these terms are incorporated into Weber's conception of the state.

Weber defined the state as "a human community that (successfully) claims *the monopoly of legitimate use of physical force* within a given territory" (Weber 1958a: 78). Weber ascribed to the state the sole right to use physical force or violence, and it is within this context that he offered an understanding of politics as the "striving to share power or striving to influence the distribution of power, either among states or among groups within a state ... the state is a relation of men dominating men, a relation supported by means of legitimate ... violence" (Weber 1958a: 78). Through its right to use violence the state presides over a situation in which the dominance of some prevails over others. But dominance is the consequence of the competition among groups to gain power, all this within an order of legitimacy. Weber identified three legitimations of domination: traditional domination by the patriarch or patrimonial prince; charismatic domination by the prophet, warlord, demagogue, or party leader; and legal domination by the bureaucrat or state servant. Weber called these "pure" or ideal types. He preferred legal domination, for it implies routinization, harmony, efficiency, and order in the bureaucratic organization of the state.

What are the characteristics of this idealized bureaucracy? A high degree of specialization prevails because of the clear division of labor in the distribution of organizational tasks. Positions are structured hierarchically into a pyramid of authority, formal rules and regulations guide decisions and actions, lines of communication are clearly established among administrative levels, and impersonal detachment and relations ensure the rational carrying out of duties. Those are the rational and efficient characteristics of Weber's typical bureaucracy.

In summary, the aspects of Weber's thinking that relate to contemporary formulations of systems theory are rationality, functional differentiation, and specialization of roles within the framework of the state. Within the state and its physical force, there are competing forces and a plurality of interests that share in the power and influence the distribution of power. This competition takes place with an order of legitimized domination. Weber's idealized conception envisions routinization, harmony, and efficiency. Marx would condemn it as an aberration of false consciousness that distorts an understanding of the modern capitalist world.

The systemic conceptions of Marx and Weber are sharply different. Although both thinkers focused on the political ramifications of the state in the society at large, Marx interpreted the structure of the state as monolithic and tied to the interests of the ruling class, whereas Weber saw that structure as sanctioning a plurality of interests. Both concerned themselves with dominance: Marx viewed all forms of dominance under the capitalist state as illegitimate, and Weber looked to the legitimate forms of dominance. Marx advocated the abolition of the state and its classes; Weber envisioned the enhancement of the state through the legitimation of its activities. Marx understood changes in the state and the ruling class as reflections of historical materialism and the conflictual interplay of social relations and forces of production that have characterized various epochs. Weber, in contrast, concerned himself with the resolution of conflict through the rationalization of the bureaucratic order, for he saw European capitalism as promoting a highly rationalized and therefore stable form of society and felt that its maintenance was tantamount to preserving order. Both Marx and Weber examined how states use physical force or violence. Weber's explanation combined state force and violence with legitimacy, but Marx offered a broader definition in which the state can be nothing but a subtle instrument of coercion to suppress the lower strata.

Culture Theory

The politics of culture constitutes another major thrust in the literature of comparative politics. In its contemporary usage, political culture has a variety of meanings. In general it refers to beliefs, symbols, and values. For Gabriel Almond, all political systems are embedded in a pattern of orientations to political action. Samuel Beer and Adam Ulam argued that the pattern consists of ideas and traditions about authority. Sidney Verba referred to political culture as the orientations of all the members of a political system. These patterns may be cognitive, involving feelings about politics, or evaluative, involving judgments about politics. They are transmitted from generation to generation by varied institutions of communication and socialization such as the family, school, and work place.

These contemporary meanings of political culture suggest a concern with general patterns, such as cultural traditions relating to authority, on the one hand, and with particular patterns such as individual preferences about politics, on the other hand. Both Marx and Weber were interested in these two levels.

The contemporary use of political culture usually encompasses the subjective or psychological milieu for politics. Marx would relate this idea of culture to his general treatment of the superstructure, which pervades society at large. At a particular level he viewed culture in the context of human alienation. In contrast, Weber related culture on a general level to authority and legitimacy; this was apparent in his examination of religion. Weber's particular treatment of culture incorporated a belief in individualism and voluntarism. At bottom, Marx defined culture in materialistic terms, while Weber defined culture in idealistic terms. We turn now to their different conceptions.

Marx perceived materialism as the basis of all history, and therefore of culture, and he conceived of materialism as including the means and modes by which people reproduce their existence through production. Culture, with its beliefs and symbols, forms part of the superstructure of a capitalist society. As such, culture is static, for it serves to legitimize the materialist base, thus protecting the interests of the privileged ruling class. Culture manifests, promotes, and perpetuates ideology as false consciousness, and culture tends to persist through time. Transformations in the mode and in the relations and means of production have characterized periods of history. The contrast between the static culture and the dynamic materialist base reveals inherent contradictions and makes apparent the increasingly irrelevant culture in relation to the actual material practices of society. Thus, Marx identified periods of history as characterized by new cultural formulations upon which the state rested and within which the dominant class—be it composed of feudal lords, merchants, or industrial capitalists—legitimized its role of exploitation.

The contradictions of the base and the culture are evident at the individual level. In *Economic and Philosophical Manuscripts,* Marx expounded on the concept of alienated labor. He saw capitalism tending toward the impoverishment of the worker, while enriching the capitalist and allowing concentration of capital. "Labor is external to the worker ... he therefore does not confirm himself in his work, but denies himself, feels miserable and not happy, does not develop free mental and physical energy, but mortifies his flesh and ruins his mind" (Marx 1975: 326). In *The German Ideology,* Marx discussed how division of labor and private property result in cleavage. "As long as a cleavage exists between the particular and the common interest, as long, therefore, as the activity is not voluntary, but naturally divided, man's own deed becomes an alien power opposed to him, which enslaves him instead of being controlled by him." Marx described the relationship between the individual and the community as undermined once the interest of the community takes the "form of the state, divorced from the real interests of individual and community" (Marx and Engels 1973: 53). In *Grundrisse,* Marx distinguished between the private individual, meaning the owner of the means of production and labor power, and the social individual, meaning the new human being or "the universally developed individual" of a classless society (Marx and Engels 1973: 161–162).

"Weber's thinking was dominated by the concept of the ideal type, which he applied to both cultural content and individual motives." In this statement Talcott Parsons (Weber 1968: lxiii) implied that Weber's attention to culture was directed to the general as well as to the particular level of thinking. The essence of Weber's concern with culture, as has been true of many of his successors who have dealt with culture and personality theory, was the use of ideal types of legitimate authority.

Weber identified three ideal types of legitimate authority that affect culture (Weber 1947: pt. 3): traditional, charismatic, and rational authority. The legitimacy of traditional authority is based on rules handed down from the past, and personal status and authority rest with an individual or chief who has been chosen on a traditional basis. The legitimacy of this traditional system of authority is questioned only when new and unmanageable crises arise, for which solutions prove impotent. When the traditional authority crumbles, the society may come under the control of a charismatic authority, resting on loyalty to the exceptional heroism or the exemplary character of an individual, who stimulates faith among his followers.

The legitimacy of charismatic authority depends upon success in coping with the crisis that toppled the traditional order. The culture propagated by this style of authority is that of the prophet leading a people to a new future. Submission to faith in charismatic authority is in contrast to the submission to the religion or mysticism of traditional authority. Charismatic authority is opposed to the routine control of action, which characterizes both traditional and rational authority. With the fall of a charismatic leader, there are alternative ways for the followers to legitimize their new social standing. They may choose to construct a new traditionalism on the basis of the teachings of the charismatic leader. In this event a return to traditional authority comes about. They may decide instead to routinize authority, rationalizing it along several lines. This latter direction necessitates a secularization or separation of religious and governmental practices, which involves a proliferation of administrative regulatory functions, the introduction of impersonal discipline and rules of procedure, and an expansion of economic activity and taxation to finance the emerging bureaucracy.

These developments promote legal-rational authority as the consequence of some religious impact, for example, the Reformation, and of the capital accumulation that brought deep changes to Europe, whose history Weber believed to be of one coherent civilization. Thus those in the comparative field who model their cultural analysis after Weber must take caution not to generalize about the directions underdeveloped nations might follow, given changes in their culture, by referring to the European experience.

Weber identified examples of authority types in the collective cultural experiences of nations, groups, and even tribes, but he also noted particular orientations toward culture. Weber condemned the Prussian Junkers, for example, for their exploitation of the farm workers, yet he emphasized their positive contributions to the evolving German state. He did not see their motives and actions as a product of economic interests, as the Marxists maintain; instead he emphasized their individualism and determination in the face of a harsh environment. He also noted the individualism and basic drive of the farm workers who opposed the Junker ruling class: "We want to cultivate and support what appears to us as valuable in man: his personal responsibility, his basic drive toward higher things, toward the spiritual and moral values of mankind, even where this drive confronts us in its most primitive form" (Weber, quoted in Bendix 1960: 44). Weber's concern with the autonomy of the individual was clearly a reflection of the liberal legacy of the nineteenth century. It also became a basis upon which liberal scholars tended to examine individual orientations toward culture in the twentieth century, and it influenced theories of rational and individual choice that permeated behavioral work in comparative politics during the 1980s.

For Weber, then, culture was an important determinant of social action and, therefore, of the historical development of civilization. Beliefs and symbols are distinctive features of his notion of authority. Authority rests on two levels, the general and the particular. Ignored in this conception is coercive power, and assumed to exist is a belief system that legitimizes control as well as a voluntary obedience and compliance of subordinates to accept the will of their superiors.

In summary, the Marxist conception explains culture by referring to the political, social, and economic settings of society, whereas the Weberian conception explains the political, social, and economic settings by referring to the culture. Marx understood dominant authority as hierarchically vested in the capitalist state in concert with the ruling class. Exploitation characterized this class's dominance and illegitimate authority. Its so-called legitimacy was simply disguised within the ideology of beliefs and symbols that pervaded the culture and ideological superstructure. Weber considered that the beliefs and symbols of the culture reinforced and legitimized the various ideal types of dominant authority. Marx emphasized that the alienation of the individual in a materialist society was the consequence of a dominant authority and the exploitation of capitalism. Weber stressed the drive of the individual within a context of voluntary obedience and legitimate controls—the parameters of a liberal society in which rationalized bureaucratic order thrives. Thus, significant differences are apparent in the Marxist and Weberian interpretations of culture. Clearly each conception yields different categories and, consequently, different assumptions and explanations that affect the outcome of study in comparative politics.

Development Theory

Theories of development cluster around a variety of themes in the comparative politics literature. Democracy is a topic found in the traditional literature of political science. Democracy usually referred to the experience of Europe and the

United States, but when comparativists turned to the many new nations, especially in the Third World, there was a reassessment. Scholars such as Lucian Pye tended to replace *democracy* with the term *political development.* Stage theories of development also were common. Walt W. Rostow set forth a number of stages through which capitalist development progresses, and A.F.K. Organski modeled an approach to political development somewhat along the lines of Rostow. Literature on nation building, nationalism, and development was widely recognized after the Second World War; it is perhaps best represented by the contributions of Karl Deutsch and Rupert Emerson. Finally, there were interpretations based on modernization, usually in the form of industrialization and other advances of the capitalist nations; the works of David Apter and Samuel Huntington exemplify this tendency. All these theories of development reflect the prevailing mainstream paradigm of comparative politics. It is also clear that the ideas and thought of Max Weber have influenced the formulation of these theories.

A counterthrust emerged to oppose these mainstream theories of development in comparative politics. The new thrust examined underdevelopment, especially in the nations of Latin America, Africa, and Asia. Although the mainstream literature understood development to be the consequence of the diffusion of capital and technology from the advanced to the backward areas, critics of this interpretation saw the consequence of such diffusion to be underdevelopment itself. Attempts of the industrialized nations to apply their models of democracy and civic culture to backward areas were also futile, resulting in increased repression and exploitation.

Writers such as André Gunder Frank focused on the development of underdevelopment, arguing that capitalism on a world scale produces developing metropoles and underdeveloping satellites. Theotônio dos Santos referred to the era of "New Dependency" in characterizing monopoly capitalism and the activities of the multinational corporations throughout the world. Fernando Henrique Cardoso argued that dependent capitalist development was evident in the underdeveloped world. Cardoso and others also began to link their theories of dependency to Lenin's theory of imperialism. Many interpretations and applications of dependency were soon adopted by social scientists of many persuasions. The confusion that ensued was partially because of the failure of many writers to root their theory in the writings of Marx.

Marx's materialistic view focused on the development process. Marx saw most theories, except his own, as bourgeois and ideological. In his *Theses on Feuerbach,* Marx rejected speculative and philosophical views of reality and indicted both idealists and materialists. The eleventh thesis states, for example, "The philosophers have only *interpreted* the world, in various ways; the point is to *change* it" (Marx and Engels 1973: 123). Marx urged the scientific study of reality, of "the actual life process," and consequently he focused most of his attention on a critique of bourgeois capitalist society rather than on speculation about the future of society. Thus Marx sought a clear and direct view, a materialist view, of the world and, in particular, its developmental process through historical periods. His perspective of development was tied to his understanding of dialectical and historical materialism.

Marx intended his understanding to be scientific in the sense of avoiding materialist or idealist abstractions in favor of "human science." With Engels in *The German Ideology*, he wrote, "Where speculation ends, in real life, there positive science begins: the depiction of the practical activity, of the practical process of development, of men." The use of science here was not positivistic in the Comtian sense. "Marx uses the word throughout his writings in such a way that it is always quite incompatible with a crude, positivistic usage, although not all of Engels' formulations are incompatible with positivism in anything like the same way" (Thomas 1976: 7).

Marx's concepts of development are not definable in positivist terms. "Neither the 'relations of production' nor the 'mode of production' is definable in terms of physical objects; and even the 'forces of production,' which seem at first glance to be more empirical, are seen not as a concatenation of things but as a development, as something in transition, a development that takes place whenever the underlying social circumstances permit" (Thomas 1976: 9).

Marx believed that economic change can transform the superstructure of ideology, because human actions are dependent on changes in economic structure, in transformations affecting the dominant mode of production. Change for Marx is a reflection of a dialectical contradiction in the diverse social forces emerging from conflict. Carl Mayer described Marx's notion of dialectic as follows: "First, the conflict is only latently and potentially present and hidden by a relative harmony of interests. Then it becomes actual. It continues to rise, finally reaching a point where it puts the existence of the society in question" (Mayer 1975: 710).

Marx intended but never did write a full explanation of the dialectic, but its use is evident throughout his work. Marx of course gave a materialist interpretation to Hegel's idealist conception of the dialectic, and he turned Hegel's conception on its head by stripping it of mysticism and rigid schema. Howard Sherman called Marx's dialectic "a non-dogmatic method of approach to problems of science or politics of everyday life." He outlined five rules of the dialectic method along with questions for inquiry. First, *interconnection:* how does a problem relate to all of society? Second, *change:* how did the problem evolve and where is it headed? Third, unity of *opposites:* what are the opposing forces, where is the conflict? Fourth, *quantity and quality:* if a quantitative change is noted, what of qualitative change? Fifth, *negation of negation:* if one aspect eliminates another, can it in turn be eliminated? (Sherman 1976: 58–62). The method thus generates questions; it does not provide answers, but it does allow for a look at dynamic, not static, and at real, not ideal, aspects of society.

One example, drawn from Marx's *Introduction to a Critique of Political Economy*, demonstrates the dialectic method. Marx refuted the perspective of those economists who tended to treat four economic activities (production, distribution, exchange, and consumption) in isolation from each other. He began by demonstrating that production and consumption are one and the same and that each provides a means of bringing the other about.

> Production is thus at the same time consumption, and consumption is at the same time production. Each is simultaneously its opposite. But an intermediary movement takes place between the two at the same time. Production leads to consumption, for which it provides the material; consumption without production would have no object. But consumption also leads to production by providing for its products the subject for whom they are products. [quoted in Marx and Engels 1973: 131]

The dialectic method stimulates a continuous reassessment of theories according to new facts. It also promotes the search for new facts and their interpretation according to new theories.

Marx's materialism emphasized the grounding of theory on the facts of historical reality, and historical materialism provided Marx with a perspective of development.

> History is nothing but the succession of the separate generations, each of which exploits the materials, the capital funds, the productive forces handed down to it by all preceding generations. ... This conception of history depends on our ability to expound the real process of production, starting out from the material production of life itself, and to comprehend the form of intercourse connected with this and created by this mode of production ... as the basis of all history. [Marx and Engels 1973: 57–58]

Marx carefully separated this material base of successive generations in history from all idealistic views of history. The materialist view "remains constantly on the real ground of history," while the idealistic view looks for a category in every period; the materialist view "explains the formation of ideas from material practice," whereas the idealistic view explains "practice from the idea" (Marx and Engels 1973: 58). Marx believed that in history human consciousness is conditioned on the dialectical interplay between human beings and the material world. Accordingly, history is a continuous process of creating and satisfying human needs. Once needs are satisfied, new needs are created:

> There is found a material result: a sum of productive forces, an historically created relation of individuals to nature and to one another, which is handed down to each generation from its predecessor; a mass of productive forces, capital funds and conditions, which, on the one hand, is indeed modified by the new generation, but also on the other prescribes for it its conditions of life and gives it a definite development, a special character. [Marx and Engels 1973: 59]

Marx analyzed various types of society, including those manifesting Asiatic, ancient, and feudal modes of production, but his principal interest lay with an interpretation of the bourgeois mode of production in a capitalist society. His theory of capitalist development is found in *Capital:* "The wealth of those societies in which the capitalist mode of production prevails, presents itself as 'an immense accumulation of commodities,' its unit being a single commodity" (Marx 1967, 1:

35). A commodity, he said, is "an object outside us" that "satisfies human wants of some sort." Every commodity has a "use-value" or utility as well as "exchange-value" or the value of a product offered in exchange for other products. Marx related both of these values to labor in the production of a commodity. Labor itself is viewed as a commodity and is exchanged on the market. The worker produces enough to cover his cost of subsistence, but whatever he produces over and beyond is surplus value. Surplus value is a source of profit and capital accumulation.

Weber's ideal types of dominant and legitimate authority have already been noted. Weber clearly considered the development of legal rationality to be a major consideration in Western civilization, upon which he focused most of his attention. Bendix suggested that "Weber was not interested in developmental theories" (1960: 326). He tended to move abruptly from one type of domination to another, somewhat in piecemeal fashion. He was not interested in explanations that traced the evolution of the European state from its feudal foundations, but he was willing to identify the distinctive characteristics of the modern bourgeois state. Although there were many types of capitalism—for example, political, imperialist, colonial, adventure, fiscal, and modern industrial capitalism (Weber 1958a: 66–68)—capitalism was the highest formal rationalization in Western civilization. Weber isolated aspects that typified rational bourgeois capitalism: secularity was one such aspect, maximization of efficiency was another. Alongside bureaucratization, professionalization also was essential in the rationalization of society. Rationalization clarifies, systematizes, and integrates ideas, thus providing societies with ideal frameworks within which action, change, and stability are achieved; for example, as ideas become consistent and integrated within a society at large, they tend to create new problems that demand resolution.

Rationality also may promote irrationality; capitalism, for instance, might be based on the accumulation of wealth but not on the enjoyment of life for a majority of individuals. Carl Mayer (1975: 710–711) accordingly characterized Weber as a theorist of conflict, not of harmony as many critics have claimed. Weber assumed that a society may continue to exist in spite of conflict or that conflict may be resolved. Tradition becomes decisive in Weber's perspective of a changing society. Mayer also believed that Weber rejected the necessity of developmental stages as well as the notion that modern societies should be more highly valued than, say, ancient civilizations. This view contrasts with Talcott Parsons's assertion that Weber contributed "a generally evolutionary view of the development of human society" (Parsons, in Weber 1968: lx).

The nuances in Weber's thought no doubt deserve careful study, for the manner by which he described the rationalization of European capitalism at the turn of the century has come to constitute a model of development of considerable influence for comparative politics today. The rationalization of bureaucracy, the separation of church and state that leads to secularization, and the gradual institutionalization of parliamentarianism all form integral elements of that model. Characteristics of the model include administrative efficiency made possible by an insistence on professional skill for advancement; impersonal discipline that elevates the office over the occupant in a clearly deniable hierarchy of authority; elaboration of unambiguous written rules of operation; and specialization of functions in response to expanding social activity. Such a model institutes in society a stabilization of the socioeconomic order to a degree sufficient for the calculated risk that is capitalist investment. At the same time Weber argued that the bureaucratization of life brings in its wake an increasing probability of democratic practice. The requisites of democratic practice are tolerance, precise legality, and representative government. Within this context, a highly efficient order extracts social resources and utilizes them in realizing socially determined goals while, at the same time, mediating the competing demands of the citizenry.

Herbert Marcuse exposed some problems in Weber's conception of development. He examined the connections among capitalism, rationality, and domination in Weber's work. Western rationality, argued Marcuse, promotes a system of material and intellectual culture that develops in industrial capitalism and tends toward bureaucratic domination. This capitalist rationality evolves through private enterprise; thus the satisfaction of human needs is dependent on the profit possibilities of capitalist enterprise and the labor at its disposal. Marcuse insisted that such a conception is outmoded today by experience in the capitalist world—industrial capitalism has become irrational, not rational, because "the struggle for existence and the exploitation of labor must be intensified more and more if increased accumulation is to be possible"; development becomes irrational because "higher productivity, domination of nature, and social wealth become destructive forces" (Marcuse 1968: 207).

Weber did not anticipate such development, according to Marcuse, even though Weber envisioned "capitalist industrialization wholly as a form of power politics, that is imperialism" (208). Large-scale industry could guarantee national independence through the international competitive struggle of imperialist power politics and the expansion of colonialism and militarism. Ultimately, domination was based on the rationality of industrial capitalism, which in modern form became inseparable from bureaucratic control. The intensification of an efficient industrial organization extends to society as a whole and to control through bureaucratic administration.

In summary, Marx offered a dynamic conception of development premised on the interaction of people with the material world of productive forces and modes of production. Weber posited a static conception of development based on the identification of distinctive rational characteristics of the bureaucratic order of industrial states. Both Marx and Weber focused on bourgeois capitalism. Some critics would characterize Marx's perspective as revolutionary and realist, Weber's perspective as evolutionary and idealist. Marx used dialectics as his method; Weber employed ideal typologies. Marx looked for transformation in the structural base and grounded his theory on the facts of historical reality. Weber gave attention to the requisites of development, emphasizing routinization, efficiency, professionalization, secularity, differentiation, and specialization; and Weber grounded his theory on ideas and their impact on society.

Class Theory

Studies of ruler and ruled have marked the comparative literature of politics from ancient times until the present. The theoretical contributions of Marx and Weber on this subject have provoked controversy and deep polemical and intellectual divisions within the social sciences. A generation of community studies revealed fundamental differences related to questions of who rules in a society. A dichotomy of positions has evolved in the theory emanating from these studies.

One position, resting upon a prevailing assumption in U.S. politics called pluralism, holds that multiple diverse interests and, therefore, a wide dispersion of power characterize the democratic order. Sometimes pluralism envisions society as made up of conflicting power groups, each group using power to further its own interests. For U.S. politics this view is found in the work of Robert Dahl, V. O. Key, and a host of other political scientists. Its origins are often traced to James Madison's *Federalist Papers* and to group theorists David Truman and Arthur Bentley. Pluralist assumptions are also indebted to the formulations of Gaetano Mosca and Vilfredo Pareto, who recognized the distinctions between a class that rules and a class that is ruled and tended to identify divisions within the ruling class, especially in democratic societies. They emphasized rule according to interests, not simply by force, and they referred to a circulation of elites or changes in elite membership over time. It is also evident that advocates of pluralism have been influenced by Weber's thinking.

The pluralist elite theory of Mosca, Pareto, and Weber served to refute Marx's conception of the ruling class. In recent times Dahl, Nelson Polsby, and others continued this critique. Marx's thought influenced a counterposition, commonly known as the ruling-elite theory, although many of its advocates did not relate directly to a Marxist framework. This position is identifiable in Floyd Hunter's study of power structure in Atlanta and in C. Wright Mills's examination of the U.S. power elite. G. William Domhoff carried on the tradition. Their interpretations challenged assumptions of democratic pluralism in the United States.

The debate between the plural elitists and the ruling elitists deflected attention from Marx's essential concern with a class analysis. Unlike Weber, who used class as a category for describing capitalist society at a particular point in time, Marx linked class to the material base in order to examine the source of changes in capitalist society. Thus under capitalism two classes stand in dialectical opposition to each other. In the *Communist Manifesto,* these classes are the bourgeoisie, "the class of modern capitalists, owners of the means of the social production and employers of wage-labour," and the proletariat, "the class of modern wage-labourers who, having no means of production of their own, are reduced to selling their labour power in order to live" (Engels, in Marx 1974a: 67 n. 12). A Marxist understanding of capitalism necessitates an examination of the conflict between the two opposing class interests. Thus the ruling-elite analysis of Hunter and Mills does not relate to a Marxist framework, for their focus on a single class is static and exclusive of masses, nor does the stratification analysis of the political sociologists who emphasize position according to income, status, and other criteria. Whereas Marx looked for opposite attributes, stratificationists examine individual and group positions in relation to similar attributes.

Marx did not fully elaborate a conception of class, but class analysis is a central concern of his work. In the *Communist Manifesto,* Marx briefly traced the history of class antagonisms: patricians, knights, plebeians, and slaves in ancient Rome; feudal lords, vassals, guild masters, journeymen, apprentices, and serfs in the Middle Ages; and bourgeoisie and proletariat under modern bourgeois capitalism. The bourgeoisie fulfilled a historical role; they put an end to feudal relations.

> The bourgeoisie cannot exist without constantly revolutionizing the instruments of production, and thereby the relations of production, and with them the whole relations of society. Conservation of the old modes of production in unaltered form, was, on the contrary, the first condition of existence for all earlier industrial classes. Constant revolutionizing of production, uninterrupted disturbance of all social conditions, everlasting uncertainty and agitation distinguish the bourgeois epoch from all earlier ones. ... The need of a constantly expanding market for its products chases the bourgeoisie over the whole surface of the globe. It must nestle everywhere, settle everywhere, establish connections everywhere. [Marx 1974a: 70–71]

In contrast, the proletariat, the working class "who live only so long as they find work, and who find work only so long as their labor increases capital," are subservient to the bourgeois class. The proletariat assimilates

> the lower strata of the middle class—the small tradespeople, shopkeepers, and *rentiers,* the handicraftsmen and peasants—all these sink gradually into the proletariat, partly because their diminutive capital does not suffice for the scale on which modern industry is carried on, and is swamped in the competition with the large capitalist, partly because their specialized skill is rendered worthless by new methods of production. Thus the proletariat is recruited from all classes of the population. [Marx 1974a: 75]

In *The German Ideology,* Marx described the ruling class as a force that rules materially over production and intellectually over ideas.

> The ideas of the ruling class are in every epoch the ruling ideas, i.e. the class which is the ruling *material* force of society, is at the same time its ruling *intellectual* force. The class which has the means of material production at its disposal, has control at the same time over the means of mental production, so that thereby, generally speaking, the ideas of those who lack the means of mental production are subject to it. The ruling ideas are nothing more than the ideal expression of the dominant material relationships, the dominant material relationships grasped as ideas; hence of the relationships which make the one class the ruling one, therefore, the ideas of its dominance. [Marx and Engels 1973: 64]

In *The Class Struggles in France, 1848–1850* and *The Eighteenth Brumaire of Louis Bonaparte,* Marx directly applied his conception of class to the revolutionary events of the midnineteenth century. His analysis focused on such class terms as the finance aristocracy, industrial bourgeoisie, petty bourgeoisie, peasantry, lumpen proletariat, industrial proletariat, bourgeois monarchy, and big bourgeoisie. An excerpt from his journalistic account of the complex struggle reveals his use of class analysis.

> In France the petty bourgeois does what the industrial bourgeois would normally have to do; the worker does what would normally be the task of the petty bourgeoisie. Who then does the task of the worker? Nobody. It is not accomplished in France; it is only proclaimed. And it will not be accomplished within any national walls. The class war within French society will be transformed into a world war in which nation confronts nation. The worker's task will begin to be accomplished only when the world war carries the proletariat to the fore in the nation that dominates the world market, i.e. England. [Marx 1974b: 111–112]

Finally, in a brief last chapter of the third volume of *Capital*, Marx attempted to set forth a conception of classes: "Wage-labourers, capitalists and landowners constitute the three big classes of modern society based upon the capitalist mode of production." He urged caution in the stratification of classes, for in highly developed England, "Middle and intermediate strata even here obliterate lines of demarcation everywhere" (Marx 1967: 3:885). Marx acknowledged the existence of less important classes—physicians and bureaucrats are two separate classes. Likewise, "the infinite fragmentation of interest and rank into which the division of social labour splits labourers as well as capitalists and landlords—the latter, e.g. into owners of vineyards, farm owners, owners of forests, mine owners and owners of fisheries" (Marx 1967: 3:886). This reference by Marx to middle and intermediate classes was to provoke later attention by Nicos Poulantzas to the notion of a new petty bourgeoisie and by Erik Olin Wright to the idea of a new middle class.

The cursory review of Marx's writings on class is not meant to be definitive or even an attempt at a reconstruction of Marx's theory of classes and class struggle. What is clear, however, is that Marx's theory and analysis of class are neither doctrinaire nor deterministic and that he applied his criteria more prudently than did many of his followers.

Weber also delineated a conception of class, especially in *Wirtschaft und Gesellschaft*, and in a discussion on the distribution of power within a community, he focused first on class.

> We may speak of a "class" when (1) a number of people have in common a specific causal component of their life chances, in so far as (2) this component is represented exclusively by economic interests in the possession of goods and opportunities for income, and (3) is represented under the conditions of the commodity or labor markets. [Weber 1958a: 181]

His reference to life chances relates to "the way in which the disposition over material property is distributed among a plurality of people, meeting competitively in the market for the purpose of exchange" (Weber 1958a: 181). Possession of goods and opportunities for income imply ownership or lack of ownership of property. For Marx, property and the lack of property signified the class relations of the material productive base of society. For Weber, they were simply "basic categories of all class situations" (182). Ultimately, Weber said, a class situation is a market situation.

Concerned that class is an economically determined concept, Weber proposed that status groups also affect the distribution of power in a community, but his definition distinguishes between class and status group.

> In contrast to the purely economically determined "class situation" we wish to designate as "status situation" every typical component of the life fate of men that is determined by a specific, positive or negative, social estimation of *honor*. This honor may be connected with any quality shared by a plurality, and, of course, it can be knit to a class situation: class distinctions are linked in the most varied ways with status distinctions. ... But status honor need not necessarily be linked with a "class situation." [Weber 1958a: 187]

All status groups exist within the confines of what, according to Weber, can be defined as economic classes. These larger classes are not precisely circumscribed, nor do they reflect a high degree of commonality in the interests, dispositions, and loyalties of their members. Each class is composed of many status groups, so that it is possible to speak of a stratification of status groups within a class, hierarchically ranked in accord with relative market advantage. As the market demands change, the relationship of the status groups within a class may be constantly rearranged. Some of the market changes might elevate one status group from a lower to a higher class. Similarly, some status groups might slip in ranking. This argument suggests that persons are more interested in the fortunes of their status group than in the overall fortunes of the class to which they nominally belong. This leads Weber to a rejection of the Marxist notion of class consciousness since, in his view, there is insufficient shared interest among a group of individuals constituting the descriptive category of one or another class.

Not only is the mobility of status groups in flux, so too are the varying fortunes of individuals within status groups. Important is the ethic of individualism and achievement inherent in, according to Weber, modern capitalist democracy. By force of talent and initiative, an individual can move to membership in a higher status group through training, profession, and change in life style.

Reinhard Bendix (1974) synthesized and interpreted these propositions by contrasting Weber's stance to Marx's position. Weber, he said, accepted Marx's assertion that property ownership and division of labor are bases for the formation of classes, but Weber's approach differed from Marx's analysis in three ways. First, whereas Marx understood class as a consequence of productive forces and relations, Weber treated class as an ideal type. Second, Marx identified three large classes (landowners, capitalists, and workers) under capitalism and noted a tendency toward the formulation of two opposing classes of bourgeoisie and proletariat, but Weber anticipated a greater variety of class situations. Third, Marx optimistically believed that class consciousness would solidify the working class into a revolutionary force, but Weber argued that nationalism, religious beliefs, and ethnic loyalties would prove stronger than class consciousness and would promote class fragmentation.

Other distinctions are discernible in the class perspectives of Marx and Weber. Ashcraft mentioned that a large segment of U.S. political sociologists have adopted the Weberian view that income is a criterion of class, a position Marx clearly rejected. Further, Weber refused to consider class as anything other than an economic grouping—thus his sharp distinction between the economic and the social orders. The Weberian position influenced Weber's successors: "in removing from 'class' the social relationships Marx had included in his definition, Weber opened the door for a sociology based conceptually on the 'infinite dissipation of interests,' which, of course, liberalism had every ideological reason to embrace" (Ashcraft 1972: 147).

The question of which precursor has influenced our understanding of class was addressed by Erik Olin Wright, who argued that Weberians have less difficulty than Marxists in forming a concept of class because their approach does not have to link to the abstract notion of mode of production; it is not based on a model of antagonistic relations; and it does not deal with a hierarchy of conceptual elements. Yet Wright argued strongly for adopting a Marxist theoretical framework that in his view leads to understanding large-scale processes of social change and offers the possibility of employing specific concepts, thereby avoiding the diffuse conceptual specifications of the Weberian approach.

Wright also considered the reformulation of Marxism that has been severely questioned, especially in the United States and in Europe during the 1990s (Wright, Levine, and Sober 1992). Some scholars such as Weisskopf (1991) have characterized this as a crisis of Marxist class theory. This crisis was proclaimed by Louis Althusser in 1977 in recognition that his own work was in decline. Althusser had stimulated new inquiry into Marxism and had substantially influenced theoretical thinking and research in the social sciences, as Gregory Elliott brilliantly showed in *Althusser: The Detour of Theory* (1987). This link of contemporary debate and past Marxist theoretical lines was nicely delineated by Howard and King (1989 and 1992).

The characterization today of Marxism in crisis must be understood in terms of its origins and evolution. Szymanski (1985) argued that Marxist theory is a response to revolutionary conjunctures and the particular contradictions of societies. Its development has not occurred in mechanical form according to some inherent logic. In periods of social and political crisis, orthodox notions prevail; in periods of stability and prosperity, open formulations make more sense. He identified the development of Marxist theory as evolving through repetitive cycles of four phases: (1) a period of energy or force provoked by a crisis in society in which there is movement to elaborate a theory of society, crisis, struggle, and transformation; (2) a period of formation of revolutionary and materialist theory, including creation of seminal theoretical works and organization of mass movements; (3) a period of undermining the revolutionary formulations, of disjunction between theory and practice, and of reformism in practice in times of prosperity and stability; and (4) a period of revisionism in which historical materialism has been rejected and the crisis in Marxist theory is obvious and mass movements are weak. Szymanski traced this cycle through six periods, each beginning with revolutionary upheaval: for example, 1843–1849 with the formation of Marxism in the work of Marx and Engels and the revolutions of 1848–1849; 1917–1921 with the wave of revolutionary crisis in Russia and Weimar Germany; 1935–1949 with the revitalization of Marxism in the wake of the depression and the upheaval of war; and 1967–1970 with the emergence of the New Left and the political mobilizations from Paris around the world.

These past trends suggest an evolution from the present phase of reformism and revisionism to a possible revitalization, perhaps in the 1990s, of Marxist theory. In fact, Marxist theory is very much alive, although the new thinking seems unlikely to establish paradigmatic alternatives (Chilcote and Chilcote 1992). Two political scientists, Manning Marable (1991) and Victor Wallis (1991), however, have set forth an agenda of questions, issues, and approaches for remaking the Left within the United States.

Ultimately one must decide if the configuration of classes leads research in useful directions, in which case Marx has provided a helpful formulation of class analysis. If, however, we see attention to classes as distractive, since it diverts inquiry from the situational and institutional nature of power in society as Weber suggested, then class analysis might be discarded. For the most part, it is Weber's model that prevails in comparative politics. Researchers look not to class divisions but to personal and institutional categories that distinguish power characteristics among countries.

In this chapter we briefly reviewed the life and thought of two precursors whose theoretical contributions have influenced contemporary comparative politics. We have identified their major works and ideas, and we have attempted to demonstrate the relationship of their thinking to the four subfields around which the comparative politics literature tends to cluster. The remaining chapters examine in some depth the origins and paradigmatic directions of those subfields.

References

Althusser, Louis. 1970. *For Marx*. Translated by Ben Brewster. New York: Vintage Books. Essays published originally in French during the early 1960s. The author stresses the scientific nature of Marx's mature works in contrast to the ideological orientation of the earlier works.

Aron, Raymond. 1964. *German Sociology*. Translated by Thomas Bottomore. New York: Free Press of Glencoe. A comparison and contrast of the systematic, historical, and interpretive schools of German sociology, with emphasis on the works of Openheimer and Weber.

Ashcraft, Richard. 1972. "Marx and Weber on Liberalism as Bourgeois Ideology." *Comparative Studies in Society and History* 14 (March), 130–168. Contrasts the theories of Marx and Weber and states that "their common agreement on the characterization of liberalism as bourgeois ideology concealed differences of historical interpretation, conflicting conceptions of methodology and opposing views of the social structure."

Atkinson, Dick. 1972. *Orthodox Consensus and Radical Alternative: A Study in Sociological Theory.* New York: Basic Books. An interpretative and critical examination of the ideas and concepts in Parsons, Marx, and Weber, as well as their influence on modern sociologists. Seeks flexible but radical alternative.

Bendix, Reinhard. 1960. *Max Weber: An Intellectual Portrait.* Garden City, New York: Doubleday and Company. A detailed analysis of the sociopolitical problems and intellectual dispositions that guide Weber in his work. Emphasis is placed on the pragmatic identification of critical social problems in the development of Weber's writing.

_____. 1974. "Inequality and Social Structure: A Comparison of Marx and Weber." *American Sociological Review* 44 (April), 149–161. Contrasts the Marxian argument on class in the organization of production with the Weberian emphasis on status differences and organized collective action.

Bendix, Reinhard, and Guenther Roth. 1971. *Scholarship and Partisanship: Essays on Max Weber.* Berkeley: University of California Press. Revisions of previously published essays that criticize Weber's substantive and methodological contributions as well as the place of his life in intellectual and political history. The first part examines his scholarship and partisanship, the second looks at authority and legitimacy, and the third deals with the intellectual influences, including that of Marx, on his thought.

Bottomore, Tom (ed.). 1983. *A Dictionary of Marxist Thought.* Oxford: Basil Blackwell. An essential source on Marxism, its origins and evolution.

Chilcote, Ronald H., and Edward B. Chilcote. 1992. "The Crisis of Marxism." *Rethinking Marxism* 4 (Summer), 84–106. Critical examination of new currents in Marxism, including post-Marxism, analytical Marxism, and new structuralism.

Cohen, Jere, Lawrence E. Hazelrigg, and Whitney Pope. 1975. "De-Parsonizing Weber: A Critique of Parsons' Interpretation of Weber's Sociology." *American Sociological Review* 40 (April), 229–241. Critique of Talcott Parsons's interpretation of the work of Weber, demonstrating that his interpretation is erroneous and misleading.

Colletti, Lucio. 1972. *From Rousseau to Lenin: Studies in Ideology and Society.* New York: Monthly Review Press. Essays translated by John Merrington and Judith White. The most useful for this study of Marx are "Marxism as a Sociology," 3–44, and "Marxism: Science or Revolution?" 229–236.

Fromm, Erich. 1961. *Marx's Concept of Man.* New York: Frederick Ungar Publishing. Includes a translation from Marx's *Economic and Philosophical Manuscripts* by T. B. Bottomore and an introductory essay by Fromm, which demonstrates the unity of thought in Marx's early and later works.

Garaudy, Roger. 1967. *Karl Marx: The Evolution of His Thought.* New York: International Publishers. A critical analysis of the evolution of Marx's thought, which identifies both its continuity and contradictions.

Giddens, Anthony. 1971. *Capitalism and Modern Social Theory: An Analysis of the Writings of Marx, Durkheim, and Max Weber.* Cambridge: Cambridge University Press. A reconsideration of the works of Marx, Durkheim, and Weber in the light of modern sociology. Affirms the intellectual contribution of Marx and the relationship of his early and later writings, then shows irremediable divergences between Marxist thought and Weber's "radical neo-Kantianism."

_____. 1976. "Classical Social Theory and the Origins of Modern Sociology." *American Journal of Sociology* 81 (January), 703–729. Reassessment of interpretations on the origins of sociology, with particular attention to Durkheim and Weber as well as Marx.

Hartsock, Nancy C.M. 1991. "Louis Althusser's Structural Marxism, Political Clarity and Theoretical Distortions." *Rethinking Marxism* 4 (Winter), 10–40. Seeks to analyze "how the defeats of Marxism in the West have come to be inscribed in its theories, and to expose the ways in which some theoretical moves foreclose new possibilities, both intellectually and politically" (11). In her reassessment of Althusser's structural Marxism, she argues that his work constituted a first step along the path later taken by poststructuralist thinkers whom she criticizes. Focuses on three themes in a helpful overview of the strengths and weaknesses in the thinking of Althusser: the concepts of last instance and overdetermination; science and ideology; and theoretical antihumanism.

Howard, M. C., and J. E. King. 1989 and 1992. *A History of Marxian Economics*. Princeton: Princeton University Press. 2 vols. An intellectual history that traces the principal strands of Marxism after Marx. Ideas and debates are related to politics, earlier Marxist thought, and broad intellectual and historical currents.

Lichtheim, George. 1961. *Marxism, An Historical and Critical Study.* New York: Frederick A. Praeger. Views Weber's framework as compatible with Marxism.

Löwy, Michael. 1989. "Weber Against Marx? The Polemic with Historical Materialism in the Protestant Ethic." *Science and Society* 53 (Spring), 71–83. Explores the methodological distinction between Marx and Weber in which the former usually is characterized as emphasizing historical materialism based on economic considerations and the latter as refuting historical materialism on the basis that the spirit of capitalism has arisen in the effects of the Protestant Reformation. Shows that this is a distortion, perpetuated by the interpretation of Talcott Parsons, and that Weber showed "the inner relationship between these two cultural structures—the Protestant ethic and the spirit of capitalism— leaving open the question of *primacy*" (74).

McLellan, David. 1973. *Karl Marx: His Life and Thought.* New York: Harper and Row. The *Grundrisse* is viewed as central to Marx's thought and linked with his alienation theory of 1844.

Marable, Manning. 1991. "Remaking American Marxism." *Monthly Review* 42 (January), 40–53. A response to new forms of Marxism and socialism that evolved among leftists in the United States after the collapse of the Soviet socialist model in Eastern Europe and the defeat of the Sandinistas in the 1990 elections in Nicaragua. These forms include a refuge in pre-Marxian forms of socialism and the search for humanism, post-Marxism or postmodern socialism, and radical democratic theory as represented in the work of Samuel Bowles and Herbert Gintis. All these forms, Marable believes, obscure the class contradiction. Suggests the need for rethinking the relationship of Marxism, especially to electoral and party politics.

Marcuse, Herbert. 1968. *Negations: Essays in Critical Theory.* Boston: Beacon Press. A Marxist critique of Weber's analysis of industrialization, capitalism, and self-preservation; the connection among these phenomena "motivates Max Weber's passionate and … spiteful fight against the socialist efforts of 1918." Marcuse's discussion is in Chapter 6, "Industrialization and Capitalism in the Work of Max Weber," pp. 201–226.

Marx, Karl. 1967. *Capital: A Critique of Political Economy.* Edited by Frederick Engels. New York: International Publishers. 3 vols.

_____. 1973. *Grundrisse: Foundations of the Critique of Political Economy.* Translated with an introduction by Martin Nicolaus. New York: Vintage Books.

_____. 1974a. *The Revolutions of 1848.* Edited with an introduction by David Fernbach. New York: Vintage Books.

_____. 1974b. *Surveys from Exile.* Edited with an introduction by David Fernbach. New York: Vintage Books.

_____. 1975. *Early Writings.* Introduction by Lucio Colletti; translated by Rodney Livingstone and Gregor Benton. New York: Vintage Books. Collection of Marx's writings of 1843 and 1844, including the *Economic and Philosophical Manuscripts.*

Marx, Karl, and Frederick Engels. 1958. *Selected Works.* Moscow: Foreign Languages Publishing House. 2 vols. Originally published in Russian.

_____. 1973. *The German Ideology, Part One.* Edited with introduction by C. J. Arthur. New York: International Publishers. Written in 1845–1846. Marx and Engels set forth a synthetic world outlook later called historical materialism. Nature and ideal are examined in dialectical relationship in an understanding of man and labor in society.

Mayer, Carl. 1975. "Max Weber's Interpretation of Karl Marx." *Social Research* 42 (Winter), 701–719. An examination of differences in the work of Weber and Marx as manifested in German criticism.

Nicolaus, Martin. 1973. "Foreword." In Karl Marx, *Grundrisse: Foundations of the Critique of Political Economy,* 7–63. New York: Vintage Books. Nicolaus, the translator, describes and analyzes this work's significance in understanding the full sweep of Marxist thought.

Ollman, Bertell. 1973. "Marxism and Political Science: Prolegomenon to a Debate on Marx's Method." *Politics and Society* 3 (Summer), 491–510. Identifies reasons for the failure of a school of Marxist political science to emerge and summarizes Marx's theory of state and capitalism in order to stress the importance of the Marxist method.

Parsons, Talcott. 1929. "'Capitalism' in Recent German Literature: Sombart and Weber." *Journal of Political Economy* 37 (February-December), 31–57. Parsons affirms Weber's refutation of Marxism.

Resch, Robert Paul. 1992. *Althusser and the Renewal of Marxist Political Theory.* Berkeley: University of California Press. A systematic assessment of structural Marxism in the work of Althusser, Poulantzas, and others.

Riazanov, David. 1973. *Karl Marx and Friedrich Engels: An Introduction to Their Lives and Work.* Translated by Joshua Kunitz with an introduction by Dirk J. Struik. New York: Monthly Review Press. Reprint of work originally published by Riazanov, a Ukrainian, in 1927. In a foreword, Paul Sweezy recommends this work not only for "the main facts about the lives and works of the founders of Marxism, but also, by way of example, something of the Marxist approach to the study and writing of history."

Ritzer, George. 1975. "Professionalization, Bureaucratization, and Rationalization: The Views of Max Weber." *Social Forces* 53 (June), 627–634. An examination of Weber's perspectives on the relationship of professionalization, bureaucratization, and rationalization.

Roth, Günther. 1965. "Political Critiques of Max Weber: Some Implications for Political Sociology." *American Sociological Review* 30 (April), 213–223. Review of political critiques of Weber from the perspectives of Marxism, fascism, and natural law.

_____. 1969. "Max Weber's Empirical Sociology in Germany and the United States: Tensions Between Partisanship and Scholarship." *Central European History* 2 (September), 196–215. An assessment of the impact of Weber and his ideas on sociology in Germany and the United States.

Schneider, Louis. 1971. "Max Weber: Wisdom and Science in Sociology." *Sociological Quarterly* 12 (Autumn), 462–472. Examines Weber's use of the dialectic even though he was neither Hegelian nor Marxist. Also looks at Weber's orientation to scientific social science and concludes that Weber probably was inclined to move away from a positivistic paradigm.

Sherman, Howard. 1976. "Dialectics as a Method." *Insurgent Sociologist* 6 (Summer), 57–66. Explanation of dialectics and its usefulness in the practice of social science. "Attempts to rescue the dialectic from the clutches of vulgar Marxists and refutes critics who see dialectics as "a useless piece of unscientific baggage."

Szymanski, Al. 1985. "Crisis and Vitalization in Marxist Theory." *Science and Society* 49 (Fall), 315–331. A reflection on the dynamics of Marxist thought through historical struggles. Argues that Marxism interacts with revolutionary movements through a series of cycles in which theory fluctuates between orthodoxy and open formulations.

Thomas, Paul. 1976. "Marx and Science." *Political Studies* 24 (March), 1–23. Argues that not Marx but his successors, beginning with Engels, popularized the term "scientific socialism" and that Marx should not be included among those who "advocated extension of the methods of natural science to history and to society."

Tiryakian, Edward A. 1975. "Neither Marx nor Durkheim ... Perhaps Weber." *American Journal of Sociology* 81 (July), 1–33. Assessment of the applicability of the perspectives on modern society of Marx, Durkheim, and Weber, with attention to the United States. Concludes that Weber is "of greatest heuristic worth in interpreting American society."

Wallis, Victor. 1991. "Marxism and the U.S. Left: Thoughts for the 1990s." *Monthly Review* 43 (June), 5–14. Shows the relevance of Marxism and class analysis.

Weber, Max. 1927. *General Economic History*. Translated by Frank H. Knight. Glencoe, Illinois: Free Press. An economic analysis of historical periods from ancient to modern times.

———. 1947. *The Theory of Social and Economic Organization*. Edited with an introduction by Talcott Parsons. New York: Oxford University Press. Reprinted by Free Press of Glencoe, 1964. Translation of Weber's *Wirtschaft und Gesellschaft*, which deals with concepts of sociology, sociological categories of economic action, and types of authority.

———. 1949. *The Methodology of the Social Sciences*. Translated and edited by Edward A. Shils and Henry A. Finch. New York: Free Press. Three of Weber's most important essays on methodology: the meaning of "ethical neutrality" in sociology and economics; objectivity in social science and social policy; and critical studies in the logic of cultural science.

———. 1958a. *From Max Weber: Essays in Sociology*. Translated and edited with an introduction by H. H. Gerth and C. Wright Mills. New York: Oxford University Press. Essays on science and politics, power, religion, and social structures as well as an introduction by the translators on the life and thought of Weber.

———. 1958b. *The Protestant Ethic and the Spirit of Capitalism*. Translated by Talcott Parsons with a foreword by R. H. Tawney. New York: Charles Scribner's Sons. A historical and sociological interpretation of the relations between Protestantism and capitalism.

———. 1962. *Basic Concepts in Sociology*. Translated with an introduction by H. P. Secher. New York: Citadel Press. A later work and a fragmentary effort at systematization of concepts, which serves as a useful, although incomplete, introduction to Weber's thinking.

———. 1965. *Politics as a Vocation*. Translation by H. H. Gerth and C. Wright Mills. Philadelphia: Fortress Press. Weber's major work that advances the distinction between the "ethics of ultimate ends" and the "ethics of responsibility." Defines the proper limits of political leadership.

———. 1967. *Max Weber on Law in Economy and Society.* Edited with introduction and annotations by Max Rheinstein; translated by Edward Shils. New York: Clarion Books, Simon and Schuster.

———. 1968. *The Sociology of Religion.* Translated by Ephraim Fischoff. Boston: Beacon Press. Contains Weber's later work on religion as well as a useful analytical introduction by Talcott Parsons.

Weisskopf, Thomas E. 1991. "Marxian Crisis Theory and the Contradictions of Late Twentieth-Century Capitalism." *Rethinking Marxism* 4 (Winter), 79–93. Review of Marx's theory of capitalist crisis, including his attention to the law of the tendency of the rate of profit to fall, international contradictions that lead to crisis, and the tendency to deplete the excess supply of labor. Examines these types of crisis theory in the light of contemporary Marxian political economy.

Wright, Erik Olin, Andrew Levine, and Elliot Sober. 1992. *Reconstructing Marxism: Essays on Explanation and the Theory of History.* London: Verso. Authors argue for a reconstruction of Marxism in order to transcend the disintegration of the theoretical unity of classical Marxism.

Zeitlin, Irving. 1968. *Ideology and the Development of Sociological Theory.* Englewood Cliffs, New Jersey: Prentice-Hall. Attempts to demonstrate, especially in Chapter 10, the proximity in the thinking of Marx and Weber.

PART THREE

Theoretical Directions

5
Theories of System and State

Philosophers and social scientists long have related some conception of state and system to their understandings of politics. Weber looked for the qualities of stability and order in a modern productive society. He saw historical change as gradualist and noted that evolutionary progress depended on the fundamental conditions of each society. He classified societies into systems of authority: traditional, charismatic, and rational-legal. He also was interested in the state and its legitimacy and power through force and coercion. For Marx, order and stability were undermined by the contradictions of each society. He classified societies into economic systems based on mode of production and relations of production manifested through social classes: feudal, bourgeois, and proletarian. Changes in the economic base, the intensification of contradictions, and the subsequent struggle among the classes would dialectically bring about changes in society. Marx also focused on the state in his critique of Hegel and in his studies of midnineteenth-century France.

The study of politics and political science has always involved interest in the state; the theorists range from Aristotle and Plato to Machiavelli to Gramsci today. This chapter briefly identifies some of the early work and its influence on comparative politics, assesses a variety of theories on the state, and affirms that indeed the state is a central focus of politics. It also delineates theories of system to show their influences and limitations. Both theories have been adopted by mainstream comparative politics, and in each case scholars have searched for and found alternatives to mainstream approaches. The focus here is first on system and later on the state.

Mainstream Theories of System

Classical conceptions divided societies into monarchies, aristocracies, and democracies. Among recent classifications, Gabriel Almond provided comparative politics with a breakdown of Anglo-American, continental European, totalitarian, and preindustrial systems. F. X. Sutton broke societies into agricultural and industrial systems. James S. Coleman wrote of competitive, semicompetitive, and authoritarian systems, and David Apter divided the world into dictatorial, oligarchical, indirectly representational, and directly representational systems. Fred W. Riggs analyzed fused, prismatic, and refracted systems. S. N. Eisenstadt offered a comprehensive classification of primitive systems, patrimonial empires, nomad or conquest empires, city-states, feudal systems, centralized bureaucratic empires, and modern systems; the last he divided into democratic, autocratic, totalitarian, and underdeveloped categories. Leonard Binder differentiated among three types: traditional, conventional, and rational systems. Edward Shils referred to political democracies, tutelary democracies, modernizing oligarchies, totalitarian oligarchies, and traditional oligarchies. In a recent classification, Arend Lijphart (1984) compared majoritarian and consensus models of democracy with focus on the experience of twenty-two democratic regimes.

System for these and other writers might represent an entity such as a legislature, political party, or labor union, but usually the term connotes nation or state. Classifications of system reveal a variety of viewpoints and interpretations, as implied above. The emergence of many new nations in the contemporary world, the amassing of information and data, and the development of many technological advances have brought increased complexity to the world. Scientists and social scientists alike have attempted to bring order to this complexity by utilizing system as a common basis for analysis and synthesis.

With the national political system as the focus, Gabriel Almond and G. Bingham Powell, Jr. (1966: 217) outlined an eclectic scheme. Drawn from the earlier classifications of Aristotle, Weber, Eisenstadt, Shils, Coleman, Apter, and others, the scheme offers a typology of systems according to primitive, traditional, and modern categories. Primitiveness is associated with a minimal structural differentiation and a parochial culture, while modernity is reflected by a substantial differentiation and a high degree of secularity. A variety of examples illustrate the many different national systems through history since classical times.

Anton Bebler and Jim Seroka (1990) joined in this search for a classification in an effort to confront "the retarded state of the discipline" and the problem of classifying political systems in contemporary work. They argued that classification is useful to comparative politics and theory building—that it enables us to organize our thoughts about reality and facilitates use of a variety of approaches rather than a single method. They looked at democratic and authoritarian capitalist systems, socialist systems, Third World systems, and institution-dominated systems.

There is no doubt that the idea of system has implanted itself firmly in social science theory, and the first part of this chapter examines in some depth the strengths and weaknesses of systems theory. After offering some general definitions of systems terminology and identifying the origins and orientations of systems theory, three major trends in the literature are analyzed. Early influences upon each trend are related to contemporary writings in comparative politics, and a critical assessment is offered. Finally, some perspectives on systems theory and its usefulness for comparative study are presented.

Understanding the Systems Terminology

Society is usually viewed as the most inclusive entity within which systems may be evaluated. *Systems* thus are abstractions of the real society. Any phenomena of society may be viewed as a system or systems. In reality all societal phenomena are interrelated, although *boundaries* may be employed to delineate different systems, for example, political, economic, social, and cultural-psychological systems. The investigator thus abstracts from the whole society some *elements* that seem to cohere more closely than others and views those elements as a system. Usually those elements exist in conceptually measurable amounts, and as such they are termed *variables*. Elements that are constant rather than variable, because they are insulated from change in society, are called *parameters*.

When we speak of a political system, an economic system, a social system, or a cultural-psychological system, we mean all those variables associated with political life, economic life, social life, or cultural-psychological life. The variables of any system may include *structures, functions, actors, values, norms, goals, inputs, outputs, response,* and *feedback.* The meaning of each of these terms will become evident in the discussion below.

Origins and Orientations of Systems Theory

The social scientists' obsession with systems theory can be attributed in large measure to compulsion to predict correctly and thereby to be able to change things for the better. Social scientists tend to emulate classical Newtonian physics in the search for general laws that have universal application. Contemporary social scientists attempt to transcend the logical positivism of Saint-Simon, Comte, and others who attempted to apply science to the study of social life. Today, however, the origins of systems theory emanate from many different sciences, including the fields of biology, cybernetics, and operations research. Systems theory in political science also is indebted to contributions from economics, sociology, and other social sciences. History, too, has exerted some influence. These fields are briefly examined in order to identify some influences and ideas that have shaped systems theory and its implementation in contemporary comparative politics (see Lilienfeld 1975 for an elaboration).

Biology. The literature of systems theory frequently refers to the contributions of Ludwig von Bertalanffy (1969) and others, who combined scientific and philosophical views to formulate a conception of system they called general systems theory. They founded the Society for General Systems Research and a journal, *Behavioral Science,* as well as a yearbook. Their basic conception differentiated the physical sciences (which deal with closed systems isolated from their environment) from biology (which concerns itself with open systems of living organisms or cells). By *open system* is implied the exchange of matter and energy in the environment. These writers sought to apply the conception of open system to society and to explain the nature of human history by seeking laws that apply to all systems, including that of the living organism or society. The fundamental aim of general systems theory is the integration of "the various sciences, natural and social," the development of "unifying principles" through the individual sciences, and the establishment of "exact theory in the nonphysical fields of science" (Bertalanffy 1969: 38).

Cybernetics. Cybernetics is the systematic study of communication and control in all kinds of organization. Developments in communications engineering led scientists to make social applications. Norbert Wiener (1961), for example, determined that the performance of machines may be corrected and guided by information in a sort of feedback process similar to the functioning of living individuals. Wiener not only drew an analogy between the nervous system and the automatic machine, both of whose performances are governed by means of communicating information, but he also concluded that the network of communications extends itself everywhere so that the world society can integrate into an organic whole. He considered his concept of cybernetic control through feedback to be a model for legitimizing government operations (Wiener 1954).

Operations Research and Systems Analysis. Operations research was an outgrowth of attempts to apply a systems approach to the use of radar installations during the Second World War. It was utilized to predict military outcomes on the basis of the design of weapons and the implementation of tactics and strategy. Operations research sought a system of minimal wastage of resources. The statistical and quantitative techniques of wartime became useful later in industries such as petroleum, chemicals, and electronics. The founding of a new profession was signified by the establishment in 1957 of the International Federation of Operations Research Societies. Soon thereafter operations research was applied to solutions of social problems, especially in education, urban areas, and health services. With the shift from military to civic applications, operations research eventually became known as systems analysis.

The Social Sciences. Among the social sciences, economics made early contributions to systems theory. Although economic problem solving today is still dominated by piecemeal and incrementalist schemes, econometric techniques have long been used to determine linear cause-and-effect relationships. These techniques, however, tend to be restricted to mechanistic systems, which do not account for the processes of change and lose touch with social reality.

In recent years computer simulation has begun to supplant many of the econometric techniques. Computers must be used, for example, in an input-output analysis such as that developed by Wassily Leontief, who sought to analyze the relations among all segments of an economic system. Such analysis was utilized in the former Soviet Union for planning at the national level. Input-output analysis usually is static in nature and thus limited to short time periods. Input-output analysis in political science generally has been limited to qualitative rather than to quantitative applications.

Game theory and formal modeling have generated mathematical explanations of strategies, especially for marketing and advertising in business firms. Game theory has had an impact on economics, and it has been widely used in political science analyses of international confrontations and electoral strategies. In fact, game theory has been used extensively by political scientists in the testing and implementation of rational-choice theory, which assumes that the structural constraints of society do not necessarily determine the actions of individuals and that individuals tend to choose actions that bring them the best results. Cooperative and competitive relations in one's bargaining with allies and opponents are emphasized by the political scientist in a fashion modeled after the economist's attention to exchange, especially through competitive market systems.

In focusing on systemic forecasting, Jantsch (1972) identified a number of tendencies in the other social sciences. For sociology, he alluded to "ways of guiding human thinking in systematic fashion," and he mentioned scenario writing, gaming, historical analogy, and other techniques. For the policy sciences, he referred to the "outcome-oriented framework for strategic planning," known as the Planning-Programming-Budgeting System, which is used by the U.S. government and other countries as well. For urban and regional planning, he stressed the computer models of "exploratory man-technique interaction" as well as environmental modeling.

We have seen that systems theory in comparative politics has its origins in physical, biological, and social schemes. We have reviewed the trends in biology, cybernetics, and operations research and systems analysis. We have identified the influences of the social sciences. Pablo González Casanova (1973), a Mexican political sociologist, referred to two types of systemic study. The first type has its roots in nineteenth-century positivist explanations and today can be called functionalism (its major theoretician is Talcott Parsons). The second type is known as systems analysis, which emphasizes the problems of decision making, and since the Second World War this type has benefited from operations research and mathematical applications. Under certain conditions both types are self-limiting and self-defeating. Thus, González Casanova studied the history of change in contemporary systems. His stress on history allowed him to introduce a radical reinterpretation of functionalism and systems analysis.

The identification of these dichotomies may be helpful in discerning the principal tendencies in the literature of systems theory, yet further discussion is necessary. Our synthesis of the literature on systems theory seeks clarity and understanding; specifically, three trends are emphasized in this chapter.

One trend, sometimes called grand theory and ahistorical in orientation, emanates from the natural and physical sciences and culminates in the contributions of David Easton in political science. The impact of Easton can be traced to several influences in comparative and international politics. In particular, these influences are exemplified by Karl Deutsch, Morton Kaplan, and Herbert Spiro.

A second trend, known as structural functionalism, strives to be holistic but tends toward ahistorical and middle-range analysis. Its roots are strongly embedded in two academic traditions. In the first academic tradition, there is the work of the anthropologists Malinowski and Radcliffe-Brown, as well as the contributions of the sociologist Parsons. In the second tradition falls the work of the political scientists Arthur Bentley and David Truman. Both traditions converge in the important writings of Gabriel Almond, which have had a significant impact upon comparative politics.

A third trend in the literature of systems theory is that of the alternative Marxist understandings of systems theory. These understandings reach toward global theory and a historical and holistic synthesis. The discussion that follows examines the critical interpretations of mainstream theory as well as orthodox Marxist and independent radical and Marxist orientations in the literature of systems.

Systems as Organic or Physiological:
David Easton and General Systems Theory

More than a generation ago sociologist Karl Mannheim (1957) addressed himself to "systematic sociology" in offering his readers an introduction to the study of society. Soon thereafter political scientist Charles E. Merriam wrote about "systematic politics." Merriam drew heavily from a variety of disciplines, for he searched into the action patterns of institutions by reaching into biology, sociology, anthropology, economics, philosophy, and other areas. Guided by "reason, reflection, experiment," he sought to utilize "both the naturalistic and the rationalistic approach." Intrigued by "the evolutionary quality of political effort and achievement," he viewed the whole life process, including government and politics, as part "of creative evolution in which the type and values of the species continually rise in the scale" (Merriam 1966: ix).

This traditional search for a systematic interpretation of society was carried on by David Easton in his application of general systems theory to politics. The following discussion of Easton's contributions includes, first, a synthesis of his fundamental ideas; second, a look at the origins of thought and the influences which shaped those ideas; third, a review of several subsequent efforts to apply Easton's ideas; and fourth, a critique of Easton's interpretation.

Easton's Framework

David Easton's efforts to build an empirically oriented political theory evolved through three phases, each represented by the publication of a major work. The first of these works, *The Political System* (1953), presented a case for general theory in political science. The second, *A Framework for Political Analysis* (1965a), set forth the major concepts for the development of such a general theory. The third, *A Systems Analysis of Political Life* (1965b), attempted to elaborate those concepts in the hope that they might become empirically applicable; in fact, Easton attempted later to move his theory toward an empirical situation with a study of how and when children's support for political authority arises in the U.S. political system. A brief outline of Easton's major contributions to political theory through a synthesis of the major ideas in each of these three phases follows.

Initially Easton argued that scientific knowledge is theoretical and based on facts, but facts alone do not explain events and must be ordered in some way. Further, the study of political life involves the political system as a whole rather than solutions for particular problems. Theory must combine with reliable knowledge and empirical data: *psychological data* on personalities and motivations of participants and *situational data* shaped by environmental influences. Political life is in disequilibrium, a status suggesting not only change or conflict but a counter-tendency to equilibrium that envisions a normal outcome of what might be. This outcome is contrasted with what actually transpires, and the differences can be explained.

Thus, Easton's quest for theory involved the formulation of a general framework, a focus on the whole system rather than merely on its parts, an awareness of environmental influences upon the system, and a recognition of the differences between political life in equilibrium and in disequilibrium. Easton rejected the concept of the state by referring to the confusion and variety of meanings; system for him permits clear conceptualization. Likewise, power is understood as only one of many significant concepts useful in the study of political life. Power, however, relates to the shaping and carrying out of authoritative politics in a society. Power rests on the ability to influence actions of others, and control of the way others make and carry out decisions determines policy. A policy, thus, "consists of a web of decisions and actions that allocates values" (1953: 130). The concepts of power, decision making, authority, and policy are essential in Easton's idea of political life as the authoritative allocation of values for a society.

Having established the need for systemic theory, Easton later (1957) identified some attributes of political systems in an attempt to move in the direction of a general political theory. These attributes were (1) properties of identification in the form of units and boundaries, (2) inputs and outputs, (3) differentiation within a system, and (4) integration within a system. Each attribute was described and illustrated through a "primitive" diagram, which is now familiar to most students of political science and is reproduced in Figure 5.1.

The diagram suggests that for analytical purposes the use of system allows the separation of political life from the rest of society, which Easton called the environment. This separation is demarcated by a boundary. The case of a political system, for example, is defined by action related to "binding decisions" of a society. The units of the political system are "political actions." Inputs in the form of de-

FIGURE 5.1
Easton's diagram of a political system

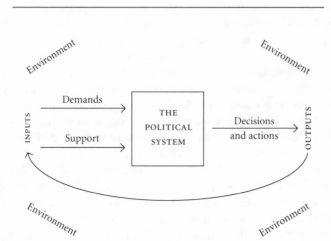

SOURCE: Reprinted from David Easton, *A Framework for Political Analysis*
(1965:112), by permission of The University of Chicago Press.

mands and supports feed the political system. Demands arise either in the environment or within the system itself. Whether externally or internally stimulated, demands become issues for discussion and resolution. Supports are "actions or orientations prompting and resisting a political system" (1957: 390). Outputs emanate from the political system in the form of decisions and policy actions. These feed back into the environment by satisfying the demands of some members of the system, and thus they generate support for the system. There may be negative consequences too, resulting in new demands on the system.

In his second work Easton set forth an integrated set of categories. Essentially the second work is an elaboration of Easton's earlier scheme, and it reiterates some assumptions related to system, environment, response, and feedback. Society as suprasystem is the most inclusive social system. The political system then is "a set of interactions abstracted from the totality of social behavior, through which values are authoritatively allocated for a society" (1965a: 57). Easton referred to closed and open systems. Political life, he argued, forms an open system, open to influences from its environment. Boundaries distinguish political systems from other systems, and boundaries serve to delimit what is included or excluded in inquiry.

Having argued the case for a general theory and having set forth concepts and diagrams, Easton next attempted to move his discussion toward the construction of a general theory (1965b). He continued to view political life as an open system subject to stress from a variety of surrounding environments. Threatened by stress, the political system, Easton argued, tends to persist, and he delved into explanations as to why systems persist in the face of frequent or constant crises. His task was to provide some generalizations in the process of theory building, but he admitted that his outcome was not yet a fully elaborated theory. That must come later. In a later work (1990), Easton reaffirmed his faith in the political system and extended his argument by focusing explicitly on structure as an essential element in political analysis. Thus, in this third phase Easton began with his broad conceptual framework and succeeded generally in the elaboration of that framework. His hope was to provide a foundation for empirical investigation.

Easton in this phase reviewed his basic categories of analysis, looked exhaustively at demand inputs, turned to support inputs, identified responses to the stress placed on support for the system, and discussed outputs as regulators of specific support. His diagrams were more complicated, but the fundamental thrust remained intact.

Origins of Thought and Influences
That Shaped Easton's Interpretation

Although Easton sought to formulate a systematic theory related to all the social sciences, in fact this effort emanated primarily from political science itself. He acknowledged that his work was stimulated by a technological and theoretical revolution in political science, the work of Charles Merriam, George Catlin, and Harold Lasswell standing out as particular examples (Easton 1965b: 19–22). Easton felt that attention to legal and formal institutions was outmoded and that political science should theorize about the political system and its processes rather than about the state and its institutions. Further, he believed that grand theory would transcend the limitations of middle-range efforts to study parties and pressure groups.

Sources outside political science were influential on his thinking. First, he looked to Talcott Parsons, whose action frame of reference was derived from Max Weber and was useful to macro theory. Parsons, however, was skeptical about the validity of political theory in attention to social systems. Their perspectives did not coincide on principles of classical liberalism; for example, whereas Parsons's notions of capacity and generalized support are "consistent" with the concepts of equality and consensus found in classical liberalism, Easton's "statements about the level of diffuse support and system persistence do not fall within the liberal perspective" (Lewis 1974: 683). Second, Easton derived the concept of function from anthropology and sociology; he made occasional reference to the anthropologists Radcliffe-Brown and Malinowski as well as to the sociologists Merton and Levy. Third, his attention to an emphasis on decision or choice drew from social psychology and was incorporated into his framework for political analysis. Fourth, he was influenced by macroeconomic conceptions in that his notion of allocation resembled "theories of income distribution and the allocation of re-sources in economics, and particularly neoclassical theory" (W. Mitchell 1961: 79). Sorzano compared Easton's approach to the classical economic model of Adam Smith: "the Eastonian model and the traditional economic approach share not only the notions of system and input-output but those of scarcity, allocation, competition, maximization, homeostatic equilibrium, functional interdependence, self-regulation, goal-seeking, and feedback" (1975: 91). Fifth, Easton's conception of system derived from the physical and life sciences: "Just as we may have a general theory of motion in physics or of life in biology, we require a general theory of the vital processes in politics" (Easton 1965b: 14).

Whatever the influences upon his work, Easton clearly placed himself in the mainstream of general systems theory, which he adapted to political science. The influence of functionalists in anthropology and sociology exists even though it may be remote, a similarity to neoclassical economic theory is apparent, and ties with the physical and life sciences are explicit. Thus, Easton joined the interdisciplinary tradition of seeking to understand the "whole" system and in contributing to the building of a paradigm in the sense used by Thomas Kuhn.

Some Criticisms of the Eastonian Framework

Easton awakened in political scientists the need to analyze complex interrelationships of political life. He shared the characteristics of many thinkers of the behavioral movement, including the rejection of traditional concepts such as state and power, incorporation of concepts such as inputs, outputs, and feedback, and emphasis on theory construction. His framework, however, is not without its critics.

First, his concern with clarifying and simplifying concepts related to an excessive preoccupation with stability, maintenance, persistence, and equilibrium, a tendency derived from biology. For example, Easton referred to the "authoritative allocation of values" as the "life processes" of the political system. Yet this idea can lead to some "misleading assumptions on which to construct an adequate theory of politics" (W. Mitchell 1961: 82). In particular, he was unable to deal with particular changes: "We can in no sense then regard Easton's theory as a theory of political change—as a theory which answers questions concerning why any particular political change occurred" (Thorson 1970: 67). His abstractions may lead to misperceptions about real situations and people (E. Miller 1971: 233). For example, the question of power may be obscured by inordinate attention to the demands of interest groups on government, when in fact the demands of government and ruling classes upon people may be more important.

Second, Easton posited some generalizations, but his framework yielded few, if any, testable hypotheses. His ideas have impacted the study of politics, but there has been little empirical consequence for comparative politics. Critics have identified some problems. Astin (1972) argued that the framework incorporates two incompatible approaches, one mechanistic and derived from Newton, the other organicist or vitalist and drawing from a view once prevalent in biology but now abandoned by most contemporary biologists. This incompatibility Astin likened to "a floating object caught up in the orbit of mechanism so long that one felt confident that, despite the vitalistic origins of his thought, he adhered to the vocabulary of cause and effect which he employed" (1972: 735). Thorson even more convincingly cast aside any illusions that the Eastonian framework offers operational possibilities: "Easton convinces us of what no mere critic ... could possibly convince us of, namely, that the enterprise is futile" (1970: 70–71).

Third, the ideological underpinnings of the framework pose a problem, as suggested by Eugene Miller (1971) who noted that early in his writings Easton (1950) was concerned with an intellectual crisis and the imminent waning of democratic liberalism. At the time Easton relegated political science to the position of an applied science or reforming discipline, and he blamed the value theory of historicism for the impoverishment of political theory while condemning the Weberian ideal of a value-free social science. In his 1953 work he emphasized science and causal theory, however, and became optimistic about the prospects for a true science of politics. In a 1969 address to the APSA, Easton placed a renewed emphasis on applied research and attention to the value assumptions of research. In his assessment, Miller concluded that Easton failed to identify "the object of political inquiry," and he questioned "if systems analysis, as a kind of political biology, is concerned with questions that are, properly speaking, political in nature" (1971: 234).

In a reflection upon the problem of the political system, Theodore J. Lowi observed: "It was everything, therefore it was nothing. Note finally that when Easton and Eastonites turned empirical within the systems context, they literally stepped outside the political system altogether and studied political socialization" (see rebuttal in Almond 1988: 888). In a full critique of systems analysis, Baruah (1987) examined the shifts in Easton's later thinking, in particular his assessment (1981) of the theory of the state in the work of Poulantzas that ultimately Easton rejected in favor of retaining an emphasis on system. This brief encounter with Poulantzas may have been an effort to reach out to alternative ideas in the field as if to anticipate such criticism, even if in the end Easton insisted that systems theory was right for political science.

These criticisms later led some commentators to reformulate the notion of political system as a theory of rational choice. William Mitchell put it this way: "As economic systems produce 'solutions' to ... problems so, too, polities provide solutions or make choices through time" (1969: 103–104). Thereafter, rational-choice models and theories were offered as alternative explanations to functionalist or structural-functional theory.

Rational-choice theory involves a number of social science approaches and thinkers. The early mainstream theory evolved from Anthony Downs's *An Economic Theory of Democracy* (1957), James Buchanan and Gordon Tullock's *The Calculus of Consent* (1962), and William Riker's *The Theory of Coalitions* (1962). Later alternative theory emerged with Robert Bates, Jon Elster, Barry Hindess, and others whose ideas and contributions have impacted the discipline (discussed more fully in Chapter 6). Rational-choice theory is normative theory concerned with behavior and assumes that all individuals are rational in choices and action. Game theory may examine the logic of choices and their consequences within constraints limited by the rules of the game. Difficulties with this approach appear, however, when the behavior of an individual actor is projected to societies as a whole or when narrowly defined models are used to predict and explain the behavior of real individuals in complex situations. To overcome these and other problems, rational-choice theorists, especially in political science and sociology, have begun to emphasize culture, history, and institutions—that is, the context in which choice occurs.

Systems as Structure and Function: Gabriel Almond and His Precursors

Influenced by the work of systems analysts in the natural sciences and the social sciences, David Easton was successful in firmly implanting a formulation of system in political science. In 1956, three years after Easton published his first book on the political system, Gabriel Almond applied a simple typology to national political systems. Together with other comparative political scientists, Almond set forth a new formulation, utilizing the political system as a base and turning to a set of concepts related to structure and function. Almond's formulation was spawned by some of the same influences that had affected Easton, but it turned away from grand theory and directed attention to middle-range concerns. It thus paralleled the Eastonian movement, although ultimately it was to exert substantially more impact upon comparative politics.

In this section the assumptions of Almond's formulation are examined, and the use of system in Almond's work is traced. Next the origins of influence upon his ideas are identified, and finally, the major criticisms of structural functionalism are summarized in an effort to assess its significance for comparative politics.

Almond's Formulation

Almond's conception of the political system evolved through a number of phases. Initially, his early typology on the political system drew from Easton the notion of system as an "inclusive concept which covers all of the patterned actions relevant to the making of political decisions" (Almond 1956: 393). For Almond, system implied "totality," interactions among units within the totality, and stability in those interactions, which he described as "changing equilibrium." He also relied heavily upon Max Weber and Talcott Parsons in his consideration of political systems of action. Instead of focusing on such concepts as institution, organization, or group, Almond turned to role and structure, roles being the interacting units of the political system and structures representing the patterns of interaction. He also introduced the concept of political culture, which he conceived of as embedded in a particular pattern of orientations to political action, with these patterns usually extending beyond the boundaries of the political system.

A second phase involved the elaboration of a set of structures and functions in a conscious effort to avoid the formalities of government institutions in areas where changes are widespread. In the introduction to a collective work coedited with James S. Coleman (Almond 1960), Almond renovated concepts of comparative politics. Political system replaced the state and the legal and institutional apparatus employed by traditional political scientists. Function substituted for power, role for office, and structure for institution. Almond employed these concepts in his thesis that political systems (advanced and backward nations) have universal characteristics: all political systems have political structures; the same functions are performed in all political systems; all political structure is multifunctional; and all political systems are mixed in the cultural sense. Almond also incorporated the Eastonian framework of inputs, outputs, and feedback, but because of its limitations outlined his own functional categories into four inputs (political socialization and recruitment, interest articulation, interest aggregation, and political communication) and three outputs (rule making, rule application, and rule adjudication). The outputs were government functions corresponding to the traditional use of three separate powers within government— categories that biased his scheme because they reflected a U.S. and European conception of Western government. The inputs, he believed, were particularly useful in characterizing the political systems of developing areas. *Political socialization*, for example, induces people to participate in the political culture of a society. *Interest articulation* is the expression of political interests and demands for action. *Interest aggregation* is the coalescing of those interests and demands articulated by political parties and interest groups. All these functions occur through *political communication*.

A third phase involved the refinement and elaboration of Almond's earlier scheme (1965) into a book widely used by specialists of comparative politics (Almond and Powell 1966). A sixfold classification of the three original outputs (government functions) and three of the four inputs (interest articulation, interest aggregation, and political communication) was worked into conversion processes that allow for the transformation of (1) the demands and supports that flow into the political system and (2) the outputs of extraction, regulation, and distribution into society that flow out of the political system, as depicted in Figure 5.2. This reformulation was an effort to contend with criticism of his earlier work, as he now stressed "interdependence" rather than "harmony" to show that his approach was neither static nor conservative because of its emphasis on equilibrium or harmony of parts. Additionally, he tried to show that his approach was dynamic in its examination of "developmental patterns," an effort to relate to the substantial lit-

FIGURE 5.2
Diagram of Almond's political system and levels of functions

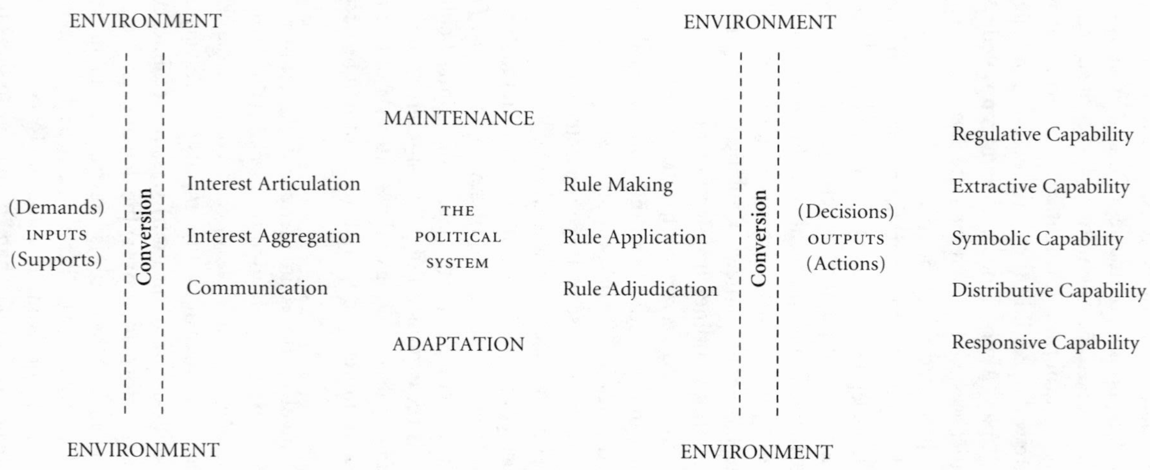

SOURCE: Adapted from Almond and Powell (1966: 16–41).

erature on political development published in the 1960s. He also desired a holistic rather than a partial theory (1966: 13–14).

During the 1980s Almond defensively reviewed newly emerging literature on the state, dependency theory, and other themes that were counterposed to his own work. These essays, gathered in his *A Discipline Divided* (1990), represented not only a careful review of the literature but also a strident reaffirmation of his earlier work and sometimes a polemical response to his critics.

Easton in his 1969 address to the American Political Science Association offered a reassessment of his early work. About the same time Almond also reviewed his own work (1969–1970). Despairing the mood of "disillusionment" that was sweeping the field of comparative politics, he lauded the impressive accomplishments of the previous two decades and asserted his faith in a systems approach to politics. In an effort to deal with the "counterproductive polemic" of the late 1960s, he proposed a research design "intended to draw us a little closer to a systematic exploitation of historical experience using a causal scheme which combines system-functional analysis, aggregate quantitative analysis and rational choice analysis at appropriate points in the explanation of developmental episodes" (1969–1970: 28). Essentially, this effort was an attempt by Almond to retain his structural-functional formulation and to combine it with other approaches so as to deal empirically with specific historical cases and to give relevance to his own theory.

Structural functionalism served to relate all social phenomena into one system of thought and to recast attention on the concept of system at a time when social scientists had become concerned with the analysis of individual behavior. Such perspectives emanated from the work of anthropologists Radcliffe-Brown and Malinowski and sociologist Parsons and his followers Levy and Merton. They influenced contemporary political science scholars, particularly William C. Mitchell (1958), Almond, and a host of comparative political scientists who pursued what might be characterized as macro-structural functionalism. A second influence upon Almond relates to the traditions of pluralism and liberalism that sprang from the *Federalist Papers* and were incorporated into contemporary political science through the seminal works of Arthur Bentley, David Truman, and Robert Dahl, whose attention to the plurality of interests within the system might be labeled a pattern of micro-structural functionalism. Briefly, an elaboration on these two structural functionalisms follows.

Origins of Thought and Influences on Almond

Macro-Structural Functionalism or Grand Theory

Almond referred to system as the interdependence of parts, inputs and outputs, boundary, and environment—all aspects of the Eastonian framework. For the concept of "political" he cited Easton's definition of "authoritative allocation of values," but he emphasized Weber's idea of legitimacy. To these roots of thought, he fused the terms *structure* and *function,* and he stuffed Easton's simplified black box with functional and structural categories while updating the classic system-functional theory of a separation-of-powers doctrine.

Although Easton and Almond diverged—Easton insisted that his framework differed from functional formulations, and Almond emphasized the divergence of his ideas from those of general systems theory—there are important similarities. For one thing, the idea of persistence runs through both tendencies. For another, there is Easton's reference to the "fundamental functions" of political systems. Then too, both Easton and Almond were influenced by the organicism in the thinking of Radcliffe-Brown, who argued that the "concept of function applied to human societies is based on an analogy between social life and organic life" (1952: 178) and who defined function as "the contribution which a partial activity makes to the total activity of which it is a part ... the contribution it makes to the total social life as the functioning of the total social system" (1935: 397). They also were interested in Malinowski's ideas on functionalism, defined in terms of needs that serve to maintain the system.

Although Almond radically restated Parsonian functionalism, two aspects of Parsons's scheme—action and social system—particularly influenced his formulation. In *The Social System* (1951), Parsons set forth a theory of action, a theory of social systems, and a theory of culture. At the root of some of his thinking were the ideas of Max Weber, the subject of his doctoral dissertation. Parsons's most influential contribution was the development of five dichotomous pattern variables as a means of describing aspects of the action theory: affectivity versus affective neutrality; self-orientation versus collectivity orientation; universalism versus particularism; achievement versus ascription; specificity versus diffuseness (Parsons 1951: 67). They formed the essence of his macro theory of social systems and of his structural functionalism, and they were utilized in Almond's own efforts to relate political systems to political culture. Terms employed by Almond such as maintenance and adaptation were inherent in the thinking of Parsons. Almond also assimilated in modified form such Parsonian aspects as functional prerequisites, structural differentiation, and specialization and was interested in the Parsonian emphasis on the cultural secularization of developing systems. Table 5.1 offers a comparison of input and output categories used by Almond, Easton, and Parsons.

Micro-Structural Functionalism
and Partial or Middle-Range Theory

Although the macro or grand theory of social scientists has focused on whole societies or systems, a growing number of social scientists have turned their attention to the study of parts rather than the whole of society. The study of groups has long been of interest to political scientists. Almond and others stimulated special-

TABLE 5.1
Categories of Inputs and Outputs: Comparison of Almond, Easton, and Parsons

	Almond		Easton	Parsons	
INPUTS	Demands		Demands	Interests-Demands	
	Supports		Supports	Supports	
				Control of productivity	
				Legitimation of authority	
				Legality of powers of offices	
OUTPUTS	Decisions	⎰ Regulations	Decisions	Policies	
		⎱ Extractions	Actions	Allocations of resources	
		Distributions		Effectiveness	
		Responses		Responsibilities	⎰ Leadership
	Actions				⎱ Operation
					Moral

SOURCE: Adapted from Mitchell (1967: 83). For an elaboration of Parsons's formulation of political system, see his essay (1966: 105–112).

ized studies on political parties, bureaucracies, labor unions, and special interest groups in countries throughout the world. Such studies of basic units or subsystems enable scholars to give attention to a "middle range" of empirical data in counterposition to abstract general theory or narrow empirical studies of behaviorism. The foundation of the middle range, Almond believed, is found in the "authors of the *Federalist papers* [who] were systems theorists as well, for they dealt with the interaction and equilibrium of the other social systems with the political system, and with the interaction of the subsystems of the polity one with the other" (Almond and Powell 1966: 10–11).

This idea of interaction and equilibrium, inherent in middle-range theory of structural functionalism, was not new to political science. David Easton noted its origins in the study of political process and the shaping of the policies of a political system, an idea he believed was traceable to the pluralism and equilibrium introduced early in Arthur F. Bentley's *Process of Government,* published at the turn of the twentieth century, and later reinforced in David Truman's monumental study of group pressures in *The Governmental Process* (1951). Those origins were explored critically by G. David Garson (1974). The assimilation by Almond of pluralist theory into a functionalist framework confirmed its universal applicability, but it also revealed that "pluralist theory is reduced to the status of partisan apologetics at worst and ideology at best" (Baskin 1970: 94–95).

Criticisms of Almond and Structural Functionalism

Functionalism and structuralism in political science derive essentially from anthropology, economics, and sociology. Critics of those approaches have found their mark, however. Functionalism frequently is identified as deterministic or ideological, conservative or restrictive, or simply false. Anthropologist I. C. Jarvie argued that functionalism is limited by "its lack of explanatory power, its unsatisfactoriness as explanation, and the constricting effect of its assumptions about the nature and working of social systems." Economist Sherman Roy Krupp warned of problems in stressing the equilibrium character of functional systems: there is a tendency to exaggerate the cohesiveness of such systems; highly integrated systems may obscure goals, resulting in vague description and lack of analysis; and ideal situations are often confused with the observed situations of systems. Sociologist Don Martindale noted four drawbacks to functionalism: the conservative ideological bias and preference for status quo; a lack of methodological clarity; an overemphasis on the role of closed systems in social life; and a failure to deal with social change (Martindale 1965). The charge that functionalism does not account for processes of change was backed up by Barber (1956), and Buckley (1966) stressed a predisposition for functionalism to assume consensus. Hempel (1959) argued that functionalism is illogical. Terry N. Clark (1972) concerned himself with the structural-functional overemphasis of institutionalized behavior, and David Apter (1971) discussed a number of weaknesses in functionalism in a critical look at developments in comparative politics.

All these problems are relevant to a critique of structural functionalism and Almond's formulation of the political system. Groth (1970), for example, referred to the difficulties of defining a system and its boundaries and to the political biases. His own concerns with the work of Almond and Powell were threefold: ambiguity in terminology, difficulties in determining political relationships, and confusion in the use of facts and values.

Functionalism blossomed in an era of consolidation and conservatism following the Second World War. C. Wright Mills (1959: 25–49) and Ralf Dahrendorf (1958) castigated Parsons and claimed that his functionalism neither was relevant to facts nor reached a level of theory. Almond's work was ethnocentric in its emphasis on stability in the light of Anglo-American norms and political tradition, a difficulty Almond acknowledged in his effort to combine structural functionalism with a theory of development. Objections to this later work, however, revealed the ideological undercurrents of the structural functionalism of Almond and Powell: "Their theory is implicitly designed to convert the reader to a belief in liberal democracy and liberal pluralism" (Sanford 1971: 5). It also was perceived as culture-bound: "establishmentarian, non-operational, formally inadequate. ... As a vehicle for research it goes nowhere, and as a language of discourse it leads to obfuscation. ... The pluralistic neutralism of structural-functionalism ... renders it useless as theory" (Powell 1971: 63). The nomenclature of Almond's political system also led to problems, according to Finer: "What Almond has to say could have been said without using this systems approach and it would have been said more clearly" (1969–1970: 4). Finally, there were operational difficulties, in particular the difficulty of refining, operationalizing, and testing hypotheses, as suggested by Holt and Turner: "It is difficult to apply on a broad basis to include both historical and contemporary cases. The formulation also tends in effect to equate the modern political system with the modern Anglo-American democratic system ... its definitions employ too many dimensions, and it neglects the problem of variation" (1966: 12–13).

Alternative Perspectives of System

U.S. conceptions of pluralist politics generally stress consensus, but some attention recently has been devoted to conflict as well. Easton recognized the limitations of systems in equilibrium. Almond, in the image of Parsons, combined his formulation of systems with perspectives on action. These efforts, however, really do not satisfy radical critics of systems theory. Lilienfeld, for example, labeled systems theory as an "ideological movement" with a "central doctrine and a syncretistic or ecumenical way of thinking" (1975: 646). The systems literature contains little relevance to the real world. Even the application of systems analysis has exerted little impact on U.S. politics, he claimed, and he cited a number of cases of system "fiascoes" and wasted expenditure. His review of the literature illustrating the failure of a practical application of systems analysis is well worth the reader's attention.

Almond, absorbed in the ideal Anglo-American model of politics, paid scant attention to Marx who also was concerned with the idea of system, which he conceived as a political economy whose changes were the consequences of class conflict according to material forces of production. Parsons also devoted little attention to Marx, but at one point Parsons acknowledged that "Marx is one of the symbolic 'grandfathers' of the theory of action" (Black 1961: 361). Easton, in his early work, was more generous. Marx and Comte, he affirmed, were preoccupied with a premature building of systems: "The complete immersion of these thinkers in something called the scientific approach distinguishes and links them." Easton summarized what he understood was the Marxist approach. Marx, he claimed,

> thought that appropriately mastered tools of inquiry, historical and dialectical materialism, which he developed from Hegel, would reveal the nature of inexorable laws and goals towards the realization of which those laws tended. ... Marx sought to prove that it [society] evolved basically from primitive communism to feudalism to capitalism and must eventuate in socialism. [Easton 1953: 12]

Although recognizing political science criticisms of Marx, Thorson, who is not a Marxist, asserted that "Marx was correct in his basic perspective" (1970: 85). Furthermore, he contrasted "the Newtonian universal-generalization paradigm of understanding with the Darwinian evolutionary-development paradigm of understanding" (209). The Newtonian paradigm he associated with Hobbes and Locke, Harrington and Madison, and Easton, while he related the Darwinian paradigm to Hegel and Marx. Marx gave political science and political philosophy "essentially a time-oriented theory of change," which differed sharply with "the static, enduring processing machine" of the Newtonian paradigm (210).

Given this latter distinction, we now discuss two orientations of a Marxist conception of system. The first orientation examines functionalism within a materialist perspective. We look at Frederick Engels's explication of a dialectical materialist explanation of the natural sciences, and then we turn to Al Szymanski's application of functionalism to Marxist dialectics. We note Marvin Harris's rejection of dialectics but his acceptance of materialism in scientific analysis. We review the efforts of Jonathan A. Sanford and others to revise a liberal perspective of structural functionalism into a radical framework. The second orientation of a Marxist conception of system examines system conceptualized as the state, beginning with a Hegelian view and the Marxist critique of Hegel's understanding of state and concluding with a summary of the contemporary approaches to an analysis of the state. Finally, we study an attempt to apply systems theory to centralized planning in the former German Democratic Republic.

System in a Dialectical Materialist Perspective

An alternative view of system, like its mainstream counterpart, roots itself in science. Science long has stressed generalization and broadly ranged theory in opposition to the partial, subjective, and irrational perspectives that pervade the orthodox underpinnings of contemporary politics. During the eighteenth century, writers moved from the Newtonian model to a deterministic view of history. Montesquieu in *The Spirit of Laws* discovered order in the histories of all nations, noted interconnected laws, and attributed changes to material causes. Marquis de Condorcet's *Outline of the Intellectual Progress of Mankind* attempted to apply the uniform and natural laws of the universe to society. He also identified ten epochs or stages in the history of civilization, a sort of incremental approach to development steeped in idealism, which nevertheless set the basis for an interpretation of evolution in the work of nineteenth-century thinkers, including Comte, Spencer, and Darwin.

Herbert Spencer focused on the themes of progress and race, laissez-faire individualism, and economic and political liberalism, and he opposed socialism and communism. Charles Darwin offered a materialist explanation of the origin of the species and emphasized progress through struggle. According to Marvin Harris (1968), who concisely summarized and interpreted all these intellectual currents, Darwin's position was confused by prevailing, yet contrasting, views related to inherited and learned traits. Nevertheless, it was Spencer and other conservatives who applied the term "social Darwinism" to an interpretation of the nature and functioning of society. Harris blamed Spencer, not Darwin, for "the onus of having crippled the explanatory power of cultural evolutionary theory by merging and mixing it with racial determinism." "The conversion of biological theory to evolutionism was an outgrowth of the social scientists' interest in progress and perfectibility, while the concept of natural selection itself arose from an interest in racial, national, and class forms of war and conflict" (Harris 1968: 129). Harris also admonished us to beware of the "myth of unilinear evolutionism," which usually characterizes classical evolutionary theory, and he argued that society and culture may skip steps in a sequence or evolve divergently (171). More recently, Carl Degler (1991) traced the application of the Darwinian concepts of heredity and biological explanation of behavior in social science and popular social thought and suggested that these concepts are employed today without the racist connotations of the past.

Darwinism and evolutionary ideas influenced Frederick Engels who, in *Dialectics of Nature* (1934), examined the achievements of the natural sciences during the nineteenth century. In particular, Engels was interested in the discovery of the organic cell as the basic structural unit of the human organism; he critiqued metaphysical and idealist conceptions in natural science, prevalent in his time as well as in ours, and drawing upon Marx's use of Hegelian dialectics, he offered a dialectical materialist explanation of natural science. His perspective focused on the development of the capitalist mode of production and advances in technology and their impact on the natural sciences.

Unlike static general systems theory, Engels combined inorganic physical science with organic life sciences into a dialectical materialist classification of the natural sciences (1934: 248–249). Emphasizing "the general evolutionary connection in nature," he interrelated all matter, organic and inorganic. Engels attacked the piecemeal arrangement of science proposed by Comte and Saint-Simon, "where one science is always exhausted before another is even broached" (250). Engels's critique, of course, counters the attempt by general systems theorists to distinguish closed (inorganic) systems from open (organic) ones. It also counters efforts by Bertalanffy, Laszlo, and others to combine scientific with philosophical views, for Engels struggled against metaphysics and the idealism, mechanism, and vulgar materialism of his contemporaries. Extracting the mysticism from Hegelianism, Engels called on scientists to apply the laws of materialist dialectics, thereby giving a dynamic method to natural science.

Engels traced the patterns of scientific revolution through historical periods (1934: 23–28 ff.), similar to the later treatment of Thomas Kuhn. Man, he argued, "reacts on nature, changing it and creating new conditions for himself" (213). Causality thus relates directly to the actions of the individual upon nature rather than to deterministic causality based on laws in nature itself.

Engels exposed as pseudoscience the "natural-philosophical systems" of the German socialist Eugen Dühring and others who wrote "in ignorance" about all ideas and put forward their thought as adhering to scientific method. Engels acknowledged the need for classifying knowledge into fields for systematic investigation, but he insisted on making clear the connections of one field to another— empiricism becomes suspect, theory necessary at this point. "Natural science enters the field of theory and here the methods of empiricism will not work, here only theoretical thinking can be of assistance" (1934: 42). Engels understood theory as "a historical product, which at different times assumes different forms and, therewith, very different contents." The science of thought is "the science of the historical development of human thought," but the laws of thought do not signify "eternal truth." Thus dialectics, following in the tradition of Aristotle and Hegel, "constitutes the most important form of thinking for present-day natural science, for it alone offers the analogue for, and thereby the method of explaining, the evolutionary processes occurring in nature, interconnections in general, and transitions from one field of investigation to another" (43).

A holistic, not segmented, view of system is essential, according to Engels, because nothing takes place in isolation. Everything affects and is affected by every other thing. An individual makes the environment serve his or her purposes and thus brings about devastating social consequences. Engels analyzed these consequences in terms of production and labor. "All hitherto existing modes of production have aimed merely at achieving the most immediately and directly useful effort of labour. ... All higher forms of production, however, led to the division of the population into different classes and thereby to the antagonisms of ruling and oppressed classes" (1934: 182).

Al Szymanski (1972) argued that Marx was a functionalist and functionalism should be employed in radical analysis when interpreted dialectically. Acknowledging the inherently conservative nature of prevailing functional theory, Szymanski believed that functionalism can be "a fundamental part of Marxist methodology, and a very powerful tool for the advance of social science" (1972: 35).

Szymanski examined the functionalism of Malinowski who saw society as culturally responding to seven basic biological needs, a formulation especially relevant for understanding classless, primitive societies. Malinowski's functionalism is not useful in the study of class societies in which needs other than biological needs develop, for example, the need to preserve and advance the interests of the class system. "When the imperatives of biology conflict with those of the preservation of class society, more likely than not, the imperatives of biology give way. Thus people go hungry so that business might make a profit" (Szymanski 1972: 38). If Malinowski's emphasis on biological needs could be combined with the historical needs of a given society, then his functionalism might become compatible with Marxist analysis, for Marx grounded his functionalism on an explanation of the contributions major institutions make to the social system of capitalism. Marx related each institution's relationship to profit maximization: religion is the opium of the people, the state is the managing force of the bourgeoisie, and the family is the replica of the greater society.

Szymanski also critiqued Parsons and Merton. Parsons's functional requisites distort reality, his schema of historical interpretation is inadequate and internally inconsistent, and his notion of culture is determinist. Further, he has no understanding of the fundamental contradictions of society. "Parsons simply fails to provide an adequate systematic theory of change that is both integrated with his abstract scheme *and* which can explain with any accuracy historical evolution" (1972: 39). In contrast, Merton is more sensitive to the problems of functionalism in his use of function and dysfunction, which moves toward an understanding of the contradictory nature of society, but Merton also has stripped functionalism of the concept of system and its holistic implications.

Finally, Szymanski introduced dialectics to functionalism, drawing upon Marx and Engels. Dialectics, he believed, is a method for understanding the physical and social world. Dialectics implies a moving back and forth between abstractness and concreteness, between theory and reality. Three principles prevail and can be related to functionalism; Szymanski called them principles of dialectical functionalism. First, things tend to be interrelated with one another, to form systems, and they must be understood as parts of a greater whole. Societies must be understood in historical context. Presently they relate to the satisfaction of biological needs and to the maintenance of the capitalist system. Second, although things are interdependent, they also have internal contradictions. In contemporary society dialectical functionalism both contributes to as well as undermines the existing system. Capitalism may result in an accumulation of real goods in society but also results in an expanded proletariat, which may struggle against those who control the means of production. Third, things tend to change as a consequence of contradictions in the system. Change emanates from the opposing forces within a given system, and change is the essential aspect of dialectical functionalism. For example, in maximizing profits through monopoly capital, the capitalist system tends to undermine its early practice of free competition.

These are the principles of Marx and contemporary Marxists who analyze racism, education, family, military, the state, and the like in functional terms; each is explained in terms of the economic requirements of monopoly capitalism. Not only are the contributions of each recognized, but the undermining and transformation of the system are also emphasized.

Marvin Harris (1968) leaned toward a materialist stance but also critically assessed the contributions of Marx and Engels to theory. He noted that they "depended upon a 'functional' model of sociocultural life," sharing with Comte and Spencer an interest in functionalism, which was compatible and subordinate to a primary interest in change. Yet all these nineteenth-century thinkers contrast sharply with the twentieth-century functionalists who are capable only of eclectic and piecemeal investigation. As to the functionalism of Marx and Engels, "As a causal, as well as diachronic and synchronic model, the economic-structural-ideological concatenation provides the basis for stipulating the more or less durable and influential parts of the system" (Harris 1968: 235). Harris noted that Marxist functionalism explicitly denies "that all the features of a sociocultural system contribute equally to its maintenance. … dysfunctional ingredients are not only accommodated, but assigned a central role as system-changing variables" (235). Conflict, he believed, is taken care of through a model that is evolutionary, not dialectical. Thus he indicted the "vague dialectical excursions" of Marx and Engels. "As a mode of analysis, which arose at the juncture of romanticism and industrialization, it is ill suited for the general history of mankind. It is a romanticized, mysticized, partisan materialism, appropriate to men who wish to

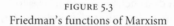

FIGURE 5.3
Friedman's functions of Marxism

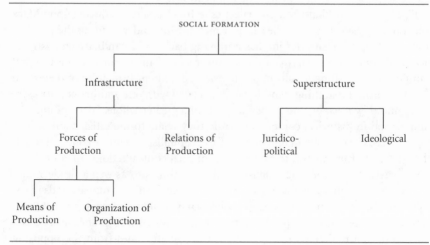

SOURCE: Adapted from Friedman (1974: 445).

foment a revolution based on mid-nineteenth-century European class structure
and ideology" (230). Harris insisted that we turn to Marx's materialism and his
distinction between economic base and superstructure.

Jonathan Friedman sketched a Marxist "model" of analytical categories that are
interrelated hierarchically into "a set of functional distinctions" (1974: 445), as in
Figure 5.3. Friedman took exception to Harris's "vulgar materialism," which he
interpreted as the "new mechanical materialism developed out of a quite understandable reaction to the almost exclusive concern for ideology and semantics
which has come to dominate much of anthropology" (444). Harris, Friedman believed, embedded himself "in a tradition of empiricist-functionalist ideology"
(465). Like Szymanski, Friedman introduced the dialectic into his formulation,
but he also attempted to elaborate a structural-Marxist model.

If Marx and Engels were functionalists, as Friedman, Harris, and Szymanski
have affirmed, then how do their conceptions relate to orthodox conceptions of
system? Sanford partially attempted to answer this question by returning to the
structural functionalism of Almond and Powell, and he offered a revision of their
formulation by breathing into it "a radical and existential ideological bias" (Sanford 1971: 27). Using similar procedures, he sharply differentiated conclusions
from the liberal pluralist findings of Almond and Powell. In his discussion Sanford referred to Marx and Engels as "the two most famous structural-functional
analysts" whose emphasis on the role of socioeconomic forces in promoting political change is echoed by Almond and Powell (Sanford 1971: 7). Sanford also
drew from the "systematic" discussions by the Russian Marxist Nikolai Bukharin,
and he cited from the works of U.S. Marxists Paul Baran and Paul Sweezy. Sanford's critique and formulation attempted to transcend the limitations of the lib-

eral pluralism of Almond and Powell, but he essentially retained their categories. His contribution is a useful example of an interpretation that moves toward the alternative paradigm of comparative politics, however.

Those who espouse an alternative paradigm, incorporating a Marxist perspective, would argue that Almond and Powell failed to see cleavages, tensions, and conflict in their analysis of systems; failed to differentiate among social classes; and failed to relate national systems to an international order, thereby offering no explanation for underdevelopment, which afflicts most countries. The pluralist assumptions in their model suggested that competing groups and interests would be dominated by ruling classes, thus isolating the masses of people. The ruling or dominant classes would perpetuate development for their own purposes, while promoting underdevelopment for the powerless and isolated lower classes. The state and its ruling classes would break through groups and organization, isolate individuals, and undermine the autonomy of the subsystems.

The radicals understand system as a whole and its holistic perspective as historical in orientation. González Casanova, for example, interpreted historical perspectives of system as dealing with process, struggle, organization, spontaneity, and other tendencies. He envisioned combinations of classical Marxism with new perspectives of social science, so that the contradictions of general systems theory, cybernetics, and even a discredited structural functionalism might be incorporated into a theory based on dialectics. Essentially, however, history is struggle.

> History as struggle emphasizes human, political categories with dialectical relations, with reciprocal actions, which are not simple relations of cause and effect, since in the midst of historical regularities a series of novelties or surprises are generated both in the structure and sequence of historical development. [González Casanova, 1973: 234]

In his effort to set forth a systematic conception of society, Mannheim also delineated a Marxist theory of social change, based on the material forces of production. "The basic organization of society is expressed in its economic structure which to a large extent determines the legal and political organization, and even the form of social consciousness ... the kind of thought and ideas people hold in any particular age" (Mannheim 1957: 136). Mannheim reminded his readers that according to Marx social change comes about as the material forces of production are subject to change, and this occurs through technical inventions. Changes in the forces of production affect class relations and result in class conflict.

Systems Analysis in a Socialist Society

Marxists might call the orthodox systems theory simply a mystification of technocrats seeking power. In an age of widespread technology, it is argued, the new technician of the United States defends the interests of a new class oriented to planning and administration and appropriates "American values based on progress through scientific rationality" (Lilienfeld 1975: 658–659). This indictment probably is acceptable to many specialists of comparative politics.

Systems theory was utilized in the former Soviet Union (Blauberg, Sadovsky, and Yudin 1977) and in Eastern Europe. For the latter, Peter C. Ludz (1975) assessed its significance and utility in the former German Democratic Republic; his findings are now reviewed, and an attempt is made to determine if the radical indictment of systems theory in the United States was relevant to that once-socialist society.

Ludz argued that the language of Marxism-Leninism provided empty formulas, even though it became the major communication pattern. Given this condition, technological concepts of the West were easily assimilated into Marxism-Leninism, in particular functionalism and cybernetic systems theory. In 1961 a Society of Cybernetics was founded, and philosopher George Klaus became the major proponent of the application of systems theory to Marxist theory. Borrowing from Ashby, Wiener, and others, Klaus envisaged a cybernetics theory of dynamic and self-regulating systems characterized by connections with the environment. This conception is formulated in terms of the biological organism, and it assumes maintenance and stability as well as control. Klaus considered information to be the link between cybernetics and dialectical materialism, and information is tied to organization. Cybernetics systems theory thus defines categories of historical and dialectical materialism precisely; serves to rationalize automation; assists economic planning and increases labor productivity; and facilitates autonomous control within organizations. Klaus also established connections between cybernetics and dialectical logic. The terminology of Western systems theory—function and structure, inputs and outputs, and feedback—was employed in the East German formulation. Eventually control of society by the state was to be replaced by the feedback system of a socialist society. Mass participation and consciousness would replace the central regulating institutions of a socialist society.

Ludz believed that systems theory threatened to undermine central control in the German Democratic Republic. Further, he noted contradictions between capitalist and socialist applications of systems theory. He admitted that "cybernetic systems theory in itself has developed characteristics which resemble the empty formulas of Marxism Leninism" (1975: 671). In any event, a ten-year experiment in the application of systems theory in a socialist country was ended in 1971, probably, he believed, because of the ideological and political implications of systems theory. He argued that "the ideas of technical rationality and economic efficiency" (1975: 674) inherent in the theory were still in effect, however. It was not clear that systems theory served to mystify and defend the interests of the German technocratic bureaucracy.

Directions for a Radical Understanding of Systems Theory

Two significant themes are suggested in criticisms of systems theory: inquiry must take into account the human condition, and theory must orient to a world system. Doris and Francis Bartlett (1971) decried the social implications of the biological determinism that has crept into social science literature. They criticized flaws in analogies of animal and human behaviors, and they condemned the "biosocial syndrome" of explanation as simply "an ideology of despair. ... Despair is the ultimate product of this application of 'science' to human affairs" (1971: 219). Baskin (1970) more emphatically denounced the absence of the human element in the pluralism upon which systems theory is often premised: "A more human politics would organize public life as an adventurous avenue for self-discovery and community-building so that men might transcend that which divides them as rivals and through citizenship in a community might experience instead that which unites them as brothers" (1970: 95).

Marx and Lenin and their followers conceived of system in international terms. This theme is carried on by several ambitious works (Wuthnow 1979), and two examples are mentioned. Immanuel Wallerstein in his *Modern World System* (1974) examined capitalist agriculture and the origins of the European world economy in the sixteenth century. In his introduction he recounted the difficulties in his past theoretical perspective. He abandoned a focus on the sovereign state or the national society, stating that "neither one was a social system. ... one could only speak of social change in social systems. The only social system in this scheme was the world system" (1974: 7). He attempted to transcend the boundaries of disciplines as he utilized a "unidisciplinary" approach—he combined all the social sciences into a historical and holistic perspective. Samir Amin in his *Accumulation on a World Scale* (1974) pursued a similar approach, utilizing an explicit Marxist framework and building a radical paradigm of understanding. He too was historical and holistic as he transcended national capitalist and socialist systems to posit the thesis, "There are not two world markets, one capitalist and the other socialist, but only one, the capitalist world market" (1974: 4). His theory of accumulation on a world scale is a theory of capitalist formations between the center and the periphery of a world system.

Implications of Approaches to Systems Theory

From ancient and medieval thought Western man derived the habit of visualizing the organic world in terms of the smallest possible units to which it could be reduced. [Martindale 1965: 144]

Don Martindale distinguished the above approaches, calling them, respectively, *holism* and *elementarism*. Holism views interrelated wholes as superior to individuals and their acts. Elementarism views social reality as consisting of individuals and their actions. In my chapter the Eastonian framework and general systems theory, the macro-structural functionalism of Almond and Parsons, and some radical orientations have been cast into a holistic context. The striving for the middle range of inquiry by many specialists of comparative politics has been cast as micro-structural functionalism and to some extent implied elementarism. Martindale's own synthesis is helpful in that it distinguishes a variety of currents linked to the positivist and historicist traditions from which emanate the mainstream and alternative paradigms of contemporary comparative politics. Combining some of his ideas with the discussions in earlier chapters, some assumptions about systems theory can be set forth:

1. The ancient and medieval thinkers distinguished between mind and matter in the construction of systems. The mind, which yields intuition and reason, for example, relates to the spiritual world and to the humanities, and matter relates to the material world and the sciences.

2. The social scientists have attempted to reconcile the intellectual distinctions between the humanities and the sciences. Auguste Comte set forth positivism as a means of transmitting the method of the physical sciences to the humanities. John Stuart Mill proposed that social science rest on physiology and physical science method. Applications of physical science continue today as the basis of positivistic social science.

3. Antipositivism emerged in the form of historicism, which objects to the intrusion of the physical science method into the social, political, and cultural disciplines. The historicists have found fault with the ahistorical interpretations of the positivists and condemned their narrow scope of inquiry.

4. Both the positivist and antipositivist positions relate to the study of whole systems or parts of systems. Orthodox holistic theory generally is organicist, and sometimes mechanistic, and dependent upon harmonious systems usually in equilibrium. Radical holistic theory focuses on systems in disequilibrium and seeks explanations that usually are not tied to organicistic or mechanistic frameworks. Orthodox narrow- and middle-range theories are concerned with parts of systems, structural functionalism being a prominent example, and radical theory attempts to relate to some parts only in the context of the whole system.

Table 5.2 illustrates these relationships and serves to summarize the discussion of the present chapter. Positivist and ahistorical perspectives, which characterize the orthodox paradigm, pervade both partial and holistic theories of system. The partial theories are liberal and pluralist in orientation and are represented by Bentley, Truman, and Almond in the tradition of Hume and Locke. The holistic theory is generally conservative in orientation and is represented by Parsons and his followers in sociology and Easton and Almond in political science in the tradition of Comte, Mill, and Spencer. Both Parsons and Easton would consider themselves to be part of the antipositivist tradition, and their early work reflects this concern; but the ahistorical abstraction and lack of concern for detail in the real world, which mark the bulk of their work, suggest the appropriateness of including them in the positivist tradition.

Partial and holistic theories of system also characterize the alternative paradigm. The French philosopher Jean-Paul Sartre and the Polish philosopher Adam Schaff are representative of partial theory in that their concerns run counter to the technocratic and scientific movement of capitalist systems, in which the indi-

TABLE 5.2

Systems Theory and Paradigms: Types, Scope, Orientations, and Representative Thinkers

Types	Scope of System	Orientations of Theory	Representative Thinkers
Mainstream (Positivist and Ahistorical)	Partial (individual group)	Liberal Pluralist	Hume, Locke, Bentley, Truman, and Almond
	Holistic	Conservative Organicist	Comte, Mill, Spencer, Easton, Almond, Parsons, Merton, and Levy
Alternative (Anti-Positivist and Historical)	Partial (individual)	Orthodox Marxist Existentialist Marxist	Sartre and Schaff
	Holistic	Collectivist Reformist Marxist	C. Wright Mills, Marx, and Engels

vidual must survive, and of socialist systems, in which individuality and collectivity must be compatible. The collectivist and Marxist orientations of holistic theory are found, respectively, in Mills and Marx.

Such a summary is indeed simplistic, but it is to be hoped that it orients the reader to recognize and distinguish among the many tendencies of systems theory.

Toward a Theory of the State

Historically, the study of politics has incorporated an understanding of the state, and political science has incorporated the concept since its inception in the nineteenth century. John Gunnell noted that "its adoption was most essentially a function of the Germanization and disciplinization of political science" (1990: 5). He traced the early work on the state to German political scientist Johann Kaspar Bluntschli (1885); Francis Lieber, a naturalized American and "the first to employ the concept of the state ... and to make it an object of theoretical analysis" (Gunnell 1990: 19); and Theodore Woolsey, who was educated in Bonn and Paris and was "the first of the major native American theorists of the state and political science" (Gunnell 1990: 22). Gunnell affirmed that "the theory of the state, as advanced by Lieber, Bluntschli, and Woolsey, constituted a distinct and influential paradigm" (38). This paradigm was to continue with the work of Westal W. Willoughby (1896), the "last 'grand' theorist of the state in American political science" (Gunnell 1990: 72).

This mainstream legacy of attention to the state was interpreted by the SSRC's Committee on Comparative Politics, whose members proclaimed that the concept of state should be replaced by political system. In his introduction to *Politics of Developing Areas* (1960), Almond argued that the state was imbued with many meanings and could not be operationalized in current comparative investigation, part of the problem being the proliferation of the newly emerging countries of the Third World as the old colonial empires of Europe collapsed after the Second World War. Later Almond reminded us that the state, conceived in its Weberian sense with attention to "the legally empowered and legitimately coercive institutions," would be assimilated in the concept of political system, together with the plethora of new institutions, extralegal and paralegal political parties, interest groups, communication media, family, school, church, and so on (1988: 885). Despite this intransigence, a campaign to "bring the state back in," mounted under the auspices of the SSRC's Committee on States and Social Structures, resulted in "a paradigmatic shift" (Evans, Rueschemeyer, and Skocpol 1985).

The campaign to retain interest in the state had in fact been evident during the 1960s and 1970s, but in the mainstream context this was largely because comparative political scientists were concerned with dictatorship and authoritarianism in the Third World and comparison with the historical experience of fascist and corporative regimes in southern Europe. At the same time, alternative perspectives on the state, based on a Marxist tradition, appeared within political science outside the United States. The following discussion reviews these currents of thinking (summarized in Table 5.3) in order to guide the student through the complexity of theory and debate that has carried forward into the 1990s. This discussion, however, will provide only a sketch of these developments because detailed syntheses of the literature are available in Carnoy (1984) and Jessop (1982 and 1990); my own elaboration of theories of the state will appear in a sequel to this book, my forthcoming work on comparative political economy.

Mainstream Theories of the State

Pluralist Capitalist Perspective

The state is a political marketplace through which filter the demands and interests of competing groups and individuals. Two views prevail. On the one hand, neutral state agencies mediate conflict that emanates from party and group competition. On the other, agencies of the state function as the bases of political power; competition among the agencies for funding determines their relationship to parties and interest groups. These views reflect the liberal, non-Marxist tradition of U.S. social science.

Although these views fall in line with the political preferences of Gabriel Almond, he nevertheless sought to rebut, indeed to discredit, the arguments of the

TABLE 5.3
Contemporary Theories of the State

Mainstream	Alternative
Pluralist Capitalist	Pluralist Socialist
Institutional	Instrumentalist
Corporatist	Structuralist
Bureaucratic Authoritarian	Feminist

statist movement. He discounted many of the arguments in favor of a programmatic shift in the discipline. J. P. Nettl (1968), for example, was the first to challenge the abandonment of the state by Almond, Easton, and others. Nettl disaggregated the state into components, but he did not succeed in operationalizing the concept. Statists such as Evans, Rueschemeyer, and Skocpol (1985), he believed, were unsuccessful in their critiques of both theoretical and empirical pluralist and structural-functional literature, and he felt their argument that Marxism is societally reductionist failed because neostatism is merely a "polemic internal to Marxism," an intellectual movement operating "from a social class reductionist set of assumptions" (Nettl 1968: 868–869). Almond (1988) bitterly despaired the impact of the statist movement for leaving a generation of young scholars with "little more than a paradigmatic farewell" and the alternative of adopting "ambiguous phraseology in the place of a hard-won tradition of operational rigor" (872).

In a view accepting of the state as a framework for analyzing a multidimensional society, Michael Mann (1986) argued against societies as totalities and therefore dispensed with orthodox ways of looking at society, such as systems theory, structuralism, structural functionalism, and so on. He took the state as one of four units for analysis; focused his concern on society as composed of four overlapping and intersecting power networks (ideological, economic, military, and political); and applied a sociospatial and organizational model and a Weberian methodology of ideal types to his analysis of the development of Europe into the eighteenth century.

In another view extending to a synthesis of state and society, Timothy Mitchell (1991) argued that neither conceptualization in the direction of political system nor the effort to reintroduce the state to mainstream political science has resolved the problem of boundary definition between the state and society. In an alternative approach, he affirmed that the state should not be seen as a coherent entity separate from society, nor should the complexity of the state lead to rejection of the state altogether; instead the "distinction between state and society should nevertheless be taken seriously, as the defining characteristic of the modern political order. ... The state should be addressed as an effect of detailed processes of spatial organization, temporal arrangement, functional specification and supervision and surveillance, which create the appearance of a world fundamentally divided into state and society" (95).

Institutional Perspective

Utilizing an "institutional perspective" to understand the sovereign state, Krasner asserted that the "range of options available to policy makers at any given point in time is a function of institutional capabilities that were put in place at some earlier period" (1988: 67). He used this position to argue against utilitarian or functional approaches that see outcomes as the consequence of individual choice. Thus, the sovereign state has come to be the form of political organization acceptable to the modern world: "Path-dependent patterns of development have been important; once Europe was committed to a form of political organization based on sovereign states, other possibilities were foreclosed" (1988: 90).

Rosenau (1988) supported the trend to reinstate the concept of state because of "diminished effectiveness of whole systems" and "a deep disillusion with systems analysis" (22). He recalled the past formulations of other political scientists, including MacIver (1926), Titus (1931), Clark and Dear (1984), and Deutsch (1986). In Rosenau's opinion, Jessop (1977) suggested a broad, somewhat confusing conceptual spectrum of views on the state, yet Rosenau affirmed that "the state is deeply embedded in our terminology and is unlikely to yield to efforts to replace it" (1988: 27).

Mainstream evidence of acceptance of the state and state theory as central to the study of comparative politics is available in the differing approaches and perspectives of international relations scholars and comparativists whose essays were collected by James A. Caporaso (1989) in a volume that examines both theoretical perspective and empirical example. An abrupt response to proponents of state theory, Almond's essay (1988) reemphasized the necessity of working with systems theory. David Easton (1981) built on this emphasis while offering a serious and critical assessment of Nicos Poulantzas's work on the state.

Corporatist Perspective

Mainstream definitions of the state include Philippe Schmitter's reference to "an amorphous complex of agencies with ill-defined boundaries, performing a great variety of not very distinctive functions" (1985: 33). Schmitter (1971) had integrated corporatism into his early work on Brazil, but later questioned its usefulness for political economy. The optimism about corporatism was based on the assumptions that planning was essential to modern capitalism; planning necessitated an effective income policy; and income policy depended on consensus and agreement among the affected groups. Thus, corporatist compromises, especially in Europe, between labor and capital sometimes evolved through the intervention of the state. Schmitter ultimately came to the view that contemporary conditions have so changed that national negotiations are of decreasing importance due to policies aimed at improving productivity and international competitiveness and to the shift of interest conflicts from class-based cleavages to social movements based on issues of gender, environment, consumer protection, and so on (1989: 70). He also noted the displacement of workers from traditional industry to services and public employment as a result of international competition. Consequently, corporatism may soon be dead: "I have become less and less concerned that corporatism ... will survive, much less be as much an imperative for the future of capitalism" (72).

In his useful overview of perspectives in the field of comparative public policy, Hancock (1983) noted a paradigmatic shift from traditional mainstream concerns toward "societal" or "liberal" corporatism, as reflected in the work of Panitch (1980) and in analysis of the state by Ashford on British (1981) and French (1982) politics. Cameron's comparative studies (1978 and 1982) of industrial nations showed how the highly developed welfare state serves a capitalist economy "by socializing collective bargaining to a degree and offering a social wage as an inducement for wage moderation by workers" (1982: 58). Andrews (1991) extended the notion of corporatism from a national to a regional context and argued that corporatism has been widely accepted in the institutions of European international organizations, particularly the European Economic Community (EEC).

Bureaucratic Authoritarian Perspective

The theory of bureaucratic authoritarianism underlies the work of Guillermo O'Donnell (1988) on Argentina during the 1960s and early 1970s and is relevant to authoritarian situations elsewhere in Latin America. Canak (1984) delved into theories of state structure and intervention in nondemocratic settings and, in particular, explored the expanding role of the state in the process of capital accumulation in Latin America. He suggested that in Latin America both theories relate to crisis caused by the exhaustion of the import-substitution model of industrialization; both theories characterize the national bourgeoisie as weak; and both theories understand the state in crisis as part of a transitional stage. In his critique he comprehensively reviewed the literature on these theories, revealing their contribution as well as limitations in characterizing the theory of the peripheral state. He suggested, however, that this characterization has become increasingly irrelevant for several reasons: dependency and capitalist development are not necessarily incompatible, as attested in the work of Cardoso and Faletto, *Dependency and Development* (1979); the increasing internationalization of production undermines industrial structures within each nation, whether core or periphery; the size of state expenditures and the extent of state intervention have increased similarly in both core and peripheral nations; and delegitimization of the state has increasingly appeared everywhere.

Alternative Theories of the State

An alternative understanding of state draws upon the thought of Hegel, Marx, Engels, and Lenin. It also focuses on recent study that expands upon the conceptions of Marx and others in order to interpret and analyze the role of the state in the contemporary world. We turn now to a review of the alternative literature on the state.

Through a critique of Hegel's notions of the state, Marx elaborated some initial assumptions that are useful to theory. Painstakingly Marx worked from within Hegel's dialectical framework to expose its contradictions and inconsistencies. Hegel distinguished between the state and civil society: the state comprises an ideal relationship of the elements of society and it aggregates the communal concerns of humanity; in contrast, civil society comprises the private world of individual interests and activities. Hegel envisioned that unity between the state and civil society would evolve through several institutions. In his example of Prussia, these institutions included the hereditary sovereign, who was considered independent of political groupings; the bureaucracy, whose interests coincided with those of the state; and an assembly of estates, which represented a consensus of the divergent interests of civil society.

In his *Critique of Hegel's Doctrine of the State,* Marx agreed with Hegel that a fundamental contradiction existed between the state and the civil society of citizens. Marx, however, separated forms of the state from an ideal or abstract conception and rooted them in "the material conditions of life." Marx stated that in ancient Greece the state and community were combined into the *polis;* there was a sense of unity between the people and the state, between private and public interests. In medieval times there was less separation between the state and civil society, "because civil society was political society; because the organic principle of civil society was the principle of the State" (Marx 1975: 137). Under capitalism, however, the state separates from civil society, and there is an estrangement between public and private life; in addition, there is an estrangement of individuals from each other as the civil society fragments into private interests competing against each other. Under such conditions the state legitimizes the right of individuals to pursue particular interests through the possession of private property. Private property promotes inequality, enhances disunity among people, and undermines the equality and general intent of the community at large. Private property dominates contemporary society.

One solution to this dilemma is the return to democracy, but not to bourgeois democracy, which stresses parliamentary government, division of powers, and equality under the law of the state. Lucio Colletti, an Italian theorist, was fascinated with this aspect of Marx's work.

> At this point in his evolution, what strikes us most forcibly is that while Marx has not yet outlined his later materialist conception of history he already possesses a very mature theory of politics and the state. The *Critique,* after all, contains a clear statement

of the dependence of the state upon society, a critical analysis of parliamentarism accompanied by a counter-theory of popular delegation, and a perspective showing the need for ultimate suppression of the state itself. Politically speaking, mature Marxism would have relatively little to add to this. [Colletti, in Marx 1975: 45–46]

Colletti compared Marx's position with that of Lenin and Engels, who also were concerned with a conception of the state, based on Marx's elaboration. Colletti argued that Engels and Lenin tended to generalize their conception, overlooking the essential distinction, drawn by Marx, in which the state becomes separated from society under emerging capitalism. In turn, this led Engels and Lenin to "their marked subjectivism and volunteerism, based on their conception of the state as a 'machine' knowingly, consciously formed by the ruling class in deliberate pursuit of its own interest" (Colletti, in Marx 1975: 45–46). This distinction between Marx and Engels, in particular, was not recognized by Hal Draper (1977), who synthesized Marx's conception of the state. Draper argued that Marx and Engels collaborated in much of their work and that any scholarly emphasis of the differences between them is of little significance.

We turn now to a summary of Draper's discussion (1977: bk. 1, 237–262), which begins with the *Critique* and evolves through *The German Ideology* and other works by Marx and Engels, in an effort to clarify their conception of the state.

Stateless societies existed before the ancient city-state of Greek times as tribal and primitive communities lacking state institutions. Such communities maintained themselves without any special means of enforcement. Their integration rested on the premise that each individual, although acting in his or her own interests, is conscious of the responsibility to maintain all society. In a stateless society specialized roles and social networks are not tolerated, and "neither economic nor political ends can be exclusively pursued by anyone to the detriment of society, because these ends are intertwined with each other" (A. Southall, quoted in Draper 1977: 238).

Coercion may be found in stateless or state societies. Nature, for example, might coerce a tribe to fish or hunt in order to avoid starvation. In primitive stateless communities, coercion is based on a collective judgment and is applied by the whole society; punishment is not relegated to a particular institution, separate from the collectivity. Once a society divides into opposing social classes, the interests of the whole society become fragmented, and the power for the enforcement of coercion separates from the collectivity, thereby ushering the state into existence. Engels described this historical process in his *Origin of the Family, Private Property, and the State*.

The state ... is rather a product of society at a certain stage of development; it is the admission that this society has become entangled in an insoluble contradiction with itself, that it is cleft into irreconcilable antagonisms which it is powerless to dispel. In order that these antagonisms, these classes with conflicting economic interests, may not annihilate each other and society in sterile struggle, a power, apparently standing above society, became necessary for the purpose of moderating the conflict and keeping it within the bounds of "order"; and this power, arising out of society, but placing itself over it, and increasingly alienating itself from it, is the state. [Engels (n.d.): 140]

Marx and Engels focused on the impact of coercion in the process of production and in economic relations. They noted that once coercion is shifted from the economic base of society, it tends to concentrate in the state or the political superstructure, a term they identify in *The German Ideology* as, "The social organization, evolving directly out of production and commerce, ... in all ages forms the basis of the state and of the rest of the ideological superstructure" (quoted in Draper 1977: 252).

Drawing upon Marx and Engels, Draper elaborated the characteristics of the state in modern history as distinguished from tribal communities. First, the state exercises power over a territory (usually with some urban concentration) rather than over a kinship group. Second, it wields power through institutions or instruments of coercion, which separate it from the collective society. Third, it is financed through taxes imposed upon the citizens. Fourth, it maintains its power through the establishment of a bureaucracy, which stands apart from and above the population as a whole. In *The Communist Manifesto,* Marx and Engels referred to the "executive" of the state as a committee for managing the affairs of the bourgeoisie. More concretely, the state serves the economically dominant class:

> Because the state arose from the need to hold class antagonisms in check, but because it arose, at the same time, in the midst of the conflict of these classes, it is, as rule, the state of the most powerful, economically dominant class, which, through the medium of the state, becomes also the politically dominant class, and thus acquires new means of holding down and exploiting the oppressed class. [Engels, quoted in Draper 1977: 257]

One of the state's major tasks is to mediate the differences and conflicts that are found within the dominant or ruling class. This class is not necessarily monolithic, especially in a competitive capitalist society, and may comprise conflicting and antagonistic individual and group interests. The state thus exists to ensure the domination of the ruling class over all society. The state acts in the interests of the ruling class, and all other interests of society are subordinated to the interests of the ruling class.

> The needs of society ... cannot be met without passing through the political (and other) institutions set up by a class-conditioned society; and it is in the course of being processed through these channels that they are shaped, sifted, skewed, molded, modeled, and modulated to fit within the framework established by the ruling interests and ideas. This is how the class nature of the state and the society asserts itself, even without malevolent purposes or sinister plots. [Draper 1977: 262]

In *State and Revolution,* Lenin succinctly summarized the theory of state elaborated by Marx and Engels. At the same time he rebutted "bourgeois" distortions of the theory. First, he insisted that the state does not reconcile class conflict but ensures the oppression of one class by another. "The state is the product and the manifestation of the *irreconcilability* of class antagonisms. The state arises when, where, and to the extent that the class antagonisms *cannot* be objectively reconciled. And, conversely, the existence of the state proves that the class antagonisms *are* irreconcilable" (Lenin 1932: 8). Second, he argued that state power must be destroyed through violent revolution, that compromise and reformist solutions will not resolve class antagonisms.

> If the state is the product of the irreconcilable character of class antagonisms, if it is a force standing *above* society and "increasingly separating itself from it," then it is clear that the liberation of the oppressed class is impossible not only without a violent revolution, *but also without the destruction* of the apparatus of state power, which was created by the ruling class and in which this "separation" is embodied. [Lenin 1932: 9–10]

The chief instruments of the force or power are a standing army and police rather than an armed power organized among all the people. The struggle against the state and its instruments of power will be carried on by the proletariat. As the development of production reaches a high stage, the existence of classes will no longer be necessary: "They will disappear as inevitably as they arose at an earlier stage. Along with them, the state will inevitably disappear" (15). The proletariat will seize power and transform the means of production from private to state property. The transition from capitalism to communism will inevitably lead to rule by the proletariat and the dictatorship of the proletariat (31). Bourgeois democracy will become proletarian democracy. The majority will suppress the oppressive minority, and the functions of state power will devolve upon the people until there is no need for such power and the state disappears altogether (37).

Drawing upon Marx's polemical writing such as *The Communist Manifesto* and *The Critique of the Gotha Programme,* Lenin outlined a theory in which communism evolves from capitalism. This was not a utopian but a scientific conception: "Marx treated the question of Communism in the same way as a naturalist would treat the question of the evolution of, say, a new biological species, if he knew that such and such was its origin, and such and such the direction in which it changed" (1932: 70). Several phases are evident in this evolution. First, a bourgeois society, capitalistically developed, emerges. Second, there is a "political transition" from a capitalist to a communist society, during which period "the state can be no other than the revolutionary dictatorship of the proletariat" (Marx, in Lenin 1932: 71). Third, in an early phase of communism, generally known as socialism, the means of production are no longer the private property of individuals but belong to the whole society, but the inequalities of bourgeois society are not eliminated altogether. Fourth, in a higher phase of "full" communism, in which bourgeois inequalities are eliminated, the state has been replaced by the rule of all society, and people work voluntarily according to their abilities and are recipients according to their needs (78–81).

With a resurgence of interest in the theory of the state, the thought of Marx, Engels, and Lenin served as a foundation for a variety of directions. Alan Wolfe suggested two trends: one embraces pluralism, the other turns to Marxism with attention to the capitalist state. Within Marxism two emphases are evident. One is influenced by Marx's early writings and the critique of Hegel and emphasizes an understanding of the human condition. The other concentrates on Marx's later writings and stresses a "scientific" rather than a "critical" perspective. Within this latter school there are two approaches, Leninist and Althusserian. Lenin emphasized the proletariat's taking control of the state. Thus the theory of Marx and Engels serves practice, that is, the implementation of revolutionary action. Louis Althusser attempted to give coherence to a theory of the state by identifying structural characteristics that ensure the stability and cohesion of the state and the dominant classes under capitalism.

Wolfe critiqued both approaches. Although the Leninist perspective "too often results in a mechanistic determinism, a confusion between form and content, and a tendency to view the state as all powerful and unchangeable" (Wolfe 1974: 136), the Althusserian view suffers from "dogmatism" and "scholasticism" as well as from an obsession with "this century's preoccupations with positivism and scientific rationality" (142). Wolfe related the capitalist state to alienation; although the state "arises out of alienated politics, it continues to exist by perpetuating alienated politics" (149). This observation leads to his suggestion that we should develop a theory of alienated politics, not a Marxist theory of the state (155).

Concern with an elaboration of a theory of the capitalist state, however, has moved many Marxists to a reassessment. Early in the twentieth century Gramsci explored various means of democratically gaining control over the state. Whereas Lenin saw hegemony as a strategy for revolution in which the working class and its representatives win the support of the majority, Gramsci extended the concept to the capitalist class and its possibilities for gaining state power. Hegemony thus is a relationship between classes and other social forces that evolves into a system of alliances to ensure hegemony over state and society.

In Germany contemporary debate traces its origins to the past century (Holloway and Picciotto 1978), and in the United States much work evolved during the 1970s around the journal *Kapitalistate: Working Papers on the Capitalist State*. Gold, Lo, and Wright (1975) synthesized this work into three traditions that have attracted the attention of Marxist scholars: the instrumentalist, structuralist, and Hegelian-Marxist perspectives. Esping-Andersen, Friedland, and Wright (1976) suggested four perspectives: pluralist, instrumentalist, structuralist, and political class struggle. We now turn briefly to a discussion of these and other perspectives.

Pluralist Socialist Perspective

The recent openings to representative and formal democracy in countries long dominated by authoritarian rule, either in fascist capitalist or existing state socialist regimes, frequently were accompanied by the view that pluralism could be compatible with a socialism in which the state filters the demands and interests of competing individuals, groups, and classes. For example, a "socialist pluralism" was the central concern of many leftist Portuguese intellectuals after the fall of the fascist dictatorship in April 1974. Although this perspective has not been elaborated in any definitive theoretical form, several critical views are helpful in working toward an understanding. The first is a Hegelian-Marxist understanding promoted by Herbert Marcuse and others representative of the Frankfurt school. Their "critical theory" exposed the mystification of the state with its emphasis on ideology and false consciousness as a means of liberating individuals and groups from the oppression of capitalism. This emphasis on the human condition emanated from the early writings of Marx and his criticism of Hegel's understanding of the state as being above particular interests and classes and as a mediator ensuring orderly competition among individuals and groups while preserving the collective interests of society within the state itself. In contrast, Marx saw the state as a political expression of class structure embedded in production.

Second, some writers emphasize the conflict between the state and social classes. For example, Claus Offe (1972) criticized interpretations that ignore mechanisms of the state that reflect its class character, structure, ideology, process, and repression. James O'Connor (1973) looked at the fiscal crisis of the state and analyzed crises of corporate profitability and state bankruptcy as a means of understanding the relationship of class struggle to the contradictions in the accumulation process. Class struggle limits the state's ability to rationalize capitalism, as Esping-Andersen, Friedland, and Wright showed in their focus on the internal structures of the state and the relationship of those structures to systemic contradictions, how those structures shape the class struggle and state policies, and the organization and content of class struggles. They located the state "within the dialectical relationship between class dominance and systemic constraints" (1976: 190).

A third view distinguishes between state capitalism (government has primary control over capital resources and carries out important industrial management functions) and military state capitalism (military activity is the primary activity of government). Seymour Melman (1991), for example, assumed that capitalism in both the Western business world and the former Soviet bureaucracy would involve the separation of decision making from production, the hierarchical organization of decision making, and a propensity of managers to enlarge their powers. Thus both U.S. and the former Soviet managers would seek to broaden their power over production and production workers. He called this the social relations of state capitalism as a dominant form of political economy.

Finally, Mark Kesselman (1982) attributed the underdeveloped state of Marxist political studies in the United States not only to the hegemony of bourgeois pluralism within North American social science but also to the lack of systematic analysis in Marx's own writings. In his view, the emergence of a radical social movement in 1968 was accompanied by rediscovery of Gramsci, who tied political analysis to advanced capitalism within a Marxist framework. Whereas traditional

Marxist studies emphasized capitalist control of material production, Gramsci stimulated focus on state activity and class struggle.

This resurgence of interest in the question of the state appeared in panels sponsored by the Caucus for a New Political Science and at the APSA's 1981 annual meeting, dedicated to "Restoring the State to Political Science." In his presidential address to the meeting, Charles Lindblom proclaimed that "conventional theory is embarrassingly defective. It greatly needs to call more heavily on radical thought" (Lindblom 1982: 20). Although political scientists and sociologists have brought the state back to the mainstream of social science inquiry, Albert Fishlow (1990) noted that economists have emphasized a smaller role for the state, less government intervention, privatization of state enterprise, and a free market. He argued that in the case of Latin America the new thrust not only is counter to the model of state-led industrialization through import substitution that has guided the region since the Second World War, but also is not the consequence of inefficiency stemming from misallocation of resources. The state assumes an active and positive role in the production of goods and services, management of revenues and expenditures, and regulation of private activity. Further, it plans levels of capital accumulation, and it adjusts for a disproportionate concentration of private power to ensure some degree of social justice, provision of public services, and equality. Fishlow attributed the principal problem to a fiscal shortfall resulting from increases in government expenditures directed toward industrialization rather than agriculture. In his analysis, an effective state, not reliance on the state, is needed, and there is no assurance that privatization will increase efficiency, a view supported by skepticism of laissez-faire: "Incomplete markets, imperfect information, strategic interactions, principal-agent problems, transaction costs, and bounded rationality take up a large part of the microeconomics literature" (1990: 65). He analyzed the state this way:

> There is still a very constructive role for the state, based upon theory and practice. ... That role effectively requires a new coalition of political support that is founded on both new and old realities: much reduced external finance and the need for larger domestic saving, especially of the public sector itself; an expanded, but more competitive, international market in manufactured products, based upon diffusion of technology and imports of capital goods; limits to the domestic tax base; and unacceptably high income inequality throughout the region. Political transformation is very much a component of redesign of the state; democratization is only a beginning. [Fishlow 1990: 72]

Instrumentalist Perspective

Lenin once referred to the standing army and police as instruments of state power. Marx and Engels alluded to the executive of the state as a committee. Paul Sweezy viewed the state as "an instrument in the hands of the ruling classes" (1942: 234). Ralph Miliband argued that the ruling class of a capitalist society uses "the state as its instrument for the domination of society" (1969: 23). A theory of corporate liberal instrumentalism focused on progressive segments of corporate capital, which determine the extent of societal reform, is attributed to G. William Domhoff (1976), his protest notwithstanding. All of these views are tied to the idea that the state is the "instrument" of the ruling or dominant class. The instrumentalist perspective thus focuses on the class that rules and on the ties and mechanisms that link ruling-class instruments and state policies. Instrumentalism has been criticized for its failure to transcend the framework of the pluralists: "The emphasis ... has been on social and political groupings rather than classes defined by their relationship to the means of production" (Gold, Lo, and Wright 1975: 34–35).

Structuralist Perspective

"The fundamental thesis of the structuralist perspective is that the functions of the state are broadly determined by the structures of the society rather than by the people who occupy positions of state power" (Gold, Lo, and Wright 1975: 36). Opposed to instrumentalism, those who advocate the structuralist perspective examine the constraints and contradictions of capitalism within the structure in which the state is embedded. This structure, rather than a struggle by individuals, classes, and the like, is of central concern. Althusser provided a foundation and Nicos Poulantzas (1973) elaborated a political side of this structuralism. He argued that the bourgeoisie is unable as a class to dominate the state, that the state itself organizes and unifies the interest of this class. The economic side of a structuralist approach is exemplified by the work of Paul Baran and Paul Sweezy; they stressed the activity of the state in resolving economic contradictions and averting crises related to monopoly capitalism. Critics of the structuralist perspective argue that it cannot explain class action that arises from class consciousness (Best and Connolly 1979).

In fact both the structuralist and the instrumentalist perspectives are criticized in terms of systemic inputs and outputs. Instrumentalists tend to relate analysis to contemporary class activity rather than to historically known constraints of the system. Structuralists tend to downplay class activity.

> The instrumentalist view of the state stresses the *political input* into the state and the importance of the unequal class distribution of power. The structuralist view of the state stresses the *political output* of state activity by which capitalist domination is reproduced and the cohesion of the social formation assured. Neither approach contains a theory of the mechanisms that link political inputs and systemic constraints to the outputs of state activity. Neither approach can analytically distinguish the extent to which class action mediates between constraints and state structures, generates those constraints and structures, or at times is irrelevant to the relationship of economic constraints to the state. [Esping-Andersen, Friedland, and Wright 1976: 189–190]

An alternative view incorporates an explanation of regulation theory, as developed by Michel Aglietta in *Régulations et crises du capitalisme* (1976) and Robert Boyer in *La théorie de la régulation: Une analyse critique* (1986). Understanding capitalism is worked out through observation of crisis and regularity. The development of capitalism is understood as a succession of periods of crisis and of periods in which a regularity of social relations and structure can be observed. A mode of regulation—that is, a set of coherent and predictable rules—corresponds to each period of stability and enables harmonious development of the system. In contrast, economic laws no longer function during the crisis because regulation is not always possible, and the system is left to the whims of "social struggle and political choices." Economic time is thus divided into two periods: periods of regularity, which are those of laws and regulation; and periods of crisis, which are those of chance (Fontvieille 1991; also see Gordon 1991 for a recent perspective on long-cycle theory).

Feminist Perspective

Feminism allows for a look at gender relations as an aspect of a power relationship, and it challenges traditional ways of studying the political by focusing on patriarchy and the domination of women by men. However, parallel with the familiar neglect of feminism in political science and comparative politics is the fact that feminists have not elaborated a theory of the state but have tended to focus on theories of gender. Kathy Ferguson (1983), for example, expressed the view that liberal feminists are being busily assimilated and coopted into the expanding bureaucratization of institutional life, and Heidi Hartmann (1979) voiced pessimism about a more radical outcome because of the inability of feminist theory to analyze the position of women within the dominant patriarchal society. Diana Coole pointed to how through the state and its apparatus men sustain male power in both the public and private sectors. Further, "many feminists have found the impersonal and bureaucratic nature of the modern state problematic in relation to the personalized and participatory style of politics which they favour" (1990: 32). V. Spike Peterson looked to "the gendered construction of the state" (1992), while Catharine A. MacKinnon contended that there is no feminist theory of the state. She explored the question of feminism and Marxism as method in a search for an understanding of the state. She emphasized the differences, noting that Marxists criticize feminism as bourgeois in theory and practice and as serving the dominant class, and that feminists view Marxism as male-dominated theory. Whereas Marxist method is dialectical materialism, feminist method is consciousness-raising. In her view, feminism becomes Marxism's ultimate critique as Marxism serves to criticize classical political economy: "Compared with Marxism, the place of thought and things in method and reality are reversed in a seizure of power that penetrates subject with object and theory with practice. In a dual motion, feminism turns Marxism inside out and on its head" (MacKinnon 1989a: 256; see 1989b for elaboration).

*   *   *

Marx and Engels distinguished between state and society in order to clarify the interrelationship of political and economic life. They envisioned the prospect of a stateless society in modern times, a notion deemed unattainable by most political scientists. For that reason, among others, the contemporary political scientist frequently downgrades the concept of state, replacing it with "system," perhaps to obscure the conditions of enforcement and constraint that society holds over individuals in a capitalist world today. However, we need not be deluded by such distractions. One of the proponents of the systems approach, David Easton, reminded us of the origins of our discipline and acknowledged our debt to Marx: "In part, political science could emerge as a discipline separate from the other social sciences because of the impetus Marx had given to the idea of the difference between state and society, an idea virtually unheard of before his time" (quoted in Draper 1977: 237).

The present generation of political scientists has also wrestled with the question of what is political and what is political science. Marx and Engels defined politics in terms of the power of the state, the superstructure that represents a bourgeois society and reflects the economic needs of the class controlling production. Marx and Engels established a relationship between the state and the class structure of society. Draper summed up their conception: "The state is the institution, or complex of institutions, which bases itself on the availability of forcible coercion by special agencies of society in order to maintain the dominance of a ruling class, preserve existing property relations from basic change, and keep all other classes in subjection" (1977: 251). Although some political sociologists and other social scientists have utilized this conception in their work, most tend to steer clear of the onus of Marxism, preferring instead to distinguish politics from economics and to avoid questions of power and coercion, class and class struggle.

References

Aglietta, Michel. 1976. *Régulations et crises du capitalisme.* Paris: Calmann-Levy. A pioneer study of the regulation school, useful in understanding long-cycle theory (see Fontvieille 1991).

Almond, Gabriel A. 1956. "Comparative Political Systems." *Journal of Politics* 18 (August), 391–409. An early attempt to offer a typology of political systems.

———. 1960. "Introduction: A Functional Approach to Comparative Politics." In Almond and James S. Coleman (eds.), *The Politics of Developing Areas,* 3–64. Princeton: Princeton University Press. Refinement and elaboration of the author's 1956 formulation. Influenced by the earlier work of Weber and Parsons, Almond sets forth a "probabilistic theory of the polity" formulated around a scheme of structures and functions.

———. 1965. "A Developmental Approach to Political Systems." *World Politics* 17 (January), 183–214. Almond recognizes the need to combine his functional theory with developmental theory in the study of comparative politics. This essay is a refinement of his 1960 contribution.

———. 1968. "Political Development: Analytical and Normative Perspectives." Boston: Benedict Lectures on Political Philosophy, Boston University, March. Reprinted in Almond, *Political Development: Essays in Heuristic Theory,* 273–303. Boston: Little, Brown and Co., 1970. Useful for the author's discussion of the influences of other social scientists upon his work.

———. 1969–1970. "Determinacy-Choice, Stability-Change: Some Thoughts on a Contemporary Polemic in Political Theory." *Government and Opposition* 5 (Winter), 22–40. Acknowledging disillusionment in the field of comparative politics, Almond sets out to defend his previous work by incorporating its approach into a new strategy for research. He proposes a "systematic exploitation of historical experience using a causal scheme which combines system-functional analysis, aggregate quantitative analysis and rational choice analysis at appropriate points in the explanation of developmental episodes."

———. 1988. "The Return to the State." *American Political Science Review* 82 (September), 853–874. Responses, pp. 875–901, by Eric A. Nordlinger, Theodore J. Lowi, and Sergio Fabbrini in "The Return to the State: Critiques." A review of the trend to refocus on theories of the state. Concludes that the statist literature fails in its attack on pluralist reductionism and, further, is not convincing. He discounts "this intellectual episode" for not searching the literature of institutional and administrative history. The replies to Almond show weaknesses in his argument and supporting sources.

Almond, Gabriel, and G. Bingham Powell, Jr. 1966. *Comparative Politics: A Developmental Approach.* Boston: Little, Brown and Co. Drawing from equilibrium theory and the influence of Newtonian mechanics, the authors set forth a functional approach to comparative politics.

Amin, Samir. 1974. *Accumulation on a World Scale: A Critique of the Theory of Underdevelopment.* New York: Monthly Review Press. A comprehensive synthesis of the world political economy viewed in terms of a Marxist perspective.

Andrews, William G. 1991. "Corporatist Representation in European International and Supranational Organizations." Paper presented at the 15th World Congress of the International Political Science Association, Buenos Aires, July 21–25, 15 pp., plus 5 pp. notes. Advances the argument that corporatism is important in European international organizations and that there has been widespread acceptance of corporatism in the institutions of the EEC. Defines modern corporatism as "a system of official representation of interest communities and associations within the formal institutions of government, and by analogy, within international organizations" (1).

Apter, David E. 1971. "Comparative Studies: A Review with Some Projections." In Ivan Vallier (ed.), *Methods in Sociology,* 3–15. Berkeley: University of California Press. Critical review of pluralist tendencies in the field of comparative politics; discussion of weaknesses in functionalism; and a look at recent developments in comparative study.

Ashford, Douglas. 1981. *Policy and Politics in Britain: The Limits of Consensus.* Philadelphia: Temple University Press. A study of public policy in Britain with emphasis on institutional power and the state.

———. 1982. *Policy and Politics in France: Living with Uncertainty.* Philadelphia: Temple University Press. Similar to his earlier work (1981) but focused on the role of the state and public policy in France.

Astin, John D. 1972. "Easton I and Easton II." *Western Political Quarterly* 25 (December), 726–737. Suggests that there are two approaches in Easton's work: the mechanist or Easton I and the vitalist or Easton II. Although these approaches are incompatible they are combined in Easton's work.

Barber, Bernard. 1956. "Structural-Functional Analysis: Some Problems and Misunderstandings." *American Sociological Review* 21 (April), 129–135. Argues that functionalism and functional theories do not account for processes of change, that these theories tend to be abstract and tend to deal with static, closed systems.

Bartlett, Doris, and Francis Bartlett. 1971. "Social Implications of Biological Determinism." *Science and Society* 35 (Summer), 209–219. Discusses the implications of interpretations that relate biology to human problems. Understands that technology has come to dominate man and that there are no options.

Baruah, Apurba Kumar. 1987. *Systems Analysis in Political Science: A Marxist Critique of David Easton.* New Delhi: Uppal. A critical examination of the problems and contradictions in American political science, with attention to the theories of David Easton and systems theory. A Marxist appraisal of Easton's thought and exposure of modifications in his thinking.

Baskin, Darryl. 1970. "American Pluralism: Theory, Practice, and Ideology." *Journal of Politics* 32 (February), 71–95. Detailed critique of pluralism, which confirms prevailing indictments of this theory.

Bebler, Anton, and Jim Seroka (eds.). 1990. *Contemporary Political Systems: Classifications and Typologies.* Boulder, Colorado: Lynne Rienner Publishers. Anthology aimed at classifying political systems in contemporary work. Divided into three sections: (1) three essays on theoretical and historical concerns; (2) nine essays on modern typologies; and (3) three essays on classification by geographic area followed by a summary conclusion that does well in its criticism of what has been achieved and what remains to be done. An impressive collection of essays on classifications and typologies of political system, a subject of limited appeal given the decline of interest in systems theory and the substantial work on theory of the state.

Bertalanffy, Ludwig von. 1969. *General Systems Theory: Foundations, Development, Applications.* New York: G. Braziller. Open (biological) systems are contrasted with closed (mechanical) systems in an effort to set forth a general systems theory. This movement combined philosophy with science to seek laws that would apply to all systems.

Best, Michael H., and William E. Connolly. 1979. "Politics and Subjects: The Limits of Structural Marxism." *Socialist Review* 9 (November-December), 75–99. A critical assessment of structuralist theory.

Black, Max (ed.) 1961. *The Social Theories of Talcott Parsons.* Englewood Cliffs, New Jersey: Prentice-Hall. Useful in-depth critiques of the work of Parsons.

Blauberg, I. V., V. N. Sadovsky, and E. G. Yudin. 1977. *Systems Theory: Philosophical and Methodological Problems.* Moscow: Progress Publishers. A surprisingly objective review of the trends and literature on systems, including scientific advances in the Soviet Union.

Bluntschli, Johann Kaspar. 1885. *The Theory of the State.* Oxford: Clarendon Press. Translation of a work originally published in German in 1851. An influential work for early American political science. Examines the conception of the state, its functions and forms, and its historical foundations (see Gunnell 1990 for a detailed review).

Boyer, Robert. 1986. *La théorie de la régulation: Une analyse critique.* Paris: La Découverte. A basic study of regulation theory by a leading contemporary proponent. Useful in understanding long-cycle theory (see Fontvieille 1991).

Buckley, Walter. 1966. "Structural-Functional Analysis in Modern Sociology." In Howard Becker and Alvin Boskoff (eds.), *Modern Sociological Theory in Continuity and Change,* 236–259. New York: Holt, Rinehart and Winston. Criticizes functionalists for their predisposition to assume consensus.

Cameron, David R. 1978. "The Expansion of the Public Economy: A Comparative Analysis." *American Political Science Review* 72 (December), 1243–1261. Analyzes the causes and outcomes of increases in the economic role and extractive resources of eighteen advanced industrial societies.

———. 1982. "On the Limits of the Public Economy." *Annals*, vol. 459, 46–62. Correlational analysis of government spending and rates of growth in nineteen industrial nations. Shows that high levels of government spending and budget deficits did not cause stagflation in Europe.

Canak, William L. 1984. "The Peripheral State Debate: State Capitalist and Bureaucratic-Authoritarian Regimes in Latin America." *Latin American Research Review* 19 (1), 3–36. Analyzes two major conceptual frameworks useful in understanding the state in Latin America: the state capitalist perspective and the bureaucratic-authoritarian perspective. Shows that the two theories are similar (state structure and policy are linked to crisis derived from exhaustion of the import-substitution model of industrialization and the weakness of the state links to the weakness of the national bourgeoisie), yet he also notes differences in justifying critical overview of each.

Caporaso, James A. (ed.). 1989. *The Elusive State: International and Comparative Perspectives.* Newbury Park, California: Sage Publications. An anthology of essays originally published in *Comparative Political Studies.*

Carnoy, Martin. 1984. *The State and Political Theory.* Princeton: Princeton University Press. A comprehensive and perceptive overview of state theory, with chapters on American political thought; Marx, Engels, and Lenin; Gramsci; Althusser and Poulantzas; the German debate; the transition to socialism; and class and state.

Clark, G. L., and M. Dear. 1984. *State Apparatus: Structures and Language of Legitimacy.* Boston: Allen and Unwin. Review and critical assessment of eighteen different theories of the state.

Clark, Terry. 1972. "Structural-Functionalism, Exchange Theory, and the New Political Economy: Institutionalization as a Theoretical Linkage." *Sociological Inquiry* 42 (3–4), 275–298. Criticizes a number of prevailing theories, including structural functionalism, and argues for a closer look at the process of institutionalization. In particular, raises questions about Parsons's work. An exchange of comments between Clark and Parsons follows the article.

Coole, Diana. 1990. "Feminism and Politics." In Adrian Leftuich (ed.), *New Developments in Political Science: An International Review of Achievements and Prospects*, 24–40. Hants, England, and Brookfield, Vermont: Edward Elgar and Gower Publications. Argues that feminism allows for a look at gender relations as an aspect of a power relationship, that it challenges traditional ways of studying the political by focusing on patriarchy and the domination of women by men. Further, feminism challenges the male dominance of politics departments within the universities and questions male values and assumptions associated with the study of politics.

Dahrendorf, Ralf. 1958. "Out of Utopia: Toward a Reorientation of Sociological Analysis." *American Journal of Sociology* 64 (September), 115–127. Critique of Parsons as a utopian in his functionalist theory.

Degler, Carl N. 1991. *In Search of Human Nature: The Decline and Revival of Darwinism in American Social Thought.* New York: Oxford University Press. Argues that Darwin's concepts of heredity and biological explanations of behavior have reappeared in social science and science without the racism of the past. Delineates the intellectual history of Darwinian ideas in popular social thought and in social science.

Deutsch, Karl W. 1963. *The Nerves of Government: Models of Political Communication and Control.* New York: Free Press of Glencoe. Argues that "it might be profitable to look upon government somewhat less as a problem of power and somewhat more as a problem of steering … that steering is decisively a matter of communication." Drawing upon classical political theory of communications and control, theory of games and decisions, and theory on international communications, Deutsch seeks "a theory of politics, both national and international."

_____. 1986. "State Functions and the Future of the State." *International Political Science Review* 7 (July), 209–222. Includes an analysis of twelve types of states.

Domhoff, G. William. 1976. "I Am Not an 'Instrumentalist': A Reply to 'Modes of Class Struggle and the Capitalist State' and Other *Kapitalistate* Critics." *Kapitalistate* 4–5 (Summer), 221–224. A rebuttal to Esping-Andersen, Friedland, and Wright (1976) and a refutation of the allegation that the author is an instrumentalist.

Draper, Hal. 1977. *Karl Marx's Theory of Revolution; Book I: State and Bureaucracy.* New York: Monthly Review Press. This first of three volumes generally covers the earlier works of Marx, focusing on politics. This volume, notable for its clarity of exposition and summary synthesis of Marx's ideas, is divided into two parts: the first deals with the young Marx and his political development from about 1842; the second deals with the Bonapartist state and the period 1848–1851.

Easton, David. 1950. "Harold Lasswell: Policy Scientist for a Democratic Society." *Journal of Politics* 12 (August), 450–477. In this, one of his early writings, Easton searches for values of democratic politics and scientific inquiry in the social sciences. He finds in Lasswell's work the "lesson" that "each social science ought to re-examine the value premises upon which its empirical research rests."

_____. 1953. *The Political System: An Inquiry into the State of Political Science.* New York: Alfred A. Knopf. The first of Easton's works on the political theory of systems, this work presents a case for general theory in political science.

_____. 1956. "Limits of the Equilibrium Model in Social Research." *Behavioral Science* 1 (April), 96–104. Views the equilibrium model as "an inarticulate theoretical framework" for political science as well as for other disciplines. Equilibrium analysis cannot be useful without more quantifiable data.

_____. 1957. "An Approach to the Analysis of Political Systems." *World Politics* 19 (April), 383–400. Following his first effort to outline the need for a theory of political systems, Easton here sets forth some concepts and a general model for an analysis of the political system.

_____. 1965a. *A Framework for Political Analysis.* Englewood Cliffs, New Jersey: Prentice-Hall. The second of the author's works on political systems, this work sets forth the major categories and concepts for the formulation of theory.

_____. 1965b. *A Systems Analysis of Political Life.* New York: John Wiley and Sons. This is the author's third work on systems theory; it elaborates on concepts set forth earlier in an effort to make them applicable to empirical situations.

_____. 1981. "The Political System Besieged by the State." *Political Theory* 9 (August), 303–325. An appraisal of Nicos Poulantzas and his conception of state and a defense of systems theory.

_____. 1990. *The Analysis of Political Structure.* New York: Routledge. Extension of his argument that structure must be taken into account in political analysis.

Engels, Frederick. [N.d.]. *Origin of the Family, Private Property, and the State: In the Light of the Researches of Lewis H. Morgan.* New York: International Publishers. A critical review of theories and histories of the family and the emergence of the state from ancient to modern times.

_____. 1934. *Dialectics of Nature*. Moscow: Progress Publishers. "It gives a dialectical materialist generalisation of the principal achievements of the natural sciences in the mid-nineteenth century, develops materialist dialectics, and criticises metaphysical and idealist conceptions in natural science."

Esping-Andersen, Gosta, Roger Friedland, and Erik Olin Wright. 1976. "Modes of Class Struggle and the Capitalist State." *Kapitalistate* 4–5 (Summer), 186–220. A review of approaches to the study of the capitalist state and an elaboration of a new approach emphasizing political class struggle.

Evans, Michael. 1970. "Notes on David Easton's Model of the Political System." *Journal of Commonwealth Political Studies* 8 (July), 117–133. A critical summary of Easton's work on systems and an assessment of conceptual, interpretative, and internal difficulties.

Evans, Peter, Dietrich Rueschemeyer, and Theda Skocpol (eds.). 1985. *Bringing the State Back In*. Cambridge: Cambridge University Press. Essays in favor of emphasizing state theory in the contemporary social sciences.

Ferguson, Kathy E. 1983. "Feminism and Bureaucratic Discourse." *New Political Science* 2 (Spring), 53–73. Sees the rise of women's movements as coinciding with the proliferation and bureaucratization of political and economic institutions. Argues that liberal feminists are absorbed in this process of bureaucratization and that radical feminists should criticize it.

Finer, S. E. 1969–1970. "Almond's Concept of 'The Political System': A Textual Critique." *Government and Opposition* 5 (Winter), 3–21. A detailed critique of nomenclature in Almond's writings on political system. Quarrels with his use of "political" and "system" and argues for a return to traditional language.

Fishlow, Albert. 1990. "The Latin American State." *Journal of Economic Perspectives* 4 (Summer), 61–74. Argues that the state has played a significant role in development and that it will continue to exercise influence in the transformation of Latin America.

Fontvieille, Louis. 1991. "Long-Cycle Theory: Dialectical and Historical Analysis." *Review* 14 (Spring), 233–261. A useful although disjointed discussion of long-cycle theory and its application in the face of the failure of economists to give answers.

Friedman, Jonathan. 1974. "Marxism, Structuralism, and Vulgar Marxism." *Man* 9 (September), 444–469. A critique of vulgar materialism, for example, that of Harris (1968), an identification of "functional distinctions" in the Marxist "model," and an attempt to relate structuralism to Marxism.

Garson, G. David. 1974. "On the Origins of Interest-Group Theory: A Critique of a Process." *American Political Science Review* 68 (December), 1505–1519. Historical review and synthesis of past and present trends in interest group theory. Useful in understanding origins of Almond's functionalism.

Gold, David A., Clarence Y.H. Lo, and Erik Olin Wright. 1975. "Recent Developments in Marxist Theories of the Capitalist State." *Monthly Review* 27 (October), 29–43, and (November), 36–51. A review of traditional approaches to the study of the capitalist state and of new theoretical directions.

González Casanova, Pablo. 1973. "Historical Systems and Social Systems." *Studies in Comparative International Development* 8 (Fall), 227–246. Identifies two thrusts in the literature of systems theory: functionalism and systems analysis. Describes mainstream interpretations of these thrusts and their weaknesses and then attempts an alternative reinterpretation by stressing history as process, as struggle, as bureaucracy, as social re-organization, and as spontaneity.

Gordon, David M. 1991. "Inside and Outside the Long Swing: The Endogeneity/Exogeneity Debate and the Social Structures of Accumulation Approach." *Review* 14 (Spring), 263–312. Examines the question of long economic swings in capitalist economies and whether they are the consequence of self-generating economic dynamics. Argues for an alternative model represented by the social structures of accumulation of which he is a principal proponent.

Grant, Wyn (ed.). 1985. *The Political Economy of Corporatism.* New York: St. Martin's. Contains an essay by Philippe Schmitter, "New Corporatism and the State."

Groth, Alexander J. 1970. "Structural Functionalism and Political Development: Three Problems." *Western Political Quarterly* 23 (September), 485–499. Focuses on three problems of structural functionalism: "terminological ambiguity; interminacy of relationships among 'things political'; and confusions of facts with values."

Gunnell, John G. 1990. "In Search of the State: Political Science as an Emerging Discipline in the U.S." In P. Wagner, B. Whittrock, and R. Riley (eds.), *Discourses on Society,* vol. 15, 123–161. Netherlands: Kluwer Academic Publishers. Examines how the concept of state evolved in nineteenth-century political science and relates this intellectual history to current debates about the state.

Hancock, M. Donald. 1983. "Comparative Public Policy: An Assessment." In Ada W. Finifler (ed.), *Political Science: The State of the Discipline,* 283–307. Washington, D.C.: American Political Science Review. A comprehensive overview of literature on comparative public policy studies, noting the diversity in scope and methods and identifying the major research themes. Includes a useful "taxonomy" of perspectives and representative scholars.

Harris, Marvin. 1968. *The Rise of Anthropological Theory: A History of Theories of Culture.* New York: Thomas Y. Crowell Co. An interpretative overview of the principal thinkers and ideas relating to culture. Harris assumes a materialist position, sympathetic to Marx but critical of the dialectical method.

Hartmann, Heidi I. 1979. "The Unhappy Marriage of Marxism and Feminism: Towards a More Progressive Union." *Capital and Class* 8 (Summer), 1–33. Argues that the relationship between Marxism and feminism has been unequal and feminism has been subordinated. Believes that it is essential to combine an analysis of patriarchy and capitalism in the understanding of capitalist societies and the position of women within them.

Hempel, Carl G. 1959. "The Logic of Functional Analysis." In Llewellyn Gross (ed.), *Symposium in Sociological Theory,* 271–307. New York: Harper and Row. Argues that structural functionalism is illogical.

Holloway, John, and Sol Picciotto (eds.). 1978. *State and Capital: A Marxist Debate.* Austin: University of Texas Press, 1978. Essays from Germany about differing theoretical perspectives. The introduction reviews and summarizes the history of the debate on the state.

Holt, Robert T., and John E. Turner. 1966. *The Political Basis of Economic Development: An Exploration in Comparative Political Analysis.* Princeton, New Jersey: D. Van Nostrand. Especially relevant is the criticism of Almond's work in the first chapter. Among its limitations are difficulties in applying his theory to historical and contemporary cases, the equation of the modern political system to the modern Anglo-American democratic system, the use of too many dimensions, and the neglect of variation in the societal functions of government.

Jantsch, Erich. 1972. "Forecasting and the Systems Approach: A Critical Survey." *Policy Sciences* 3 (December), 475–498. Begins with a typology of internal self-organizing systems—mechanistic, adaptive, and inventive; then turns to external self-organizing systems, which are discussed in terms of planning—normative or policy planning, strategic planning, and operational or tactical planning. Approaches useful in systems analysis and forecasting are identified—in economics, sociology, policy science, urban and regional planning, and other areas.

Jessop, Bob. 1977. "Recent Theories of the Capitalist State." *Cambridge Journal of Economics* 1 (December), 353–373. Identifies six conceptions of the state in the Marxist literature.

———. 1982. *The Capitalist State*. Oxford: Martin Robertson. A review of the literature on theories of the state.

———. 1990. *State Theory: Putting Capitalist States in Their Place*. University Park: Pennsylvania University Press. An updating and expansion of his earlier work (1982) with very useful criticism and interpretation of the various lines of state theory.

Kesselman, Mark. 1982. "Socialist Pedagogy." *New Political Science* 9–10 (Summer-Fall), 113–136. A critical examination of themes relevant to Marxism, with attention to the state, democracy, and socialism. Turns to Gramsci and others in order to resolve the lack of systematic political analysis in Marx's thought.

Krasner, Stephen D. 1988. "Sovereignty: An International Perspective." *Comparative Political Studies* 21 (April), 66–94. Argues for an "institutional perspective" and against utilitarian and functionalist perspectives in affirming that the sovereign state was chosen long ago as the fundamental form of political organization.

Lenin, V. I. 1932. *State and Revolution*. New York: International Publishers. Lenin's synthesis and analysis of the state, based on Marx and Engels, with a critique of Kautsky.

Levy, Marion J., Jr. 1952. *The Structure of Society*. Princeton: Princeton University Press. Attempts a synthesis of Parsons and Merton.

———. 1958. "Some Aspects of 'Structural-Functional' Analysis and Political Science." In Roland Young (ed.), *Approaches to the Study of Politics*, 52–65. Evanston: Northwestern University Press. The author, a sociologist, applies his concepts and understanding of structural functionalism to the study of politics.

Lewis, Thomas J. 1974. "Parsons' and David Easton's Analyses of the Support System." *Canadian Journal of Political Science* 7 (December), 672–686. The author discusses the concepts of equality and consent as used in classical liberalism and relates them to Parsons's and Easton's concepts of the support system. He concludes that Easton's concepts are nonliberal, whereas Parsons's concepts are liberal.

Lijphart, Arend. 1984. *Democracies: Patterns of Majoritarian and Consensus Government in Twenty-One Countries*. New Haven: Yale University Press. A comparison of the majoritarian and consensus models of democracy. Despite the subtitle, the focus is on the experience of twenty-two democratic regimes. Especially useful for introductory and undergraduate comparative courses.

Lilienfeld, Robert. 1975. "Systems Theory as an Ideology." *Social Research* 42 (Winter), 637–660. Identifies the origins of systems theory in biology, cybernetics, economics, communication and information theory, and operations research. Systems theory is examined as a social movement and a social philosophy. The author concludes that systems theory cannot be described as empirical science, that it has no relation to concrete human history, and that it can only be understood as an ideology.

Lindblom, Charles E. 1982. "Another State of Mind." *American Political Science Review* 76 (March), 9–21. Presidential address to the APSA in 1981.

Ludz, Peter C. 1975. "Marxism and Systems Theory in a Bureaucratic Society." *Social Research* 42 (Winter), 661–674. Critical examination of systems analysis in the light of the experience of Marxist East Germany.

MacIver, R. M. 1926. *The Modern State*. Oxford: Oxford University Press. Identifies seven conceptions of the state in the traditional literature.

MacKinnon, Catharine A. 1989a. "Feminism, Marxism, Method, and the State: An Agenda for Theory." In Elizabeth Abel and Emily K. Abel (eds.), *The Signs Reader: Women, Gender and Scholarship*, 227–256. Chicago: University of Chicago Press. A powerful analysis of the incompatibility between Marxist theory and feminist theory. Suggests that both are theories of power and its unequal distribution. Sees Marxist method as dialectical materialism and feminist methods as consciousness-raising. Shows the strengths of feminist theory in this essay.

_____. 1989b. *Toward a Feminist Theory of the State*. Cambridge: Harvard University Press. An elaboration of her criticisms of traditional feminist approaches and Marxist theory.

Macridis, Roy C. 1961. "Interest Groups in Comparative Analysis." *Journal of Politics* 23 (February), 25–45. Critique of the revival of interest group inquiry, which warns of its theoretical limitations.

Mann, Michael. 1986. *The Sources of Social Power: A History of Power from the Beginning to A.D. 1760*. Cambridge: Cambridge University Press. The first of three projected volumes on a history and theory of power relations in human societies. Argues that "societies are constituted of multiple overlapping and intersecting sociospatial networks of power" (1) but insists that societies are neither unities nor totalities.

Mannheim, Karl. 1957. *Systematic Sociology: An Introduction to the Study of Society*. Editorial preface by J. S. Eros and W.A.C. Steward. New York: Grove Press. Based on lectures given at the London School of Economics. Mannheim focuses on "man and his psychic equipment," elementary social processes, social integration, and social stability and social change.

Martindale, Don (ed.). 1965. *Functionalism in the Social Sciences: The Strength and Limits of Functionalism in Anthropology, Economics, Political Science, and Sociology*. Monograph 5. Philadelphia: American Academy of Political and Social Science. Collection of critical essays on functionalism in anthropology, economics, sociology, and political science. Reviews by I. C. Jarvie, Sherman Roy Krupp, Robert T. Holt, William Flanigan and Edwin Fogelman, Don Martindale, and others. Martindale's concluding essay is an excellent analysis of the origins and influences of structural theory upon the social sciences.

Marx, Karl. 1975. *Early Writings*. Introduction by Lucio Colletti. New York: Vintage Books. Includes *Critique of Hegel's Doctrine of the State* and *Economic and Philosophical Manuscripts*, along with other early writings of 1843 and 1844.

Marx, Karl, and Frederick Engels. 1970. *The German Ideology*. Edited with introduction by C. J. Arthur. New York: International Publishers. A very useful synthesis of Marxist thought. Especially appropriate for understanding forces and modes of production, division of labor, and class struggle.

Meehan, Eugene J. 1968. *Explanation in Social Science: A System Paradigm*. Homewood, Illinois: Dorsey Press. Attacks prevailing interpretations and uses of social science theory as "the deductive paradigm of explanation," but Meehan sets forth his own systems theory as the basis of explanation.

Melanson, Philip H., and Lauriston R. King. 1971. "Theory in Comparative Politics: A Critical Appraisal." *Comparative Political Studies* 4 (July), 205–231. Criticism of contemporary comparative theory with attention to problems in Almond and Powell. In particular, examines ambiguity of terms, the resurgence of hyperfactualism, and the implicit assumptions that shape inquiry.

Melman, Seymour. 1991. "Military State Capitalism." *The Nation* 252 (May 20), 664. A brief piece that distinguishes between state capitalism and military state capitalism. Offers a characterization of capitalism itself and distinguishes between the decision-making power of top managers in U.S. and Soviet industry.

Merriam, Charles E. 1966. *Systematic Politics.* Chicago: University of Chicago Press. The author sets out "to analyze political behavior in the light of the factors that surround institutional forms, ideologies, political patterns, or clusters of patterns in particular political societies," and he uses "both the naturalistic and the rationalistic approach. ... they are inseparable in the understanding of politics."

Merton, Robert K. 1949. *Social Theory and Social Structure.* Glencoe, Illinois: Free Press of Glencoe. Revised and enlarged, 1957. Clear exposition of structural functionalism as the author seeks a middle range of analysis.

Miliband, Ralph. 1969. *The State in Capitalist Society: An Analysis of the Western System of Power.* New York: Basic Books. The author's line of thinking follows an instrumentalist view of the capitalist state, that is, the ruling class uses the state to ensure its dominance over society.

Miller, Eugene F. 1971. "David Easton's Political Theory." *Political Science Reviewer* 1 (Fall), 184–235. A detailed and in-depth critical review of Easton's major work on systems through three stages: preparation, construction, and reappraisal. Identification of difficulties in Easton's methodology and an assessment of his theoretical position.

Miller, James G. 1969. "Living Systems: Basic Concepts." In William Gray, D. F. Duhl, and N. Rizzo (eds.), *General Systems Theory and Psychiatry,* 51–134. Boston: Little, Brown and Co. The author, who initiated interdisciplinary efforts that involved Easton in the search for systems theory, sets forth concepts that run parallel to those of Easton.

Mills, C. Wright. 1959. *The Sociological Imagination.* New York: Grove Press. Chapter 2 presents a devastating indictment of Parsons's "grand theory."

Mitchell, Timothy. 1991. "The Limits of the State: Beyond Statist Approaches and Their Critics." *American Political Science Review* 85 (March), 77–96. Offers a third approach, between that of the political system and that of the return to the state, and argues that "we need to examine the detailed political processes through which the uncertain yet powerful distinction between state and society is produced" (78). Gives a useful review of the demise of the state concept in the work of Easton and Almond as well as the actions of the state to social science.

Mitchell, William C. 1958. "The Polity and Society: A Structural-Functional Analysis." *Midwest Journal of Political Science* 2 (November), 403–420. Sets forth "a conceptual scheme for the analysis of political action," which draws from Easton and Lasswell but relies on Parsons, with illustrations limited to the U.S. polity.

_____. 1961. "Politics as the Allocation of Values: A Critique." *Ethics* 71 (January), 79–89. Critical examination of the "allocative approach to politics." Identifies the major postulates of the approach, indicates some reservations, and suggests consequences for the future of political science. Discussion particularly relates to the work of Easton and Parsons.

_____. 1967. *Sociological Analysis and Politics: The Theories of Talcott Parsons.* Englewood Cliffs, New Jersey: Prentice-Hall. Contemporary Political Theory Series, David Easton, editor. Summary synthesis and critique of the work of Talcott Parsons in an effort to convince other political scientists of the usefulness of that work. This is a coherent statement of what Parsons has to say about polity.

_____. 1969. "The Shape of Political Theory to Come: From Political Sociology to Political Economy." In Seymour Martin Lipset (ed.), *Politics and the Social Sciences,* Chapter 5, 101–136. New York: Oxford University Press. Identifies the paradigm of "new political economy" based on exchange models of politics.

Moore, Barrington, Jr. 1955. "The New Scholasticism and the Study of Politics." *World Politics* 6 (October), 122–138. Parsons is castigated as the New Scholastic.

Nettl, J. P. 1968. "The State as a Conceptual Variable." *World Politics* 20 (July), 559–592. A rebuttal to political scientists such as Almond and Easton who had abandoned the concept of state.

Nicholson, M. B., and P. A. Reynolds. 1967. "General Systems, the International System, and the Eastonian Analysis." *Political Studies* 15 (February), 12–31. The authors find little basis for Easton's claim that his systems formulation has an applicability to international systems.

O'Connor, James. 1973. *The Fiscal Crisis of the State.* New York: St. Martin's Press. Attempts to relate state structures and policies to class struggle.

O'Donnell, Guillermo A. 1988. *Bureaucratic Authoritarianism: Argentina, 1966–1973, in Comparative Perspective.* Translated by James McGuire in collaboration with Rae Flory.

Offe, Claus. 1972. "Advanced Capitalism and the Welfare State." *Politics and Society* 2 (Summer), 479–488. Examines the class character of the capitalist state and looks at mechanisms within the state that reflect its class relationships. Critical of the instrumentalist and structuralist perspectives of the capitalist state.

Ostrom, Elinor. 1990. "Rational-Choice Theory and Institutional Analysis: Toward Complementarity." *American Political Science Review* 85 (March), 237–243. A review and sympathetic critique of the literature on rational choice, in particular contributions by Jon Elster and Barry Hindess. Argues that these theories are normative, that a convergence is occurring in political science with the acceptance of the proposition that individuals are rational, but that rational-choice behavior can be explained through a deep understanding of institutions.

Panitch, Leo. 1980. "Recent Theorizations of Corporatism: Reflections on a Growth Industry." *British Journal of Sociology* 31 (June), 159–187. A useful critical overview of corporate theory.

Parsons, Talcott. 1937. *The Structure of Social Action.* New York: McGraw-Hill. Reprinted by Free Press of Glencoe, 1949. Parsons's initial effort to set forth a theory of action, focused on the actor; considered to be the first of two stages in the formulation of this theory.

_____. 1951. *The Social System.* Glencoe, Illinois: Free Press. Systematic and general outline of a conceptual scheme for the analysis of structure and processes or functions of social systems.

_____. 1966. "The Political Aspect of Social Structure and Process." In David Easton (ed.), *Varieties of Political Theory,* 71–112. Englewood Cliffs, New Jersey: Prentice-Hall. Parsons attempts to apply his concept of system and structural functionalism to the study of politics.

Parsons, Talcott, and Edward A. Shils (eds.). 1951. *Toward a General Theory of Action.* Cambridge: Harvard University Press. Sets forth an elaboration of earlier Parsonian ideas, now in a somewhat positivist fashion. Herein is the second-stage theory of action and the revision of Parsons's earlier notions.

Parsons, Talcott, Robert F. Bales, and Edward A. Shils. 1953. *Working Papers in the Theory of Action.* Glencoe, Illinois: Free Press. This work gives more attention to politics as a sub-system and provides conceptual detail on the internal structure and function of systems in general.

Peterson, V. Spike (ed.). 1992. *Gendered States: Feminist (Re)Visions of International Relations Theory.* Boulder, Colorado: Lynne Rienner Publishers. Perspectives on "the gendered construction of the state" with criticism of key concepts of political and international relations theory.

Poulantzas, Nicos. 1973. *Political Power and Social Classes.* London: New Left Books and Sheed and Ward. The author develops a structuralist perspective on the capitalist state.

Powell, Charles A. 1971. "Structural-Functionalism and the Study of Comparative Communist Systems: Some Caveats." *Studies in Comparative Communism* 4 (July-October), 58–67. Critical of culture-bound "theory" of structural functionalism and its misapplications to cases of socialist society.

Radcliffe-Brown, A. R. 1935. "On the Concept of Function in Social Science." *American Anthropologist* 37 (July-September), 394–402. Demonstrates explicitly the analogy between social life and organic life in formulating a conceptualization of function.

_____. 1952. *Structure and Function in Primitive Society.* New York: Free Press. Collection of essays on structural functionalism as drawn from the author's field and other work.

_____. 1957. *A Natural Science of Society.* Glencoe, Illinois: Free Press. Posthumously published work that makes clear the organicist influences upon the author's conception of the social system.

Rosenau, James N. 1988. "The State in an Era of Cascading Politics: Wavering Concept, Widening Competence, Withering Colossus, or Weathering Change?" *Comparative Political Studies* 21 (April), 13–44. Emphasis on "the norms governing relationships, the habits of voluntary and coerced compliances, and the practices of cooperation through which large numbers of people form and sustain a collectivity that possesses sovereign authority" (15). He applies these features to an "adaptation framework" as a way of synthesizing diverse perspectives of the state.

Sanford, Jonathan A. 1971. "Political Development and Economic Change: A Radical Interpretation of Almond and Powell's Developmental Approach." *Journal of International and Comparative Studies* 4 (Summer), 1–36. Critical comments of the liberal structural functionalism of Almond and Powell. Offers a radical revision of this theory and attempts to operationalize it.

Schmitter, Philippe C. 1971. *Interest Conflict and Political Change in Brazil.* Stanford, California: Stanford University Press.

_____. 1985. "Neo-Corporatism and the State." In Wyn Grant (ed.), *The Political Economy of Corporatism,* 32–62. New York: St. Martin's. A critical review of past and present thinking on corporatism.

_____. 1989. "Corporatism Is Dead! Long Live Corporatism!" *Government and Opposition* 24 (Winter), 54–73. An interpretative overview and insightful piece that offers a reassessment of Andrew Shonfield's *Modern Capitalism* (1965) and his insights into modern corporatism.

Shannon, Thomas Richard. 1989. *An Introduction to the World-System Perspective.* Boulder, Colorado: Westview Press. A basic text and useful synthesis in world-system theory.

Sorzano, J. S. 1975. "David Easton and the Invisible Hand." *American Political Science Review* 69 (March), 91–106. Analysis of the similarities between the Eastonian framework and that of traditional economics. The concepts and assumptions of Easton are recognized in the characteristics of the classical economic model of Adam Smith.

Spiro, Herbert J. 1962. "Comparative Politics: A Comprehensive Approach." *American Political Science Review* 56 (September), 577–595. Obviously influenced by Easton's search for a systemic approach to politics, the author sets forth his own scheme for comparative politics. At the heart of this scheme is his flow-of-policy process, involving formulation of an issue, deliberation, resolution, and solution.

Sweezy, Paul. 1942. *The Theory of Capitalist Development: Principles of Marxian Political Economy.* New York: Monthly Review Press. An examination of value and surplus value, the accumulation process, crises and depressions, and imperialism using an instrumentalist perspective.

Szymanski, Al. 1972. "Malinowski, Marx, and Functionalism." *Insurgent Sociologist* 2 (Summer), 35–43. Argues that functionalism has been and still is conservative, but if interpreted dialectically, "is a fundamental part of Marxist methodology, and a very powerful tool for the advance of social science."

Thomas, Lewis. 1978. *The Lives of a Cell: Notes of a Biology Watcher.* New York: Penguin Books. 1st ed., Viking Press, 1974. See especially "On Societies as Organisms," pp. 11–15, which stresses that ants, bees, and termites appear to live two kinds of lives—"individuals going about the day's business without much evidence of thought for tomorrow, and they are at the same time component parts, cellular elements, in the huge, writhing, ruminating organisms of the hill, the nest, the hive" (12)—yet human beings "do not like the notion that there can be collective societies with the capacity to behave like organisms" (12).

Thorson, Thomas Landon. 1970. *Biopolitics.* New York: Holt, Rinehart and Winston. A critical examination of "the Newtonian universal-generalization paradigm of understanding," "the Darwinian evolutionary-developmental paradigm of understanding," and the utility and nonutility of these paradigms in contemporary political science.

Titus, C. H. 1931. "A Nomenclature in Political Science." *American Political Science Review* 25 (February), 45–60. Identifies different definitions of the state.

Truman, David B. 1951. *The Governmental Process.* New York: Alfred A. Knopf. Seminal work on pluralism in U.S. politics, which revives the tradition of Bentley and others.

Wallerstein, Immanuel. 1974, 1980, 1989. *The Modern World-System: Capitalist Agriculture and the Origins of the European World-Economy in the Sixteenth Century.* 3 vols. New York: Academic Press. An ambitious "unidisciplinary" overview, which places system into a framework of international capitalism.

Wiener, Norbert. 1954. *The Human Use of Human Beings.* Garden City, New York: Doubleday Anchor Books. Systems theory viewed in terms of cybernetics and communications as related to machines and people.

———. 1961. *Cybernetics.* New York: John Wiley. Mathematics and cybernetics are combined to demonstrate that communications patterns relate to both machines and man.

Willoughby, W. W. 1896. *An Examination of the Nature of the State.* New York: Macmillan. One of the "grand" theorists of the state in early American political science who believed that the state was a principal focus of study in political science.

Wolfe, Alan. 1974. "New Directions in the Marxist Theory of Politics." *Politics and Society* 4 (Winter), 131–160. An overview of writings concerned with a Marxist theory of the state.

Wuthnow, Robert. 1979. "The Emergence of Modern Science and World System Theory." *Theory and Society* 8 (September), 159–214. An essay on the origins of world system theory.

6

Theories of Political Culture: Individual and Movement in the Struggle for Collectivity and the New Person

Contemporary mainstream and alternative theories of political culture are the concern of this chapter. First, these theories are related to some basic assumptions about culture in the works of Marx and Weber. Then a variety of views emanating from anthropology, sociology, and psychology are examined in seeking the origin of the term *political culture*. Our discussion traces these views since the end of the Second World War and shows the relevance of traditional interpretations to contemporary work on culture and politics. Major interpretations of political culture, as conceived on a general or macro level as well as interpretations on a more particular or micro level, are identified while assessing current research on socialization and communication. Finally, a critique of mainstream interpretations and evolving alternative theories of political culture and socialization are dealt with.

On a general level, Marx conceived of the beliefs and symbols of culture in capitalist society as part of a superstructure of ideology and false consciousness. The superstructure, representing the interests of the bourgeoisie, assimilates the ideology inherent in the dominant mode of production and social class relations. Culture therefore becomes static, because it protects the interests of the ruling bourgeoisie or capitalist class. Only through historical changes in the material base, through a transformation in the mode of production and in class relations, are changes in the generally persistent culture possible. Culture thus derives from the material practices of society and, more particularly, from the consequences of the relationship of the workers to their production. Although the capitalists are free to exploit labor, the workers are forced to sell their labor and thus are alienated from the product of their work and from themselves.

Weber as well as Marx dealt with general and particular levels of culture. On the general level, he viewed culture as being composed of the beliefs and symbols of ideal types of authority: traditional, charismatic, and rational. Those ideal types of authority are legitimized by the actions of individuals who shape the collective society. Individual actions are conditioned by custom and tend to become increasingly rational. Consequently, individual actions are oriented to beliefs that support and maintain the collective society at large. A rationalization of authority accompanies a secularization of this society: rules of procedure become routine, and administrative activities are specified. In sum, Weber explained the political, social, and economic setting by referring to a somewhat autonomous culture shaped by individual orientations of rational self-interest, whereas Marx explained culture in terms of its dependence on the political, social, and economic setting of the society at large.

The Mainstream Conceptualization of Culture and Political Culture

Political culture theory originated with conceptualizations and studies of culture itself. Therefore, this section begins with a discussion of culture, then political culture. A plethora of meanings has emanated from the anthropological use of the term *culture*. In 1871, E. B. Taylor introduced the concept of culture to anthropology as "that complex whole which includes knowledge, belief, art, morals, law, custom, and any other capabilities and habits acquired by man as a member of society" (quoted in Kluckhohn 1964: 165–168).

Among the hundreds of definitions that were introduced thereafter, Kroeber and Kluckhohn (1952: 43–55) reviewed some 160 meanings offered by social scientists. Anthropologist Franz Boas's descriptive definition is similar to that of Taylor: "Culture embraces all the manifestations of social habits of a community, the reactions of the individual as affected by the habits of the group in which he lives, and the products of human activities as determined by these habits." Boas viewed culture in its totality with an emphasis on cultural content. In contrast, Ralph Linton stressed a historical feature of culture, such as social inheritance or social tradition. O. Klineberg emphasized a normative connotation; culture is "that whole 'way of life' which is determined by the social environment." C. S. Ford presented culture in terms of its psychological implications, as a means of satisfying needs and solving problems: "Culture consists of learned problem-solutions."

Dissatisfaction with efforts to characterize national character or national culture of various countries prompted a reformulation of concepts and a substantial effort in comparative politics to view culture in a political context. Gabriel Almond and Sidney Verba preferred political culture rather than national character because that term allowed them to draw related concepts such as socialization, culture conflict, and acculturation from anthropology, psychology, and sociology (1963: 13). Lucian Pye saw political culture as a means of transcending "the complex subtleties of individual psychology to … the traditional plateau of political science" (1965: 9).

Political culture thus was shaped around the cultural contributions of Weber, Kroeber, Parsons, and others. A macro level of political culture related to "psychological orientations" and "cognitions, feelings, and evaluations" of people in relation to their political system. The conceptual premises of political culture were clearly identified by Almond and Verba (1963: 4–11): first, civic virtue and responsibility in a world of warm attitudes toward people, sharing of values with others, trust and confidence in one's fellow being, and freedom from anxiety; second, participatory and pluralistic democracy based on the toleration of individual freedoms and consensus among the governed; third, order through rational bureaucracy, in the spirit of Weberian thought; and, fourth, stability through modernization as related to the degree of modernization, rate of literacy, and level of education. This foundation of ideas leads to general macro and specific micro levels of analysis of political culture studies.

Interpretations of Political Culture at a General Level

Gabriel Almond first introduced the concept of political culture in 1956 in his early attempt to offer a classification for comparing political systems. "Every political system is embedded in a particular pattern of orientations to political action. I have found it useful to refer to this as the political culture" (Almond 1956: 396). Almond suggested that the political culture had a certain autonomy and yet was related to the general culture; it did not "coincide" with the political system since patterns of orientation to politics transcend the boundaries of political systems. Yet he related political culture to his classification of political systems. The political culture of the Anglo-American system, for example, is homogeneous and secular, that of continental Europe is fragmented, that of the preindustrial system is mixed, and that of the totalitarian system is synthetic. Almond intended that his concept should replace less useful terminology such as national character and cultural ethos.

In *The Civic Culture* (1963), Almond and Verba refined this conception of political culture and used it in an empirical study and survey of attitudes in five nations. They defined political culture in terms of political orientations and attitudes held by individuals in relation to their political system. "When we speak of the political culture of a society, we refer to the political system as internalized in the cognitions, feelings, and evaluations of its population. People are induced into it just as they are socialized into nonpolitical roles and social systems" (Almond and Verba 1963: 14). *Cognitive orientations* include knowledge and beliefs about the political system, its leaders, and operation. *Affective orientations* involve feelings about the system such as attachment or alienation. *Evaluative orientations* comprise judgments and opinions about the system and might, for example, include the application of values such as democratic norms. These orientations become the basis for types of political culture. Three types are postulated: *parochial,* implying that individuals have low expectations and awareness of government and generally are not involved; *subject,* in which individuals are aware of the outcomes of government but do not participate in the processes that result in policy decisions; and *participant,* in which individuals are active and involved in the system as a whole, that is, in both the input and output processes.

In a collaborative effort with G. Bingham Powell, Jr., Almond elaborated further his conception of political culture, tying it both to the political system and to political development (Almond and Powell 1966: 50–72). "Political culture is the pattern of individual attitudes and orientations toward politics among the members of a political system. It is the subjective realm which underlies and gives meaning to political actions" (50). Political culture is explained in terms of its relationship to the capabilities of the political system. Development is a reflection of the degree of secularization of the political culture. Cultural secularization implies bargaining and give-and-take interactions, a kind of "marketplace attitude which permeates the conduct of politics" (57). Additionally, cultural secularization is seen in the movement from diffuseness to a specificity of orientations and a differentiation of roles in the polity; diffuseness characterizes parochial cultures in which there is little or no awareness of the political system as a separate entity, whereas specificity and differentiation characterize subject and participant political cultures. In newer nations a "cultural dualism" is evident, in which a small elite is modernized or "socialized in the specific, universalistic, and pragmatic orientations which typify 'modern' culture—while the vast majority remains tied to the rigid, diffuse, and ascriptive patterns of tradition" (72).

At this point Almond defended the explanatory potential of political culture. He argued that his categories were not merely descriptive; they could be measured through public opinion surveys, interviews, and other techniques. Further, political culture is a conceptual tool that bridges the gap between studies of the individual and studies of the political system as a whole.

Other writers have reiterated Almond's formulation of political culture. Pye, for example, viewed political culture as providing "an ordered subjective realm of politics," which is found on two levels. "For the individual the political culture provides controlling guidelines for effective political behavior, and for the collectivity it gives a systematic structure of values and rational considerations which ensures coherence in the performance of institutions and organizations" (Pye 1965: 7). Political culture thus is the product both of collective histories and of individual life histories of the political system. It evolves from conscious learnings about politics. Analytically, it gives a behavior form of analysis to such terms as ideology, national spirit, and values of people.

Sidney Verba concurred that political culture "consists of the system of empirical beliefs, expressive symbols, and values which defines the situation in which political action takes place" (Verba 1965: 513). Political culture is a system of control, related to the beliefs held by individuals. In focusing on beliefs, Verba suggested a number of dimensions of political culture, including beliefs identifying with politics, especially with the nation-state; with one's fellow citizens; with governmental output and operation; and with the process of making decisions—the political input.

Interpretations of Political Culture at a Specific Level

Mainstream political scientists have applied their culture theory to empirical studies of communication and socialization. Briefly, we examine some of these studies and assess their contributions to theories of political culture.

Communication Studies

Communication permeates human relations and, according to Lucian Pye, is "the web of human society" providing a framework for an orderly establishment of power relationships in society. Communication applies to mass media institutions: press, radio, television, popular arts, and the like. Pye (1963) also posited a "world culture" as an ideal type of what we think of as "modern life." He envisaged a world culture that incorporates the rational bureaucracy of Weber and the civic culture of Almond into a formulation that transcends the nation-state. Communication diffuses this world culture throughout different societies and ensures the political development of nations everywhere. Pye broke this world culture into traditional, transitional, and modern communication stages, and he and other comparativists elaborated communications theory in terms of interest articulation and aggregation, recruitment, mobilization, participation, and influence. Most of these processes were incorporated by Almond as input functions in his model of the political system.

Communication studies often identified ideas about systems and cybernetics, especially as formulated by David Easton but more specifically as directed to comparative politics by Karl Deutsch in his *Nerves of Government* (1963) and *Nationalism and Social Communication* (1965). These classical studies were complemented by Lucian Pye's work in the comparative study of communications (1956, 1963, and 1964). Inkeles (1969), Rokkan (1960), and Verba (1962) combined theory with data in comparative study.

Communication studies also relate to comparative study of participation. Two wide-ranging surveys produced analysis on participation in a multitude of countries. Through survey data on six nations (Argentina, Chile, India, Israel, Nigeria, and Bangladesh), Alex Inkeles and David Smith examined the proposition that "a modern nation needs participating citizens, men and women who take an active interest in public affairs and who exercise their rights and perform their duties as members of a community larger than that of the kinship network and the immediate geographical locality" (1974: 4). They emphasized the individual and how people pass from traditional to modern states of existence. In another study, intended as a follow-up that both built upon and attempted to transcend *The Civic Culture,* Verba, Nie, and Kim (1978) examined a model of individual preferences and institutional constraints among seven nations (Austria, India, Japan, Netherlands, Nigeria, United States, and Yugoslavia) and assessed the degree to which the population was politically participant.

Socialization Studies

The study of communication, especially within the mass media, contributes to an understanding of political socialization, a subject of intense interest to specialists of comparative politics. In capitalist countries like the United States, the political scientist examines political socialization as a means of verifying assumptions about the democratic polity. Studies of socialist countries like China and Cuba focus on patterns of thought that socialize the populations so that they adopt the beliefs and values about revolutionary society. In the less developed Third World, the U.S. social scientist views the mass media as the instrument for socializing backward peoples into the modern world. Historically, the term *socialization* derives from two approaches, each with different emphases and disciplinary roots.

The sociopsychological approach emanates from the tradition of work in sociology and psychology as well as anthropology, and this discussion draws from the excellent review by John Clausen (Clausen et al. 1968). The term *socialization* apparently was in vogue before its use by social scientists. The *Oxford Dictionary of the English Language* dates the term to 1828, giving socialization the connotation of "to render social, to make fit for living in society" (Clausen et al. 1968: 21). Other early uses emphasized a moral thrust, with socialization understood as the process of perfecting the individual for society. The early conceptual usage of socialization was identified in the United States about 1895 in a paper by G. Simmel, which influenced F. P. Giddings and E. W. Burgess to elaborate the term in sociological textbooks.

Although socialization received attention in the major sociological writings thereafter, its application was relegated to studies of culture and personality in the late 1920s, and during the 1930s it was the concern of many interdisciplinary studies. With the publication of two articles that focused on socialization in the July 1939 issue of the *American Journal of Sociology,* the term came to be widely used in sociology. In psychology, socialization was not widely utilized until the 1930s, when it was incorporated into theories of learning and personality. In recent decades anthropologists have shown an interest in socialization. Their concern with combining culture and personality was initially evident in the late 1920s. The relevance to political science of the sociopsychological approach to socialization is found in its attention on why and how individuals acquire beliefs about politics. Research in this area tends to be meticulous and narrowly focused.

The general political approach, in contrast, assesses the consequences of socialization for the whole political system. It is less concerned with individual beliefs about politics and instead directs attention to those institutions that shape the patterns of authority and legitimacy. Research in this area is broad or macro in orientation. The political approach emanates from the traditional concerns of political science with ideology, stability, and civic training. In the United States interest in civic training was reflected in the educational literature at the turn of the twentieth century, when the assimilation of large immigrant populations was an issue. Even today formal civic education remains a concern of schools, in which attention to patriotism, for example, is a common theme. Greenstein (1968) neatly summarized the main lines of thought that run through political studies of socialization. The first dates to the late 1920s and early 1930s when political scientists such as Charles Merriam directed attention to formal aspects of civic training. A second line revolves around the studies of personality and politics and national character (Inkeles and Levinson 1954) made during the Second World War and the decade thereafter. A third orientation developed in the late 1950s when behavioral studies of the political socialization of children and adolescents were conducted. Herbert Hyman (1959), for instance, stimulated considerable interest in political socialization.

Given these two approaches, what definitions guide the study of political socialization? A general study of socialization by social psychologists, sociologists, and some anthropologists would focus on the learning process whereby new members of society, such as infants, interact and acquire a social behavior. In that kind of study, individual socialization equates with all social learning, although some social scientists would narrow the process to individual learning based on behavior that a group approves, and others would identify socialization as the process whereby a child internalizes parental norms. Although the concept generally is used in relation to children, it also is applicable to adults. Thus socialization might be simply the inculcation of skills, motives, and attitudes for the performance of roles in society.

There have been some ambitious attempts to examine political socialization through data comparisons of two or more countries. For example, Greenstein and Tarrow (1970) utilized semiprojective interviews with children in Britain, France, and the United States; and Langton (1969) compared national samples of high school students in Jamaica and the United States.

A Critique of Culture Theory

Anthropologist Anthony Wallace applied Kuhn's formulation of paradigmatic processes to the experience, study, and theory of culture. Rather systematically he identified stages in the evolution of a paradigm of culture and the pervasive influence that paradigm has exerted upon social science (Wallace 1972). In the present work the political culture basis of the mainstream paradigm, which has come to dominate comparative politics, has been outlined, but a critique of culture theory has not yet been offered. Thus, I now raise some questions and illustrate the concern about culture theory with some comments from students. These questions and comments serve as a basis for assessing both the general theory of political culture and political socialization studies. Does the theory not tend to be purely descriptive or classificatory? Are not the classificatory schemes of political culture far too simplistic and static? What about the relationship of political culture to systems analysis? Does the literature offer any analytical possibilities for dealing with political culture, especially given that political scientists working with such theory have failed to apply it as such?

Criticisms of political culture theory cluster in four areas relating to reductionism, bias, explanatory value, and autonomy. Lehman, for example, argued that studies of political culture "reduce cultural factors ... to social system characteristics" (1972: 362). Easton warned that most social science is culture-bound and that most generalizations are valid only within particular cultural situations. Greenstein (1970), Hitchner (1968), and Lehman (1972) referred to cultural bias in the form of Western preconceptions of modernity. Bostock (1973) indicted political scientists for asserting weak and naive assumptions in their explanations of political culture; specifically he argued that the typology of political culture suggested by Almond and Verba is based on descriptive rather than analytic criteria, does not employ any theoretical construct, and therefore is nonexplanatory and nonpredictive. Finally, in his emphasis on the autonomy of political culture, Almond suggested that the political system of society is embedded in its political culture. This view may lead to the biased position that the ideal political culture is found in the attributes of a democratic environment, a rational bureaucratic development, and popular sovereignty usually associated with advanced industrial societies.

Political socialization studies have been criticized as conservative because they focus on continuities rather than discontinuities among agencies during different periods of an individual's life. For example, attention to parents may show that they impart only what they have learned, and thus major changes in society and culture may be ignored. Another problem has been emphasis on childhood and adolescence rather than adult learning. Socialization theory has tended to be speculative, tentative, and imprecise. The mainstream of socialization research has tended to incorporate the methodological thrust of liberal democratic theory or to focus almost exclusively on attitudes in stable, democratic societies and the experience of the United States and Western Europe. The result, according to Connell and Goot, is that important questions and issues often are overlooked: "The investigators rarely ask hard political questions about who benefits, who controls, and who attempts to control, the processes they study. That children have a 'benevolent' image of the political world is mostly a myth. But it is dead certain that political socialization theorists do" (1972–1973: 181).

In their reassessment of civic culture, Almond and Verba reminded us of the historical traditions of the concept, dating to ancient writings of Greek philosophers and others, upon which a theory of stable democracy could be examined in recent history. They argued that political culture is not a theory but relates to variables used in the positing of theory, that it contributes to an understanding of the psychological or subjective dimension of politics, and that its explanatory power is an empirical question open to hypothesis and testing (Almond and Verba 1980: 26).

The Almond and Verba reassessment (1980) also collected commentary by other scholars. In a sympathetic defense (53–54) of the original civic culture studies, Arend Lijphart suggested in hindsight that the causal direction of democracy and stability in selected countries might have been perceivable through repetitive studies every five years and that additional countries might have been included in the surveys. Carole Pateman, however, provided a critical assessment in her observation that we lack a democratic "theory ... of civic, participatory practice of the people and for the people" (98). She argued that a theoretical alternative to conventional empirical theory must be developed. Further, it is understandable that Almond and Verba do not succeed in their treatment of liberal democracy as a system in which the relationship between the civic culture and political structure can be identified: in particular, their liberal theory of democracy emphasizes individual preferences yet obscures political realities, such as correlations between class and civic tendencies. She noted, for example, that their work "is systematically divided along lines of class and sex" and that it does not question how in fact the relation of class to civic orientations and participation might challenge a view of history based on liberal ideology that assumes politics can protect the interests of all citizens (60). Further, in their emphasis on "the political culture of democracy," the meaning of democracy is never explicated. Jerzy J. Wiatr expanded on this criticism and emphasized the tendency of Almond and Verba to base their findings on the status quo, the consequence of their definition of citizen participation within the established system; their failure to note social conflicts and political polarization; and their tendency to attribute differences between normative standards of democracy and political reality in terms of psychological deficiencies rather than structural contradictions (117). In a retrospective essay, Sidney Verba (1980) characterized *The Civic Culture* as a product of mainstream political science concerned with mass politics in the turn of the discipline away from legal and historical studies; as such the study was part of the behavioral movement of the times, more concerned with policy inputs rather than policy process.

Thompson, Ellis, and Wildavsky (1990) referred to the revival of political culture as a concept in the work of Ronald Inglehart (1988), Lucian Pye (1988), and Robert Putnam and others (1988). They presented a pluralistic conception that accounts for hierarchy, egalitarianism, fatalism, individualism, and autonomy in cultural life. To them, *The Civic Culture* is "a model of scientific inquiry" that helps explain why democracy persisted in the face of its failure in continental Europe during the Second World War. In a contrasting perspective and an attempt to explain the worldwide "crisis of authoritarianism," Lucian Pye predicted the emergence of postauthoritarian regimes that are not necessarily democratic. He suggested that the outcome of any particular crisis, in this case of authoritarianism, depends on the character of the political culture. As an example he noted "the new authoritarian" thinking in China about 1988 that was influenced by the work of Samuel P. Huntington, who in Pye's view "did not have in mind the arbitrary ways of China's personalized government and its rule by men rather than by law" (Pye 1990: 17). Another useful contribution to the revival of political culture was worked out by Glenda Patrick (1984), who examined various conceptions—first of culture in the work of Kroeber and Kluckhohn, later in the understanding of Parsons—and produced a helpful table (282) identifying a broad range of conceptions and emphases by the major writers on this theme.

The possibilities of integrating the continuity patterns of culture with social and revolutionary processes of change were explored by Harry Eckstein (1988), who suggested a tendency toward retrenchment and the mainstream. In a more optimistic account of politics and culture, Michael Ryan (1989) offered an argument for a practical utopianism in his "working hypotheses" for a postrevolutionary and postmodern society. Arguing that whereas a civic culture emerged in the rise of capitalism, contemporary prosperous societies tend to evolve with postmaterialist values in which capital accumulation is not necessarily held as a high value. Ronald Inglehart (1988) also insisted that rational-choice models based on economic variables have ignored cultural aspects, especially personal life satisfaction, political satisfaction, interpersonal trust, and support for the existing social order.

Toward an Alternative

A challenge to the mainstream theories of political culture and political socialization initially might begin by summarizing the above criticisms of such theories as:

- Idealized as capitalist-technological political secularization
- Inadequate, ambiguous, unproven, or false in assumption
- Reductionist, culture-bound, nonexplanatory, and descriptive
- Particularistic rather than holistic, speculative
- Static, limited in method, and oriented to passive and conditioned rather than active and spontaneous behavior

Beyond these characterizations, the critical observer might probe into the ideological implications of culture and socialization. Education in particular might be understood to be crucial to state-sponsored socialization. Socialization might be simply some ideological induction into the political system. In the United States, for instance, values and norms of liberal democratic pluralism might be induced into the system so that culture and socialization become not independent of but dependent on the state or system itself. This pervasive diffusion of ideology could contribute to the passivity and false consciousness of the world in which individuals live. Individuals, for example, might be socialized to view needs or problems as unimportant. For an elaboration of these themes, see Kanth (1978) and Mattelart (1979).

Freire referred to the dialectic between determinism and freedom and how consciousness and action lead to change: "Only beings who can reflect upon the fact that they are determined are capable of freeing themselves. Their reflective-ness results not just in a vague and uncommitted awareness but in the exercise of a profoundly transforming action upon the determining reality" (1970: 453). He argued that therefore "Revolution is always cultural, whether it be in the phase of denouncing an oppressive society and proclaiming the advent of a just society, or in the phase of the new society inaugurated by the revolution" (476). The cultural revolution, of course, seeks to counter the pervasive influence of education as it emanates from the capitalist state (Shapiro 1980).

Such problems prompt an exploration of the alternatives. A look at the tenta-tive directions suggested by a few writers leads to the conclusion that Marxist the-ory usefully contributes to a radical view of culture and socialization. The vulgar and humanist Marxist interpretations of culture are examined, and then Marxist theory is assessed in the light of experiences in three socialist countries.

In distinguishing culture from civilization's material and tangible manifesta-tions, Bostock concluded that culture is "an abstract concept, consisting of ideas, and therefore incapable of material observation" (1973: 44). Political culture is made up of central values that give meaning to the individuals who are socialized for it and thus "unwittingly become its transmitters" (48). These observations imply serious consequences for researchers who may manipulate their findings to preserve a status quo society. Connell and Goot (1972–1973) indicted those aca-demics whose world view may be shaped by their class position so that they see working-class children as "incompletely socialized," resulting in feelings of in-competence. Is it surprising, Connell and Goot asked, that such children feel un-able to influence a capitalist state? They despaired of the academic effort to con-tain socialization that might disrupt stable conditions.

Connell and Goot sought an alternative approach to political socialization the-ory. They recognized that both capitalist and socialist orders may make use of po-litical socialization. The formation of consciousness or false consciousness among the masses may affect both established and revolutionary societies. Rather than suppress the concreteness of the present, Connell and Goot advocated an ap-proach that deals "with people acting in history." This emphasis on political con-sciousness is found in two strands of Marxist theory: one combines the thought of Marx with that of Georg Lukács and Antonio Gramsci and the other integrates Marxist and Freudian ideas in the thought of Karl Mannheim, Erich Fromm, Herbert Marcuse, and Jean-Paul Sartre. Connell and Goot opted for the latter but raised some questions about the acquisition of delusions or distortions about pol-itics—or false consciousness and the extent to which consciousness is imposed upon a population in relation to patterns of domination and freedom that people have in determining their own choices (1972–1973: 182–187).

The relevance of politics to culture is more likely to be found in a Marxist framework than in articles in the professional journals of political science, according to John Meisel (1974: 614). Legros (1977) argued that the cultural evolutionism of U.S. anthropologists is quite inconsistent with Marxist theory despite assertions to the contrary. Given this state of the disciplines, we now turn to a discussion of Marxist theories of culture. Two levels, individual and societal, are of especial concern.

The Marxist view of the individual often is dichotomized along two lines. Marx replaced Hegelian idealism with a concrete interpretation of material society by rooting analysis in the mode of production and the process of labor within it. Some Marxists would state that material forces determine the extent of an individual's consciousness. Kovel argued that such a conception is linear and deterministic, relegating people to a situation of passivity and being unable to act alone. This view, he believed, reflects a "vulgar" Marxism and is profoundly not Marxist, for the individual under such conditions "is a robot as ripe for the domination of bureaucratic socialism as for that of corporate capital" (Kovel 1976: 223). The alternative view, Marxism humanism, suggests that the individual is shaped not only by the material conditions of history but also by social activity in the present and future. People do not exist in passivity, subject to their material relation, but may become active in transforming their situation.

An extensive debate has evolved around the two views. Most notably, Freudian and Marxist theoreticians have differed in their interpretations, probably because Freudians usually align themselves with bourgeois society. Some Marxist scholars, however, have investigated the extent to which Freudian psychoanalysis is compatible with the historical materialism of Marx and whether psychoanalysis is compatible with proletarian revolution and class struggle. Notable in this regard are an essay by Wilhelm Reich (1966), an assessment of the differences by Kovel (1976), and an overview by Brown (1973). A Marxist conception of individual and culture as drawn from Marx's writings will now be outlined.

Marx first dealt with the individual by positing a theory of alienation in *Economic and Philosophical Manuscripts*, but in *Capital*, published more than twenty years later, Marx did not focus on alienation. Thereafter a controversy ensued in which some writers argued that the mature Marx had abandoned his earlier theory; others insisted that the vital theory was rooted in the works of the young Marx. This dispute was resolved in part by the publication of *Grundrisse*, a transitional work and the basis for the ideas elaborated in *Capital*; therein a theory of alienation is evident (Marx 1973: 161–162, 172–173, 325, 487–488, 540–542). What seems apparent is that there is both a continuity and an evolution of thought between Marx's young and mature phases.

A theory of alienation rests upon economic, political, and social conditions, and such a theory may be found in all historical periods. Marx, however, was interested in alienation in a capitalist society. In particular he examined the consequences for human labor of commodity production, economic scarcity, and social division of work. Essentially, alienation is a reflection of the relations between the classes of owners and workers.

> We have shown that the worker sinks to the level of a commodity, and to a most miserable commodity; that the misery of the worker increases with the power and volume of his production; that the necessary result of competition is the accumulation of capital in a few hands, and thus a restoration of monopoly in a more terrible form; and finally that the distinction between capitalist and landlord, and between agricultural laborer and industrial worker, must disappear and the whole of society divide into the two classes of property *owners* and propertyless *workers*. [Marx 1961: 93]

Implied in a theory of alienation is the possibility of the gradual disappearance of alienation brought about through the creation of conditions for a classless society and a world socialist revolution. It should be clear that such conditions do not exist in capitalist societies today, nor are they found in China and Cuba where private property has been abolished for the most part but where society continues to have different social levels, division of labor, and commodity production— thereby permitting alienated labor to persist.

What are the prospects for the elimination of alienation? Bruce Brown (1973) referred to a "new praxis" of practice and theory that begins with an individual's experience with oppression, then turns to the discovery of alienation, and ends with the refusal of alienation through a process in which the self is politicized to attain "a truly social dimension, uniting the struggle for the creation of a new self with the struggle for the creation of a new society" (Brown 1973: 189). Frank Lindenfeld (1973) argued that in highly industrialized societies it is possible to eliminate alienation in work. He assumed that alienation is the consequence of job specialization and bureaucratization in industry under capitalism or socialism. Further, workers may not be conscious of their alienation because they receive high pay and fringe benefits. Lindenfeld believed, however, that work can be satisfying if large factories are decentralized into small units and if democratic self-management is established for the employees. Automated and decentralized production along with a free distribution of the basic necessities of life to all workers can liberate them from the need to work for income. Such an approach, he felt, might be implemented in the United States, where technological capacity could be combined with freely available necessities, voluntary work, and the workers' control of the productive process.

Although Brown alluded to a process in which the individual is politicized to reshape society and Lindenfeld suggested a means of contending directly with alienation, alienated labor and alienated people continue to characterize the contemporary world. Lindenfeld cited the case of the Spanish Republic to illustrate his approach. Other observers might look to the practice of socialism in China as a solution to the problem. Yet alienation cannot be abolished in those societies without ending commodity production and social division of labor as well as eliminating differences between manual and intellectual labor and between producers and managers. Once these conditions are achieved, the prospects brighten

for disalienation and a milieu in which people voluntarily work not only to provide for the needs of themselves and others in the society at large but also to ex-
press their talents in creative human activity.

Rational-Choice Theory and Formal Modeling

Rational-choice theory is primarily normative theory and assumes that all individuals can be rational. Around 1950 economist James Buchanan began to focus
on decision making in government institutions, and in articles and books he and
Gordon Tullock (1962) carved out a niche around public- or rational-choice theory. They argued that an analysis of the market should be based on rational individuals who pursue their own self-interests. Further, they were concerned with
how efficiently government institutions function to shape individual preferences
about public goods and policies. Subsequent work stemmed largely from James
Buchanan (1975), Anthony Downs (1957), Mancur Olsen (1965), William Riker
(1962), and Gordon Tullock (1965) and was based on models of rational-choice
theory and methodological individualism in which benefits and costs are considered before taking action. In tracing the evolution of rational-choice theory, Almond alluded to the metaphor of the invisible hand in the thought of Adam
Smith as a means of expressing the ideal of democratic politics and the competitive struggle for power and the metaphor of market in descriptions of democratic
politics in the thought of Pendleton Herring and Joseph Schumpeter. Rational-
choice political scientists in the 1960s and 1970s turned toward economics and
formal models to describe political behavior. Almond warned that reducing politics to a market or game, however, may result in exaggerated claims: "rational
choice analysis may lead to empirical and normative distortions, unless it is used
in combination with historical, sociological, anthropological, and psychological
sciences, which deal with the values and utilities of people, cross-culturally, cross-
nationally, across the social strata, and over time" (Almond 1990: 121). He illustrated this proposition through the work of Robert Bates (1981) on Africa and
Third World political economy, who discovered that conventional economics
provides a weak foundation for the study of agrarian questions; likewise, radical
political economy fails to provide analysis of a peasantry whose class action is
problematic, and Almond recognized the need to combine the rational-choice
tradition with cultural studies. Almond (1990) expressed despair that the rational-choice school has neglected "social science literatures that display the variety
of values, preferences, and goals in time and space—in different historical
periods, in different cultures and societies, and among different social groupings.
... This failure of rational choice theorists ... leaves them with theories that cannot travel very far in space and time, and cannot deal effectively with political
change" (135).

Marxist Rational Choice

An alternative to conservative rational-choice theory has evolved through the work of progressive intellectuals who call themselves "rational-choice Marxists," among whom Jon Elster and Adam Przeworski are of particular interest to comparative political scientists. Their work resembles neoclassical economics in its emphasis on equilibrium analysis and rational decision making. Elsewhere (Chapter 8) I have elaborated on their contributions, but a brief summary of their attention to individual preference and the implications for political culture is offered here.

Marxist rational-choice theory focuses on the utility of individual choice in attaining goals and on the principle that all people act rationally to achieve their preferences. In *Making Sense of Marx* (1985), Elster tried to show that Marx himself was a founder of rational-choice theory. Przeworski placed more emphasis on structurally determined positions that influence individual decision-making parameters. For example, in *Capitalism and Social Democracy* (1985), his analysis of the failures of social democracy, he emphasized the lack of choice as an evolutionary, structurally determined phenomenon. For Przeworski, choice exists but is structurally determined by limits outside the realm of individual choice. Przeworski also emphasized problems of unity but focused more on the empirical realities of contemporary life than on philosophical propositions.

This form of Marxism suggests the possibility of a political culture in which individual choice is the norm. Social classes and class struggle are not determinant. The approach is appealing to academics not only because it fits well with analysis of advanced capitalist societies seeking reform along social democratic lines but also because it approximates positivist theory and the emphasis of mainstream social science on quantitative analysis, statistical application, and mathematical formal models. Marxists who work in a mathematical and statistical language find legitimacy in postulating an argument. Critics contend that the rational-choice approach is dogmatic and unaccepting of traditional or structural Marxism and its conceptions of exploitation and class. Indeed, it is alleged that these Marxists seek to reorient Marxist epistemology, abandon the old assumptions and premises, and convert Marxism to the realm of subjective social analysis.

New Social Movements

The early discussion on the new social movements included work by Jürgen Habermas (1981) and his affirmation of their "newness." David Slater later set forth criteria for a definition: the movements must demonstrate political leadership and organizational capability; they must articulate a political project for change; they must identify sociopolitical forces in the process of struggle for change; they must impact on prevailing power relations; and they are historically more temporal than political parties (Slater 1991: 49–50). These movements are involved in three types of social struggles: against domination, against exploitation, and against subjugation and submission. Social movements are also associated with issues of democracy and power. For instance, early political activity and movements are discernible in the resistance to established policies and practices, as Don Nonini (1988) demonstrated in the absenteeism of people from elections, in military draft evasion, and in the underground economy. Scholars often turn to the new social movements in an effort to move away from reductionist tendencies of class analysis; for example, they may reject a determinist assumption that societal change is dependent on the consciousness and actions of the proletariat.

It is useful to identify the new social movements, theoretical directions, essential issues of debate, and the principal literature (much of which began to appear in the 1980s). In 1989 Timothy Luke distinguished the new from the old movements of labor unions, worker-class parties, and proletarian organizations inspired by Marxism, which nevertheless integrated themselves into central bureaucratic networks; the new movements, in contrast, tend to be innovative and operate through noninstitutional and extraparliamentary ways. Luke (1989: 129) assessed various theories of new social movements, contrasting the perspectives of Alain Touraine (who deemed the new social movements organized collectives struggling for social control in "a concrete community") and of Jürgen Habermas (1981) (who characterized them as "segments of civil society working on the periphery of institutionalized state-corporate structures"). Luke identified seven traits of the new social movements: new political opposition; programs of post-Marxist, postproletarian, and postindustrial theory and practical politics; struggle against labor and statist sectarianism; organization along new territorial, cultural, and functional cleavages; linkage between empowered planners and producers and disempowered citizens and consumers; mobilization to achieve a qualitatively new phase of modernization; and reflection on a crisis of rationalization (1989: 132–133). These new movements "articulate the ideologies and class interests of a contradictory and complex social bloc: informational 'new middle class' workers; anti-industrial resistance groups, local hi-tech entrepreneurs, anti-life world colonization movements, and traditional culture defense groups" (149).

Useful among other important studies of the new social movements are Stanley Aronowitz (1992) on class and culture in social movements organized around race and gender; Carl Boggs (1986) on political power and the movements in Europe and the United States organized around issues of economic stagnation, ecological devastation, nuclear threat, and bureaucratic impasse; and Jeremy Brecher and Tim Costello (1990) on grassroots coalitions between labor and community movements. Stanley Aronowitz (1973) analyzed working-class consciousness under conditions of U.S. capitalism, and André Gorz (1980) questioned the role of the ever-weakening working class under capitalism and suggested that groups based on gender, race, age, and community will be decisive in the struggle to bring about a transition to socialism.

Alternative perspectives on culture and its potential for overcoming societal problems include Stuart Hall (1992) on the importance of studying race and ethnicity; Peter Hitchcock (1992) in a review of cultural studies and their potential for undermining disciplinary hegemony; and Barry Hindess (1987) in an attempt to transcend traditional class analysis by focusing on the problems of the middle class and the position of women. Michael Burawoy and others (1991) revealed the disruptive impact of capitalism on individual social, economic, and political life in urban environments as well as how people confront and respond to the deterioration of daily life. Elizabeth Martinez (1990) exposed the cultural politics of "cultural diversity," Patrick Mason (1991) demonstrated how race and competition under capitalism affect differences in wages, and Oliver Loud (1991) speculated on the prospects for a socialism in the 1990s that transcends traditional cultural and political limits.

A prolific literature on women and ecological movements includes Mary Mellor (1992) on how ecofeminist theory and politics evolved out of the radical feminist movement and the peace and environmental movements of the early 1970s and Tokar (1990) and Cockburn (1989) on how the environmental movement has been coopted by advanced capital. The role of gender in comparative political analysis was analyzed by Barbara Nelson (1992), Kathy Ferguson (1987) indicted political science for its "male-oriented politics," and Mary Lyndon Shanley and Carole Pateman (1991) identified feminist interpretations from classical to contemporary political theory. Eli Zaretsky (1976) suggested a theory of patriarchy as a basis for understanding the impact of capitalism on the obscured public and private role of women throughout history; Jacquelyn Zita (1981) placed a feminist analysis of patriarchy alongside Marxist accounts of class and capitalism. Elizabeth Fox-Genovese (1991) argued that feminism has been undermined by individualist premises, and she attacked feminism as an elitist enterprise in the hands of a small group of women who seek equal opportunity. Norma Stoltz Chinchilla (1990) provided comparative perspective with an incisive analysis of revolutionary popular feminism in Cuba after 1959 and under the Sandinistas in Nicaragua prior to 1989 and suggested that these experiences have implications for the international feminist movement.

In Latin America, culture has assimilated many traditions. For example, the base or grassroots of the liberation theology movement incorporates not only Western Christianity but also African religious cults and intellectual traditions. Lehmann (1990) claimed the evolving social movements are assimilating these tendencies within their ideological thrust while weakening Marxist class analysis, dependency interpretations, and revolutionary change. For a full exposition of the urban movements in Latin America, see Assies, Burgwal, and Salman (1990); and see Foweraker and Craig (1990) for a focus on the women's movement, peasant struggles, workers, and other social movements; Guimarães (1991) for a study of ecopolitics in Brazil; Hewitt (1991) for understanding of the lay groups that evolved out of the institutional framework of the Roman Catholic Church; and Corcoran-Nantes (1990) for analysis of women and popular urban social movements in São Paulo.

Radical Views of Culture

Radical critics take issue with some of the new direction in culture study. In particular, the capitalist foundations of most societies are understood as undermining attempts to find satisfactory individual and collective outcomes. For instance, in an innovative view of the criticism of the fragmentation of modern culture, Louis Dupré showed how Marx criticized the fragmentation of modern culture and attempted to reintegrate culture with human activity in a manner that "continues to challenge our attitudes today" (1983: 13). Suspicious of "postmodern" interpretations and arguing that our conceptions of culture may be outmoded, Fredric Jameson (1991) warned of a persisting capitalism associated with a presumably vanishing modernism. In fact, even cultural resistance succumbs to the capitalist system: "not only punctual and local countercultural forms of cultural resistance and guerrilla warfare but also even overt political interventions ... are somehow secretly disarmed and reabsorbed by a system of which they themselves might be considered a part, since they can achieve no distance from it" (1991: 49).

Long ago Daniel Bell argued that cultural contradictions arise from the historical development of self-discipline and work motivation as requisites in the sphere of capitalist production. That the world has not evolved into a free and unified universal world culture was explicitly proclaimed by Fred Halliday (1989), who cited as evidence the proliferation of "particularisms" in the advanced capitalist countries with "their pervasive racism and chauvinism"; the Third World "awash in indigenous conflicts and ideological regressions"; and the socialist world whose stress on internationalism, fraternity, and equality are undermined by the "pluralism" of "nationalistic frenzy and hatred" (1989: 234). Finally, Edward Said (1993) delved into the cultural centrality of the British, French, and U.S. imperial experience to show how imperialism shaped the novel, modernism substituted art for the empire, and postmodernism obscures imperial history altogether. The American example was expanded by Ted Solotaroff with his observation that although "publishing is our most representative cultural institution," it is changing its mission and course and thereby confirming "the general feeling of decline in the midst of expansion, of a whole culture selling out" (1991: 399).

An important aspect of political culture is its persistent claims to traditional ideas and thought and its pervasive influence on progressive intellectuals that results in their renunciation of the Left, withdrawal from Marxism, retreat from socialism, and withdrawal from political activism, as was the case of the New York intellectuals during the 1930s and 1940s who during the Cold War turned against their ideals. This intellectual transformation was vividly described in a series of important books: Alexander Bloom, *Prodigal Sons* (1986); Terry A. Cooney, *The Rise of the New York Intellectuals* (1986); and Alan M. Wald, *The New York Intellectuals* (1987). The New Left after 1968 also declined, and its collapse was described in a number of retrospective accounts: Todd Gitlin, *Sixties: Years of Hope, Days of Rage* (1987); Maurice Isserman, *If I Had a Hammer* (1987); George Katsiaficas, *The Imagination of the New Left* (1987); James Miller, *Democracy in the Streets* (1987); and Gregory Nevala Calvert, *Democracy from the Heart* (1991). This process of intellectual transformation of notable English progressives was analyzed by Perry Anderson (1990) and that of intellectuals in the Caribbean by Alex Dupuy (1991).

Samir Amin (1977) identified three universal models of social organization and ideological formulation: the North American, the former Soviet, and the Chinese. Departing from an analysis of the relations between the economic base and the ideological superstructure, Amin saw the first model as rooted in the capitalist formation and ideology of Europe and its philosophy of the Enlightenment based on a tradition of mechanistic materialism. This tradition assumes that science and technology will diffuse into every aspect of social life and transform social relations until a conscious, nonalienated, and classless society emerges. But, argued Amin, "bourgeois 'science' has never transcended this primitive materialism because it conditions the reproduction of alienation, enabling capital to exploit labor" (1977: 27). The Soviet model shared with the first model the ideas that consumption, technology, and labor derive from the development of the productive forces and that capitalism distinguishes itself from socialism in relation to the private or public ownership of the means of production. The Chinese model, in contrast, did not initially anticipate that socialism could take over capitalism's patterns of consumption and labor.

Each of these models represents a different cultural sphere, according to Amin. In assessing each sphere, a Marxist approach combines materialism with dialectics and thus distinguishes itself from classical interpretations of materialism and from idealism. Marxism "demystifies" materialism and idealism by relating these terms to class struggle. This emphasis on class struggle is essential in a refutation of vulgar Marxism, which postulates, first, that the development of productive forces determines the changes in the relations of production and, second, that the superstructure reflects the demands of the economic base. Instead class struggle alters the relations of production, thus making possible the development of productive forces, and the relationship of base to superstructure must pertain to every mode of production. Amin also refuted the belief of some Marxists that society is governed by "laws": such laws take us "back to bourgeois philosophy and religion" (1977: 28). Given this perspective, let us now examine culture theory in the experience of three socialist situations: the former Soviet Union, China, and Cuba.

Cultural Spheres and Socialist Experiences

The Soviet Union

Marxist analysis concentrates on the mode of production, forces of production, and the social relations of production; thus the concept of culture is applicable to Marxism, not at the level of base but at the level of superstructure. Lenin understood culture as class culture, created in the image of the ruling class. In capitalism, the bourgeoisie uses culture to increase its wealth and to intensify the exploitation of those who work. In imperialism, bourgeois culture undergoes decay, and the cultural level of the population declines. In socialism, culture is directed toward the satisfaction of the needs of the popular masses. Thus Lenin saw culture as generated, on the one hand, in a democratic and socialist culture of the mass of working and exploited people and, on the other, in the ruling culture of the bourgeoisie.

Lenin criticized the use of culture by nationalists:

> The class-conscious workers know that the slogan of "national culture" is clerical or bourgeois bluff ... when nations were not yet divided into bourgeoisie and proletariat, the slogan of national culture could be an unifying and total call to battle against feudalism and clericalism. But since then the class struggle of the bourgeoisie and the proletariat has broken out everywhere. The split of the "united" nation into exploiters and the exploited has become an accomplished fact. Only clericals or bourgeois can talk about national culture at all. The working masses can talk only about the international culture of the world movement of workers. [quoted in Meyer 1952: 214]

In this sense culture implies a struggle against bourgeois ideology, art, and philosophy. Culture involves socialization and resocialization. It also signifies leisure activities and enjoyment in the broadest context. International culture seeks to raise class consciousness and to make all people into proletarians.

Lenin developed his conception of class culture in the early years of the Russian revolution; the theme was later elaborated by Charles Bettelheim in his *Class Struggles in the USSR* (1976). Stalin modified Lenin's conception by giving attention to the national traditions and the many nationalities of the Soviet Union. His recognition of national culture transcended the use of culture by Lenin and Marx and juxtaposed his "national" position with the "international" stance of Lenin. Stalin developed a theory of nations in which he attacked reformist nationalism, for example, the tendency to substitute national for revolutionary aims. Stalin also set forth a theory of national minorities, calling an ethnic group a national minority if it did not possess the characteristics of a nation; the Jews of Russia, for example, constituted a national minority.

Stalin's theory of national minorities did not pertain to colonies, which Lenin incorporated into his theory of imperialism. Lenin associated bourgeois nationalism with oppressor nations in an age of imperialism, whereas nationalism in the oppressed nations took the form of a struggle for national liberation. Stalin's theory of national minorities has been described as incompatible with Lenin's theory of imperialism. The theory of national minorities, it is argued, was useful for describing an early period of rising capitalism in Europe; in contrast, a theory of imperialism includes all nations under contemporary capitalism and imperialism. These different theories have influenced the varying perspectives on national culture, from the melting-pot notion, in which immigrants lose their original nationalities and become ethnic minorities within the new nation, to the idea that the conditions of national assimilation are giving way to an increased imperialist exploitation and oppression of workers in a colony such as Puerto Rico (Blaut 1977).

The shaping of a socialist culture is dependent upon changes in education and ideology. Mainstream political scientists do not usually combine these considerations with the theoretical perspectives of Marx, Lenin, and Stalin on the questions of national and class culture. Kenneth Jowitt (1974), for example, differentiated three types of political culture: elite, regime, and community political culture—these types are described in jargonistic terms and are not effectively utilized in his analysis. However, he turned to tasks that shape the character of a regime and its relationship to socialist society. He identified attempts to transform or destroy values and behaviors as well as efforts to define problems and politics along procedural lines. He also examined the ideological commitment of Marxist-Leninist regimes to such principles as the dictatorship of the proletariat and democratic centralism. He concluded that most Marxist-Leninist regimes continued to use the authoritative model shaped by Stalin.

If an authoritative model was shaped by Stalin, what then was the nature of political socialization in the Soviet Union? Robert W. Clawson (1973) examined the early childhood experiences of Russian children in family and preschool institutions. He was concerned with how one generation shapes the political standards and beliefs of successive generations, and he examined six historical periods. At the outset of the Russian revolution, three groups with differing viewpoints prevailed: "radical-communalists," based in Petrograd (Leningrad), who favored the early separation of children from the conservative prerevolutionary milieu of the average family; "traditionalists," who supported the system of child rearing and education that prevailed prior to the revolution; and the "progressive-individualists," who favored freedom for the individual youth to develop according to personal motivations.

During 1917 to 1921 the Soviet leadership, including Lenin, hesitated to intervene in education, and the period was characterized by "decentralized experimentation" and "pedagogical anarchy." During 1921 to 1932 the progressive-individualists intervened, and the radical-communalists were virtually eliminated; emphasis centered on liberating the individual child and on eliminating competition between individuals. There followed, from 1932 to 1936, a period of transition to discipline under Stalin. Experimentalism was abolished as "collective-traditionalists" took command to advocate a traditional approach toward learning, including a formal curriculum, texts, exams, grades, and discipline as well as respect for traditional parental authority. From 1936 to 1953 there was official recognition of the significance of the family experience for the child. The collective-traditionalist pattern received broad exposure along with conservative family legislation, which placed constraints on divorce and abortion. This promotion of a stable family continued under Khrushchev, from 1953 to 1964, although there was an abandonment of the inculcation of a Stalinist image.

The end of that period reflected the rise and influence of a new group of data-oriented "empirical-progressives." According to Clawson, Soviet education specialists recognized that deliberate political socialization during early childhood was ineffective, and they stressed the role of the family in the socializing experience. Clawson believed that changes in the family's role as political socializers would be more the consequence of the impact of urbanization (affecting housing, income distribution, and the like) than of official intervention into the affairs of the family.

> The likelihood of any substantial change in future specific Soviet policy toward the existence of the family is slight, if only because the radical communalist impulse seems to be rare in both the population as a whole and within the ruling elite. In addition, the ideological roots found in Marxist literature on the child-rearing family have been ignored by virtually everyone who has ever held top political power in the USSR. [Clawson 1973: 711]

Some writers in the Soviet Union and Eastern Europe turned their attention to questions about the individual and the meaning of life. This renaissance of a Marxist humanism centered around Marx's *Economic and Philosophical Manuscripts* and was a response to the constraining influences of the Stalin period. One of those Marxists, Adam Schaff of Poland, wrote: "Marxism is humanism, a *radical* humanism" (Schaff 1970: 168). Schaff believed that Marxist humanism is autonomous in the sense that the individual creates his or her own development. The Marxist humanism is militant and committed and therefore rooted in practice. Marxist humanism thus is revolutionary in its struggle against the dehumanization of life. These characteristics suggest a theory of the new person. Such theory has been explicitly related to the experiences of China and Cuba.

China

After Mao and the Chinese revolutionaries came to power in 1949, they initially were influenced by the Stalinist orthodoxy and attempted to emulate the Soviet model of building heavy industry while deemphasizing light industry and the production of consumer goods. Application of this model in the Soviet Union had diverted attention from the peasantry, thus interfering with efforts to tie the peasant and working classes into an alliance. At the same time a repressive state emerged. The Chinese soon discovered that such a model was unrealistic in light of their concern with agriculture and the peasantry. Priorities were rearranged so that industry was related to agriculture, located in the countryside as well as in the cities, and employed surplus rural labor. Thus the capital or surplus needed to develop the Chinese economy was generated from increases in the productivity of all Chinese labor, agricultural and industrial alike. This made possible an alliance of worker and peasant.

The Chinese revolution incorporated class struggle: first, in the overthrow of the old ruling feudal order; second, in efforts to eradicate the counterrevolutionary ideas of the elites who took the place of the old ruling classes but continued to espouse their values and behavior; and, finally, in contending with the bureaucratic and vested interests of the administrators, managers, and technicians who run the postrevolutionary society. Thus it is a myth that the abolition of private property in the means of production will necessarily result in a classless society harmoniously evolving toward socialism.

Under Chinese socialism the ongoing class struggle aimed not only to raise the material level of the population but also to promote the development of human beings on an egalitarian basis. According to John Gurley, a Maoist perspective placed value on breaking down specialization, dismantling bureaucracies, and undermining centralizing and divisive tendencies.

> The proletarian world view, which Maoists believe must replace that of the bourgeoisie, stresses that only through struggle can progress be made; [that] selflessness and unity of purpose will release a huge reservoir of enthusiasm, energy, and creativeness; that active participation by "the masses" in decision-making will provide them with the knowledge to channel their energy most productively; and that elimination of specialization will not only increase workers' and peasants' willingness to work hard for the various goals of society but will also increase their ability to do this by adding to their knowledge and awareness of the world around them. [Gurley 1971: 19]

Thus will emerge the new person, the making of the "Communist man," thereby eroding the alienation that besets human beings everywhere (Gurley 1970).

However, any illusions about the end of alienation were shattered in June 1989 by the dramatic demonstrations in Beijing and elsewhere in China and the repressive and tragic response by the government. But before and after that event, the process of implementing reforms and opening up the economy to the international capitalist system was associated with rapid economic growth and a rise in the material existence of most Chinese. The Chinese revolution evolved from the overturning of the feudal order to a phase of some thirty years of political consolidation and hard work, which resulted in a substantial infrastructure, and eventually to a phase of reforms and building of a socialist market economy. Accompanying material progress were distinctions among high party cadres of ministers and other important officials, middle-cadre division heads, and low-level cadres. Further, the class nature of Chinese society was increasingly discernible among remnants of the old capitalist classes outside the country; the new capitalist classes within, including the relatively affluent agrarian middle and big capitalist farmers; the mass of subsistence peasant farmers or small producers, workers, and small merchants; and an emerging petty bourgeoisie in urban and rural areas. These differences were being played out through an extraordinary development process. Whether it would evolve toward capitalism or socialism probably depended on the commitment of a divided leadership within the Communist Party and government, but in early 1994 it was too early to dismiss the socialist implications of what was happening in China, which stood in stark contrast both to the dismal failure of capitalism to solve the problems of poor nations everywhere and to socialist failures not only in Eastern Europe and the former Soviet Union but in the Third World.

Cuba

With the triumph of the Cuban revolution in 1959, Ché Guevara placed emphasis on individual sacrifice in a collective society. "It is rather that the individual feels greater fulfillment, that he has greater inner wealth and many more responsibilities. In our country the individual knows that the glorious period in which it has fallen to him to live is one of sacrifice" (Guevara 1967: 42). Sacrifice implies overcoming feelings of individualism and placing emphasis, above all else, on a sense of solidarity among people. Political beings must be politically conscious and socially responsible, devoid of vestiges of selfishness and egotism. The new person must work for the benefit of the collectivity and must struggle against injustice and against the exploitation of person by person and the division of society into classes.

In Cuba, alienation was to disappear with the formation of the new person. Alienation did not disappear, however, with the break in Cuba's dependent relations with the capitalist world. Nor did it dissolve with the nationalization of the principal means of production and the shift from private to state ownership.

Alienation did diminish with the Cuban emphasis on changing patterns of consumption. All persons who so desired were given an opportunity to work. At the same time basic necessities for the population were provided to assure at least a minimally sufficient material standard of living. Income differences continued to exist, but luxury consumer goods were not available for purchase. Economic gains were not distributed to a few but to many through an increasing variety of goods and services, which were either free or made available without reference to income. Rather than being bombarded with media messages designed to create a desire for material goods, Cubans were encouraged to find satisfaction in contributing to their society.

Along with the changing consumption patterns was an emphasis on moral rather than material incentives. Workers would contribute to the development of the revolution rather than to their own personal gain. The new work ethic was the worker's desire to serve society, not the individual. Monetary incentives such as

munity larger than that of the kinship network and the immediate geographical locality" (4). The emphasis here is on the individual rather than the elite and on how people pass from traditional to modern states of existence.

Jameson, Fredric. 1991. *Postmodernism, or the Cultural Logic of Late Capitalism.* Durham, North Carolina: Duke University Press. A critical examination of the cultural implications of modernism and postmodernism, with attention to culture and ideology.

Jowitt, Kenneth. 1974. "An Organizational Approach to the Study of Political Culture in Marxist-Leninist Systems." *American Political Science Review* 68 (September), 1171–1191. Reviews orientations and definitions of political culture, then outlines an analytic framework to study political culture in Marxist-Leninist regimes.

Kanth, Rajani. 1978. "Political Culture Revisited: Notes on a Coercive Ideology." *Indian Journal of Political Studies* 39 (January-March), 89–98. Attacks the concept of political culture and political culture studies as a reflection of imperialist intervention in the internal affairs of the Third World.

Kluckhohn, Clyde. 1964. "Culture." In Julius Gould and William Kolb (eds.), *Dictionary of the Social Sciences,* 165–168. New York: Free Press of Glencoe. Synthesis of past conceptions and trends related to culture and its analysis.

Kovel, Joel. 1976. "The Marxist View of Man and Psychoanalysis." *Social Research* 43 (Summer), 220–245. Examines the Marxist views of man, the limits of Marxist psychology, and the compatibility of Marxism and Freudianism.

Kroeber, Alfred L., and Clyde Kluckhohn. 1952. *Culture: A Critical Review of Concepts and Definitions.* Cambridge, Massachusetts: Peabody Museum. A review of nearly a century of definitions and conceptions of the term culture. Begins with a historical overview of the term, then identifies definitions according to six categories: descriptive, historical, normative, psychological, structural, genetic.

Langton, Kenneth P. 1969. *Political Socialization: Studies in Behavioral Political Science.* New York: Oxford University Press. Focuses on the influence of different social agencies in the political socialization process. Cross-cultural in orientation, with an emphasis on national samples of high school students in Jamaica and the United States. Langton argues that the manipulation of children is justified and works out ideas designed to further the aims of elites and segregate social classes—Connell and Goot (1972–1973) call them "fascistic."

Legros, Dominique. 1977. "Chance, Necessity, and Mode of Production: A Marxist Critique of Cultural Evolutionism." *American Anthropologist* 79 (March), 26–41. Attempts to demonstrate that Marxism radically differs from cultural evolutionism: first, in definition of concepts such as society and mode of production; second, in interpretation of superstructure and base; and third, in perspectives of materialism.

Lehman, Edward W. 1972. "On the Concept of Political Culture: A Theoretical Reassessment." *Social Forces* 50 (March), 361–370. Critiques the pitfalls of reductionism and normative bias found in current usage of political culture; examines dimensions of political culture—participational and institutional, power and legitimation, general culture; assesses generalizations between general culture and political culture and between symbols of political institutions and political legitimizations.

Lehmann, David. 1990. *Democracy and Development in Latin America: Economics, Politics, and Religion in the Post-War Period.* Philadelphia: Temple University Press. A provocative account of social movements and their impact on the developmental process in Latin America, with emphasis on the Brazilian case and liberation theology as the basis for grassroots participation.

Lindenfeld, Frank. 1973. "Work, Automation, and Alienation." In Lindenfeld (ed.), *Radical Perspectives on Social Problems*, 238–249. 2d ed. New York: Macmillan Company. An examination of Marxist and other theories of alienation and an argument for workers' control of what and how they shall produce.

Loud, Oliver S. 1991. "Socialism in the 1990s: Where Do We Go from Here?" *Monthly Review* 43 (June), 45–53. Addresses the problem of how socialism can transcend the constraints of traditional culture.

Luke, Timothy W. 1989. "Class Contradictions and Social Cleavages in Informationalizing Post-Industrial Societies: On the Rise of New Social Movements." *New Political Science* 16–17 (Fall-Winter), 125–153. Argues that the new social and popular movements of Left and Right have manifested opposition outside traditional courses of action. Although they are relatively weak in impacting "informational society," they are "an initial expression of incipient class conflicts and periphery versus core cleavages in the emergent informational society of Western Europe, North America, and Japan" (149).

Lutjens, Sheryl L. 1992. "Democracy and Socialist Cuba." In Sandor Halebsky and John M. Kirk (eds.), *Cuba in Transition: Crisis and Transformation*, 55–76. Boulder, Colorado: Westview Press. A historical review of the struggle for decentralization, reform, and political democracy in socialist Cuba that reveals the contradictions and tensions among state, party, and the people.

Martinez, Elizabeth. 1990. "The Cultural Politics of 'Cultural Diversity': Old Poison in New Bottles." *Z Magazine* 2 (July-August), 35–40. An exposé of racist currents that undermine the struggle for educational reforms that affect minorities and cultural diversity, such as ethnic studies and bilingual programs.

Marx, Karl. 1961. *Economic and Philosophical Manuscripts*. Translated by T. B. Bottomore and included in Erich Fromm, *Marx's Concept of Man*. New York: Frederick Ungar Publishing. A Marxist humanist stance and review of the manuscripts are presented by Fromm in a lengthy introduction.

————. 1973. *Grundrisse: Foundations of the Critique of Political Economy*. Translated with a foreword by Martin Nicolaus. New York: Vintage Books. Originally seven notebooks drafted as an outline of Marx's attempt to elaborate fully a conception of political economy.

Mason, Patrick L. 1991. "Race, Competition, and Differential Wages: A Marxian Model." Riverside: University of California. November 18, 1991. Revives attention to the internal colony model, drawing especially on Donald Harris (1972), to reveal the nature of racial discrimination in economic activity.

Mattelart, Armand. 1979. *Multinational Corporations and the Control of Culture: The Ideological Apparatuses of Imperialism*. Atlantic Highlands, New Jersey: Humanities Press. Comprehensive analysis of the impact of multinational corporations on culture and ideology.

Meisel, John. 1974. "Political Culture and the Politics of Culture." *Canadian Journal of Political Science* 7 (December), 601–615. Presidential address to the Canadian Political Science Association. Describes four meanings of culture: anthropological, aesthetic, political, and leisure culture. Discusses implications of culture for political science by examining the reciprocal interaction between culture and politics; cultural policy and class; culture and the international context; cultural policies and values. Concludes that a Marxist framework is likely to focus more on cultural concerns than is U.S. political science.

Mellor, Mary. 1992. "Eco-Feminism and Eco-Socialism: Dilemmas of Essentialism and Materialism." *Capitalism, Nature, Socialism: A Journal of Socialist Ecology* 3 (June), 43–62. Shows how ecofeminist theory and politics evolved out of the radical feminist movement and the peace and environmental movements of the early 1970s. Discusses ecofeminist philosophy and its prospects for promoting understanding of ecological problems.

Meyer, Alfred G. 1952. "The Use of the Term Culture in the Soviet Union." In Alfred Kroeber and Clyde Kluckhohn, *Culture: A Critical Review of Concepts and Definitions*, 213–217. Cambridge, Massachusetts: Peabody Museum.

Nelson, Barbara J. 1992. "The Role of Sex and Gender in Comparative Political Analysis: Individuals, Institutions, and Regimes." *American Political Science Review* 86 (June), 491–495. A critical review of six books on women and politics that are relevant to comparative study.

Nonini, Don. 1988. "Everyday Forms of Popular Resistance." *Monthly Review* 40 (November 1988), 25–35. A plea to the Left to pay attention to poor people, women, blacks, skilled workers, and even the middle class in their resistance, evasion, and even neutralization of the oppressive measures of American capitalism and the capitalist state. Notes absenteeism in elections, noncompliance with the military draft, and the underground economy as examples that pervade the arena of resistance.

Ogles, R., M. Levy, and T. Parsons. 1959. "Culture and Social System: An Exchange." *American Sociological Review* 24 (April), 246–250. Three communications that criticize Kroeber and Parsons.

Olsen, Mancur. 1965. *The Logic of Collective Action.* Cambridge: Harvard University Press. A political economy approach to public choice and one of several seminal works that served as a basis for rational-choice theory and comparative research on voting behavior.

Patrick, Glenda M. 1984. "Political Culture." In Giovanni Sartori (ed.), *Social Science Concepts: A Systematic Analysis*, 265–314. Beverly Hills, California: Sage Publications. A useful conception of political culture as it evolved in the literature on politics. Examines various conceptions, first of culture in the work of Kroeber and Kluckhohn, later in the understanding of Parsons. A useful table (282) identifies a broad range of conceptions and emphases by the major writers on this theme.

Putnam, Robert, et al. 1988. "Institutional Performance and Political Culture: Some Puzzles About the Power of the Past." *Governance* 1 (July), 221–242. A review of ideas and literature on power and political culture, representative of the revival in political culture studies.

Pye, Lucian W. 1956. "Communication Patterns and the Problems of Representative Government in Non-Western Societies." *Public Opinion Quarterly* 20 (Spring), 249–256. The culture of Third World society is characterized by traditional patterns of communication and special problems of political communication affected by Westernization and urbanization.

———. 1963. *Communications and Political Development.* Princeton: Princeton University Press. Contains an introductory overview as well as description of models of traditional, transitional, and modern communication systems by Pye. In addition there are articles by Wilbur Schramm on communication development; by Herbert Hyman on mass media and political socialization; and by Daniel Lerner on a communication theory of modernization. A selected bibliography is appended.

————. 1964. "The Non-Western Political Process." In Harry Eckstein and David E. Apter (eds.), *Comparative Politics,* 657–665. New York: Free Press of Glencoe. Originally published in *Journal of Politics* 20 (August 1958), 468–486. Presents a series of propositions that attempt to distinguish between politics in the Western and non-Western worlds.

————. 1965. "Introduction: Political Culture and Political Development." In Pye and Sidney Verba (eds.), *Political Culture and Political Development,* 3–26. Princeton: Princeton University Press. Offers definitions of political culture and political development, then synthesizes patterns of political culture that emanate from ten country essays, which follow.

————. 1988. *The Mandarin and the Cadre: China's Political Culture.* Ann Arbor: University of Michigan Press. The traditional concept of political culture applied to China's complex society.

————. 1990. "Political Science and the Crisis of Authoritarianism." *American Political Science Review* 84 (March), 3–19. Argues that political culture will shape future postauthoritarian regimes that will be constrained by modernization and not necessarily be democratic.

Pye, Lucian W., and Sidney Verba (eds.). 1965. *Political Culture and Political Development.* Princeton: Princeton University Press. Studies in Political Development (5). Exploratory essays on political culture from a symposium sponsored by the Social Science Research Center.

Reich, Wilhelm. 1966. "Dialectical Materialism and Psychoanalysis." *Studies on the Left* 6 (July-August), 5–46. Publication of a paper originally issued in German in 1929. Searches for compatibility of Freudian psychoanalysis and Marxist historical materialism.

Riker, William. 1962. *The Theory of Coalitions.* New Haven, Connecticut: Yale University Press. A political economy approach and a model of public choice that served as a major contribution to rational-choice theory.

Rokkan, Stein (ed.). 1960. "Citizen Participation in Political Life." *International Social Science Journal* 12 (1), entire issue. An introduction (7–14) to a series of country studies dealing with citizen participation. Concerned with the threatening decline in participation and increasing public apathy about public affairs.

Rosenau, Pauline M., and Robert Paehlke. 1990. "The Exhaustion of Left and Right: Perspectives on the Political Participation of the Disadvantaged." *International Political Science Review* 11 (1), 123–152. Finds contradictions in five ideologically defined intellectual tendencies so that Western Marxists and liberals are optimistic about human nature and favor participation of the disadvantaged, conservatives and Marxist-Leninists are pessimistic and discourage it, and the perspective of the New Right is contradictory.

Ryan, Michael. 1989. *Politics and Culture: Working Hypotheses for a Post-Revolutionary Society.* Baltimore: Johns Hopkins University Press. Explores the political implications of culture and offers an argument for a practical utopianism in his "working hypotheses" for a postrevolutionary and postmodern society.

Said, Edward W. 1993. *Culture and Imperialism.* New York: Knopf. Emphasizes the unique coherence but also the special cultural centrality of British, French, and U.S. imperial experience. Argues "that imperialism invented the novel, that modernism substituted art for empire, that postmodernism is a reactionary denial that any of this ever happened." See review by John Leonard, *The Nation* 256 (March 22, 1993), 384.

Schaff, Adam. 1970. *Marxism and the Human Individual.* Introduction by Erich Fromm; edited by Robert S. Cohen. New York: McGraw-Hill Book Co. An important statement by a Polish philosopher.

Shanley, Mary Lyndon, and Carole Pateman (eds.). 1991. *Feminist Interpretations and Political Theory.* University Park: Pennsylvania State University Press. Provocative feminist essays on political theorists from the classical writings of Plato to the contemporary work of Habermas.

Shapiro, H. Svi. 1980. "Education and the State in Capitalist Society: Aspects of the Sociology of Nicos Poulantzas." *Harvard Educational Review* 50 (August), 321–331. Reviews the work of Poulantzas to show his criticism of sectarian Marxism and, in particular, of the linear argument that educational policy is coherent; to the contrary, this policy "is the outcome of an incoherent, irrational, and contradictory process" as shaped within capitalism by various class and other elements, including political power and ideologies.

Slater, David. 1991. "New Social Movements and Old Political Questions: Rethinking State-Society Relations in Latin American Development." *International Journal of Political Economy* 15 (Spring), 32–65. Reviews the major literature and theoretical trends on the new social movements. See also his "Power and Social Movements in the Other Occident: Latin America in an International Context." Amsterdam: Center for Latin American Research and Documentation. Paper presented at the meetings of the International Political Science Association, Buenos Aires, August 1991.

Solotaroff, Ted. 1991. "The Paperbacking of Publishing." *The Nation* 253 (October 7, 1991), 399–403. Explores the notion that "publishing is our most representative cultural institution" but that it is changing its mission and course and thereby confirming "the general feeling of decline in the midst of expansion, of a whole culture selling out" (399). An indictment of the publishing industry, its change of mission, its expansion, and its contribution to a decline in culture.

Thompson, Michael, Richard Ellis, and Aaron Wildavsky. 1990. *Cultural Theory.* Boulder, Colorado: Westview Press. The authors emphasize five ways of life (hierarchy, egalitarianism, fatalism, individualism, and autonomy) and employ a grid-group typology proposed by Mary Douglas. Examination of the contributions of major thinkers, from Montesquieu, Comte, and Spencer to Durkheim, Marx, Weber, and others. Authors argue that cultures are plural, not singular; they cover most of the literature on political culture, including the principal studies on the American polity.

Tokar, Brian. 1990. "Radical Ecology on the Rise." *Z Magazine* 1 (July-August), 12–18. Distinguishes between environmentalists who focus on life-style changes and whose ideas have reached the mainstream and those who see green politics as a means to build bridges among diverse and fragmented social and ecological movements.

Tullock, Gordon. 1965. *The Politics of Bureaucracy.* Washington, D.C.: Public Affairs Press. Utilizing a political economy approach to public choice, the author focuses on bureaucratic politics; this work serves as a basis for rational-choice theory.

Valdés, Nelson P. 1992. "Cuban Political Culture: Between Betrayal and Death." In Sandor Halebsky and John M. Kirk (eds.), *Cuba in Transition: Crisis and Transformation,* 207–228. Boulder, Colorado: Westview Press. A perceptive overview of traditional beliefs and practices in Cuban political culture and their assimilation into the revolutionary period after 1959.

Verba, Sidney. 1962. "Political Participation and Strategies of Influence: A Comparative Study." *Acta Sociologica* 6, 22–42. An examination and analysis of the perceptions and behavior of the ordinary citizen in five countries—the United States, Britain, Germany, Italy, and Mexico; in particular looks at the extent to which citizens in a nation perceive themselves as "competent" to influence government and the strategies they would employ.

————. 1965. "Comparative Political Culture." In Lucian Pye and Sidney Verba (eds.), *Political Culture and Political Development*, 512–560. Princeton: Princeton University Press. Detailed examination of political culture: approach, dimensions, political beliefs, political style, origins, and political crises.

————. 1980 (1989). "On Revisiting the Civic Culture: A Personal Postscript." In Gabriel A. Almond and Sidney Verba (eds.), *The Civic Culture Revisited*, 394–410. Boston: Little, Brown. 2d ed., Sage Publications, 1989.

Verba, Sidney, Norman H. Nie, and Jae-on Kim. 1978. *Participation and Political Equality: A Seven-Nation Comparison*. Chicago: University of Chicago Press. A survey of attitudes and information in seven nations (Austria, India, Japan, Netherlands, Nigeria, United States, and Yugoslavia) with attention to a model of individual propensities and institutional constraints. Intended as a follow-up that both built upon and attempted to transcend *The Civic Culture* (1963). A study of contrasts and differences among nations as to the degree to which the population is politically participant.

Wallace, Anthony F.C. 1972. "Paradigmatic Processes in Culture Change." *American Anthropologist* 74 (June), 467–478. Synthesizes generalizations into a paradigm of cultural change and outlines some applications, with reference to England and the United States.

Zaretsky, Eli. 1976. *Capitalism, the Family, and Personal Life*. New York: Harper and Row. Rev. ed., Perennial Library, 1986. In the first edition the author argued that capitalist development impacted on women in relation to public and private life. In the revised edition she reviews the major lines of thought on the history of the family since the 1970s, including feminist thinkers who use psychoanalysis as well as the history of women and develop a theory of patriarchy. This work is an important overview of trends among feminist thinkers and the prospects for socialism.

Zita, Jacquelyn. 1981. "Dual Systems Theory." *New Political Science* 5–6 (Winter-Spring), 78–88. A bibliography on dual systems theory formulated by leftist women dissatisfied with Marxist accounts of "the woman question." Thus, radical feminist analysis of patriarchy develops alongside Marxist accounts of class and capitalism.

7

Theories of Development and Underdevelopment

A prolific literature exists on the subject of development and underdevelopment. Contemporary writers have tended to differ according to their preference for capitalism or socialism. Thus, conservative and liberal social scientists and policymakers from the advanced industrial countries have proclaimed the need to diffuse capital and technology outward as a means of promoting development in the less developed parts of the world. Third World intellectuals and policymakers, including some Marxist social scientists, have argued that diffusion of capital and technology can produce negative consequences for backward areas. Indeed, development and underdevelopment might be conceived in terms of the advance of the forces of production through the accumulation and reproduction of capital along alternative paths of capitalism or socialism. Competitive, manufacturing, monopoly, and welfare forms appear in capitalism; all are guided by the capitalist market, the drive to make a profit, and the rule that under capitalism the threat of unemployment serves as a means for incentive in raising productivity despite worker alienation. In contrast, social democratic, democratic socialist, bureaucratic command, and revolutionary forms appear in socialism; central planning, state hegemony, and sometimes a partially open socialist market usually characterize socialist economies.

These distinctions may help initially in grasping many of the meanings in the literature on development. For example, within American political science, development usually is equated with political democracy or formal and representative institutions, often under capitalism and sometimes under socialism, based on a division of powers in government (executive, legislative, and judicial) and a parliamentary system based on political parties and coalitions of parties. This sort of development may be measured in terms of the number of parties (usually two but also a multitude of parties), the degree of interest group competition, and recognition of individual (but not necessarily collective) rights. Among the problems of this approach is that the hegemony of the state usually is not addressed; neither is the alienation of civil society from decision making due to the actions of elected or appointed officials who lose contact with the people. Class distinctions are not examined so that exploitation and inequality between dominant and dominated classes are overlooked. Participation is measured in political terms, not according to social needs or equitable distribution of available resources and economic achievements. Development is also often referred to as modernization. Traditionally, it was measured in terms of per capita income and other criteria that would distinguish advanced industrial nations from backward and less developed nations. Within capitalism this form of development emphasized private ownership of the means of production, sometimes in conjunction with state agencies that coordinate and plan societal activities leading to competition for profit and exploitation. Modernization is sometimes also associated with socialism, usually in social-democratic regimes that are willing to distribute resources to people to meet some needs (ensuring high levels of learning and education for all, medical service for all, food distribution so as to prevent hunger, housing for all, and so on) while at the same time advancing the forces of production. China has promoted "modernization" through reforms aimed at creating a socialist market while maintaining central planning and opening up the economy to foreign capital investment. Finally, development may be understood in terms of human needs, a concept promoted by development specialists at the United Nations where indicators are tabulated country by country in relation to literacy, schooling, health services, housing, provision of food, and growth. According to these criteria, the United States would score low—no universal health care (as of early 1994), millions of unemployed, homeless people in the streets—and would fall well down the list of advanced industrial nations.

A reassessment of development, together with criticism of capitalism and socialism, was prompted by traumatic upheavals in the world, including the overthrow of conservative dictatorships in southern Europe (Spain, Portugal, and Greece) during the mid-1970s and in the southern cone of South America (Argentina, Brazil, Chile, and Uruguay) during the early 1980s as well as the popular uprisings that overcame the dominance of intransigent socialist and communist regimes in Eastern Europe and the Soviet Union in 1989. The political changes in southern Europe and South America from formerly conservative, fascist-leaning dictatorships to democratically representative regimes were also accompanied by capitalist transformations from relatively stagnant and retarded economies under the aegis of a strong state to growing economies under neoconservative policies that favored the wealthy and dominant classes. The fall of the regimes in Eastern Europe and the Soviet Union was accompanied initially by euphoria over freedom and bourgeois democracy, the abandonment of socialism, and the adoption of neoconservative practices in the West in a push toward the capitalist market. Later, this enthusiasm was dampened by disruptions that undermined basic social services, limited prospects for employment, and brought food shortages.

The complexity of these issues becomes awesome for the student recently initiated to the literature on development. In an attempt to clarify the issues, this chapter sets forth a synthesis and an assessment of six general themes that run through the literature.

- Political development
- Development and nationalism
- Modernization
- Underdevelopment
- Dependency
- Imperialism

Mainstream comparativists favor the first three of these topics, progressive comparativists prefer the last three, although differences are obscured by overlapping theory as well as by contradictions and imprecisions of terminology.

Some comparativists seeking alternative theories and frameworks have turned to theories that emphasize modes of production, class struggle, the world system, and internationalization of capital. As noted in Chapter 4, these perspectives of development are demarcated by the varying interpretations of Marx and Weber. Marx concerned himself with development premised on the interaction of people with the material world of productive forces and modes of production. Weber identified distinctive rational characteristics of the bureaucratic order of industrial states. Both thinkers focused on bourgeois capitalism, but Marx looked for transformations in the structural base and attempted to ground his theory on facts of historical reality, and Weber dealt with the requisites of development—emphasizing routinization, efficiency, professionalization, secularity, differentiation, and specialization—and related his theory to ideal conceptions. Some critics would characterize Marx's perspective as revolutionary and realist, his conception of development as dynamic, his method as dialectical; and Weber's understanding would be seen as static, his conception of development as evolutionary and idealist, and his method as rooted in ideal typologies. The influence of these different approaches is evident in the contemporary literature on development.

Political Development

The traditional literature on political development emphasizes a political dimension, distinguishing political from economic development. This literature clusters into at least three types: one associating with notions of democracy; another focusing on aspects of political development and change; and a third examining the crises and sequences of political development.

Traditionally political scientists have addressed questions of democracy. James Bryce's *Modern Democracies* (1921) and Carl J. Friedrich's *Constitutional Government and Democracy* (1937) are representative of this trend. Attention to democracy incorporates issues of elections and constitutional legitimacy into political analysis. Seymour Martin Lipset (1959) outlined the requisites of democracy in the context of economic development and political legitimacy. His conditions of democracy included an open class system, economic wealth, and a capitalist economy; the higher the level of industrialization, wealth, and education, the greater the prospects for democracy.

These premises about democracy continue to pervade conceptions of political development. The effort of Almond (1965) to tie orthodox systems and culture theory to political development exemplifies this unchanged view of reality. In his *Aspects of Political Development,* Pye (1966, especially chap. 4) revealed his biases toward Western democracy while acknowledging a diversity of definitions, generally associated with change. For example, he referred to political development as institution building and citizen development; mass mobilization and participation are essential to democracy and order. He argued for pluralistic participation, multiparty systems, and competitive politics, as well as political stability and an avoidance of excessive tension. Democratic development, however, must balance with strong government and ordered authority. Inherent in the references to democracy are value-laden and Western-oriented assumptions, and, thus, attention to political development rather than to democracy implies a more value-neutral basis.

What is clear from these and other studies of change is that no single mainstream theory of change prevails in comparative politics. This lack of theory was recognized by the Committee on Comparative Politics of the Social Science Research Council, which turned to the study of crisis and sequences of development.

The product of the committee's deliberations comprised contributions by Leonard Binder, James S. Coleman, Joseph LaPalombara, Lucian Pye, Sidney Verba, and Myron Weiner. Their studies were published in a series of volumes on political development (Binder et al. 1971). While attempting to transcend "the formal and institutional bias" of comparative studies, these specialists searched for a theoretical basis. Their conception centered on a "development syndrome" or the three dimensions of a political system—differentiation, equality, and capacity. Differentiation refers to "the process of progressive separation and specialization of roles, institutional spheres, and associations in societies undergoing modernization." Equality relates to "national citizenship, a universalistic legal order, and achievement norms." Capacity involves how the polity manages tensions and stimulates new change. As the polity develops through increases in differentiation, equality, and capacity, crises may occur: crises of identity, legitimacy, participation, penetration, and distribution.

Each of these crises is described separately. An identity crisis relates to mass and elite culture in terms of nationalist feelings about territory, cleavages that undermine national unity, and conflict between ethnic loyalty and national commitments. A legitimacy crisis arises because of differences over authority—for example, when a ruling group is forced to compete for power with other groups or a ruler's claim to authority is rejected as illegitimate by the masses. A crisis of participation occurs when "the governing elite views the demands or behavior of individuals and groups seeking to participate in the political system as illegitimate." A crisis of penetration is characterized by "pressures on the governing elite to make institutional adaptation or innovations of a particular variety" (quotes in Binder et al. 1971: 77–80, 187, 205–206). A crisis of distribution is analyzed in terms of such problems as ideology, physical and human resources, and the institutional environment.

Binder and his colleagues raised questions about the sequential or evolutionary theory that underlies the attention to a development syndrome. Two decades of study and hundreds of thousands of dollars worth of research funds did not result in a new theory of development. Holt and Turner offered a critique of this conceptual framework by noting the lack of emphasis during the early stages on rigorous concept formation, systematic analysis, or the development of interrelated propositions (1975: 987). As to the conceptualization of the five crises, Holt and Turner argued that "the categories are not defined with sufficient sharpness, and there is considerable overlap" (992). Only the broad outline of a conception was revealed. Kesselman argued that although Binder and his colleagues were able to transcend prevailing assumptions that pluralism, political stability, and the end of ideology would inevitably characterize development, they emphasized change and crises yet gave "no satisfactory explanation … for the dynamics of change. … In the absence of a theory of structural change, change appears to occur in a random, inexplicable, and ahistorical fashion" (Kesselman 1973: 148–149). Moreover, Kesselman argued, those comparativists were ideological in their desire "to freeze alternatives and reduce irregularity" (153). They placed priority on "an implicit belief in the superiority of American political values, institutions, and processes," an ethnocentric premise that "originated during the cold war, a war the United States was never in danger of losing" (153–154).

Development and Nationalism

Development often is associated with nationalism, and this relationship has been emphasized in reference to the emerging national states in Africa, Asia, and Latin America, where a "new nationalism" seeks a common political loyalty for groups divided by major linguistic, ethnic, and religious differences through a struggle for independence and nationhood. The "classical" origins of nationalism, however, are European and are based on common cultural traditions such as a single language or closely related dialects; a heritage of customs and interests common to people; symbols of national experience, including the flag, anthem, parades, processions, pilgrimages; institutional solidarity, including a single government; sovereignty of the "state" or nation; a territorial unit; and a creed of loyalty and a common feeling or will associated with the consciousness of the nation in the minds of the people. Such characteristics are identified by major writers on nationalism, including Carlton Hayes in *Nationalism* (1960) and Hans Kohn in *The Age of Nationalism* (1968).

Most historians date nationalism to the French Revolution, although national-ism sometimes is associated with primitive peoples or was submerged in the city-state, local villages, or region. Some writers root nationalism in midseventeenth-century England where new institutions emerged such as Parliament, civic inter-ests, and new national symbols. Classical nationalism, however, was spurred on by the French Revolution as well as by Napoleon's expansion into Europe, which brought together opposing states into bonds of national unity and a shared com-munity interest. According to Hayes, nationalism evolved through four historical periods thereafter: 1815 to 1871, when nationalism and an emerging capitalism unified states formerly subject to feudal division; 1871 to 1900, when nationalism forged unity in Germany and Italy and prompted other nationalities to call for in-dependence based on unity of geography, language, and culture; 1900 to 1918, a period of international rivalry in which imperialism was disguised in the form of supranationalism; and 1918 to date, when the new nationalism challenged colo-nialism and imperialism with the formation of new states.

Historians and social scientists have suggested a classification of nationalisms, and at least nine types of nationalisms are identifiable in the general literature. *In-digenous nationalism* is associated with primitive and tribal organizations, which are small but homogeneous and held together through a system of beliefs and practices that shape the loyalty and devotion of individual members to their "na-tion." *Traditional nationalism* favors the preservation of an aristocracy, upholds God as the supreme arbiter of a nation, and encourages the "civilizing" of back-ward peoples. *Religious* or *symbolic nationalism* is characterized by emotion-laden symbols and, in secular form, is like a religion whose god is the national state. *Hu-manitarian nationalism* arose from eighteenth-century thought and is similar to traditional forms of nationalism; it promises an escape from present evils to a fu-ture millennium, substitutes the natural for the supernatural and science for the-ology, and exalts human reason and promises for the perfection of the human race.

Liberal nationalism also originated with eighteenth-century thought, and it stresses political democracy, humanitarian values, and individual liberties as well as patriotism and sovereignty as the bases for the nation-state. *Integral national-ism* rejects liberalism, insists on patriotic allegiance, is hostile to foreign influ-ences, and exalts the nation as a stepping-stone to a new order, which will evolve through physical force, militarism, and imperialism. *Bourgeois nationalism* is ex-pressed through old and new forms. The old variant is supported by the commer-cial and professional middle classes who profess national unification and political and economic liberalism; they profess national unification while believing that the nation can be strengthened through foreign investment, enterprise, and cul-ture. The newer form of bourgeois nationalism is manifested by the "national bourgeoisie" whose interests are rooted in private capital tied to the nation rather than to foreign influences. *Technological nationalism* is evident in industrializing countries where progress is promoted through centralized planning and development; this nationalism believes that heavy industry will provide a panacea to developmental problems and that an infrastructure of transportation and power should be established as the base of all development. Finally, *Jacobin* or *radical nationalism* is identified with contemporary liberation movements; it advocates disciplined political and economic centralization, popular sovereignty, liberty, and equality as well as a reliance on force to attain its ends. (For elaboration of these nine types of nationalism, see the synthesis in Chilcote 1969.)

The "new nationalism" caught the attention of comparative politics specialists. Karl Deutsch wrote, "Nation-preserving, nation-building, and nationalism. ... these still remain a major and even a still growing force in politics which statesmen of good will would ignore at their peril" (1953: 4). This theme runs through Deutsch's writings. Other contributions include Reinhard Bendix's *Nation-Building and Citizenship* (1969), Leonard Doob's *Patriotism and Nationalism* (1964), and Rupert Emerson's *From Empire to Nation* (1960).

The literature on nationalism usually interprets development as an incremental or asynchronous process of change and growth. Incremental development implies a linear progression from traditional to modern stages, and asynchronous development involves a complex series of changes in the rates of growth from sector to sector in society; the establishment of a manufacturing plant, for example, may lead to pressures for the training of a new type of labor force.

Comparative political scientists tend to emphasize political development in relation to nationalism. They stress socialization as the means through which nationalism provides the ideological impetus and motivation for development. They also give attention to patterns of inculcating behavior so that people not only will recognize their nation with pride but also will render respect and obedience to authority and governmental legitimacy. The literature, however, also examines the impact of nationalism on economic development (through demands for higher levels and varied styles of production and consumption, egalitarian distribution, and degrees of specialization); on social development (through an awareness of the gaps between classes and the potential for mobilization and aggregation); and on cultural and psychological development (through learning and the common patterns of life and thought shaped by the day-to-day and generation-to-generation experiences).

Thus nationalism provides an ideological impetus for all development—political, economic, social, cultural, and psychological. Although some nationalism may be more effective than others in stimulating national development, a basic assumption runs through the literature: the stronger the nationalism, the greater the probability that new demands and actions will arise for involvement in national life; these demands and actions may lead to change and development.

The pervasive nature of nationalism gave relevance to the study of nationalism in emerging socialist societies. Horace Davis analyzed the connections between nationalism and socialism by initially distinguishing destructive tendencies from constructive ones. "While nationalism has been used as a cloak to cover up some of history's greatest crimes, it has also inspired constructive movements. The problem of the Marxist is to distinguish between these two aspects of nationalism—to learn to harness nationalist movements where possible to serve the interests of progress while condemning and curbing them when they are used for antisocial ends" (1967: xi). Nationalism therefore may be progressive. Citing Marx and Engels, Davis described how nationalism becomes the necessary condition for the emergence of an internationalism with the harmonious cooperation of people under the rule of the proletariat. The nation is the basis for the building of the international society of the future. Although the internationalism of the advanced industrial nations accompanies ruthless imperialist expansion and capitalist development in the undeveloped nations, the contradictions inherent in this process may eventually permit the rise of socialism.

The question of nationalism as a force leading to socialist development is much debated in the literature. Lenin, Luxemburg, Stalin, and Mao held divergent views on the question. Marx and Engels generally viewed nationalism in relation to the development of West European nations, but the revolutions in Russia and China brought new conditions and necessitated new theoretical perspectives. The breakup of the European empires and the emergence of many new nations provoked more interpretations and theories. Consequently, considerable confusion continues to characterize the literature on nationalism and development today, and a clear theory has yet to establish itself in comparative study.

Modernization

The experience of Western Europe has suggested a linear path toward modern development. Nineteenth-century theories of evolution asserted that the Western world had pursued a path through successive stages of development. Implied in this view of "progress" was the belief that the Western world could civilize other less developed areas, and conquest and expansion would combine with the spread of European values to these areas. In social science Max Weber contrasted traditional and modern societies, and Talcott Parsons offered dichotomous variables so that ascriptive statuses, diffuse roles, and particularistic values of traditional society were juxtaposed with achievement statuses, specific roles, and universalistic values of modern society. This ideal typing of traditional and modern societies influenced the orthodox approaches to the study of development as modernization. For example, S. N. Eisenstadt (1964) identified the major structural characteristics of modernization somewhat along the lines suggested by Weber and Parsons. He associated modernization with a highly differentiated political structure and the diffusion of political power and authority into all spheres of society. In *Modernization and the Structure of Societies,* Marion J. Levy, Jr. (1966), known for his neo-Parsonian structural-functional framework in *The Structure of Society* (1952), assimilated his basic categories in a two-volume work that presents a comprehensive outline of propositions for the analysis of societies undergoing modernization.

Although the literature on modernization is extensive and varied, three examples will reflect the contrasting approaches.

Stage Theory and Modernization

After the Second World War the interest of the Western capitalist nations in the poorer nations focused not only on profits, extraction of raw materials, and new markets, but on the assumption that massive financial and technical assistance would transform the agricultural subsistence societies into modern industrial societies. Western scholars have described this transformation in terms of developmental stages. Inherent in this theory are some premises: through change higher levels of order may be achieved, change continuously and necessarily occurs through a sequence of stages and toward certain qualities characteristic of Western Europe, and change emanates from uniform causes.

The most influential proponent of this theory was the U.S. economic historian Walt W. Rostow, who in his *Stages of Economic Growth: A Non-Communist Manifesto* (1960) outlined five stages: (1) traditional society, (2) preconditions for takeoff, (3) takeoff, (4) drive toward maturity, and (5) age of high mass consumption. The takeoff stage is especially relevant to new nations, when growth becomes a reality. A decade later Rostow added "the search for quality" as a sixth stage in his treatise on *Politics and the Stages of Growth* (1971). Rostow's stage theory has been adopted by many political scientists. A.F.K. Organski examined the role of government through four stages in his *Stages of Political Development* (1965): (1) primitive national unification, (2) industrialization, (3) national welfare, and (4) abundance. Organski defined political development in terms of increasing government efficiency in the mobilizing of human and material resources toward national ends. His notion of development assumes, as was the case for the new advanced nations, that the Third World will grow from a stage of underdevelopment to one of capitalist democracy, abundance, and mass consumption. C. E. Black (1966) described phases of modernization in an effort to avoid the unilinear and evolutionary implications of the simplistic stage theory. He referred to criteria that facilitate the assessment of such phases as (1) the challenge of modernity to traditional society, (2) the consolidation of modernizing leadership as traditional leaders decline in significance, (3) the transformation of economy and society from rural and agrarian to urban and industrial, and (4) the integration of society.

Modernization and Decay of Society

Samuel P. Huntington in *Political Order in Changing Societies* (1968) placed emphasis on stability in the face of the rapid social and economic changes that accompany modernization. Modernization implies industrialization, economic growth, increasing social mobility, and political participation. He advocated a control and regulation of the process of modernization by constraining new groups from entering into politics, limiting exposure to mass media and access to higher education, and suppressing the mobilization of the masses. Preferring the status quo to the uncertainty of instability and revolution, Huntington focused on the issue of political decay. Political decay is a reflection of instability, corruption, authoritarianism, and violence and is the result of the failure of development, which is defined as the enhancing of the capacity to sustain the continuous transformation necessitated by the challenge of modernization and the demands of expanding participation. An imbalance toward institutionalization and order, thereby enhancing capacity, may result in repression, whereas an excessive increase in demands leading to greater participation may lead to decay and instability.

Huntington's complex model attempts to avoid the pitfalls of writers who understand political change as the outcome of social and economic conditions or of those who emphasize unilinear growth. Yet Huntington revealed an emphasis on containing change. His fundamental understanding of development was essentially conservative, resting upon values of stability, order, balance, and harmony. Notwithstanding claims that his approach to development was dialectical, fluctuating between demand and capacity, Huntington ultimately leaned toward institutional stability rather than toward the potentially disruptive demands of a participating and mobilizing society. Curiously he repeatedly referred to Leninism and the ability of communist societies to govern, provide effective authority, and legitimize a mobilizing party organization. In fact, he emphasized (especially military) order and institutionalization as essential to all political systems and as such he slighted modernization in the form of mobilization and participation.

In a later work Huntington and Nelson (1976) examined participation in relation to five models of development. The *liberal* model, evident in U.S. society, assumes that modernization and development will enhance the material conditions of society and correct the inequality, violence, and lack of democratic participation found in backward societies. Such a model, however, "has been shown to be methodologically weak, empirically questionable, and historically irrelevant" (1976: 20). The *bourgeois* model of development accounts for the political needs of an emerging middle class whose demands center on urban economic growth and the development of electoral and legislative institutions. In the *autocratic* model, government authority may use the power of the state to suppress middle-class participation and to secure the support of the lower classes. The *technocratic* model of development is characterized by low political participation and high foreign investment; participation is restrained in favor of economic development and increases in income inequality. In contrast, the *populist* model emphasizes high political participation as well as economic equality along with low economic growth. Huntington and Nelson applied these models to two phases of development, one in which economic development begins and economic inequalities appear and the other in which social classes begin to demand access to political participation and power. All models were cast as ideal types, but the authors attempted to distinguish the positivist and determinist liberal type from the other four, thus trying to explain how the expansion or contraction of political participation affects the degree of socioeconomic equality.

The Politics of Modernization

David Apter in *The Politics of Modernization* (1965) presented a typology of government and some theories about change. He distinguished between development and modernization.

> Development, the most general, results from the proliferation and integration of functional roles in a community. Modernization is a particular case of development. Modernization implies three conditions—a social system that can constantly innovate without falling apart ... ; differentiated, flexible social structures; and a social framework to provide the skills and knowledge necessary for living in a technologically advanced world. Industrialization, a special aspect of modernization, may be defined as the period in a society in which the strategic functional roles are related to manufacturing. [1965: 67]

Apter identified two models: "secular-libertarian" or pluralistic systems and "sacred-collectivity" or mobilizing systems. These models are formulated as a dichotomy of ideal types along a continuum of authority. The secular-libertarian model is represented by the modern reconciliation system, characterized by diversified power and leadership, bargaining, and compromise as exemplified by a liberal democracy such as the United States. The sacred-collectivity model is represented by the modern mobilization system, characterized by personalized and charismatic leadership, political religiosity, and the organization of a mass party. China under Mao, Ghana under Nkrumah, and Egypt under Nasser are examples of mobilization systems. Apter conceded that reconciliation systems do not seem to work in the new nations; many parties, for example, tend to fragment and disunify a political order. The mobilization system tends to involve people in rallies and demonstrations; involvement in a single-party system enables the voter to engage in tangible, albeit largely symbolic, participation.

Apter remained optimistic about the future of democracy and the reconciliation system, however. On the one hand, he believed that the reconciliation system will lead to new "consummatory values" and to a search for humanness in ending the alienation of the individual. On the other hand, he assumed that the reconciliation system will benefit from science and that science will regenerate democracy. Apter described this scientific ethic in terms of rationality and empirical research. In this notion of science, Apter appeared to be affirming the prevailing scientific paradigm of comparative politics.

In his appraisal, Gianfranco Pasquino linked Apter's political system types to Rostow's stages of economic growth. Rostow's preconditions for the takeoff stage are created by Apter's reconciliation system or, alternately, by a modernizing autocracy or a military oligarchy. The takeoff stage is achieved by a mobilization system that draws on national resources, disrupts social stratification, and destroys the agrarian sector. Apter's reconciliation and mobilization systems are in effect during Rostow's stage of the drive to maturity. Both systems may be replaced by the final stage of development, that of the age of high mass communication. Pasquino offered a fourfold critique of Apter's concept of mobilization. First, the concept is too broad and not operational in research. Second, Apter focused exclusively on the capability of the system rather than on its demands. Third, Apter imprecisely and loosely formulated three stages—traditional, transitional, and modern. Fourth, Apter resorted to the use of ideal types, which sometimes are mistaken for accurate descriptions (Pasquino 1970: 308–318).

Criticism of Mainstream Theories

The mainstream theories of development were uncritically and nearly universally accepted during the early 1960s, when they experienced their greatest reception by the specialists of comparative politics. A synthesis (Chodak 1973) suggests five currents of thinking. One deals with the evolutionary theories of development, including the formulations of Lewis H. Morgan, Marx, Comte, Spencer, and others. Another approach concerns the macrosociological theories of industrialization found in the writings of Durkheim, Bendix, and Neil Smelser. A third approach looks at the mechanisms of development, relying especially on the psychological explanations found in Max Weber's study of capitalism and the Protestant ethic or David McClellan's theory of achievement motivation. A fourth approach emphasizes political and economic development, in particular in planning and goal-oriented actions. A last approach emphasizes theories of modernization as found in the writings of Levy, Bendix, Apter, and Eisenstadt.

There has been abundant criticism of these theories of development since the late 1960s, even though they continue to pervade policy areas of government and the classrooms of mainstream political science. The following discussion concentrates, first, on some modest assessments, then turns to several indictments that appeared to put the old questions to rest, and, finally, looks at the effort of mainstream intellectuals to revive old ideas two decades later.

Dissatisfaction was clearly evident among younger scholars who searched for alternative views. Some critics reached for middle ground, sympathetic to a leftist view that had indicted the idea of progress through a diffusion of capital and technology from the advanced industrial nations to the less developed nations. Chalmers (1972), for example, acknowledged the exploitative relationship of developed to underdeveloped nations; noted the failure of developmentalism to deal with the special conditions and cultural backgrounds of the underdeveloped na-

tions; and questioned the assumptions and values of developmentalism, in particular the emphasis on stability. The search for a theory of development remains a
worthy enterprise, he believed, although the advocacy of developmentalism by the
United States and other developed nations in the underdeveloped parts of the
world should be avoided. Schmitter (1972) discussed varying types of modern
politics, ranging from pluralist democratic to corporatist authoritarian to collectivist monocratic. He favored the corporatist-authoritarian explanation for Latin
America and suggested that Latin Americans need not continue, as in the past, to
employ alien conceptions and theories but now can utilize their own models.
Tipps (1973) found that modernization theory was a product of an ethnocentric
world view and representative of the expansion of U.S. interests throughout the
world. Sachs (1972) observed that development theories were crude and simple
interpretations based on a grossly mechanistic and materialist understanding of
history. Coulter (1972) suggested a tendency toward reductionism. O'Brien (1972)
showed that the theories inclined toward authoritarian solutions and totalitarian
regimes.

Leftist intellectuals offered a blistering attack on development theory through
scrutiny of principal approaches in social science. One was the ideal typical approach conceived by Weber, systematized by Parsons, and elaborated by Bert
Hoselitz and others, all of whom were faulted on theoretical as well as on empirical grounds because their attempts to apply theory to underdeveloped countries
proved to be totally ineffective. The stage theory of Rostow was criticized for its
assumption that underdevelopment is an original stage of traditional society
when in fact underdevelopment in the underdeveloped countries is the consequence of the economic and political expansion of Europe since the fifteenth century. Stage theory ignores both historical conditions as well as the relations of the
underdeveloped countries with the now developed countries. The fallacies of a
second approach were exposed—the diffusionist view that development can
evolve through the spread of knowledge, skills, organization, values, technology,
and capital from the advanced to the backward areas of the world. Finally,
weaknesses of psychological approaches to a theory of development were revealed. By utilizing the jargon and terminology of the very theory he sought to
demolish, André Gunder Frank penetrated and revealed the weaknesses of mainstream theories of development. His solution rests with the underdeveloped
countries themselves.

> If the developed countries cannot diffuse development, development theory, or de-
> velopment policy to the underdeveloped countries, then the people of these coun-
> tries will have to develop them by themselves. These three modes of approach are the
> emperor's clothes, which have served to hide his naked imperialism. Rather than
> fashion the emperor a new suit, these people will have to dethrone him and clothe
> themselves. [Frank 1967b: 73]

Criticisms abound of political scientists for their failure to build a theory of development and for dealing with trivia, abstractions, and obscure terminology.

Dennon sounded the tone: "The literature is not only ahistorical and apolitical, but, behind all the analytical techniques, it is consciously or unconsciously prostituted to the goals of American foreign policy" (1969: 285). Apter, for example, relied on static categorization, with catastrophic results. "On the particular level, a country once placed in the appropriate box is frozen in time and cannot be discussed as a living entity with a past and a future—it has only an eternal present; on the general level, once a model has been raised to such a level of abstraction that its historical significance is obliterated, it makes just as much sense for it to occur at one time as at another, and a multitude of useless generalizations can be deduced from speculation on its occurrence at any given time" (1969: 288). Black's criteria of development became irrelevant to his concept of modernity. Further, he imposed ideas upon his data, uncritically fit countries to his typologies, and projected a utopian conception of modernization that restricts attention to political conflict. As to Pye, "his preoccupation with the surface characteristics and formal institutions ... developed to the point where he believed the government capable of acting independently of society" (291).

Bodenheimer examined the "ideology of developmentalism," in particular criticizing the "notion that knowledge is built up through patient, piecemeal accumulation of new observations, which has reached its triumphant culmination in the modern data bank" (Bodenheimer 1970: 100). Such practice lends credence to theory that stresses continuous and linear progression from traditional to modern stages through an irreversible process. The idea that development can be diffused from developed to underdeveloped nations also was debunked.

The debates on mainstream theories of development have not faded away. The old ideas on industrialization, urbanization, modernization, and growth were largely dehumanized, so that a reconceptualization might incorporate the means for obtaining the good life and sustaining life in terms of food, shelter, health, survival, esteem or recognition, self-respect, dignity, and freedom from oppression (Goulet 1968). Thus, development evolves primarily through the realization of human needs (Park 1984) and by means of struggle for liberation (Kruijer 1987).

This theme served to expose "mythical undercurrents" on which both capitalist and socialist models of development might be premised because Western capitalism's "anemic" formulations are weak and of little use, and Marxism's synthesis of science and socialism often becomes relegated to bureaucratic formulas because revolutionary leaders fail when they turn to the practical concerns of administration and planning (Berger 1976: 28–29). For example, underdeveloped countries may need foreign aid in order to achieve higher rates of growth. Their problem is to transcend the negative impacts of foreign aid strategies that may serve the interests of other nations and lead to the concentration of income in a few hands and other contradictions. They must avoid this income dilemma and implement a policy leading to self-sustained growth as well as to equity and social justice within a capitalist or socialist framework (Hamid 1974). As another example, Barrington Moore, Jr., in *Social Origins of Dictatorship and Democracy: Lord and Peas-*

ant in the Making of the Modern World (1966) traced three distinct paths to development and modernization, each leading to a political outcome: democracy, fascism, and communism through particular national experiences. Thus, Moore did not postulate one path through which the national experiences and development of all nations pass; nor did he rely on a single class, say the bourgeoisie or the proletariat, to carry out the modernizing revolution. Consequently, his work stands as "virtually the only well-elaborated Marxist work on the politics of modernization to which one can point" (Skocpol 1973: 1).

The old ideas have been recycled in recent years. The decline of the political development school was due not only to the popularity of alternative approaches but to the need for terminology and conceptualization (Riggs 1981). David Goldsworthy picked up on this issue and argued that clarity in terminology might be achieved once development is recognized as "a political problem, a political issue, and a political process" (1988: 526).

The field of political development has been both a success and a failure, but today it generally is "a muddle" and the consequence of "all the traits of too-rapid, jerry-built growth, and of its concomitant, 'decay'" (Eckstein 1982: 451). Yet the liberal development theory of political science is drawn from the belief that pragmatic pluralism is the basis of a science of politics as well as a justification of the American political system, according to Binder (1986). He showed how both liberals and conservatives emphasize culture rather than class or political institutions so that political development came to be defined more conservatively by Samuel Huntington and others in terms of control, planning, technology, and stability (see Weiner and Huntington 1987). Tony Smith affirmed that developmentalism failed because its models were formal and abstract: "loose and incomplete at a heuristic level on the one hand, and deficient in genuinely interdisciplinary empirical propositions at the level of comparative theory on the other" (1985: 542). Although he deemed the dependency school "coherent and complex" and "an alternative paradigm of study" (550), he argued that one must expose dependency's "myth of imperialism at the same time as its myth of the logic of change on the periphery" (557). Undeterred by these views, Lucian Pye, in his 1989 presidential address to the American Political Science Association, looked at the crisis of authoritarianism and events during the 1980s that were throwing into question the legitimacy of all authoritarian regimes and attributed the changes to modernization. Pye's appeal was not in vain if one turns to recent serious efforts to recast modernization to show its strengths and weaknesses in the search for alternative theory (for example, Dube 1988 and So 1990).

This synthesis and assessment of the mainstream theories of political development, development and nationalism, and modernization leave the student with the choice of revising or rejecting most of these contributions to comparative politics. A major problem has been the attempt to apply theories and ideas drawn from the experience of the advanced nations to an understanding of the rapid and perplexing events in the underdeveloped nations. The results have been unsatisfactory, prompting scholars and political leaders to turn to alternative theories and interpretations of underdevelopment, dependency, and imperialism. Radical perspectives proliferated, but the issues and debates that ensued have stimulated a new generation of thought and intellectual and practical activity that deserve serious consideration in the field of comparative politics. Thus, we now turn to a critical overview of underdevelopment, dependency, and imperialism, themes that are manifest in this new thought and that also have been largely incorporated today into the thinking of mainstream comparative and international politics (see Caporaso 1980, for example).

Underdevelopment

Theories of development generally relate to the experience of the advanced nations. Thus traditional perspectives of development in the less developed nations usually assume the possibility of development everywhere; capital and technology might filter down from the advanced to the less developed nations. Diffusion of capitalism, it is believed, will resolve the problems of poverty, hunger, health, and the like. After the Second World War, however, it was clear that this approach was not resolving the problems of the less developed nations. The intellectual reaction that followed (principally from the less developed nations) included differing perspectives, both non-Marxist and Marxist.

The non-Marxist reaction sprang from the economists associated with the United Nations Economic Commission for Latin America (ECLA), under the aegis of Raúl Prebisch of Argentina. Essentially ECLA accepted the proposition that a new bourgeoisie, commercial and industrial in character, would emerge as a supporter of national interests in the face of foreign penetration into the domestic economies of the less developed nations. ECLA thus assumed a nationalist yet an anti-imperialist stance. ECLA, figuratively speaking, divided the world into an industrial center and a periphery producing raw materials and assumed that both could benefit from the maximizing of production, income, and consumption. This bifurcation of the world kindled an interest in underdevelopment as well as in development. The writing of Celso Furtado, a Brazilian economist once active in ECLA, is representative of this approach.

Furtado criticized bourgeois neoclassical as well as Marxist theories in his *Development and Underdevelopment* (1964). Furtado examined various trends in the development of the European industrial economy and noted that expansionism led to dualism—some structures characterize the capitalist system and others perpetuate the features of the previous precapitalist system. European industrial development manifested itself in various stages so that underdevelopment was not necessarily a stage in the formation of the modern capitalist economies. Furtado then went on to analyze the structural causes of the external disequilibrium in the underdeveloped economies. Elaborating a contrasting perspective to traditional bourgeois theory, Furtado essentially favored autonomy as a solution to national development. He opposed imperialism and foreign penetration into the domestic economy, but his approach did not embrace a Marxist framework.

It has been argued that the idea of development is firmly rooted in Marxist origins but that underdevelopment is essentially non-Marxist in its original conception, and thus, Marxist attention to underdevelopment should be viewed as critically as bourgeois theory. Aiden Foster-Carter (1974: 69) noted Marx's aversion to dealing with forms of underdevelopment, yet acknowledged that Marx was aware of the tendency of capitalism to generate both wealth and poverty. Foster-Carter argued that Marx saw such a dichotomy as occurring within national societies, not in the international sphere. Further, Marx saw capitalism as inherently progressive and not as a process in which the relationship between unequal partners would allow one to develop at the expense of the other—as in the less developed nations of Africa, Asia, and Latin America, areas that are not the major concern of his writings. According to Marx:

> Capital strives after the universal development of productive forces, and thus becomes a prerequisite for a new means of production. This means of production is founded not on the development of productive forces in order to reproduce a given condition and, at best, to extend it, but is one where free, uninhibited, progressive and universal development of productive forces itself forms the prerequisite of society and thus of its reproduction. [1976: 111]

Samir Amin, the Egyptian scholar, who reminded us to look for understanding of development outside Eurocentric thinking, stressed Marx's "brilliant insight" about non-European societies, given the dearth of knowledge at the time Marx wrote. Amin argued that Marx foresaw that no colonial power would be able to preclude for long the local development of capitalism. With the rise of monopolies, however, the "development of capitalism in the periphery was to remain extraverted, based on the external market, and could therefore not lead to a full flowering of the capitalist mode of production in the periphery" (1976: 199).

A view on both progressive and negative development emerges in the thinking of Marx: "A new and international division of labor, a division suited to the requirements of its chief centers on modern industry, springs up and converts one part of the globe into a chiefly agricultural field of production, for supplying the other part which remains a chiefly industrial field" (1967: 1:451). Marx wrote that merchant capital exploits and destroys but does not necessarily transform precapitalist social formations in a backward country such as India. British rule in India created misery and backwardness along with the conditions for capitalist development, but full-fledged capitalism and industrialization never took hold there. However, as Brewer noted: "While merchant capital and its allies exploit and destroy without transforming, industrial capital destroys but at the same time transforms" (1990: 50). In contrast to his view on India, Marx's writing on the Irish question more closely resembled contemporary writing on underdevelopment, as Mohri (1979) observed. Marx argued that the Irish needed self-government and independence, agrarian revolution, and protective tariffs against England.

Marxism, as interpreted by Lenin, was concerned with precapitalist societies, and Russia, in spite of its long European tradition, was viewed as a backward nation at the time of the 1917 revolution. David Lane (1974) synthesized Lenin's views on social change in backward areas. First, despite his condemnation of the evils of capitalism, Lenin recognized the benefits of advanced forms of industrial organization, even under capitalism, which he opposed. Second, Lenin's theory of imperialism condemned capitalism as it affected the less developed countries. Third, his theory embraced centralized decision making. Fourth, his theory envisioned mass participation. These views led to the belief that industrialization on a large scale and modern technology constituted elements of a model for development that was implemented by the Soviet Union, but the model did not conform to all of Lenin's original concerns. State ownership and control, the facilitation of rapid economic growth, and direct forms of political participation for social equality must be combined in the less developed areas. The consequence may be a policy of industrialization without capitalism in combination with greater participation and equality than was evidenced in the Soviet Union.

Several theories of underdevelopment have become influential. Three overlapping theoretical tendencies will now be looked at: capitalist development in the center and underdevelopment in the periphery, unequal development, and uneven development.

Capitalist Development in the Center and Underdevelopment in the Periphery

While Celso Furtado and other ECLA economists critiqued, then modified, bourgeois theories of development, André Gunder Frank and a handful of others attempted to formulate a theory of underdevelopment. Frank (1966) distinguished center and periphery by referring to metropole and satellite. He argued that an adequate theory of development could not be formulated without attention to the past economic and social history of underdevelopment suffered by the majority of the world's population. He was concerned that most theory fails to account for the relationship between metropolis and colony in times of mercantilist and capitalist expansion.

Frank set forth a number of premises. First, underdevelopment is not original or traditional. The now developed countries may once have been undeveloped, but they were never underdeveloped. Contemporary underdevelopment is a consequence of the relationships between the now developed metropolitan countries and the underdeveloped satellite countries, a reflection of the development of the capitalist system on a world scale. Second, the view of dual societies—one modern, capitalist, and developed and the other isolated, feudal or precapitalist, and underdeveloped—is false because the underdevelopment of backward areas is a product of the same historical process of capitalist development that shaped the development of the progressive areas. Third, metropole-satellite relations thus are found at the international level as well as in the economic, political, and social

capitalist progress who maintained that all activist peoples would emerge from their precapitalist state to a world of bourgeois capitalism and free competition. Events of the twentieth century have demonstrated the accumulating effects of world capitalist development and have manifested extreme irregularities, because capitalist commerce, banking, and industry have concentrated in Western Europe and the United States while the majority of people have been relegated to backward conditions. Marx, Engels, as well as Lenin, and Trotsky all noted uneven development. But Trotsky went so far as to formulate his understanding into the law of uneven and combined development.

The uneven and combined features of development were succinctly described by George Novack. For uneven development,

> The mainspring of human progress is man's command over the forces of production. As history advances, there occurs a faster or slower growth of productive forces in this or that segment of society, owing to the differences in natural conditions and historical connections. These disparities give either an expanded or a compressed character to entire historical epochs and impart varying rates and extents of growth to different peoples, different branches of economy, different classes, different social institutions and fields of culture. This is the essence of uneven development. [Novack 1966: 5]

For combined development,

> These variations amongst the multiple factors in history provide the basis for the emergence of exceptional phenomena in which features of a lower stage are merged with those of a superior stage of social development. These combined formations have a highly contradictory character and exhibit marked peculiarities. They may deviate so much from the rule and effect of such an upheaval as to produce a qualitative leap in social evolution and enable a formerly backward people to outdistance, for a certain time, a more advanced. This is the gist of the law of combined development. [Novack 1966: 6]

In an analysis of the early phase of the Russian revolution, Lenin attributed the success of the revolutionary events to an unusual historical conjuncture involving the combination of dissimilar movements, different class interests, and opposed political and social tendencies. In his *History of the Russian Revolution,* Trotsky related those laws to his theory of permanent revolution, which was applicable to the period of transition from capitalism to socialism.

Dependency

Dependency is a concept popularly used in comparative analysis of the Third World countries in Asia, Africa, and Latin America. It evolved in Latin America during the 1960s and later it found favor in some writings about Africa and Asia. Both mainstream as well as progressive writers have assimilated dependency into their interpretations of development and underdevelopment, resulting in consid-

erable confusion. This effort concentrates on distinguishing among various us-
ages of dependency. Briefly I trace its origins and attempt to differentiate between
a non-Marxist and a Marxist view of dependency; I look at some applications and
finally conclude with some critical observations and affirm that there is no unified body of thought called dependency theory.

Definitions of Dependency

In his elaboration of a theory of imperialism, Lenin referred to the concept of dependency. He understood capitalist imperialism to be a manifestation of the
struggle among the colonial powers for the economic and political division of the
world. Although the colonial powers were sharply distinguishable from the colonies, formally independent yet dependent countries also were evident. "Not only
are there two main groups of countries, those owning colonies, and the colonies
themselves, but also the diverse forms of dependent countries which, politically,
are formally independent, but in fact, are enmeshed in the net of financial and
diplomatic dependency" (Lenin 1967: 1:742–743).

Contemporary perspectives of dependency reveal the contrasting forms of
dominance and dependence among the nations of the capitalist world. Capitalism
may be either progressive or regressive. Dependent nations may develop as a reflection of the expansion of dominant nations or underdevelop as a consequence
of their subjective relationship. Brazilian social scientist Theotônio Dos Santos affirmed the duality:

> By dependence we mean a situation in which the economy of certain countries is con-
> ditioned by the development and expansion of another economy to which the former
> is subjected. The relation of inter-dependence between two or more economies, and
> between these and world trade, assumes the form of dependence when some coun-
> tries (the dominant ones) can do this only as a reflection of that expansion, which
> can have either a positive or a negative effect on their immediate development. [Dos
> Santos 1970: 231]

Those who employ dependency in the analysis of development and underdevelopment often focus on the problem of foreign penetration into the political
economies of the Third World. Outside economic and political influences affect
local development and reinforce ruling classes at the expense of the marginal
classes. Chilean economist Osvaldo Sunkel elaborated on this interpretation.

> Foreign factors are seen not as external but as intrinsic to the system, with manifold
> and sometimes hidden or subtle political, financial, economic, technical and cultural
> effects inside the underdeveloped country. ... Thus the concept of "dependencia"
> links the postwar evolution of capitalism internationally to the discriminatory nature
> of the local process of development, as we know it. Access to the means and benefits
> of development is selective; rather than spreading them, the process tends to ensure a

TABLE 7.1
Approaches to Dependency

Non-Marxist Anti-Imperialist	Marxist Anti-Imperialist
Desarrollista, structuralist, and nationalist autonomous development (Prebisch, Furtado, and Sunkel)	Monopoly capitalism (Baran and Sweezy)
	Subimperialism (Marini)
Internal colonialism (González Casanova)	Capitalist development of underdevelopment (Frank, Rodney)
Poles of development (Andrade)	New dependency (Dos Santos)
Dependent capitalist development (Cardoso)	

self-reinforcing accumulation of privilege for special groups as well as the continued existence of a marginal class. [Sunkel 1972: 519]

Marxists as well as anti-Marxists might find that these definitions depict the world today. At the same time, it is clear that there is no consensus about a theory of dependency. Indeed no common theory exists; the literature on dependency moves in many directions, and critics set forth a multitude of positions. Some critics attack the nationalist inclinations of some advocates of dependency who oppose outside influence. Many argue that attention to external considerations of dependency avoids considerations of the internal class struggle, and others believe that dependency obscures the analysis of imperialism.

Approaches to Dependency Theory

Table 7.1 outlines the major approaches to a theory of dependency. All these approaches assume an anti-imperialist stance, yet they are distinguishable through non-Marxist and Marxist categories. These categories are suggested because many of the diffusionist theories of development are incorporated into a theory of dependency. The consequence has been a great deal of confusion and contradiction in the writing on dependency. For example, Marxists seeking to influence radical bourgeois reformers frequently have utilized bourgeois social science concepts. Marxists who have opposed such an approach have associated *dependentistas* with non-Marxist perspectives of imperialism. At the same time social scientists unfamiliar with Marxist thought often have assumed that *dependentistas* were Marxist because of a common opposition to foreign penetration. Some clarification of this problem is found in Brenner (1976), Chilcote (1984), and Blomström and Hettne (1984). We turn now to the non-Marxist anti-imperialist approaches to dependency, then look at the Marxist anti-imperialist approaches.

Desarrollista, *Structuralist, National Autonomous Development*

For centuries dominant nations have intervened in the internal affairs of other nations. In the case of the United States during the nineteenth and twentieth centuries, intervention occurred with the advances of U.S. manifest destiny. The establishment of international financial institutions helped ensure the hegemony of dominant nations over dependent ones, and the establishment of aid programs such as the Alliance for Progress served as a facade for old strategies to serve U.S. capitalism. The United States was to serve as benefactor to rid the backward world of underdevelopment and to diffuse civilization everywhere.

Since colonial times Latin America has depended on its export of raw materials and agricultural commodities in pursuit of development, but this strategy of outward *desarrollo* (development) was undermined by a decline in export earnings during the depression of the 1930s. Under ECLA, and Argentine economist Raúl Prebisch, strategy turned to inward *desarrollo*. The new strategy was premised on the achievement of national autonomy through state control and planning of the political economy under the petty bourgeois intelligentsia and the industrial bourgeoisie. Under the modernizing state the bourgeoisie would become progressive and a supporter of national interests as capitalist development diffused itself into rural areas and as economic and political policies restricted the influence of foreign interests.

The ECLA approach was based on two essential propositions. One held that the developing nations are structured into dual societies, one advanced and modern and the other backward and feudal. Under the capitalist state and the growing autonomy of national interests, an infrastructure of roads, power, and other essentials could be established to ensure the path toward industrialization. The other proposition divided the world into an industrial center and a periphery. Under unrestrained competition the center tends to appropriate most of the increment in world income to the disadvantage of the periphery.

The ECLA approach was anti-imperialist in that it linked Latin American underdevelopment to the international economic system. Its preference for autonomous capitalist development was echoed by the democratic leftist or social democratic politicians of the times, such as Haya de la Torre of Peru, Rómulo Betancourt of Venezuela, and Arturo Frondizi of Argentina. Although Haya was prevented from coming to power by the military, Betancourt and Frondizi were elected to the presidencies of their respective countries. All three believed that the capitalist stage must be promoted and that a dynamic bourgeoisie would emerge under the leadership of the anti-imperialist state.

Osvaldo Sunkel and Celso Furtado elaborated upon the ECLA position. Furtado examined the inequalities in Brazil throughout historical periods, tracing the shift of major economic activity and production from the Northeast to the Center-South region where São Paulo is situated. Before the 1964 military intervention and Furtado's exile, an attempt to rectify the economic imbalance was made by Furtado as head of SUDENE, a regional agency in the Northeast whose principal task was to mediate on behalf of the state the future course of capitalist development. In this way the state was to serve the masses by preventing a concentration of income in the privileged sectors, by widening the market to all segments of the population, and by influencing technological change (Furtado 1970).

Sunkel agreed that this transformation of the existing structures was necessary for autonomous growth; he believed that participation of the masses, including the marginal population, was essential. Underdevelopment, he argued, is not a stage in the evolution of an autonomous society.

> We postulate that development and underdevelopment are the two faces of the same universal process ... and that its geographic expression is translated into two great polarizations: on the one hand the polarization of the world between industrial, advanced, developed and metropolitan countries and underdeveloped, backward, poor, peripheral and dependent countries; and on the other hand, a polarization within countries in terms of space, backward, primitive, marginal and dependent groups and activities. [Sunkel, quoted in P. O'Brien 1975: 14]

Sunkel seemed to assume that underdevelopment is a part of the process of world capitalist development, that the manifestations of underdevelopment are normal. He saw a complex of structures, held together by laws and composing a system that is affected by change. Change in a structure is identifiable once one relates the parts to the whole system. Thus, planning and control can result in structural transformations and make development possible.

Internal Colonialism

Sunkel alluded to polarization within countries, reminiscent of the theory of internal colonialism proposed by the Mexican sociologist Pablo González Casanova (1969). The same conditions of traditional colonialism, he argued, are found internally in nations today. These conditions include monopoly and dependence (the metropolis dominates the isolated communities, creating a deformation of the native economy and decapitalization); relations of production and social control (exploitation plunders the land and discriminates everywhere); and culture and living standards (subsistence economies accentuate poverty, backward techniques, low productivity, lack of services). These are the conditions of marginal peoples who suffer from low levels of education, unemployment and underemployment, and lack of nourishment. Such peoples experience a sense of resignation and fatalism similar to that of colonized peoples. González Casanova believed that external conditions no longer have a great impact in Mexico, so that a national solution is possible. This will occur as the marginal peoples are assimilated into a collective society through the formation of a national bourgeoisie. Thus, resistance can be mounted against monopoly capitalism turned inward and capitalist exploitation. (See Love 1989 for an elaboration of theories of internal colonialism.)

Poles of Development

A derivation of internal colonialism is the theory of poles of development, first set forth by the French economist François Perroux (1968) and elaborated by the Brazilian geographer Manuel Correia de Andrade (1967). Andrade was concerned especially with unequal development, which, he believed, was evident between nations as well as between regions within a single country. The experience in capitalist nations of a concentrated growth of people and markets in areas of natural resources and in socialist nations of planned industrial centers served as the basis of a poles-of-development theory.

This theory assumes that underdeveloped economies are characterized by a lack of infrastructure in transportation and communication; by a dual economy, with advanced areas existing alongside subsistence ones; and by dependence upon external decisions that pertain to the production of primary products. These conditions may be overcome by diffusing capital and technology to undeveloped centers that promise potential for industrialization. Through careful planning a balance in the economy can be achieved, resulting in autonomous development.

Dependent Capitalist Development

Fernando Henrique Cardoso and Enzo Faletto (1979) contended with the idea that capitalism promotes underdevelopment. To the contrary, they argued that capitalist development can occur in dependent situations. They believed that dependent capitalist development has become a new form of monopolistic expansion in the Third World. Development thus takes place within the new dependency. This development benefits all classes associated with international capital, including the local agrarian, commercial, financial, and industrial bourgeoisie and even the working class employed in the international sector, but it undermines national interests that are not linked to the multinational corporations, such as local entrepreneurs. The consequence is a fragmentation of interests into a structural dualism between those associated with the multinationals and those marginalized by them. Under such conditions the bourgeoisie often becomes unstable, prompting military intervention and rule.

Cardoso defended his approach by suggesting that modern capitalism and imperialism differ from Lenin's earlier conceptions. Capital accumulation is largely the consequence of the activities of multinational corporations rather than of financial control, and investment has moved away from raw materials and agriculture to industry. Further, new trends in international capitalism have resulted in an increased interdependence in production activities at the international level and in a modification in the patterns of dependence that limit developmental policy in the peripheral countries of the international capitalist system. He agreed that international capitalism has obtained a disproportionate influence in industry in the peripheral areas, but he found misleading the assumption that there is a lack of growth in dependent economies because of imperialism (Cardoso 1972: 94).

Clearly Cardoso's approach is anti-imperialist, but is it Marxist? Cardoso probably would respond in the affirmative, arguing that his ideas constitute an updating of a foundation of theory established by Marx and Lenin. Certainly he attempted to transcend the writings of Celso Furtado and Helio Jaguaribe, who Cardoso felt "contributed to conceptual confusion" with "overly static, mechanistic views of the relationship between the economy and the polity" (Cardoso 1973a: 143). He considered unrealistic the possibility that the state, supported by the bourgeoisie, might confront the excesses of international capitalism and promote development along national autonomous lines. And he considered his approach to be flexible in the face of orthodox and dogmatic Marxist conceptions. He was critical of many of the dependency writers, including Frank, and unlike many *dependentistas,* he attempted to combine his theory with empirical analysis (Cardoso 1971). The test of this theory, then, may rest with its revolutionary potential. One critic, for example, suggested that Cardoso's theory is simply a "non-revolutionary response" (Myer 1975: 47).

Monopoly Capitalism

Although Cardoso's thought might be marginally Marxist, the writings on monopoly capitalism of several independent socialists fall more clearly into a Marxist framework, even though some critics have found fault with them for not following a "pure" Marxist or Leninist line. Lenin of course developed a theory of imperialism. Imperialism, in his view, was simply the monopoly stage of capitalism; this stage combined bank capital with capital of monopolist industrialists. Lenin called this a merger of finance capital under a financial oligarchy. Today such a merger would be represented by the multinational corporations, which are referred to later in this chapter. Some writers on the Left argue that corporate capital today has replaced finance capital as the dominant form of capital, a view that has not been without dissent from economists who write from a classical Leninist position. Perhaps the major contemporary line of thinking on the subject was set forth by Paul Baran and Paul Sweezy (1966) as they attempted to update and refine Lenin's earlier thought.

Baran and Sweezy revitalized what they called the stagnation of Marxian social science. They credited Lenin with advancing Marxist theory from an analysis of capitalism based on an assumption of a competitive economy, generally of small firms, to the proposition that imperialism constitutes a monopoly stage of capitalism composed of large-scale enterprises. Marx acknowledged that monopolies are remnants of the feudal and mercantile past, not intrinsic segments of capitalism. Engels commented on monopolies in the late nineteenth century, but he did not integrate them into Marxist theory. Baran and Sweezy turned to the generation and absorption of surplus under monopoly capitalism. Surplus is "the difference between what a society produces and the costs of producing it" (1966: 9). Attention to surplus, they believed, allows for an analysis that links the economic base of society with the ideological superstructure.

Baran and Sweezy examined the United States in the light of this approach, but their work also serves as a foundation for understanding the external impact monopoly capitalism of the center exerts upon the peripheral nations of the world. Harry Magdoff (1969) traced imperialism from its beginnings to the modern period and attempted to relate the behavior of private enterprise to U.S. foreign policy. Each line of thinking arises from a separate concern, but they converge in their analysis of the large multinational corporations of modern capitalism and their domestic governments. Cardoso related this concern with multinational corporations to a theory of dependency and also attempted to update Lenin. Samir Amin (1974) provided even greater depth in an analysis of monopolies and dependency in an accumulating capitalist world of center and periphery.

Subimperialism

Theories of imperialism in the literature on development and underdevelopment are discussed later in this chapter, but this discussion of the approaches to dependency must not overlook Ruy Mauro Marini's notion of subimperialism as it pertains to Brazilian capitalist development. He characterized Brazilian capitalism as superexploitative, with a rapid accumulation of capital benefiting the owners of the means of production and an absolute poverty accruing to the masses. With the diminution of the internal consumer market and a related decline in surplus, the Brazilian economy reached an impasse in 1964. At that time the military regime initiated its subimperialist scheme on two fronts: first, to further exploit mass consumption and, second, to penetrate foreign markets. Compromised by the interests of the multinationals and the exploitation of the proletariat, Brazilian expansion depended on the ability of the bourgeoisie to compete in foreign markets (Marini 1969: 122–129).

Whatever the successes and failures of this model, subimperialism implies a means for military rulers and bourgeoisie to promote national and semiautonomous development. Marini analyzed the difficulties of an escape from dependency and underdevelopment in the face of ties to international capitalism and imperialism. His approach combined a dependency perspective with a Marxist anti-imperialist framework.

Capitalist Development of Underdevelopment

The early writing of André Gunder Frank (1966) provided another foundation for dependency theory. Frank emphasized commercial monopoly rather than feudalism and precapitalist forms as the economic means whereby national and regional metropolises exploit and appropriate surplus from the economic satellites. Thus capitalism on a world scale promotes developing metropolises at the expense of underdeveloping and dependent satellites.

Frank (1975) certainly was influenced by the ECLA structuralist approach and reaction to the orthodox perspectives of development, as demonstrated by David

Booth (1975). Frank's dichotomy of metropolis and satellite paralleled the ECLA formula of center and periphery. Frank, however, was a critic of ECLA, which led him to an anticapitalist and an apparent Marxist position. He rejected the stage theory of Rostow and others and also indicted orthodox Marxist theory as placing the history of capitalism into deterministic formulas. Frank was influenced by Paul Baran's early work (1957) and by the efforts of Baran, Sweezy, and others to set forth original and imaginative ideas within a Marxist tradition. In this spirit, Frank took exception to the notion of a dual society. He also outlined the major contradictions of capitalism that led to underdevelopment.

New Dependency

Theotônio Dos Santos took exception to Frank's emphasis on surplus extraction as the principal cause of underdevelopment: "The process under consideration, rather than being one of satellization as Frank believes, is a case of the formation of a certain type of internal structure conditioned by international relationships of dependence" (Dos Santos, quoted in P. O'Brien 1975: 71). Dos Santos outlined several types of dependency. Colonial dependency characterized relations between Europeans and the colonies whereby a monopoly of trade complemented a monopoly of land, mines, and manpower in the colonized countries. Financial-industrial dependency consolidated itself at the end of the nineteenth century with, on the one hand, a domination of capital by the hegemonic centers and, on the other, the investment of capital in the peripheral colonies for raw materials and agricultural products, which in turn would be consumed by the centers. The new dependency, which emerged after the Second World War, was based on investments by multinational corporations. The theory of the new dependency is elaborated in Dos Santos's writings.

This theory understands industrial development to be dependent on exports, which generate foreign currency to buy imported capital goods. Exports are usually tied to the traditional sectors of an economy, which are controlled by the landed bourgeoisie and which, in turn, are tied to foreign capital. Since that bourgeoisie remits its capital abroad, it is not surprising that foreign capital controls the marketing of exported products, even though the dependent countries have attempted to impose policies of exchange restrictions and taxes on foreign exports and have leaned toward the nationalization of production. Industrial development is conditioned by fluctuations in the balance of payments, which in dependent countries often lead to deficits caused by trading in a highly monopolized international market, the repatriation of foreign profits, and the need to rely on foreign capital aid. Industrial development also is conditioned by the technological monopoly of the imperialist centers.

The theory of new dependency attempts to demonstrate that the relationship of dependent countries to dominant countries cannot be altered without a change in internal structure and external relations. Further, the structure of the dependency deepens, leads dependent countries to underdevelopment, and aggravates the problems of the people as those countries conform to an international and internal structure strongly influenced by the role of multinational corporations as well as by the international commodity and capital markets. In particular, the dependent structure affects productivity, according to Dos Santos.

> In the first place, the need to conserve the agrarian or mining export structure generates a combination between more advanced economic centers that extract surplus value from the more backward sectors, and also between internal "metropolitan" centers and internal interdependent "colonial" centers. The unequal and combined character of capitalist development at the international level is reproduced internally in an acute form. In the second place, the industrial and technological structure responds more closely to the interests of the multinational corporations than to internal developmental needs. … In the third place, the same technological and economic-financial concentration of the hegemonic economies is transferred without substantial alteration to very different economies and societies, giving rise to a highly unequal productive structure, a high concentration of incomes, underutilization of installed capacity, intensive exploitation of existing markets concentrated in large cities, etc. [Dos Santos 1970: 234–235]

The Lack of a Unified Dependency Theory: A Critical Assessment

This discussion reveals no unified theory of dependency, a reflection of the various approaches introduced above. We turn now to a critique of those approaches.

In setting forth its center-periphery thesis, ECLA correctly linked underdevelopment to the international system and thus affirmed an underlying assumption of dependency theory. Yet the thesis neglects a close examination of the policies and specific needs of the nations of the center, and it mistakenly attributes backwardness to traditional or feudal oligarchies, assumes that development would be promoted by a progressive national bourgeoisie, and advocates import substitution as a solution to consumptive dependence on the outside world. The early work of Prebisch and others argued against specialization in primary products and advocated government intervention in the internal economy in support of the private industrialization effort, for industrialization would provide the basis for the establishment of a genuinely national economy.

Sunkel elaborated on the need for national development but departed from the mainstream of ECLA thinking by advocating (1) regional economic integration and national investment in heavy industry, such as steel and petrochemicals; (2) a redistribution of income and land to the agricultural population; (3) state intervention and even nationalization in traditional export sectors; (4) joint national-multinational arrangements for the introduction of foreign technology and the development of national technology; and (5) the formation of large, specialized units under joint national and multinational control. Sunkel referred to mechanisms of dependency (agricultural stagnation, commodity concentration of ex-

ductive and a priori determinism drawing on a few global propositions about the world system (and its history), and a verificationist empiricism in which any set of facts illustrates and 'proves' these global propositions" (1983: 620); theoretically Frank's version of "world systems" "lacks concepts of relations of production, contradictions and class struggle; its form is that of a mechanical and deductive determinism" (621); methodologically Frank "essentially packages facts in a few global categorical boxes" (621); politically he offers a voluntarist conception of development and socialism that "neither starts from the concrete struggles of the exploited and oppressed nor puts them at the centre of analysis" (621). Simon and Ruccio (1986) pointed to similar weaknesses, and Stern (1988) situated these problems in his historical overview of underdevelopment theory. Foster-Carter (1985) backed up his critique of Frank by reference to the newly industrialized countries in East Asia, such as Taiwan, Singapore, Hong Kong, and South Korea. Hettne (1983) argued that these countries have been taken seriously as models of development, although one must consider the favorable economic and political support given them by the United States and the capitalist world as strategic consideration of the "free world" mentality.

New directions in Marxism include the mode-of-production approach, evident in Laclau's criticism (1971) of Frank and in French and English anthropological writings on modes of production (Foster-Carter 1978 and Taylor 1979) and the theory of internationalization of capital (Palloix 1977 and Marcussen and Torp 1982). Other emphases include the role of the state as a mediator between global- and local-level forces, and the shift from analysis of dependency and focus on individual nations or groups of nations to analysis of global accumulation or world accumulation, as evidenced in the writing of Amin, Frank, and Wallerstein.

Alice Amsden, an economist and specialist on East Asia, suggested in a *New York Times* article (April 6, 1990: A15) that Eastern Europe might benefit from the experience of countries like South Korea and Taiwan where institutions were implemented that used the impetus of the market but restrained its impact so that new industries eventually could compete with foreign firms. In her view, late industrializing countries require government intervention to ensure competition, full employment, and price limitations. The vision of a free market may lead to control by big corporations and foreign investors and to unemployment and other problems. Thus, "an authoritarian politics of industrialization" may advance not only industrialization and economic betterment but eventually also popular democratic governments—in which case the course for East Asia and for Eastern Europe is popular control of government but also government discipline to prevent domination by big corporations.

In 1985 Booth wrote of an "impasse" in the theory, and although it is clear that many of these problems continue with work on dependency, it is premature to proclaim its demise altogether. First, there has been a resurgence of interest and reappraisal—for example, Frank's retrospective examination (1991) of his earlier contributions as well as important new scholarship on dependency and underdevelopment by Hunt (1989), Kay (1989 and 1991), Larraín (1989), Lehman (1990),

Mittelman (1988), and Post (1989). Second, those who question what has happened to dependency can turn to Packenham's impassioned review (1992) and learn that the "movement" is very much alive. Although he acknowledged some dependency propositions as "innovative, interesting and correct," he voiced deep concern about its "Marxist socialism" and impact on intellectuals and, in particular, on mainstream social science and development studies. His is an unusually strong polemical, critical, and contentious perspective featuring defense of liberal and conservative views in the search for scholarship and truth; the view that partisan activities are illegitimate; and affirmation that dependency scholars are misled in their policy preferences and theoretical understandings. In an effort to overcome two decades of silence and frustration with an academic community perceived by him as infused with radical views and committed to combining scholarship with activism and change in the real world, Packenham cast his net widely, presumably with the intention of influencing academics to return to the traditional mainstream of their disciplines. Yet he ignored much of the Marxist literature appearing from the mid-1970s on that either rejected or transcended the dependency question through different approaches, such as the theories of internationalization of capital, state, or new social movements.

Packenham offered a useful, detailed, and critical textual analysis of the work of Fernando Henrique Cardoso but exaggerated his influence on dependency thinking by focusing on U.S. social science. He contrasted Cardoso's thinking with that of Frank but only cursorily referred to Dos Santos, Marini, González Casanova, and other writers who also were prominent and should be dealt with more carefully in a study of the dependency movement. Further, he did not fully examine how the positions of dependency thinkers changed, especially after the democratic transitions from dictatorships in the early 1980s. For example, Bowles and Gintis (1986) argued for a postliberal position between liberalism and Marxism; Becker and colleagues (1987) transcended dependency with their theory of postimperialism; and Laclau and Mouffe (1985) established a post-Marxist position premised on pluralistic politics and pluralism. Packenham's assertion that the dependency approach is fundamentally about capitalism versus socialism is correct, but the assumption that all *dependentistas* envisage a socialist rather than capitalist system distorts the fact that many of them initially preferred reformist and peaceful capitalist development, while others have argued for revolution as the means to overcome dependency and eventually reach socialism.

Imperialism

A variety of interpretations cloud a definitive theory of imperialism. Jonah Raskin (1971) contrasted the highlights of liberal and radical perspectives of imperialism as they are reflected in the contemporary novel: The world of imperialism "came crashing through the walls of the nineteenth century novel." For example, although Kipling hid the "truth of imperialism," Joseph Conrad examined the expansion of international capitalism, the extraction and expropriation of wealth by foreigners, and the conflict between imperial and colonial lands. Both writers reflected "the broad and deep tensions within the culture of British imperialism."

> Both were dedicated to the British Empire, but Conrad saw beyond its limits to imperialism, exploitation, racism. ... Kipling wanted order and a hierarchical society which negated conflicts. ... they both saw the extremes, the contrasts, but Conrad immersed himself in them, squeezing his art from the clash of opposites. Kipling retreated from the extremes, from the conflicts. He ensured that they were frozen, separated, they would never rebound against one another. [Raskin 1971: 36]

Theories of imperialism generally relate to the activities of some dominant nations in the world. Along this line imperialism might be defined as a "relationship of effective domination or control, political or economic, direct or indirect, of one nation over another" (Cohen 1973: 15). The relationship could be that of dominance and dependence, of big and small, of industry and agriculture, or of rich and poor.

George Lichtheim described empire or imperialism as "the relationship of a ruling or controlling power to those under its domination" (1970: 1:42). He traced imperialism from its classic roots in the Greek and Roman empires. He believed that domination and subjection constitute the elements of imperialism. The loss of sovereignty or autonomy implies that a nation is under imperial domination, which may come about through direct and overt intervention by one nation into the affairs of another, by diplomatic advantage or treaty, or by economic means. Lichtheim insisted that most theories of imperialism are fragile. He argued, for example, that the liberal view has been proved theoretically inadequate and that the fusion of social imperialism with social Darwinism in the theory and practice of European fascism during the 1930s and 1940s was discredited. He also argued that the Marxist-Leninist analysis of capitalist imperialism had become suspect once the Soviet Union manifested its imperial pretensions in the less developed areas of the world. In contrast, he saw some hope for the ultraimperialism of Kautsky, who envisioned a unified ruling elite of managers who leave their national loyalties behind and form a global cartel of the industrial centers of the world.

That conception of imperialism, as a relationship of domination and subjection, derives not only from the traditional understandings of imperialism dating from the Greek and Roman empires but also is associated with the influence of mercantile interests, along with the rise of the nation-state and the spread of European power overseas to Africa, Asia, and Latin America. Indeed the terms *empire* and *imperialism* cannot be limited "to one particular form of domination over conquered peoples, let alone to overseas colonization prompted by mercantile interests" (Lichtheim 1970: 1:55). Once mercantilism faded away, one might ask why imperialism survived into the nineteenth and twentieth centuries. The answer rests with the forms and manifestations of capitalism that took root.

The principal forms of imperialism are identifiable in history. First, during the sixteenth and seventeenth centuries European mercantilism was characteristic of the old or classical imperialism. Portugal, as one of the first mercantile states, briefly established commercial dominance in the first half of the sixteenth century. In an early phase Portugal implemented an imperialism of "exchange," especially in Africa and in the Far East where major trading points along the coasts were seized and controlled. In a later phase exchange imperialism evolved into an imperialism of "extraction," whereby the Portuguese penetrated inland areas to assure their hegemony over the source of raw materials—gold, ivory, and later slaves.

Second, a period of new or "transformer" imperialism emerged in 1870 and thereafter with the European empire building, and it represented a shift from informal to formal mechanisms of control and influence in the colonies. The new imperialism focused on economic considerations, and two theories were evident. One, Marxist in conception, argued that imperialism was a reflection of an expanding capitalism, necessitated by the contradictions in the capitalist mode of production. The other, liberal in thrust, played down the consequences of the Marxist interpretation and argued that the inequalities of the capitalist system could be readily adjusted.

Writers also speak of modern imperialism in reference to the breakup of empires and the rise of neocolonialism. A theory of modern imperialism emphasizes two views. The view from the center or metropolis stresses that imperialism is necessary for the advanced capitalist economies, and the view from the periphery focuses on the negative consequences of capitalism in the poorer economies of the world. Notions of dependency generally have been assimilated or subsumed under the latter view.

The liberal and Marxist theories of imperialism emerge in the writing of a number of important thinkers. Liberal theory is found in J. A. Hobson's work at the turn of the twentieth century. Karl Kautsky drew his ideas from Marx and others who followed in a Marxist tradition, but his belief in a peaceful reconciliation of international capital interests has also tended to influence the liberal conception of imperialism. Joseph Schumpeter used Marxist terminology but assumed an anti-Marxist stance in his polemic against Otto Bauer and Rudolf Hilferding on the Left and Hobson and others on the Right. Johan Galtung built on those theories by empirically examining imperialist relationships between the center and the periphery. In contrast to liberal theory, Marxist theory was consolidated by Lenin, who combined the contributions of Marx with those of Hobson and Hilferding. Rosa Luxemburg and Nikolai Bukharin also contributed to the Marxist theory of imperialism, and later contributions by Paul Baran, Paul Sweezy, and Harry Magdoff carried on that tradition. These theories are outlined in Table 7.2, and a review of them follows.

TABLE 7.2

Theories of Imperialism

Liberal Non-Marxist	Radical Marxist
Domestic underconsumption (Hobson)	Continuous capital accumulation and penetration in primitive societies (Luxemburg)
Peaceful resolution by the capitalist class (Kautsky)	Finance capital (Hilferding)
Withering away of imperialism under progressive capitalism (Schumpeter)	Monopolies of banks and corporations in advanced stage of capitalism (Bukharin, Lenin)
Structural view of collectivities in center and periphery (Galtung)	Monopoly and oligopoly and impact of capital surplus (Baran and Sweezy)
	Multinationals and U.S. expanding trade and aid (Magdoff)

Hobson: Domestic Underconsumption as a Cause of Imperialism

In 1902 J. A. Hobson offered an interpretation of imperialism that shaped ensuing non-Marxist conceptions and influenced some Marxist conceptions as well. Prior to Hobson, two "neutral" connotations of imperialism existed: one was used by those who desired to keep British settlements under imperial control rather than allowing them to become independent states, and the other was associated with expansionism and the control of the "uncivilized" parts of the world (Fieldhouse 1961: 187–188). Although these connotations continue to shape some thinking on imperialism, the more contemporary and common understanding dates from Hobson, who emphasized that the drive to invest capital abroad was dependent on underconsumption at home.

> As one nation after another enters the machine economy and adopts advanced industrial methods, it becomes more difficult for its manufacturers, merchants, and financiers to dispose profitably of their economic resources, and they are tempted more and more to use their Governments in order to secure for their particular use some distant undeveloped country by annexation and protection. [Hobson 1965: 80]

Hobson believed that if an increase in domestic consumption were to occur, then there would be no excess of goods or capital. There would be no expansion into foreign markets, savings would be used at home to ensure full employment among the working class, and imperialism would fade away. Thus, Hobson's understanding of underconsumption became an alternative to the Marxist concept of surplus value.

Even critics sympathetic to Hobson's work do not hesitate to attack his theory. Fieldhouse labeled Hobson's doctrine of imperialism "a dogmatic interpretation," and one that cannot be explained in terms of economic theory and capitalism; yet he also acknowledged that Hobson's non-Marxist theory became generally ac-

cepted (Fieldhouse 1961: 188). Lichtheim considered the Leninist theory of imperialism as more firmly grounded because it avoids Hobson's "theoretical mistake
of making capital investment abroad dependent on underconsumption at home"
(Lichtheim 1970: 39). Tarbuck valued Hobson's "material explanation for imperialism, rather than a vulgar, jingoistic or militaristic one" (Tarbuck in Luxemburg
and Bukharin 1972: 34). However, one major defect is this theory's emphasis on
policy and the assumption that changes in policy rather than in the class relationships in English society can be used to eliminate imperialism.

Kautsky: Peaceful Resolution of Imperialism

Karl Kautsky, born of Czech parents, spent most of his life in Germany where he
was associated with the German Social Democrat Party. After the death of Marx
and Engels, he was a leading advocate of many of their theories. Until 1914 Lenin
associated himself with many of Kautsky's views, but thereafter the two thinkers
engaged in written polemical debates. Kautsky attacked Lenin and the Bolsheviks
for undermining the democratic essentials of Marxism. He believed that the rise
of the Bolsheviks to power in Russia was followed by a dictatorship, not of all the
proletariat as Marx had envisaged but of only a segment of the proletariat represented by the party. This dictatorship was unacceptable because it lacked universal suffrage and popular participation in politics. In this regard Kautsky assumed
an orthodox Marxist position, arguing that a democratic revolution could not occur until certain conditions of advanced capitalism were evident, namely large-
scale industry and a majority of the proletariat interested in socialism. Kautsky
believed that the class conflicts of capitalism and capitalism itself would diminish
through peaceful processes.

> This so-called peaceful method of the class struggle, which is confined to nonmilitant
> methods, Parliamentarism, strikes, demonstrations, the Press, and similar means of
> pressure, will retain its importance in every country according to the effectiveness of
> the democratic institutions which prevail there, the degree of political and economic
> enlightenment and the self-mastery of the people. On these grounds, I anticipate that
> the social revolution of the proletariat will assume quite other forms than that of the
> middle class, and that it will be possible to carry it out by peaceful economic, legal
> and moral means, instead of by physical force, in all places where democracy has
> been established. [Kautsky 1964: 37–38]

Kautsky's pacifism was clearly evident in his view of imperialism. His explanation of imperialism in 1914–1915 was more complex and sophisticated than that of
Hobson, for it was couched in Marxist rather than in liberal terminology. Kautsky
utilized some of Hobson's lines of thinking, however, especially the emphasis on
imperialism as a manifestation of protectionism and militarism. Kautsky envisioned an imperialism in which there might be collective exploitation of the
world by international finance. The interests of the capitalist class as a whole

conflicted with those of capital—a minority of powerful capitalists who relied on military means to support their expansionist efforts. An internationally united finance capital thus might lead to a peaceful resolution of real and potential conflict generated by the rivalry of national finance capitals. Lenin attacked this position, arguing that the struggle among the leading powers would inevitably lead to a collapse of capitalism. Although Lenin's assumption has not yet become a reality, Kautsky's hopes for a benevolent and peaceful alliance of international finance capital have been undermined by the events of the past half century.

Although devastated by events of the twentieth century, Kautsky's view continues to carry weight. S. M. Miller, Roy Bennett, and Cyril Alapatt (1970) questioned the necessity of imperialism in their criticism of Harry Magdoff's *The Age of Imperialism* (1969). They examined economic penetration only in underdeveloped countries and limited their discussion to exports and direct private investment. Their theoretical position is illustrated by a reference to Kautsky's belief that the majority of capitalists will eventually oppose and prevent military imperialist expansion. They distinguished between a minority of capitalists who need expansion and a majority who do not need expansion. Thus capitalism should be able to exist without imperialism. Magdoff (1970) rebutted their "limited and crude" economic interpretation of imperialism and argued that capitalism prospers by molding the world to the needs of the advanced capitalist countries, that the less developed countries become dependencies of the industrial and financial centers, and that imperialism is characterized by the rise of an intensive competitive struggle among advanced capitalist nations. Thus the prospects of an antiimperialist coalition of capitalists were diminished by developments.

Schumpeter: Withering Away of Imperialism

Joseph Schumpeter acknowledged the significance of Marxist theory, which "views imperialism simply as the reflex of the interests of the capitalist upper structure, at a given stage of capitalist development" (1955: 7). However, he disassociated this view from an economic interpretation of history. His line of thinking is traced as follows. First, he examined types of imperialism, ranging from the empires of antiquity to modern experiences that are rooted in precapitalist economics. Turning to the England of the midnineteenth century, Schumpeter established the basis of his thesis. "Even in England imperialism will remain a plaything of politics for a long time to come. But in terms of *practical* politics, there is no room left for it there—except possibly as a means for defense—nor any support among the real powers behind the policies of the day" (1955: 22). Historically, imperialism has been irrational, a reflection of the needs of people who want to survive, and a response to the social and economic interests of ruling classes and individuals. Imperialism stems from conditions of the past, not the present. It is precapitalist and thus will disappear in a rational and progressive era of capitalism.

Since the vital needs that created it have passed away for good, it too must gradually disappear, even though every warlike involvement, no matter how non-imperialist in character, tends to revive it. It tends to disappear as a structural element because the structure that brought it to the fore goes into a decline, giving way, in the course of social development, to other structures that have no room for it and eliminate the power factors that supported it. ... If our theory is correct, cases of imperialism should decline in intensity the later they occur in the history of a people and of a culture. [Schumpeter 1955: 65]

Schumpeter developed his argument by contrasting eras of absolute autocracy and industrial revolution. With capitalism and the industrial revolution, the working masses emerged to transform the earlier milieu of guild and aristocracy. The production of commodities and the market of consumers that developed in the second half of the nineteenth century brought about a specialized, mechanized world. The people of that world were democratized, individualized, and rationalized.

They were democratized because the picture of time-honored power and privilege gave way to one of continual change, set in motion by industrial life. They were individualized, because subjective opportunities to shape their lives took the place of immutable objective factors. They were rationalized, because the instability of economic position made their survival hinge on continual, deliberately rationalist decisions. [1955: 68]

Thus the world of capitalism represses imperialist impulses, although there may be interests that advocate imperialist expansion. Schumpeter cited evidence for this assumption. Opposition to war, expansion, armaments, and professional armies arise under modern capitalism. Strong peace parties and vigorously anti-imperialist workers characterize the politics of the modern epoch. No class desires expansion if free trade prevails. Even the alliance of "high finance and the cartel magnates" is untenable and will disappear either peacefully or by revolution. Monopolies, wars, and imperialisms will eventually "wither and die." The modern capitalist world will destroy all these irrational "precapitalist elements" and endure (98).

Although he was critical of Schumpeter, Henry Pachter nevertheless also rested his case with progressive capitalism. He examined imperialism as "a deliberate, well-profiled policy, executed with powerful means and accompanied by an ideology that justifies the striving for empire and domination" (Pachter 1970: 461). His focus on policy negates, on the one hand, the optimistic interpretations that he attributed to reformist liberals and pacifists, including those on the democratic Left as well as isolationists and others on the Right, and, on the other hand, the "pessimist" and "determinist" view of militants on the Left who adhere to Lenin's perspective of imperialism as the last stage of capitalism.

What then is the crux of Pachter's position? He argued that the underdevelopment of nations is not a consequence of imperialism but of the population explosion. The less developed nations, therefore, "must telescope the three industrial revolutions through which the West has passed into the lifetime of one generation" (1970: 485). Among the reforms that might enhance this process are common-market arrangements that would allow the less developed nations to protect their markets, agreements to stabilize prices and allocate the production of raw materials and foodstuffs, the transfer of military budgets to development projects, the establishment of each nation's control over its national resources, and a shift from foreign to state ownership of industry in those nations. These reforms will not necessarily eliminate rivalries among the advanced nations, nor will they immediately close the economic gaps among nations. Imperialism thus is not necessarily a consequence of economic activity but reflects polemics that "are nothing but exaggerated, perverted, unleashed functions of the legitimate security interests of national states" (487).

Galtung: Structural Theory of Imperialism

Johan Galtung (1971) offered a structural theory of imperialism that has had wide acceptance among non-Marxists. He argued against the "reductionist" thrust of the Leninist view of imperialism as an expanding economic force under capitalism; instead, he understood imperialism as a structural relationship between collectivities. "Imperialism is a system that splits up collectivities and relates some of the parts to each other in relations of *harmony of interest,* and other parts in relations of *disharmony of interest,* or *conflict of interest*" (Galtung 1971: 81). Collectivities may be nations of the center and the periphery, and each nation in turn may have its own center and periphery. Imperialism is defined in terms of a number of relationships between the center and the periphery. For example, a harmony of interests is evident in the centers of both center and periphery nations. Disharmony exists between the periphery of the center nation and the periphery of the periphery nation (1971: 83). The relationship of a peripheral nation to a center nation is characterized by dependency.

Galtung outlined some dimensions and effects of that relationship and related them to five types of imperialism: (1) *economic,* in which new means of production develop in the center and nothing develops in the periphery; (2) *political,* where there is a reinforcement of position, respectively, in the center and the periphery; (3) *military,* signified by a production of the means of destruction in the center, with no production in the periphery; (4) *communication,* easily developed in the center and undeveloped in the periphery; and (5) *cultural,* reflected in education and training so that a feeling of self-reliance and autonomy pervades the center while a feeling of dependence runs through the periphery. Galtung went on to identify phases of imperialism. His concepts are applied to two nations, then to three nations and three classes (including the middle class). Variables are examined qualitatively and quantitatively, and a number of strategies for change and development are offered.

Galtung's approach defines terms, identifies relationships between center and periphery, then examines data to test some generalizations and hypotheses. As such the approach is static in its reliance on descriptive categories. The fragmentation of a single notion of imperialism into a variety of types tends to neutralize the term, deprive it of theoretical significance, and deemphasize its economic thrust. Nevertheless, the approach follows in the tradition of political science, with its reliance on mystifying abstractions and description that offers little analytical potential. Its influence, however, is clearly apparent in the writing of Klaus Jürgen Gantzel (1973), who viewed relations of dominance and dependency between centers and peripheries of capitalist and socialist societies. An appendix to Gantzel's article identifies some forty studies undertaken by German social scientists, many of whom seem to follow the structural approach of Galtung and Gantzel.

Luxemburg and Bukharin:
Accumulation of Capital and Imperialism

As early as 1913 Rosa Luxemburg, a Polish Marxist whose late years were devoted to German socialism, began to elaborate a theory of imperialism in order to explain continuous capital accumulation. Her central concern was the examination of capital penetration into primitive economies. She distinguished three phases of capital accumulation. The first involves the struggle of capital with natural economy in areas where there are primitive peasant communities and a common ownership of land or a feudal system or an economic organization oriented to internal demand and where there is little surplus production or demand for foreign goods. In a second phase capital struggles with a commodity economy. Finally, there is the imperialist phase of capitalist accumulation.

> For capital, the standstill of accumulation means that the development of the productive forces is arrested, and the collapse of capitalism follows inevitably, as an objective historical necessity. This is the reason for the contradictory behaviour of capitalism in the final stage of its historical career: imperialism. [Luxemburg 1951: 417]

Luxemburg saw imperialism as the conversion of surplus into capital, which finds itself everywhere in the world economy and does not limit its accumulation to an isolated capitalist society. The drive of capital to expand is the outstanding feature of modern development, and in its final phase capitalism "has adopted such an unbridled character that it puts the whole civilization of mankind in question. Indeed, this untamable drive of capital to expand has gradually constructed a world market, connected the modern world economy and so laid the basis for socialism" (Luxemburg and Bukharin 1972: 143).

Luxemburg offered a wealth of detail and description, but what is the significance of the theory? One critic concluded that "Luxemburg's works offer very little
theory to explain the specific capitalist forms of imperialism" (Tarbuck in Luxemburg and Bukharin 1972: 33). Nikolai Bukharin, a leading Bolshevik theoretician,
argued that Luxemburg's theory of imperialism led her to the position of those
who believe in the harmonious development of capitalism and that her theory is
"voluntaristic" and similar to that of Hobson.

Bukharin's work on imperialism (1929) was written in 1915 and included a preface by Lenin, a year before Lenin prepared his own treatise on the subject.
Bukharin related the world economy to imperialism, which was seen as an advanced stage of capitalism. His argument follows: The world economy consists of
a system of production relations and exchange relations on a world scale. Exchange relations constitute the most primitive form and trusts and cartels represent the highest form of capitalist organization at the international level. Uneven
development reflects differences in the productive forces of various countries, yet
a rapid development of the productive forces of world capitalism has accounted
for the expansion of the world economy since the end of the nineteenth century.
This expansion is the consequence of new economic formations, namely, capitalist monopoly organizations such as cartels and trusts and the banks that finance
them—banking capital transforms into industrial capital to become finance capital. This formation of capitalist monopolies transcends national boundaries and
results in a consolidation of developed powers at the center and undeveloped
countries in the periphery: "a few consolidated, organised economic bodies ('the
great civilized powers') on the one hand, and periphery of underdeveloped countries with a semi-agrarian or agrarian system on the other" (Bukharin 1929: 74).
National capitalism seeks expansion, extending itself into three spheres of the
world economy: markets for the sale of commodities, markets for raw materials,
and capital investment. The inevitable result is conflict, capitalist expansion, and
imperialism.

> It follows that the recent phase of capitalism sharpens the conflicts also in this sphere.
> The faster the tempo of capitalist development, the stronger the process of industrial-
> ization of the economic life and urbanisation of the country, the more disturbed is
> the equilibrium between industry and agriculture, the stronger is the competition
> between industrially developed countries for the possession of backward countries,
> the more unavoidable becomes an open conflict between them. [Bukharin 1929: 95]

Bukharin criticized two "vulgar" interpretations of imperialism, relating to
race and conquest. Then he demonstrated how a Marxist should approach the
analysis of imperialism, and he defined imperialism as a policy of finance capital.
"It upholds the structure of finance capital; it subjugates the world to the domination of finance capital; in place of the old pre-capitalist, or the old capitalist
production relations, it put the production relations of finance capital" (1929:
114).

Lenin: Imperialism, the Highest Stage of Capitalism

In his work on imperialism Lenin acknowledged his debt to Hobson's description of imperialism: "This author, whose point of view is that of bourgeois social-reformism and pacifism which, in essence, is identical with the present point of view of the ex-Marxist, Karl Kautsky, gives a very good and comprehensive description of the principal specific economic and political features of imperialism" (Lenin 1967: 1:684). At the same time Lenin also recognized Hilferding's suggestion that imperialism in the form of finance capital is a stage of capitalism in its latest and most highly developed form. "In spite of a certain inclination on his part to reconcile Marxism with opportunism, this work gives a very valuable theoretical analysis of 'the latest phase of capitalist development'" (684). Hilferding argued that finance capital struggles against any "harmony of interests." "As an ideal there now appears the conquest of world mastery for one's own nation, a striving as unlimited as capital's striving for profit from which it springs. Capital becomes the conqueror of the world, and with every new land conquered sets a new border which must be overstepped" (Hilferding 1910: 376).

Lenin's theory of imperialism as the highest stage of capitalism is based on a close analysis of several principal economic features. One is the rapid concentration of production in large industrial monopolies. Another feature is the role of the banks, which concentrate into powerful monopolies with control over money, raw materials, and a means of production. The capital of industrial and bank monopolies combines into finance capital, a term Lenin attributed to Hilferding, who wrote, "Finance capital is capital controlled by banks and employed by industrialists" (Hilferding, in Lenin 1967: 1:711).

In his explanation of finance capital, Lenin defined capitalism as "commodity production at its highest stage of development, when labour-power itself becomes a commodity" (1967: 1:723). Characteristic of old capitalism, in an era of free competition, is the export of goods. Under the new capitalism, characterized by monopolies, capital is exported. This export of capital is another major feature of imperialism (723–724); it is associated with uneven development and the accumulation of a surplus of capital in the advanced nations under the control of a financial oligarchy of bankers who increasingly invest their money in industry and transform themselves into industrial capitalists (710–711). Thus, finance capital and the financial oligarchy reign supreme over all other forms of capital (721). Under monopoly capitalism, cartels, syndicates, and trusts divide the domestic market and take control of industry in their own countries, but capitalism also creates a world market. Domestic markets are tied to foreign markets, and the export of capital increases, resulting in the economic division of the world among the international capitalist associations.

For Lenin "imperialism is monopoly capitalism. This in itself determines its place in history, for monopoly that grows out of the soil of free competition, is the transition from the capitalist system to a higher socio-economic order" (1967:

pendent and metropolitan countries and, on the other, the specific mode of production of each one of the dominant and dependent countries. Fifth, underdevelopment is not the result of a lack of entrepreneurial spirit but the consequence of objective historical conditions and, in particular, of centuries of capitalist exploitation.

López Segrera set forth his principal hypotheses to clarify the nature of Cuban capitalist underdevelopment. First, since the arrival of the Spaniards, Cuba had been characterized by dependent capitalism. Second, Cuban capitalist underdevelopment began early in the sixteenth century. Third, once a country such as Cuba has initiated capitalist underdevelopment, it can advance toward development only by isolating itself from the world capitalist structure. Fourth, from the beginnings of capital accumulation until 1959, metropolitan capital (through the foreign bourgeoisie) associated itself with indigenous capital (the dependent bourgeoisie), first exploiting the colony (under Spanish mercantile capitalism) and later the neocolony (under North American imperialism). Fifth, dependency related almost exclusively to a single commodity (first gold, then livestock and sugar). Sixth, as the metropolis developed through Cuban underdevelopment, so too did some regions, cities, classes, groups, and individuals benefit from the underdevelopment of others. Seventh, underdevelopment does not precede capitalism but, on the contrary, is a consequence of capitalism. Eighth, production in the colony is subordinate to the needs of the foreign market.

López Segrera's case study is addressed principally to dependency and capitalism and analyzes the consequences of historical relationships between metropolis and colony or neocolony. It does not attempt to analyze developments after the Cuban revolutionaries under Fidel Castro came to power and confronted the realities of a transition from capitalism to socialism. That task is the concern of Clive Thomas in his *Dependence and Transformation: The Economics of the Transition to Socialism* (1974).

Thomas was not concerned with the debates over the transition to socialism in industrial societies in Eastern Europe and to a lesser extent in China. Instead he focused on the problems of underdeveloped societies. Unlike many other dependency theorists, Thomas analyzed the productive forces and relations of production in the periphery of the capitalist system. He attempted to assimilate dependency theory and a Marxist framework and to link his Marxist dependency synthesis to social practice. His effort represents a considerable contribution to the discussion of the nature of the transition to socialism in the less developed nations.

The thrust of Thomas's work is prescriptive. He wanted to avoid a developmental strategy that might be influenced by the ECLA import-substituting industrialization solution, the Soviet model of heavy industry, or neoclassical economic notions of comparative advantage. Specifically, he wanted to deal "exclusively with the problems of developing the productive forces that would confront what would contemporaneously be described as an underdeveloped economy during the 'transition to socialism'" (1974: 27). He limited himself to countries like Cuba and

Tanzania in which "a political revolution has been initiated and has succeeded in transferring state power to a worker/peasant alliance, thereby fundamentally altering production relations so that the struggle to bring the productive forces under their control and direction, to disengage from international capitalism, and to raise the material levels of welfare of the population are central economic issues at that stage in constructing socialism" (29).

The three works above represent serious efforts to construct a theory of development in the contemporary world. They assess the relevance of both mainstream and alternative theories of dependency and underdevelopment. They suggest the possibility of an analysis that combines theory with practice in the examination of case studies. Finally, they move us toward a critical examination of the issues and problems of revolutionary societies that attempt to escape capitalism and mold their future in a socialist direction.

Let us now draw some findings from this chapter. First, mainstream perspectives have been found to be abstract and lacking in applicability to concrete situations, ethnocentric in their preference for the Anglo-American system, and favorable to capitalism. Some of these problems are due to conceptual difficulties—for instance, political scientists who emphasize the "political" dimensions and policy rather than theory, or economists who ignore the political side and also lean toward policy considerations in the direction of capitalism. Yet these views continue to be influential today, and indeed, they have been prolifically recycled in the literature on development. For example, Apter (1987) took up anew the question of modernization; Binder and Eckstein, despite criticisms, expressed hope for developmental theory; and Almond, Huntington, and Packenham reasserted the hegemony of mainstream developmental theory. The breakup of the Soviet Union and the states of Eastern and Central Europe has aroused renewed interest in nationalism as well. Some new ideas have emerged, such as Bates's (1981) regarding individual choice and capitalist markets in Africa.

Second, developmental writings that emphasize dependency and underdevelopment have certain tendencies: to look at conditions of exploitation, poverty, and inequality; to stress exchange, circulation, and trade rather than production and relations of production; to ignore relevant classical theories of political economy, including Marxism; to overlook issues around the role of the state and class in the planned economy or market mechanisms; to emphasize capitalist accumulation and its consequences; and to project idealistic and inevitable outcomes without concrete analysis (Dussel 1990). These deficiencies led to other alternatives, including work on the world system. For example, Wallerstein (1974) developed a model of the world system broken into a center, semiperiphery, and periphery, and he suggested that the world is in transition from capitalism to socialism, a process that will evolve over the next hundred years or so. He identified three strategies for this transformation: state intervention; enticement of capital on the promise of low wage levels and other investment advantages; and self-reliance.

Third, work on imperialism has been joined with developmental theory, initially by Warren (1980) who stressed the progressive aspects of capitalism as releasing individual creativity and organized cooperation in production as well as serving as the basis for the advance to socialism; and, second, by Brewer (1990) who turned the old polemics of imperialism upside down and looked at underdevelopment and dependency in terms of theories of imperialism. Griffin and Gurley (1985) provided a detailed literature review of these themes, and Smith (1981) exposed what he characterized as dependency's myth of imperialism.

A further problem has been the miscasting of development as political or representative democracy with attention to Western-style governmental institutions and political parties, thereby diverting attention from capital accumulation and capitalism and their impact (negative and positive) on people. Such a problem can be corrected by shifting analysis to a focus on the structure of the state and class forces. Democracy is also used in its formal sense, implying representative and indirect forms of political involvement, yet there is need to transcend this conception and to examine participatory democracy in its political, social, and economic implications. The work on the new social movements (women, ecology, peace, and so on) has carried on in this tradition (see Fuentes and Frank 1989). Sen and Grown (1987), for example, argued that there has been little structural realignment since colonialism. They looked for a more equitable and humane future for women by drawing lessons from feminism and the experiences and struggles of women's organizations. Lehman (1990) examined liberation theology, the progressive Catholic movement in Latin America, as a force for change in less developed areas of the world. The old ideas are challenged by the new social movements and by postmodernism in the West and by alternative developmental strategies in the South:

> What these pairs of perspectives—modernization theory and Marxism, development thinking and dependency theory—have in common is economism, centrism, and teleology; economism because economic growth is the centerpiece of social change, teleology in that the common assumption is goal-oriented development, centrism because development (or underdevelopment, according to the dependency view) is led from where it is furthest advanced—the metropolitan world. This testifies to the strength and complexity of developmentalism as a paradigm. [Pieterse 1991: 15]

The policy implications of the early theory of dependency and underdevelopment suggested revolution and socialism as responses to capitalism and autonomy. The United States resorted to counterinsurgency during the 1960s in order to confront the influences of the Cuban revolution in Latin America and the Third World. Policy considerations in the West turned to other strategies under authoritarian regimes, and the idea of associated dependent capitalism evolved. A combination of state, domestic bourgeoisie, and international capital undermined the possibilities for broad revolutionary coalition movements. Many of the recent writings on development (Chilcote 1992 and Evans and Stephens 1988) thus have turned toward the study of the international capitalist order or system, its reorganization and consolidation. There is need to combine analysis of international capitalism with internal aspects, including state, class, and mode of production in the city and countryside. There should also be attention to development and the transition to socialism in Third World revolutionary situations since the Second World War (see Fagen, Deere, and Corragio 1986). This necessitates a careful critique of capitalism itself and its weaknesses as well as a rethinking about questions of socialism and Marxism so that analysis during the 1990s will relate more directly to problems in terms of both theory and strategies designed to change the world order.

Theories of development and underdevelopment should serve future analysis as they have benefited past understanding dating to the nineteenth century. Although these theories do not stand as polished or unified, they may help in understanding unequal development in an evolving consolidation of capital in the international order. They may stimulate awareness of problems associated with delayed capitalist development and lead to theoretical and practical thinking on ways for deprived peoples to relate to and resist oppressive manifestations of capitalism and to search for transitions to democracy and socialism.

References

Acuña, Rodolfo. 1972. *Occupied America: The Chicano's Struggle Toward Liberation.* San Francisco: Harper and Row. A history of the exploitation of the Chicano in the United States, relevant to the model of internal colonialization.

Almaguer, Tomás. 1971. "Toward the Study of Chicano Colonialism." *Aztlán* 2 (Fall), 7–21. An early effort to apply the internal colonial model to the Chicano minority in the United States.

Almond, Gabriel A. 1965. "A Developmental Approach to Political Systems." *World Politics* 17 (January), 183–214. An effort to deal with criticisms suggesting that systems theory is static. Almond ties systems to development by dressing his old framework and terminology in a "new" conception of development and change.

Amin, Samir. 1974. *Accumulation on a World Scale: A Critique of the Theory of Underdevelopment.* New York: Monthly Review Press. An ambitious critique of bourgeois economic theory and a serious synthesis and assessment of contemporary issues and theories of underdevelopment in the periphery of the less developed world.

———. 1976. *Unequal Development: An Essay on the Social Transformations of Peripheral Capitalism.* New York: Monthly Review Press. Amin argues that the confrontation with imperialism must start from the periphery rather than from the center. His book is a theoretical exploration into precapitalist formations, laws of the capitalist mode, dependency, the development of underdevelopment, and social formations in the periphery.

Andrade, Manuel Correia de. 1967. *Espaço, polarização e desenvolvimento: a teoria dos polos de desenvolvimento e a realidade nordestina.* Recife: Centro Regional de Administração Municipal. Sets forth a description of Northeast Brazil, identifying potential poles of development and following in the thought of François Perroux.

Apter, David E. 1965. *The Politics of Modernization.* Chicago: University of Chicago Press. Emphasizes two models of modernization—the Western democratic and the sacred col-

Dussel, Enrique. 1990. "Marx's Economic Manuscripts of 1861–63 and the 'Concept' of Dependency." *Latin American Perspectives* 17 (Spring), 62–101. Illustrates the relevance of the dependency concept in the thought of Marx.

Eckstein, Harry. 1982. "The Idea of Political Development: From Dignity to Efficiency." *World Politics* 34 (July), 451–486. Argues that the field of political development is a "muddle," especially where it does the most harm "to the very meaning of political development" (451). Offers a way out of the dilemma: "The long trajectory from social polity to political society can also be considered a modulation from 'dignity' to 'efficiency' ... and each stage of the process can be treated as a changing balance between the two. In parallel, politics change structurally from personage to court, to machine, to system" (486).

Eisenstadt, S. N. 1964. "Modernization and Conditions of Sustained Growth." *World Politics* 16 (July), 576–594. Theoretical observations of modernization and growth.

Emerson, Rupert. 1960. *From Empire to Nation.* Cambridge: Harvard University Press. A major study of nationalism and its emergence in Africa.

Emmanuel, Arghiri. 1972. *Unequal Exchange: A Study of the Imperialism of Trade.* New York: Monthly Review Press. Discusses various cases of exchange through trade of products in light of current theory. Demonstrates that unequal exchange is a reflection of relations of developed to underdeveloped nations. Includes critical views of Charles Bettelheim and rejoinders by Emmanuel.

Evans, Peter B., and John D. Stephens. 1988. "Development and the World Economy." In Neil J. Smelsor (ed.), *Handbook of Sociology,* 739–773. Newbury Park, California: Sage Publications. An extensive review of development theory in the light of a changing international capitalist economy.

Fagen, Richard R., Carmen Diana Deere, and José Luis Coraggio (eds.). 1986. *Transition and Development: Problems of Third World Socialism.* New York: Monthly Review Press. A collection of excellent essays that examine the problems of transition to socialism, with attention to Third World revolutionary situations since the Second World War.

Fieldhouse, D. K. 1961. "'Imperialism': An Historiographical Revision." *Economic History Review* 2d ser. 14 (2), 187–209. A critical examination of the pros and cons of Hobson's theory of imperialism. Concludes that his theory was "defective" and that it is unacceptable as a historical interpretation of the expansion of European empires between 1870 and 1914. See also his *The Theory of Capitalist Imperialism.* London: Longman, Green, 1967.

Foster-Carter, Aiden. 1974. "Neo-Marxist Approaches to Development and Underdevelopment." In Emanuel De Kadt and Gavin Williams (eds.), *Sociology and Development,* 67–105. London: Tavistock Publications. A detailed examination of neo-Marxist thought, namely, that thought that has reassessed Marxism's practical successes and failures since 1945.

_____. 1976. "From Rostow to Gunder Frank: Conflicting Paradigms in the Analysis of Underdevelopment." *World Development* 4 (March), 167–180. Within the Kuhnian concept of scientific revolution the author examines the paradigmatic conflict between the theories of Rostow and André Gunder Frank.

_____. 1978. "The Modes of Production Controversy." *New Left Review* 107 (January-February), 47–77. A useful synthesis of the origins and evolution of the modes-of-production school, with attention to English and French anthropologists and their contributions.

———. 1985. *The Sociology of Development*. Lancashire: Causeway Press. An overview of development theory, initially setting forth definitions and a descriptive taxonomy of underdeveloped societies, then turning to theoretical issues around the modernization and dependency schools, and finally offering a criticism of the stagnationist thesis of André Gunder Frank by illustrating the success of newly industrialized countries such as Taiwan, Singapore, Hong Kong, and South Korea.

Frank, André Gunder. 1966. "The Development of Underdevelopment." *Monthly Review* 18 (September), 17–31. Here Frank first sets forth his influential and controversial theory of capitalist development of underdevelopment.

———. 1967a. *Capitalism and Underdevelopment in Latin America: Historical Studies of Chile and Brazil*. New York: Monthly Review Press. The author's pioneer effort to set forth a theory of capitalist underdevelopment, with case studies of Brazil and Chile.

———. 1967b. "Sociology of Development and Underdevelopment of Sociology." *Catalyst* 3 (Summer), 20–73. An exhaustive critique of prevailing orthodox conceptions of development in the social sciences.

———. 1974. "Dependence Is Dead, Long Live Dependence and the Class Struggle: An Answer to Critics." *Latin American Perspectives* 1 (Spring), 87–106. A rebuttal to critics of the Right, traditional Marxist Left, and new Left.

———. 1975. "Development and Underdevelopment in the New World: Smith and Marx vs. the Weberians." *Theory and Society* 2 (Spring), 431–466. Reviews contrasting interpretations of development and underdevelopment.

———. 1991. "The Underdevelopment of Development." *Scandinavian Journal of Development Alternatives* 10 (September), 2–148. Special issue containing an autobiographical essay by Frank with attention to his contributions on development theory. Includes a full bibliography of his published writings.

Fuentes, Marta, and André Gunder Frank. 1989. "Ten Theses on Social Movements." *World Development* 17 (2), 179–191. Sets forth a series of assertions about the importance of the new social movements.

Furtado, Celso. 1963. *Economic Growth of Brazil: A Survey from Colonial to Modern Times*. Berkeley: University of California Press. Historical analysis of economic growth and decline in Brazil, a case study of dependency and underdevelopment within a non-Marxist context.

———. 1964. *Development and Underdevelopment*. Translated by Ricardo W. de Aguiar and Eric Charles Drysdale. Berkeley: University of California Press. Theoretical essays on classical and Marxist interpretations of underdevelopment.

———. 1970. *Economic Development of Latin America: A Survey from Colonial Times to the Cuban Revolution*. Cambridge: Cambridge University Press. An overview of development and underdevelopment in Latin America.

Galtung, Johan. 1971. "A Structural Theory of Imperialism." *Journal of Peace Research* 8 (2), 81–117. Non-Marxist but detailed theory of imperialism based on the definition that "imperialism is a system that splits up collectivities and relates some of the parts to each other in relations of *harmony of interest*, and other parts in relations of *disharmony of interest*, or *conflict of interest*."

Gantzel, Klaus Jürgen. 1973. "Dependency Structures as the Dominant Pattern in World Society." *Journal of Peace Research* 10 (3), 203–215. Examines dependency and imperialism in terms of center and periphery with attention to four perspectives: relations between capitalist center nations; relations between capitalist center nations and the periphery; relations between capitalist and socialist centers; relations between socialist societies.

Gilbert, Guy J. 1974. "Socialism and Dependency." *Latin American Perspectives* 1 (Spring), 107–123. Refutation of the criticism of Ray (1973), who argues that socialist dependency must be studied alongside capitalist dependency.

Girvan, Norman. 1970. "Multinational Corporations and Dependent Underdevelopment in Mineral-Export Economies." *Social and Economic Studies* 19 (December), 490–526. Analyzes the anatomy of dependent underdevelopment for economies structured around mineral export industries operated by large multinational firms in Venezuela, Chile, Surinam, Guyana, Jamaica, Trinidad and Tobago, and the Netherlands Antilles.

Goldsworthy, David. 1988. "Thinking Politically About Development." *Development and Change* 19 (July), 504–530. Argues that most "thinking about development remains politically uninformed, to its clear detriment" (504). He delves into a number of concepts in order to reach clarity in terminology, and he sets forth a series of questions to guide future study.

González, Gilbert. 1974. "A Critique of the Internal Colony Model." *Latin American Perspectives* 1 (Spring), 154–161. An indictment of the internal colonial model as a means of understanding exploitation of Chicanos in the United States.

González Casanova, Pablo. 1969. "Internal Colonialism and National Development." In Irving Louis Horowitz et al. (eds.), *Latin American Radicalism*, 118–139. New York: Vintage Books. Sets forth his thesis on internal colonialism. Drawn from his *Sociología de la explotación*, 2d ed. Mexico City: Siglo Veintiuno Editores, 1970.

Goulet, Denis A. 1968. "Development for What?" *Comparative Political Studies* 1 (July), 295–312. Searches for a definition of development based on values and goals that affect individual survival, esteem, and freedom.

Griffin, Keith, and John Gurley. 1985. "Radical Analyses of Imperialism, the Third World, and the Transition to Socialism: A Survey Article." *Journal of Economic Literature* 23 (September), 1089–1143. An exhaustive review of the literature on imperialism and development.

Hamid, Naved. 1974. "Alternative Development Strategies." *Monthly Review* 26 (October), 31–52. Demonstrates the contradictions in attempting to balance foreign investment with domestic control over economy and welfare and concludes that an underdeveloped country must first mobilize its domestic resources.

Harris, Donald I. 1972. "The Black Ghetto as Colony: A Theoretical Critique and Alternative Formulation." *Review of Black Political Economy* 2 (Summer), 1–33. Examines the Afro-American ghetto in terms of the internal colonial model.

Hayes, Carlton. 1960. *Nationalism: A Religion*. New York: Macmillan Company. A major treatment of nationalism that examines its European origins and evolution.

Hettne, Björn. 1983. "The Development of Development Theory." *Acta Sociologica* 26 (3–4), 209–354. An overview of the underdevelopment theory from "its early economistic and eurocentric phase to the present more interdisciplinary and global ... debate" (247). Equates modernization theory to evolutionism as a central tradition in Western social thought. Dependency theory, he believes, was derived from Baran and had its roots in a diversity of Latin American positions. Baran based his major example on India, and although dependency is not especially important in India today, the dependency idea is found among Indian thinkers—for example, the drain theory of Naoroji and others who elaborated on this idea.

Hilferding, Rudolf. 1910. *Das Finanzkapital.* Pages 426–429 translated into English in Paul Sweezy, *The Theory of Capitalist Development: Principles of Marxian Political Economy,* 375–378. New York: Monthly Review Press, 1942. The notion of finance capital influenced Lenin in his study of imperialism.

Hobson, J. A. 1965. *Imperialism: A Study.* Ann Arbor: Ann Arbor Paperbacks, University of Michigan Press. Reprinting of Hobson's classic study, first published in 1902, with an introduction by Philip Siegelman. A Liberal interpretation that was to influence Lenin in his own study of imperialism.

Holt, Robert T., and John E. Turner. 1975. "Crises and Sequences in Collective Theory Development." *American Political Science Review* 69 (September), 979–994. A critical review of the work on development by the Social Science Research Council.

Horowitz, Irving Louis, and Ellen Kay Trimberger. 1976. "State Power and Military Nationalism in Latin America." *Comparative Politics* 8 (January), 223–244. Sees in dependency theory a failing in the emphasis on forces of external capital and not analyzing national differences. Looks at an autonomous military bureaucracy and successful development, which follows three patterns: state-initiated national capitalist development; state-initiated dependent development; and state-directed socialist development.

Hunt, Diana. 1989. *Economic Theories of Development: An Analysis of Competing Paradigms.* Hemel Hempstead: Wheatsheaf. An assessment of past and present development theory.

Huntington, Samuel P. 1965. "Political Development and Political Decay." *World Politics* 17 (April), 386–430. Examines the relationship between institutionalization and stability, on the one hand, and mobilization and participation, on the other. Where mobilization and participation outpace institutionalization, political decay sets in.

————. 1968. *Political Order in Changing Societies.* New Haven: Yale University Press. Elaboration of his thesis (1965), in which he notes political decay appears with an imbalance toward mobilization and participation. Argues for stability and order.

Huntington, Samuel P., and Joan M. Nelson. 1976. *No Easy Choice: Political Participation in Developing Countries.* Cambridge: Harvard University Press. Attempts to depart from Huntington's earlier analysis of political instability (1968) by turning to political participation in countries of the Third World.

Jackson, Steven, Bruce Russett, Duncan Snidal, and David Sylvan. 1979. "An Assessment of Empirical Research on *Dependencia.*" *Latin American Research Review* 14 (3), 7–28. Reviews the origins of dependency theory through the work of Frank, Cardoso, Amin, and the Economic Commission for Latin America; examines case studies by Quijano on Peru, Leys on Kenya, and Biersteker on Nigeria; and assesses U.S. empirical applications of dependency theory. Describes the Yale project that has applied statistics and mathematics to dependency analysis.

Kaufman, Robert R., Harry I. Chernotsky, and Daniel S. Geller. 1975. "A Preliminary Test of the Theory of Dependency." *Comparative Politics* 6 (April), 303–330. Attempts to operationalize and test bivariate propositions of dependency theory by looking at data for seventeen Latin American nations. Concludes that the concept of dependency requires refinement and redefinition, that attention should be directed to political, social, and cultural variables that may intervene between economic dependency and its alleged consequences, and that new techniques should be devised for a systematic exploration of dependency hypotheses.

Kautsky, Karl. 1964. *The Dictatorship of the Proletariat.* Ann Arbor: University of Michigan Press. This was the initial polemic in the debates between Kautsky and Lenin and their interpretations of Marxism. Attacks the undemocratic regime of the Bolsheviks in Russia.

Kay, Cristóbal. 1989. *Latin American Theories of Development and Underdevelopment.* London: Routledge. A synthesis and critical appraisal of the origins and evolution of Latin American theory on development and underdevelopment.

———. 1991. "Reflections on the Latin American Contribution to Development Theory." *Development and Change* 22 (January), 31–68. Argues that development theorists have ignored the theories emanating from the Third World. Here he looks at the Latin American contribution. Dependency theory has been distorted and important dependency writers have been ignored. He examines a number of themes in the Latin American thinking: the debate on reform or revolution, the structuralist or center-periphery paradigm, the analysis on internal colonialism and marginality, and dependency studies.

Kay, Geoffrey. 1975. *Development and Underdevelopment: A Marxist Analysis.* London: Macmillan Press. Systematically analyzes both merchant and industrial capital in the process of underdevelopment, unequal exchange, and other aspects of classical and contemporary Marxist theory.

Kesselman, Mark. 1973. "Order or Movement: The Literature of Political Development as Ideology." *World Politics* 26 (October), 139–154. A critical review of Binder et al. (1971) and Huntington (1968).

Kohn, Hans. 1968. *The Age of Nationalism: The First Era of Global History.* New York: Harper and Row. A classical study of nationalism in historical perspective.

Kruijer, Gerald J. 1987. *Development Through Liberation: Third World Problems and Solutions.* Atlantic Highlands, New Jersey: Humanities Press International. Third World liberation struggle for spiritual and material progress serves as the foundation for development.

Laclau, Ernesto. 1971. "Feudalism and Capitalism in Latin America." *New Left Review* 67 (May-June), 19–38. Critical of Frank's theory of underdevelopment.

Laclau, Ernesto, and Chantal Mouffe. 1985. *Hegemony and Socialist Strategy: Towards a Radical Democratic Politics.* London: Verso. The authors assume a "post-Marxist" view in defense of socialism and the extension of democracy through a radical politics involving not only the working class but other social movements.

Lall, Sanjaya. 1975. "Is 'Dependence' a Useful Concept in Analyzing Underdevelopment?" *World Development* 3 (November-December), 799–810. A sympathetic but critical assessment of dependency. Argues that many conclusions about the impact of dependence on development apply to particular cases but cannot be generalized.

Lane, David. 1974. "Leninism as an Ideology of Soviet Development." In Emanuel de Kadt and Gavin Williams (eds.), *Sociology and Development*, 23–37. London: Tavistock Publications. Identifies the major aspects of Lenin's views about social change in backward areas, then examines the ways in which Soviet policies of social change deviated from Lenin's intentions.

Larraín, Jorge. 1989. *Theories of Development: Capitalism, Colonialism, and Dependency.* London: Polity Press. A Marxist interpretation of development theories emanating especially from the Third World.

Leaver, Richard. 1977. "The Debate on Underdevelopment: On Situating André Gunder Frank." *Journal of Contemporary Asia* 7 (1), 108–115. Reassesses Laclau's criticism of

André Gunder Frank and examines Frank's theory of underdevelopment and dependency.

Lehman, David. 1990. *Democracy and Development in Latin America: Economics, Politics, and Religion in the Postwar Period.* Philadelphia: Temple University Press and London: Polity Press. An interpretative study of development, with attention to social movements and liberation theology, especially in Brazil.

Lenin, V. I. 1967. *Selected Works in Three Volumes.* Moscow: Progress Publishers.

Leys, Colin. 1977. "Underdevelopment and Dependency: Critical Notes." *Journal of Contemporary Asia* 7 (1), 92–107. Critical assessment of theories of underdevelopment and dependency. Argues that these theories must be transcended.

Lichtheim, George. 1970. "Imperialism." *Commentary* 49, Part 1 (April), 42–75; Part 2 (May), 33–58. The first part outlines the background relevant to a general understanding of imperialism in the contemporary world; the second part deals with the ideas and theories of imperialism since the late nineteenth century. These essays were included in the author's *Imperialism.* New York: Praeger Publishers, 1971.

Lipset, Seymour Martin. 1959. "Some Social Requisites of Democracy: Economic Development and Political Legitimacy." *American Political Science Review* 53 (March), 69–105. Presents some requisites for democracy. This paper represents a major synthesis of criteria relating to democracy and development.

Long, Norman. 1975. "Structural Dependency, Modes of Production, and Economic Brokerage in Rural Peru." In Ivar Oxaal, Tony Barnett, and David Booth (eds.), *Beyond the Sociology of Development,* 253–282. London: Routledge and Kegan Paul. Using Peru as a case example, the author criticizes various approaches to the interpretation of problems of underdevelopment and structural dependency.

López Segrera, Francisco. 1972. *Cuba: capitalismo dependiente y subdesarrollo (1510–1959).* Havana: Casa de las Américas. A case study of Cuba under dependent capitalism, as early as the sixteenth century. Examines each historical period systematically for the impact of dependency, underdevelopment, and imperialism.

Love, Joseph L. 1989. "Modeling Internal Colonialism: History and Prospect." *World Development* 17 (June), 905–922. An excellent historical overview of the concept of internal colonialism, its origins and various conceptualizations, with attention to Celso Furtado and Hans Singer. Emphasis on an economic rather than ethnic conceptualization.

Luxemburg, Rosa. 1951. *The Accumulation of Capital.* Translated by Agnes Schwarzschild. New Haven: Yale University Press. Reprinted by Monthly Review Press, 1964. A useful introduction by Joan Robinson summarizes and criticizes the theories of Luxemburg. The central thesis of this book is set forth in chapter 26 on the reproduction of capital, in which Luxemburg argues that capitalism subsists on its penetration of primitive economies and their subsequent underdevelopment.

Luxemburg, Rosa, and Nicolai I. Bukharin. 1972. *The Accumulation of Capital—An Anticritique* and *Imperialism and the Accumulation of Capital.* Edited with an introduction by Kenneth J. Tarbuck. New York: Monthly Review Press. Two volumes dealing with Marx's theory of accumulation.

√ Magdoff, Harry. 1969. *The Age of Imperialism: The Economics of U.S. Foreign Policy.* New York: Monthly Review Press. A contemporary Marxist statement of imperialism.

———. 1970. "Is Imperialism Really Necessary?" *Monthly Review* 22 (October), 1–14. Reply to an article by S. M. Miller, Roy Bennett, and Cyril Alapatt (1970), who take a liberal stance and deemphasize the economic implications of imperialism. This article was originally published in *Social Policy* 1 (September-October 1970), 19–29.

Marcussen, Henrik Seecher, and Jens Erik Torp. 1982. *The Internationalization of Capital: The Prospects for the Third World.* London: Zed Press. An explication of the theory of internationalization of capital, drawing upon case studies in Africa.

Marini, Ruy Mauro. 1969. *Subdesarrollo y revolución.* Mexico City: Siglo Veintiuno Editores. Examines underdevelopment and revolution, the dialectic of capitalist development in Brazil, and the impact of subimperialism on the working masses. An excerpt from this work appeared as "World Accumulation and Sub-Imperialism," *Two Thirds* 1 (1978), 29–39.

Marx, Karl. 1967. *Capital: A Critique of Political Economy.* 3 vols. New York: International Publishers.

_____. 1976. "The Potentialities of Capitalist Development." Excerpt from *Grundrisse* reprinted in M. C. Howard and J. E. King (eds.), *The Economics of Marx: Selected Readings of Exposition and Criticism,* 111–113. Harmondsworth, Middlesex, England: Penguin. Delineates the nature of development of the capitalist forces of production. For an analysis, see Donald J. Harris, "On Marx's Scheme of Reproduction and Accumulation," *Journal of Political Economy* 80 (1972), 505–522.

Miller, S. M., Roy Bennett, and Cyril Alapatt. 1970. "Does the U.S. Economy Require Imperialism?" *Social Policy* 1 (September-October), 13–19. A liberal critique of Magdoff (1969); argues that capitalism will transcend world conflict generated by imperialism. Magdoff offers a rebuttal in the same issue, pages 19–29.

Mittelman, James H. 1988. *Out from Underdevelopment: Prospects for the Third World.* New York: St. Martin's Press. A review of theory and practice in the search for a means to overcome underdevelopment.

Mohri, Kenso. 1979. "Marx and 'Underdevelopment.'" *Monthly Review* 30 (April), 32–42. Compares and contrasts Marx's writing on India and Ireland to show the potential relevance to contemporary theories of underdevelopment.

Moore, Stanley W. 1957. *The Critique of Capitalist Democracy: An Introduction to the Theory of the State in Marx, Engels, and Lenin.* New York: Paine-Whitman Publishers. A tight synthesis of the theory of the state with attention to dictatorship, capitalist exploitation, capitalism and democracy, and ideology and alienation.

Muñoz, Carlos, Jr. 1970. "On the Nature and Cause of Tension in the Chicano Community: A Critical Analysis." Published in summary form in *Aztlán* 1 (Fall), 99–100. Contains the first reference to the internal colonialism of the Chicano, according to the author in his *Youth, Identity, Power: The Chicano Movement.* London: Verso, 1989.

Myer, John. 1975. "A Crown of Thorns: Cardoso and Counter-Revolution." *Latin American Perspectives* 2 (Spring), 33–48. A review and critique of the works and thoughts of Cardoso. Exposes the alleged non-Marxist tendencies in his theory.

Nathan, Otto. 1966. "Marxism and Monopoly Capital." *Science and Society* 30 (Fall), 487–496. A critical review of Baran and Sweezy's treatise on monopoly capitalism (1966).

Novack, George. 1966. *Uneven and Combined Development in History.* New York: Merit Publishers. Full discussions of these laws as elaborated by Trotsky and others.

O'Brien, Donald Cruise. 1972. "Modernization, Order, and the Erosion of a Democratic Ideal." *Journal of Development Studies* 8 (July), 351–378. Notes a shift from the study of democracy to a normative emphasis on authoritarianism as the explanation of U.S. politics for an ideology of authoritarianism and institutional order.

O'Brien, Philip J. 1975. "A Critique of Latin American Theories of Dependency." In Ivar Oxaal, Tony Barnett, and David Booth (eds.), *Beyond the Sociology of Development,* 7–85.

London: Routledge and Kegan Paul. A review of the dependency literature from ECLA to the present. Classifies the literature into theories around ECLA structuralism, Marxist dependency, and the Marxist-structuralist synthesis.

O'Connor, James. 1966. "Monopoly Capital." *New Left Review* 40 (November-December), 38–50. A critique of the work of Baran and Sweezy on monopoly capital (1966).

————. 1968. "Finance Capital or Corporate Capital?" *Monthly Review* 20 (December), 30–35. Identifies and contrasts two Marxist approaches, one that looks to corporate capital and the other that sees bank capital as the dominant form of capital in the world. O'Connor favors the position of Baran and Sweezy, which focuses on corporate capital, but argues that there is a need to develop a systematic theory of corporate capital.

Organski, A.F.K. 1965. *The Stages of Political Development*. New York: Alfred A. Knopf. An application of stage theory to politics, influenced by Rostow's theory of economic stages (1960).

Pachter, Henry. 1970. "The Problem of Imperialism." *Dissent* 17 (September-October), 461–488. Argues that Lenin has misled an entire generation of anti-imperialists by insisting that the root was always economic and looks for non-Marxist explanations to describe different types of imperialism.

Packenham, Robert A. 1992. *The Dependency Movement*. Cambridge: Harvard University Press. An indictment of the dependency movement, which is viewed as Marxist-inspired and out of touch with mainstream social science.

Palloix, Christian. 1977. "The Self-Expansion of Capital on a World Scale." *Review of Radical Political Economy* 9 (Summer), 1–28. Translation of chapter 2 and appendix 1 from his book *L'Internalisation du capital*. Paris: François Maspero, 1975. An initial effort to develop a theory of internationalization of capital.

Palma, Gabriel. 1978. "Dependency: A Formal Theory of Underdevelopment or a Methodology for the Analysis of Concrete Situations of Underdevelopment." *World Development* 6, pp. 881–894. A careful examination of the roots of underdevelopment theory, in particular turns to the thinking of Lenin and his influence on contemporary theory.

Park, Han S. 1984. *Human Needs and Political Development: A Dissent to Utopian Solutions*. Cambridge, Massachusetts: Schenkman. An elaboration of development, conceptualized as the meeting and sustaining of human needs.

Pasquino, Gianfranco. 1970. "The Politics of Modernization: An Appraisal of David Apter's Contributions." *Comparative Political Studies* 3 (October), 297–322. Rejoinder by Apter, in the same issue, pages 323–332. A critical review of Apter's work, from his field studies in Africa to his attempt to evolve a theory of modernization.

Perroux, François. 1968. "Multinational Investment and the Analysis of Development and Integration Poles." In Inter-American Development Bank, *Multinational Investment, Public and Private, in the Economic Development and Integration of Latin America*, 95–125. Bogotá: Inter-American Development Bank. Synthesizes Perroux's work on development poles and integration poles, setting forth theory and methods of application.

Pieterse, Jan Nederveen. 1991. "Dilemmas of Development Discourse: The Crisis of Developmentalism and the Comparative Method." *Development and Change* 22 (January), 5–29. Argues that developmentalism is a theory of linear progress that has taken several forms (evolutionism, modernization, development) in line with different historical periods of Western hegemony. He sees developmentalism as universalist, ahistorical, teleological, and ethnocentric.

Post, Ken. 1989. *Socialism and Underdevelopment*. London: Routledge. Theories of underdevelopment are examined in the light of socialist examples.

side was the bourgeoisie of modern capitalists and owners of the means of production, and on the other side there were the modern wage workers who sell their labor to live and have no means of production. Marx examined the conflict between these opposing forces. At the same time he acknowledged the existence of smaller classes—bureaucrats and professionals, for example—and he used such class terms as the finance aristocracy, industrial bourgeoisie, peasantry, lumpenproletariat, industrial proletariat, and so on. At the heart of his analysis was a focus not on ruling classes alone, but on ruling classes and ruled masses in conflict and the struggle generated by one class's dominant rule materially over production and intellectually over ideas, resulting in an exploitation of a repressed class.

Weber argued that status groups as well as classes affect the control over a community. Status groups are found within economic classes, stratified and hierarchically ranked according to the demands of the market and reflecting a diversity of interests and preferences. With changes in market, status groups are rearranged within a class so that a lower group might be elevated to a higher one, and others might drop in ranking. The status groups as well as the individuals within them are mobile and in flux; individual talent and initiative may bring about changes in individual and group position in society. Weber thus saw class as an ideal type, not a consequence of the productive forces and relations. Weber anticipated unlimited class and group situations in contrast to Marx who emphasized two or three large classes. Weber also argued that class fragmentation would result from nationalism and ethnic loyalties, whereas Marx believed that class consciousness would solidify the proletariat into a revolutionary force.

Preferences for one approach or another are manifested in the contemporary literature. Two examples may help in understanding the differences. Jean Cohen, for instance, argued for "a post-Marxist critical stratification theory" in place of a Marxist theory that tends to reduce "the workers' movement to the logic and contradictions of a mode of production—the capitalist economy," which in turn "accounts for the transformation of an originally critical analysis of the specific modern principles of stratification into a dogmatic class theory" (1982: 2–3). In contrast, Erik Olin Wright offered a defense of the Marxist tradition and commitment to class analysis, arguing that politically a Marxist approach allows for "the most comprehensive and compelling theoretical framework within which to understand the possibilities for and obstacles to emancipatory social change"—theoretically it does well in analysis of "both epochal social change and systematically structured social conflict," and methodologically it provides for the development and reconstruction of "specific concepts within a clearly specified set of constraints" (1991: 31).

These differences have been played out in recent and past historical events. Even before the fall of bureaucratic state socialism in Eastern Europe and the former Soviet Union, an analysis based on a rigid two-class formulation was being questioned. In the *Manifesto* Marx and Engels had anticipated an eventual class struggle between the bourgeoisie and the proletariat as capitalism fully developed.

Followers of Marx assumed that socialism and eventually communism would ensue. The Bolshevik leaders of the Russian revolution implemented state ownership of the means of production and economic planning, but they did not carry
out a democracy of workers. They had to confront many outside pressures, and
under Stalinism a new ruling clique of state bureaucrats was organized through
the Communist Party. Under the reforms of Mikhail Gorbachev during the 1980s,
the privileges of this class were undermined and dissipated in many directions.
Given the existence of a relatively well-developed working class of wage and salary
earners, constituting perhaps three-fourths of the working population, then what
was needed, according to Paul Sweezy, were "general principles—continued public ownership of the commanding heights of the economy, overall but decentralized and flexible planning, creative use of controlled markets, and ... genuine as
distinct from merely formal democracy." He argued for analysis within a Marxist
framework: "from a Marxist point of view, you have got to identify the class structure, the subordinate and dominant classes, the modes of extracting surpluses"
(Sweezy 1991: 8–9). He considered the working class as the most clearly formed
class in the Soviet Union, whereas the best examples of a monopoly class in the
sense of a class "for itself" were in the United States, Germany, and Japan: "you
need a class analysis to understand our capitalist class, the most powerful class the
world has ever seen, but one which has no thoughts, no way of understanding itself" (16).

An understanding of class can be worked through divergent lines of thought.
Analysis could elaborate on the followers of Marx and Weber and their applications of a class analysis according to the respective approaches. It could turn to
heuristic schemes, with attention to production-determinative, functional, and
process-oriented formulations as a means for coping with the complexity of contrasting positions. This chapter, however, pursues a different approach and examines the following principal lines of thought, their origins, epistemological
strains, and influential ideas in the search for a theory of class:

- Pluralism
- Instrumentalism
- Structuralism
- Criticalism
- Statism and class struggle

It should be clear that the concern with class and class struggle inevitably becomes entangled with the effort to understand the nature of the state. (Various
approaches to the study of the state are identified at the end of Chapter 5.) Although Marx never fully elaborated a theory of state and class, his work focused
directly on those vital themes. His early thought is in *Critique of the Doctrine of
State in Hegel's Philosophy of Right,* and a clearer statement, revealing the theoretical underpinnings of his position, appears in his joint effort with Engels, *The German Ideology.* Certainly *The Eighteenth Brumaire* and *Class Struggles in France,*

1848–1850 are representative works on state and class that reveal an ingenious linking of theory to historical experience. In those and later writings, including *Capital,* reference to state becomes a backdrop for discussion of class. The concept of state allowed Marx to focus on bourgeois or capitalist politics, and the concept of class served as the foundation of Marx's understanding of political economy. A class commonly is identified as a group of people sharing common characteristics, although in a Marxist context a class of people constitutes a component of society. Marx differentiated between a class of producers or a working class and a class that controls the means of production or the ruling class. As the working class produces beyond its needs, the ruling class appropriates the surplus. Inevitably, according to Marx, conflict and struggle will characterize the relationship between these two classes. Engels, in *Origin of the Family, Private Property, and the State,* and Lenin, in *The State and Revolution,* synthesized and popularized Marx's theory on state and class.

Inadequate attention to state and class perhaps accounts for the dearth of serious Marxist literature on these themes since Lenin. Stanley Moore's *Critique of Capitalist Democracy: An Introduction to the Theory of the State in Marx, Engels, and Lenin* (1957) offers a synthesis of past theory and paves the way toward a reassessment. Hal Draper's *Karl Marx's Theory of Revolution* (1977) is an outstanding restatement of Marx's theories of state and class. Perry Anderson's *Lineages of the Absolutist State* (1974) analyzes the emergence of the absolute state and the centralized monarchies in western Europe during the sixteenth century; those regimes constituted a form of state power to rule over the class struggle between the old feudal nobility and the new urban bourgeoisie. In *Late Capitalism* (1975), Ernest Mandel traced the role of society from mercantilist times to the present. E. P. Thompson in his important study, *The Making of the English Working Class* (1968), argued that history can be rescued from "below" through a focus on class consciousness and the creativity and initiative of the mass of people. Thompson thus examined subjective aspects of class and in the process turned against structural interpretations and theoretical and practical deformations that run through history. He insisted that class must be envisaged as a relationship and a process to be observed over time.

Although American political science has not been much concerned with questions of class, in a review of new directions in political science and comparative politics, Alan Wolfe (1974) stressed a Marxist theory of politics by synthesizing critical and scientific perspectives and affirming the importance of state and class. Jean-Claude Girardin (1974) assessed humanist and structuralist understandings, while Ralph Miliband (1969) argued that at the core of Marxist politics are the state, class, and class conflict. Al Szymanski emphasized those themes in his lucid text, *The Capitalist State and the Politics of Class* (1978). In an effort to bring the class back into social science analysis to recapture "the central elements of a Marxist class analysis and show how and why it is more efficacious than other approaches for understanding class in comparative and historical perspective," McNall, Levine, and Fantasia (1991: 1) also observed that the division between

288 Theories of Class

Weberian and Marxian perspectives has faded with focus on problems of prole-
tarianization, the role of culture in preserving class boundaries, and the independent position of bureaucracies in shaping the middle classes.

The argument that class is obscured because the majority of the American population has been led to believe that it is somewhere between the rich and the poor
is perpetuated, according to Vicente Navarro, by U.S. government data, organized
by race, gender, and region, but not by class: "The absence of class analysis and
class discourse is a victory for the capitalist class, in whose interest the myth of the
'middle-class society' is reproduced" (1991: 5). The attention to middle class also
obscures the fact that, despite stability in the world capitalist system, the ranks of
the poor are swelling, as reported in a United Nations survey: 1.1 billion people
living in poverty in the Third World, more than half of them classified as "extremely poor"; the industrialized world home to more than 200 million poor people; and the percentage of poor to population ranging from 51 percent in South
Asia to 47 percent in sub-Saharan Africa, 31 percent in the Middle East, and 19
percent in Latin America (*Los Angeles Times*, November 23, 1991).

Each of the major theoretical schools roots itself in a particular intellectual tradition. For example, pluralism is a distinctly U.S. phenomenon; instrumentalism
has its origins in studies of community power structures in the United States, but
also has been advanced in England; structuralism stems from influential social
science circles in France; criticalism owes its debt to a number of German thinkers; and the school of statism and class struggle represents an attempt to synthesize and transcend the other schools.

Pluralism

Political scientists generally allude to the pluralist character of Anglo-American
politics. Pluralism holds that democracy is premised on diverse interests and the
dispersion of power. Theories of pluralism stem from liberal economic and political thought. On the one hand, John Locke and Jeremy Bentham stressed individual property rights and private initiative. On the other, James Madison envisioned competing interests in the struggle for power. Those thinkers provided a
basis for group and interest theory, enhanced by the contributions of Arthur
Bentley and David Truman to contemporary political science in the United States.
Several positions are evident among pluralists. One, often called an elitist theory
of democracy, distinguishes between rulers and ruled but emphasizes changes in
elite membership over time; Vilfredo Pareto called this a theory of circulating
elites, and Gaetano Mosca's theory of ruling classes was similar. Another position
examines pluralism as a fundamental practice in Western plutocratic society and
is represented in the work of Robert Dahl and other prominent U.S. political scientists and sociologists. Lastly, pluralism sometimes relates to certain lines of socialist thought, and in this position theories of conflict and consensus may be ap-

calling themselves "analytical Marxists," "rational-choice Marxists," and "subjective Marxists." Its ranks include G. A. Cohen, Jon Elster, Adam Przeworski, John Roemer, and Erik Olin Wright. This current claims to follow Marxism, emphasizes rational choice, approximates positivist approaches to social science, and tends to build on micro foundations (Roemer 1989) or individual decisions.

For example, Elster (1985) argued that the actions of classes are reducible to the actions of individuals, and he attempted to demonstrate that Marx himself was a founder of rational-choice theory. In contrast to Elster, Przeworski and Wright placed emphasis on structurally determined positions that influence individual decisions. Cohen based his theory of history (1978) on the forces of production, thus making it functional in its core. Roemer employed rational-actor assumptions to show that capitalist exploitation occurs as a result of whether an individual buys or sells labor power; the exploitative relationship is the consequence of unequally distributed property relations. Roemer (1988) argued that the injustices of capitalism occur in property relations that determine class, income, and welfare, not in what happens at the point of production. In his recent attention to class, Wright (1985) shifted from his earlier emphasis on structure and contradictory class locations (1978) to a more subjective realm of class analysis, a methodological shift that reoriented his analysis from classes and the labor process to political power groups and the power they wield.

Critics have suggested that this rational-choice approach is unaccepting of traditional or structural Marxian conceptions of exploitation and class and is oriented to the realm of subjective social analysis. Attention to class shifts from the process whereby groups of people become differentiated through the labor process to a focus on the development of groups of people into collective units. Burawoy (1989) suggested that the rational-choice approach purges Marxism of its dogmatic elements by introducing the clear and rigorous thinking of analytical philosophy and the logico-deductive models of neoclassical economics. He noted the attention to methodological individualism and micro foundations through the rational-choice models of general equilibrium theory, game theory, and the formal modeling of neoclassical economics, but concluded that the claims for micro foundations are misleading because the importance of relations of production is obscured in attention to politics. Ellen Meiksins Wood provided a comprehensive and exhaustive criticism of analytical Marxism, which in her view is converging with post-Marxism—two approaches that "began as an effort to establish 'rigor' in Marxist theory and ... ended for many in a general repudiation of Marxism in theory and in practice" (1989: 87).

Instrumentalism

Instrumentalism assumes that the state is controlled by and serves the interests of the capitalist class. Instrumentalists argue that an elitist or minority class rules in most societies, a position not dissimilar to the views of Pareto and Mosca. This assumption also is found in a generation of studies of power structure in U.S. communities. It is a central premise of the work of C. Wright Mills and of the work of G. William Domhoff, both of whom have elaborated on power-structure theory. Much of instrumentalist theory skirts Marxist premises, but the work of Ralph Miliband takes an explicit Marxist stance. According to Miliband, the capitalist ruling class exercises the power to use the state as its instrument for a domination of society. His view is drawn from *The Communist Manifesto* in which Marx and Engels asserted that "the modern state is but a committee for managing the common affairs of the whole bourgeoisie."

The Legacy of Power Structure in the Community

Traditionally, community studies have addressed the question of who rules, and generally these studies employ stratification theory. Nelson Polsby (1963: 8–11) alluded to some important assertions of stratification studies of power in the United States. A ladder of strata usually is envisaged with an upper class at the top that rules the local community. This class is identifiable by such criteria as income, occupation, housing, and consumption pattern. As a consequence of its economic position the upper class has greater power than do the political and civic leaders. Sometimes this upper class is thought of as a power elite that stands at the apex of a pyramid of power. This upper class rules in its own interests, and its dominance and position ensure its separation from the lower classes of a community; this separation leads to social conflict.

Among the community studies that employ stratification theory, that of Middletown or Muncie, Indiana, remains a classic. Conducted by Robert and Helen Lynd, first in the mid-1920s and again a decade later, the study of Middletown identified the "business class," which in turn was controlled by one family, as dominant in every sphere of community activity. William Lloyd Warner and associates published during the 1940s and 1950s five studies of Yankee City or Newburyport, Massachusetts, in which attention is directed to position and social status. These studies demonstrate a dominance of the upper classes, even though conflict between the upper and lower classes sometimes is evident. Warner also studied the small town of Morris, in northern Illinois, during the late 1930s and early 1940s. He called it Elmtown. Hollingshead confirmed that the upper classes controlled community life. Digby Baltzell observed that Philadelphia businessmen constitute a ruling class of families with high status and old wealth. He identified them through *Who's Who in America* and the *Social Register*. During the early 1950s Floyd Hunter utilized panels of persons knowledgeable about community life to identify decision makers in Regional City or Atlanta, Georgia. This reputational approach served to describe community power structure.

These studies tend to view power as being in the hands of a ruling class or elite, and thus these studies have established the orientation of most community research in the United States. The existence of a single center of power or a tight co-alition of groups that wield power in U.S. communities is, of course, a proposi-tion that has been challenged by many pluralists. Arnold Rose (1967: 483–492) asserted that a power structure is found at every level of U.S. life—national, re-gional, state, and local. Although small numbers of persons hold the greatest amount of power within this variety of power structures, their power depends on the extent to which they interact in order to influence public opinion. Rose be-lieved that power structure in the United States is highly complex and diversified rather than unitary and monolithic. In their studies of New Haven, Robert Dahl, Nelson Polsby, and Raymond Wolfinger offered an alternative perspective, noting multiple centers of influence and limits on the power of leaders. Dahl solidified a consensus around pluralist theory with his attack on the ruling-elite model (1958: 463–469). Dahl's emphasis on pluralistic patterns of decision making was chal-lenged by Peter Bachrach and Morton Baratz (1962), who argued that "two faces of power" characterize decision making. One is manifested overtly in the deci-sion-making process, and the other is evident in the capacity of powerful individ-uals and groups to prevent issues that threaten their interests from arising. Using power-structure methodology G. William Domhoff (1978) replicated Dahl's study of New Haven (1961) and concluded that evidence of pluralism does not contra-dict a ruling-class view that suggests that a ruling class often struggles to imple-ment its policies.

Power Structure and Instrumentalism: Mills and Domhoff

The attention of many community studies on power structure has provided an initial impetus for an instrumentalist theory of class. The state becomes an instru-ment in the hands of the ruling class and allows that class to dominate in its own interests. Power-structure studies tend to show that such a class exists, especially in a capitalist society. Direct personal links between the ruling class and the state apparatus are identified. Sometimes the actions and nature of the ruling class are studied. Mechanisms that tie this class to the state are described, and class inter-ests are related to state policies. C. Wright Mills and Floyd Hunter focused on some of these concerns, and G. William Domhoff elaborated their work in greater sophistication. Their work concentrated on showing the social connections among the individuals who occupy positions of power.

Mills's *The Power Elite* (1956) offered a general analysis of elites in the United States. Hunter in *Top Leadership USA* (1959) extended his research on community power structure to the entire United States and utilized empirical research with few theoretical underpinnings to demonstrate his thesis of dominance by a ruling elite. Thomas R. Dye, in *Who's Running America?* (1976), followed this approach, hesitated to confirm or deny the tenets of either pluralist or elitist models of na-tional power, and in fact skirted theoretical implications altogether. Mills, however, provided a more sophisticated study and theoretical framework. Miliband has summarized Mills's central thesis: "that in America some men have enormous power denied to everyone else; that these men are, increasingly, a self-perpetuating elite; that their power is, increasingly, unchecked and irresponsible; and that their decision-making, based on an increasingly 'military definition of reality' and on 'crackpot realism,' is oriented to immoral ends" (Miliband, in Domhoff and Ballard 1968: 5). Mills examined vertical and horizontal dimensions of the power structure in the United States. The structure of vertical power comprises an elite at the top, a middle level of special interest groups, and a mass society. The structure of horizontal power embraces three groups at the top—an interlocking power elite consisting of a political directorate of politicians and bureaucrats, high corporate executives, and prominent military figures. These groups are bound together by common interests, for example, corporate interest in military armaments.

Criticism of Mills's power-structure theory includes liberal and radical perspectives. Dahl (1958) launched an attack on Mills's methods by suggesting a number of tests of Mills's thesis. Pluralists like Rose (1967) also claimed that Mills exaggerated the influence of the corporate elite. Radical critics of the power elite manifested a critical stance as well. Robert Lynd (in Domhoff and Ballard 1968: 103–115) addressed unanswered questions and vagueness about class. Paul Sweezy expressed concern that although Mills appeared to hold the military in contempt, his theory of the military was similar to that of Cold War liberals: "Semi-elitists like Mills—people who think they can adopt the terminology without any of the basic ideas of elitist theory—tend to get bogged down in confusion from which the only escape is to borrow the most banal ideas of their opponents" (Sweezy, in Domhoff and Ballard 1968: 127). He also indicted Mills for blurring his analysis of class and class relations.

Domhoff (in Domhoff and Ballard 1968: 251–278) departed from this criticism and affirmed that in fact Mills's own position ranged between the positions of his liberal and radical critics. The liberals challenged Mills to focus on an analysis of decisions—decisions by the power elite would be based on the input of a variety of interest groups, they argued. Radicals argued that Mills should relate institutions and leaders to socioeconomic classes—Mills did not carry his analysis far enough, they believed. Although both liberals and radicals rejected Mills's theory, Domhoff in Who Rules America (1967) attempted to build upon some of Mills's premises. Empirically he linked members of the upper class to control of the corporate economy, thus affirming the idea that U.S. life is dominated by a relatively unified corporate elite rather than by a "managerial revolution." He also demonstrated the existence of an interacting national power structure through interviews in which the respondents acknowledged they personally knew each other. He showed unity among the various institutions of the power elite. Persons who run the corporate world are involved in foundations, political parties, and civic associations. Domhoff believed that the concept of the power elite is a bridge between pluralist and radical positions. He saw the power elite as an extension of the concept of the ruling class.

In his early study Domhoff utilized the concept of governing class. In a later work he appeared to equate ruling class and governing class and turn to what he described as a Marxist position. In addition to *Who Rules America*, Domhoff's *The Higher Circles: The Governing Class in America* (1970) exemplifies his early emphasis on the governing class. The work looks at the social institutions of the upper class and identifies the members of such a class through contingency, reputational, and positional analysis. Contingency analysis examines the association of people listed in various biographies and social registers with schools and clubs. Reputational analysis is personal and subjective and involves asking knowledgeable persons whom they believe to be important. Positional analysis identifies influential people on the basis of their position in a corporation, bank, foundation, or the like. Domhoff not only identified the upper class through these techniques, but he also demonstrated that the upper class is a cohesive governing class or power elite, by which he meant "a social upper class which owns a disproportionate amount of the country's yearly income, contributes a disproportionate number of its members to governmental bodies and decision-making groups, and dominates the policy-forming process" (Domhoff 1970: 109). In contrast to this early emphasis on the governing class, Domhoff later turned to the ruling class, which he claimed is a term "roughly interchangeable" with power elite (Domhoff 1975: 173). One of his concerns was to show the cohesiveness of the ruling class by studying small-group settings such as summer resort residential patterns, private school attendance, overlapping club memberships, and interlocking directorships in major charitable, educational, and cultural organizations. Domhoff focused on "networks" of clubs and policy groups that are tightly interlocked with corporate directorships.

Domhoff replied (1976: 221–224) to criticisms that his work is instrumentalist and limited to identifying ties among persons in important positions, arguing that his notion of ruling class should be understood in a Marxist context: the ruling class is based on the national corporate economy and its institutions, and the ruling class manifests itself through what Mills called the power elite, a term Domhoff redefined as "the leadership group" of the upper or governing class. Domhoff objected to the characterization of his work as corporate liberal instrumentalist, arguing that his perspective incorporates an analysis of class struggle that is not incompatible with power-structure research conceptualized in terms of networks. Further, Domhoff took exception to leftist critics who allege that his work is "personalistic" and "voluntaristic," and although he proclaimed that he is not an instrumentalist, he acknowledged that his approach allowed readers to view class in static, one-dimensional terms rather than as a dynamic dialectical relationship involving more than a single class.

Marxist Instrumentalism: Miliband

Ralph Miliband's *The State in Capitalist Society* (1969) is firmly rooted in instrumentalism. The work attacks pluralistic theory and contributes to a Marxist theory of the state and class under capitalism. The state is understood in terms of the instrumental use of power by people in important positions. In citing the famous passage in *The Communist Manifesto,* Miliband sided with Marx and Engels: "They never departed from the view that in capitalist society the state was above all the coercive instrument of a ruling class, itself defined in terms of its ownership and control of the means of production" (Miliband 1969: 5). The ruling class of a capitalist society thus holds the reins of economic power and uses the state as its instrument for the domination of society. Miliband wrote about two classes under capitalism—the class that owns and controls and the class that works. Between these "polar" classes one finds two elements of a "middle class," one consisting of professional people and the other made up of businessmen and farmers of small and medium enterprises. In addition, there is a mass of professional people who run the state.

Miliband did not deny the position of Marxist instrumentalism that critics attributed to him, yet he probably would object to this characterization. In fact his debate with Nicos Poulantzas, a well-known structuralist, cast Miliband in an instrumentalist position. Until recently the instrumentalist interpretation of the executive-committee idea in Marx and Engels dominated Marxist thinking on the relationship of class to state. However, Miliband reminded us that Marx and Engels referred to the executive of the state as a committee for managing the affairs of the *whole* bourgeoisie, that the idea of a whole bourgeoisie implies the existence of separate parts as well as a degree of autonomy so that the state may act in the interests of capitalists but not necessarily at their command (1973: 85). This interpretation differs from a central instrumentalist premise, that the ruling class manipulates the state in its own interests.

Criticism of Instrumentalist Theory

Power-structure researchers and instrumentalists have encountered conceptual difficulty with the loose categories that they indiscriminately employ. The terms ruling elite, circulating elite, power elite, upper class, governing class, and ruling class are not always distinguishable in studies of community power and structure. Furthermore, those terms are used abstractly in isolation from other levels of socioeconomic class. This one-dimensional focus on class results in static and sometimes insignificant perspectives.

At the heart of Marxist theory is class dynamism. Marx referred to class in a popular and a formal sense. On the one hand, a social class shares certain characteristics, for example, related to income, so that Marx frequently wrote of the moneyed or industrial class; sometimes he mentioned ideological classes, unproductive classes, uneducated classes, and so on. On the other hand, Marx showed that historically the differentiation of classes occurs with the development of the forces of production and the creation of a surplus product beyond the needs of the direct producers or workers. In this light two basic classes appear—the ruling class and the class of workers—and these classes are described in terms of relations of production. A mode of production is socially structured around such a relationship. It should be clear, however, that one cannot determine a mode of production by the structure of classes in a particular society. Classes are understood in terms of a society's mode of production. Thus, an abstract consideration of certain criteria in order to identify a particular class of a society may be misleading, as is the problem found in the instrumentalist interpretation. Marx offered no formal definition of class, avoiding definitions for categories and abstract ideas.

This emphasis on class and production differs from the emphasis of Max Weber and a host of followers who locate class in the market and relations of circulation. A focus on market implies bargaining power so that classes may compete on common ground, which of course leads to pluralist premises and to a fundamental argument against power-structure theory as well as Marxist instrumentalist theory. This problem was discussed by Therborn (1976). Curiously, scholars in some socialist countries have attempted to combine pluralist and Marxist theory in their attention to the ruling class. Consequently, the contrasting paradigms of bourgeois and Marxist thought have been blurred by this attempt to fuse opposing theory.

Structuralism

Theories of structuralism and power structure differ substantially. Rather than be subject to the manipulation of the ruling bourgeoisie under capitalism, the state may operate in a way determined by the development of capitalism itself. Nicos Poulantzas (1969), for instance, argued that the direct participation of members in the ruling class does not necessarily account for the actions of the state. In fact, he affirmed that "the capitalist state best serves the interests of the capitalist class only when the members of this class do not participate in the state apparatus" (1969: 74).

The origins of structuralism have been traced to Marx and the French anthropologist Claude Lévi-Strauss. Within the structuralist school political and economic currents are evident. Political structuralists like Althusser and Poulantzas focus on state mechanisms of repression and ideology and the way they provide an ordered structure for capitalism. This political structuralism contrasts with the economic structuralist approach, examples of which are found in the writings of Baran and Sweezy and O'Connor. In addition there is the effort to develop a class analysis of world economy introduced by Wallerstein. All of these aspects of structuralism are described below, along with the assessments of them by critical observers.

Structuralism in Marx and Lévi-Strauss

In an essay on structure and the contradictions of capitalism analyzed in Marx, Maurice Godelier (1973) outlined the proximity of structuralism and Marxism. Marx, he claimed, described social life in terms of structure by reference to infrastructure and superstructure. Marx also offered a scientific understanding of the capitalist system by discovering "the internal structures hidden behind its visible functioning" (1973: 336). Godelier suggested that Marx and Lévi-Strauss find common ground.

> For Marx, as for Claude Lévi-Strauss, "structures" should not be confused with visible "social relations" but constitute a level of *reality* invisible but present behind the visible social relations. The logic of the latter, and the laws of social practice more generally, depend on the functioning of these hidden structures and the discovery of these should allow us to "account for all the facts observed." [1973: 336]

Godelier believed that Marx initiated the modern structuralist condition; he carefully distinguished this tradition from the U.S. and British belief in empirical social science in which a structure must be directly visible.

The early texts of Claude Lévi-Strauss clearly reveal the contradictory effects of his work. On the one hand, Lévi-Strauss's attention to structuralism at a time when functionalism was in decline within anthropology "served to shore up the discipline's crumbling edifice." On the other hand, in France "it was appropriated by a left-wing intelligentsia still hesitant in its ideological and political commitment" (Keleman 1976: 859). The thought of Louis Althusser and Nicos Poulantzas is representative of this latter trend and is examined below.

Lévi-Strauss's work represents a significant theoretical contribution to contemporary anthropology, and although it is not Marxist, it has been incorporated into a Marxist model. Jonathan Friedman (1974) analyzed similarities in the thought of Marx and Lévi-Strauss and concluded that although works such as Lévi-Strauss's *Les Structures élémentaires de la parenté* (1967) and Marx's *Capital* are different, "they both attempt to explain reality in terms of what are conceived of as fundamental underlying relations" (1974: 453).

Political Structuralism: Gramsci, Althusser, and Poulantzas

Antonio Gramsci was a founder of the Italian Communist Party in 1921, a parliamentary deputy in 1925, and a prisoner under Mussolini's fascist government throughout the late 1920s until near the time of his death in 1937. During his imprisonment under difficult conditions he wrote a series of political tracts that have been translated and published in English as *Selections from the Prison Notebooks* (1971) and *Selections from Political Writings 1910–1920* (1977). Giuseppe Fiori's *Antonio Gramsci: Life of a Revolutionary* (1970) provides us with a sympathetic and revealing biography of Gramsci's life.

Gramsci's notes on the state provide one basis for structuralist thought and have influenced Althusser and Poulantzas. Gramsci directed us toward a Marxist theory of politics. His emphasis on hegemony or dominance of some social group or class in power has prompted some critics to suggest he was advocating reformist interpretations or undialectically separating politics from economics. Gramsci tended to utilize categories of analysis, for example, in distinguishing between state and civil society, as did Hegel and Marx, in his early work. Gramsci's conception of state is varied, however. Crises occur in the hegemony of the ruling class because it fails in some political undertaking and the masses become discontented and actively resistant. Such a crisis of hegemony is a crisis of authority or crisis of the state. Under such conditions a ruling class may seize control and retain power by crushing its adversaries. Gramsci examined this activity in terms of the experiences of Italy and other nations in Europe. He seemed to be agreeing with the structuralist position that the activities of the state are determined by the structures of society rather than by persons in positions of state power.

> The fact that the State/government, conceived as an autonomous force, should reflect back its prestige upon the class upon which it is based, is of the greatest practical and theoretical importance, and deserves to be analyzed fully if one wants a more realistic concept of the State itself. ... It can, it seems, be incorporated into the function of elites or vanguards, i.e. of parties, in relation to the class which they represent. This class, often, as an economic fact ... might not enjoy any intellectual or moral prestige, i.e. might be incapable of establishing its hegemony, hence of founding a state. [Gramsci 1971: 269]

There are scattered references to Gramsci in the work of French structuralist Louis Althusser. For example, in *For Marx* (1970), Althusser commented, "The jottings and developments in his *Prison Notebooks* touch on all the basic problems of Italian and European history: economic, social, political and cultural. There are also some completely original and in some cases general insights into the problem, basic today, of the superstructure. Also, as always with true discoveries, there are *new concepts,* for example, hegemony: a remarkable example of a theoretical solution in outline to the problem of the interpenetration of the economic and the political" (1970: 114). Althusser's major works in English, in addition to *For Marx,* include *Reading Capital* (with Étiènne Balibar, 1970), *Lenin and Philosophy and Other Essays* (1971), and *Politics and History: Montesquieu, Rousseau, Hegel, and Marx* (1972). Althusser's thought was shaped by an attack on Marxist humanists and by an effort to sharply distinguish the humanist ideas in Marx's early writings from the structuralist formations found in the later writings. Mark Poster (1974) characterized Althusser's structuralism as "an escape from ideology into science," and "a theoretically more sophisticated Marxism that could analyze various segments of society without reducing them all to the economy" (1974: 397).

Althusser's thought is difficult to comprehend, subject to changing conceptualization, and burdened with jargon and philosophical terminology. One essay (1971) on the state and ideology outlines the structuralist approach to state and class and reveals some differences with Marx. Whereas Marx understood ideologies as illusions, Althusser saw them as systematic elements of every society. This perspective and Althusser's elaboration of structuralism are evident in the following summary.

In his essay on ideology and the state, Althusser sketched Marx's representation of the structure of every society in terms of levels: infrastructure or economic base composed of productive forces and relations of production, on the one hand, and superstructure composed of politico-legal and ideological aspects, on the other hand. Althusser referred to this representation as a spatial metaphor, that is, it remains descriptive, and he set forth a different formulation. Following Marx he conceived of the state as a repressive apparatus that permits the ruling classes to dominate over and exploit the working class. This apparatus includes the bureaucracy, police, courts, prisons, and the army, which intervenes in times of crisis. The state then is a force of repression and intervention that shields the bourgeoisie and its allies in the class struggle against the proletariat. Indeed the whole of the political class struggle revolves around the state. The objective of the class struggle concerns state power, for the proletariat must seize state power, destroy the bourgeois state apparatus, replace it with a proletarian state apparatus, and then in the end destroy the state itself.

Althusser thus distinguished between state power and repressive state apparatus, and he identified the structural elements of this state apparatus. In conjunction with the repressive state apparatus he alluded to a plurality of ideological state apparatuses, which appear to the observer in the form of distinct and specialized institutions, including the religious system of churches, schools, family, political parties, trade unions, communications, and cultural enterprises. These ideological state apparatuses operate generally in the private domain in contrast to the repressive state apparatuses, which are public. The former function predominantly by ideology; the latter, by violence. Such diversity should not disguise the real unity of the ruling class, which holds state power and may utilize both the repressive and ideological state apparatuses. These conditions ensure the reproduction of relations of production through historical periods.

> The role of the repressive State apparatus, insofar as it is a repressive apparatus, consists essentially in securing by force (physical or otherwise) the political conditions of the reproduction of relations of production which are in the last resort relations of exploitation ... , but also and above all, the State apparatus secures by repression ... the political conditions for the action of the Ideological State Apparatus. [Althusser 1971: 142]

In a late or mature capitalist society the ruling bourgeoisie has installed the educational ideological apparatus in the dominant position. The schools of an advanced capitalist society have assumed the role of the church in a precapitalist society. Althusser noted the paradoxical nature of this thesis, in view of the common belief that parliamentary democracy with its universal suffrage and party struggle represents the dominant ideological apparatus or force under contemporary capitalism. Lurking behind this democratic facade is the powerful and pervasive educational apparatus.

Althusser's emphasis on structure has evoked among critics the charge that he is a positivist. He isolated social phenomena so that they appear to be static, and critics have alleged that he elevated the scientific method as an absolute means for knowledge. Poster defended Althusser on these matters. "Althusser avoids positivism, I would argue, because he does not leave the choice of historical subject either to the accident of facts not previously uncovered or to a fetish of available methodology. ... In any case, Althusser's investigations seem to avoid both mechanical, economic determinism and the moralism of many Marxist humanists" (Poster 1974: 406).

Girardin (1974), who looked to Jean-Paul Sartre's *Critique de la raison dialectique* (1960) as a basis for a humanistic approach to Marx, contended with Althusser on a number of grounds. First, Althusser distinguished his conception of state from the class struggle. His methodology "cannot rediscover the real world of class struggle ... in the congealed world of superstructures systematized by Althusser, no contradictions can arise since the indeterminations which emerge are always in the last instance controlled from a distance by the ultimately dominant economic structure" (1974: 198). Second, Althusser's "bureaucratic conception of social relationships ... is more Weberian than Marxist." Violence is obscured by the state apparatus, which regulates social relations. The state must be taken over by the working class through legal electoral means, a position Girardin called "reformism" and "a bourgeois view of working class politics" (196–197). "The radical anti-humanism of Althusser, aiming at a scientific reconstruction of historical materialism, has placed him in the reassuring world of objectivity" (198).

Today Althusser's work has been somewhat obscured by the decline of leftist intellectuals in France and England and a conscious desire of many writers to avoid a structural analysis. His ideas, however, stimulated a return to Marx and an effort to revitalize Marxism. His contribution was exhaustively assessed in 1987 by Gregory Elliott, who based his excellent appraisal on a critical reading of Althusser's texts and an examination of the historical context and the political and personal struggles that shaped his thinking, including his ambiguous position within the French Communist Party, his criticism of Stalinism, and his affinity to Maoism under the Chinese cultural revolution: "If Althusser's constructions were problematic, the majority of his criticisms were pertinent and powerful. They released Marxists from more than one conceptual prison, re-establishing historical materialism as a research programme" (1987: 184). Elliott also

mentioned Althusser's understanding of dialectical materialism as "a highly sophisticated anti-empiricist epistemology which posited abrupt discontinuities between science and ideology … and within the history of science … via the category of overdetermination." He noted other achievements: "a reconceptualization
of the structure of social formations which respected their constitutive complexity through the assignment of relative autonomy to irreducible political and ideological regions, the totality being governed by a structural causality wherein determination in the last instance, but not dominance, was the preserve of the
economic; an anti-teleological theory of modes of production as articulated combinations of relations and forces of production … ; and a distinctive conception
of ideology" (1987: 324–325).

Nevertheless, these accomplishments must be balanced against the problems of
Althusserianism: the disjunction between his focus on the maintenance of capitalism and his insistence on the possibility of undermining it through ideological
and political class struggle; the unresolved tension between functionalism
through the apparatuses of the state and voluntarism; the exaggeration of the role
and form of the ideological state apparatuses so as to obscure distinctions between the state and civil society; the inadequacy of his history and proposals for
reforming bureaucratic centralism; the crude indictment of the Western Marxist
tradition; the undiscriminating typology of Marxism; and his defective reconstruction of historical materialism (Elliott 1987: 225, 233, 311, 337). Elliott also observed that Althusser "retreated from the most original … aspects of his initial
project with Marxism, and offered no alternative of comparative novelty and
power" (313); resorted to "an astringent theoretical anti-humanism which oc-
cluded human agency in its prioritization of structural necessity" (325); and also
"queried the Marxist and Leninist legacies and relinquished Althusserianism, effectively effacing the epistemological break whose vindication had been the object
of the Althusserian exercise" (327). Despite these reservations, Elliott concluded
that "The history of Althusserianism … now shorn not only of its original *élan*
but of many of its pretensions and vices, continues—to the undoubted benefit of
Marxist and Socialist culture" (1987: 341).

Elliott also summed up "the continuing productivity and vitality" of the
Althusserian research program by recognizing a number of prominent works and
authors who have been influenced in their research and writing by Althusser, citing among a plentitude of examples, scholarly studies by Guy Bois on Norman
feudalism and analysis of the feudal mode of production; Robert Linhart on reassessment of the peasant question and industrial labor under the Bolshevik state;
Peter Schöttler on application of propositions on ideology and class struggle to
France under the Third Republic; Perry Anderson on comparative historical
study of feudalism and the formation of the state in Western and Eastern Europe;
Gareth Stedman Jones on the English working class; Pierre-Philippe Rey on the
impact of French colonialism in the Congo; Nicos Poulantzas on the capitalist
state; and Göran Therborn on state structure and ideology (see Elliott 1987: 331–

335, notes 9–15 for identification of the major works, too numerous to cite here in detail).

Nicos Poulantzas elaborated an Althusserian structuralist model of the state and class. In line with the French structuralist perspective, Poulantzas believed that the structures of society rather than influential people generally determine the functions of the state. He examined the structure of class in society in order to identify the contradictions in the economy and to analyze how the state attempts to mitigate or eliminate those contradictions. Poulantzas's theory of the capitalist state was introduced in his *Political Power and Social Classes* (1973). Other contributions include his *Fascism and Dictatorship* (1974) and *Classes in Contemporary Capitalism* (1975). Although Poulantzas's writings have been received with interest if not acclaim, it is clear that English and U.S. critics recognize their contribution to a Marxist theory of politics, especially in conceptualizations of state, class, and power. His work, however, suffers from an abundance of formal terminology, abstraction, and a failure to elucidate and explicate many terms. The writing is obscure and often redundant (Barbalet 1974). Despite these limitations, some essential aspects of his thought are summarized below.

In *Political Power and Social Classes,* Poulantzas offered a theory that relates to the functions of the capitalist state and to the impact of the state on the capitalist and working classes. The state functions in several ways to reproduce the capitalist society as a whole. The state maintains cohesion and equilibrium on behalf of the political interests of the dominant class. The state characterizes all social relations as competitive so that workers and capitalist owners appear to be free and equal, thereby isolating them as individuals and obscuring their division into classes. Second, the state attempts to represent itself on behalf of the "unity" of the mass of isolated individuals as if a class struggle could not exist. Third, the state functions to allow classes to organize their own parties, which left to themselves promote internal contradiction and fractionalization, resulting in struggles within the working class and disunity within the bourgeoisie so that it is unable to rise to hegemonic domination as a united class. Thus the structure of the state permits the working class to organize and place demands on the state in ways that may conflict with the economic interests (but not the political interests) of the dominant classes. This demonstrates that the state is not simply the instrument of the dominating classes. Instead the state through its relative autonomy is able to ensure the stability of the interests of the dominating capitalist classes. The state structure stands above the special interests of individual capitalists and capitalist class fractions.

In his *Classes in Contemporary Capitalism,* Poulantzas systematically examined classes in capitalist society. This work has been digested by Erik Olin Wright (1976), who identified three basic premises. First, classes are defined in terms of class practices as reflected in antagonistic social relations, division of labor, and class struggle. Second, classes hold positions in the division of labor, these positions representing the structured determination of class. Third, classes are structured at economic, political, and ideological levels. Poulantzas argued that a new petty bourgeoisie of white-collar employees, technicians, and civil servants has arisen as the traditional petty bourgeoisie of artisans and small shopkeepers has declined. He analyzed the relationship of this new petty bourgeoisie to the working class, distinguishing between productive and unproductive labor. He also looked at the economic ownership and control that the bourgeoisie has over the means of production. Wright attacked this distinction between productive and unproductive labor and argued further that Poulantzas's use of political and ideological criteria undermines the primacy of economic relations in determining class position. He also questioned Poulantzas's insistence that the traditional and new petty bourgeoisie are of the same class.

Other criticisms of Poulantzas abound. Although acknowledging that Althusser and Poulantzas seek to rescue Marxism from empiricist, idealist, and historicist tendencies, Dale Johnson (1978) concluded that structuralism "is seriously deficient in terms of historical grounding and dialectical conception" (41). He expressed interest in the "Weberian-sounding conception of the three-dimensional determination of social class," whereby the new petty bourgeoisie appears as a sort of new middle class. Finally, he indicted structuralism for its static formalism or functionalism in which the "Marxist concept of reproduction becomes transformed into an almost Parsonian preoccupation with 'system maintenance'" (43). Gold, Lo, and Wright (1975) were concerned with the failure of Poulantzas to explain the social mechanisms that guarantee that the state will function autonomously to protect the interests of the dominant class (1975: 38). Amy Bridges (1974) argued that Poulantzas was antimaterialist, antihumanist, ahistorical, and descriptive in his view of the state as a dual structure that is both cohesive and transforming (178–181). Ernesto Laclau (1975) condemned Poulantzas for theoreticism and formalism, which result in a neglect of concrete analysis. In admitting the validity of some of these criticisms, Poulantzas (1976a) retorted with his own criticism and self-criticism. In this process he rebutted Miliband's (1973) charges and argued that the debate between them was based on false and misleading premises.

These criticisms are balanced against the serious inquiry of Bob Jessop (1985) into the life and thought of Poulantzas, who applied a class analysis in his comparative study (1976b) of the democratic openings made possible by the crisis and fall of the dictatorships in Spain, Portugal, and Greece. These events may have influenced Poulantzas to abandon a Leninist position that emphasized a dual-power system in which workers and popular forces build their revolutionary power base outside the state apparatuses and confront state power. In particular, the Portuguese revolutionary period during 1974 and 1975 demonstrated the possibility of a bloodless revolution through penetration and occupation of key state apparatuses. Jessop (1985) noted that this perspective, evident in Poulantzas's last book, *State, Power, and Socialism* (1978), may have inspired some leftist intellectuals in the early 1980s to move beyond structured new social movements and evolve theory within a post-Marxist terrain.

Structuralism and the Middle Classes

Many followers of Marx emphasized only two classes, polarized around labor and capital, and the ensuing dissatisfaction with this simplistic approach dissuaded many scholars from applying class to their analyses of society. Marx did refer to intermediate strata, however, and in recent times scholars have elaborated old and new categories of class (see Burris 1987 for an important and useful synthesis of different perspectives).

Five Marxist and three Weberian approaches to understanding the middle class were identified by Wacquant (1991). The effort to deal with questions unresolved in Marx's reference to salaried intermediaries includes, first, the view of Harry Braverman (1974) and others that the middle class will progressively erode into the working class as monopoly capitalism takes hold. Second is the position of Guglielmo Carchedi (1975), an elaboration of that of Braverman, that delineates the "collective laborer" or the complex coordination of workers under monopoly capitalism; the "global capital" or complex bureaucratic apparatus that controls labor to ensure accumulation; and the middle class that performs both functions of collective laborer and global capital but that becomes proletarianized because of technological changes spurred on by accumulation. The third approach is the perspective of Nicos Poulantzas (1977) that sees the professional, technical, and bureaucratic workers as a "new" segment of the petty bourgeoisie. The fourth is Erik Olin Wright's theory (1978) of contradictory locations in which the new middle class contends for power in a class society through collusion with capitalists or alliances with labor. Fifth is the notion of Barbara and John Ehrenreich that technical and cultural producers form a distinctive professional-managerial class under monopoly capitalism, distinct from clerical and sales employees as well as the petty bourgeoisie, whose "function in the division of labor may be described broadly as the reproduction of capitalist culture and capitalist class relations" (1977: 12).

Three influential approaches represent the Weberian effort to focus on the middle class, which is generally understood as white-collar workers, professionals, and others who fall in the middle of the statistical distribution of income and status. The first, which is similar to the distinction C. Wright Mills made in his *White Collar* (1956), is the approach of David Lockwood (1958), who noted differences in consciousness between clerical and manual workers and suggested that each segment corresponds to a different class. Using an empirical focus, with emphasis on data rather than on a theory of class, he qualified the distinction along three lines: occupation and mobility in the market; position in the division of labor; and status defined in terms of prestige. Second is Ralf Dahrendorf's (1959) view of classes not as economic groups but as "groups of social conflict" whose participation is related to authority association. Only two classes derive from this authority; thus those in between align either with those who exercise authority (bureaucrats) or those who are subject to it (workers). The third approach, represented by Anthony Giddens, refers to market capacities and a structure of three classes: an upper class demarcated by its ownership of the means of production; a working class that holds labor power; and a middle class characterized by its technical and educational expertise (1973: 107). In his assessment of all these approaches, Wacquant reminded us that the agenda for study of the middle class should not be oriented to the search for improved theoretical maps but that we should instead "engage in historical and comparative investigations of how agents situated at various points of the 'middle' zones of social space can or cannot be assembled ... into a collective resembling something like one or several 'middle classes'" (1991: 58).

The New Structuralism

Some scholars prefer not to be labeled with the theoretical legacy of structuralism. Nevertheless, the discourse and theoretical categories of structuralism (social formation, modes of production, and overdetermination, to name just a few) are pervasive in contemporary Marxian literature. The new structural Marxism embodies diverse and often contradictory theories and strives to transcend the limitations of rigid theoretical formulations, reductionism, and intransigent policy, yet it incorporates an explicitly structural framework (see Chilcote and Chilcote 1992). In their *Knowledge and Class* (1987), Stephen Resnick and Richard Wolff illustrated these concerns. In their 1982 review of Marx's theory of class, they emphasized the class process of extracting surplus labor through different forms ranging from primitive communist, ancient, feudal, slave, and capitalist, and they distinguished between fundamental classes (performers and extractors of surplus labor) and subsumed classes (persons who neither perform nor extract surplus labor but who share in the distribution of extracted surplus labor and carry out certain social functions in society). They identified examples of subsumed classes in Marx's writings—merchants, money lenders, supervisory managers of joint-stock companies—and delineated Marx's explanation of how these classes produced neither value nor surplus value; this analysis led them to a distinction of productive and unproductive labor. Drawing from Althusser and Marx, Resnick and Wolff employed the term *overdetermination* to suggest that "each process has no existence other than as the site of the converging influences exerted by all the other social processes. Of each process it can be said that all the other processes that combine to overdetermine it are 'its conditions of existence' ... the class process is a condition of existence of each and every other social process" (1982: 2). This notion of overdetermination led them to an understanding of class struggle, which to them is basic in Marxist theory. In their view, Marxist theory begins with the class process and contradictions that produce struggles in the social formation:

> We conceive each and every class and non-class process of the social formation to be in a process of contradictory change. ... The fundamental and subsumed class pro-

cesses in any social formation define the different class positions occupied by individuals. These class processes and positions are conceived to exist as the combined effort of all other social processes. Overdetermined in this way, each class position is constituted to be in tension, movement, and change. ... We use the notion of struggle or conflict to refer to a particular moment or conjuncture in which the overdetermined contradictions embedded in social processes have fused to motivate intense collective effort to change the process in question. [Resnick and Wolff 1982: 14–15]

Economic Structuralism:
Sweezy and Baran and O'Connor

In *The Theory of Capitalist Development* (1942) Paul Sweezy distinguished between a theory of class mediation and a theory of class domination. Liberal theorists advocate a class-mediation conception of the state, which assumes the existence of a certain class structure and recognizes the state as the mediator of conflicting interests of various classes. Marxist theorists employ a class-domination conception of the state. As the instrument of the ruling classes the state maintains and guarantees a given set of property relations and enforces and ensures the stability of the state itself. In this view the state is an *economic* instrument within capitalism. Specifically the state may act to solve particular crises of capitalism, it may be used on behalf of the interests of the bourgeoisie, and it may serve to blunt class antagonisms and revolution by providing concessions to the working class. Sweezy, whose criticism of power-structure research has already been mentioned, thus alluded to Marxist theory, which had largely been ignored. His perspective of the state as an economic instrument of the ruling classes also accounted for the constraints of bourgeois democracy. Democracy, he argued, brings the contradictions and conflicts of capitalist society into the open so that capitalists may not freely use the state in their own interests.

This perception of state response to economic contradictions also reflects a view of economic structuralism. In this view political influences on economic policy are considered to be of secondary importance. In *Monopoly Capital* (1966) Sweezy and Baran combined instrumentalist and structuralist analysis.

> The particular actions of capitalist groups are seen as being in conflict with the need for the state to act for the class as a whole, so that the actual ways in which the state attempts to absorb the rising surplus are a result of an interaction between the structural needs and the particular interests. But the economic contradictions dominate the analysis and the instrumentalist evidence is interpreted within that framework. Other contradictions, such as those arising from ideology or class conflicts, play a minor role. The thrust of the work, then, is basically that of economic structuralism. [Gold, Lo, and Wright 1975: 39–40]

Baran and Sweezy focused on how the state facilitates the process of surplus absorption. The state acts to avert crises of monopoly capitalism, thereby guaranteeing absorption of surplus.

James O'Connor in *The Fiscal Crisis of the State* (1973) expanded on this view by arguing that the state is a complex structure of authority relations and itself possesses some autonomy. O'Connor did not see the state as merely an instrument for the ruling class or even specific segments of that class. O'Connor argued that the state does not produce but instead appropriates surplus to enhance the conditions requisite for capital accumulation. The state shapes the conditions for monopoly and competitive capitalism. Although the monopoly sector constantly reproduces the conditions for the competitive sector, competitive capitalism occupies a subordinate role to monopoly capitalism, which is the driving force in the productive process.

Class Analysis of the Modern World System: Wallerstein

Somewhat related to economic structuralism is the work of Immanuel Wallerstein (1975) on class in the capitalist world economy. His argument runs as follows. Class is a concept historically linked to the capitalist world economy or the modern world system. This world system consists of three basic elements: a single market, a series of state structures or nations that affect the workings of the market, and three levels (core, semiperiphery, and periphery) in an exploitative process involving the appropriation of surplus labor. Class struggle emanates from the relationship among these levels. "Those on top always seek to ensure the existence of three tiers in order the better to preserve their privilege, whereas those on the bottom conversely seek to reduce the three to two, the better to destroy this same privilege. This fight over the existence of the middle tier goes on continually, both in political terms and in terms of basic ideological constructs" (Wallerstein 1975: 368). In this struggle classes are formed, consolidated, disintegrated, and reformulated as capitalism evolves and develops. This changing struggle is located in the capitalist world economy.

> The capitalist world economy as a totality—its structure, its historical evolution, its contradictions—is the arena of social action. The fundamental political reality of that world economy is a class struggle which however takes constantly changing forms: overt class consciousness versus ethno-national consciousness, classes within nations versus classes across nations. [1975: 375]

Wallerstein expanded a conception of center and periphery that originated with the Argentine economist Raúl Prebisch and the UN Economic Commission for Latin America. He came close to the formulations of the unequal-development thesis of Samir Amin who, however, attempted to give weight to the productive process of capitalism as well as the market. Wallerstein also attempted to move beyond a conception of class within nations, thereby escaping some of the problems in a class analysis of internal colonialism, such as advocated by the Mexican political sociologist Pablo González Casanova, or the attention to national bourgeoisie found in writings by Marxists and non-Marxists alike.

Terence K. Hopkins (1977) clarified and elaborated on this formulation of class in the capitalist world economy. He argued that Wallerstein provided a theory of the global capitalist economy as a world system, not a theory of the development of national economies or of an international economy. Hopkins believed that with the evolution of this world system there has been the establishment of an organized world capitalist class in contrast to alliances among national bourgeoisies. A parallel development has been the formation of an international movement of labor through the organization of a worldwide labor market. The multinational corporations have proved effective in organizing this world system along such class lines.

This imaginative yet somewhat eclectic theory of Wallerstein has been widely criticized for its attention to market rather than to production as a basis for analyzing class relations in the contemporary capitalist world. Wallerstein cited Marx for support of his theory and attempted to disassociate his thought from the ideas of Max Weber. His concern with structure transcended national state boundaries and attempted to explore the roots of the world capitalist economy. Wallerstein elaborated and recast dimensions of the dependency theory and thus has influenced many mainstream social scientists to alter their perspectives of development, state, and class. The reader, however, will discover significant differences, theoretically and methodologically, between Wallerstein and other structuralists such as Althusser and Poulantzas.

Criticism of Structuralist Theory

A major problem of structuralist theory is that it does little to explain class action arising from class consciousness, a concern of Marx, especially in his early works, and of the critical school, which is examined later in this chapter. Esping-Andersen, Friedland, and Wright (1976) deplored a lack of theory that ties political inputs and constraints to outputs of state activity; neither structuralist nor instrumentalist theory solves this problem (1976: 189). John Mollenkopf believed that structuralists have offered useful critiques of instrumentalism, which studies of power structure exemplify. At the same time both economic and political structuralism remain inadequate. First, economic structuralism limits the state to a superficial conception, to a kind of systemic checklist. "It assigns solely economic, rather than political motives to the state in the face of substantial evidence to the contrary. It also projects an economistic 'inevitability' for crises which politics should not be able to allay, but somehow does." Second, political instrumentalists such as Poulantzas focus on the ideological and repressive institutions that sustain capitalism. This emphasis on the political aspects of structuralism leads to what Miliband called structuralist "abstractionism" or "superdetermination." "The state becomes an all pervasive political/ideological realm shorn of institutional location, visible boundaries, or even political struggle" (Mollenkopf 1975: 256). The structuralist work tends to be highly abstract and oriented to conceptual schemes rather than theory. It permits an understanding of the workings of the capitalist state and its agencies and policies. It also allows for distinctions between class and group interests, although Mollenkopf advocated work on a theory of class political action that would explain the aims and actions of late capitalism. Finally, Amy Beth Bridges (1974) summed up the reservations of many U.S. critics.

> A sterile functionalism—marxist or not—cannot inform either social understanding or revolutionary politics. In fact, the structuralist framework, presenting the social formation as self-reinforcing, can lead only to anarchist politics or to the worst kinds of reformism. Those who struggled against this kind of analytic perspective in mainstream sociology ... will find its antihumanism no more acceptable when couched in marxist terms that when it was unabashedly bourgeois. [1974: 180]

Criticalism: Ideology and Consciousness

Although some structuralists like Althusser and Poulantzas dwelt on political questions of state and class, in particular relating to ideology, they attacked the loose conceptions that characterized Marx's early writings as well as a host of successors, most of whom are associated with the Frankfurt school. The brief discussion below returns to the "critical" studies of the early Marx and his followers who concentrated attention on the nature of the superstructure, the activities of the state, ideology, and class consciousness.

The critical school draws from the early Marx who contended with Hegel. Marx's critique of Hegel's notions of state gives the school its "critical" orientation. Hegel distinguished between the institutions of civil or private society (family, for example) and the state but showed that the split between them could be overcome, a proposition Marx argued was false. Marx believed that the state is separate from civil society and is the organization the bourgeoisie adopts for the protection of its property and interests. Despite Marx's criticism, he was indebted to Hegel for attention to a political theory of the state, for elaboration of dialectical method, and, finally, for seeking meaning in the concept of freedom and the unfolding of human consciousness. For this reason critical thought is often referred to as emanating from a Hegelian-Marxist tradition.

What then are the major lines of thought within this Hegelian-Marxist tradition? In the sense that Marx desired to expose the false consciousness or ideology that accompanies the capitalist era, the objective of contemporary Marxism becomes the creation of a genuine consciousness (Cornforth 1963). Marx uncovered the meaning of consciousness in the *Economic and Philosophical Manuscripts of 1844* in his analysis of the alienation of labor. Work is external to the worker who thus cannot satisfy himself and feels miserable, physically exhausted and mentally depressed. The alien nature of work is shown by the fact that the worker produces for someone else, not himself. Eric Fromm in *Marx's Concept of Man* (1961) analyzed this phenomenon, but Georg Lukács in *History and Class Consciousness,* first published in 1923, offered a seminal work on class consciousness. Later contributions include István Mezáros's *Marx's Theory of Alienation* (1970) and Bertell Ollman's *Alienation* (1970).

In the preface to the 1967 edition of his study, Lukács offered a self-assessment. His theoretical formulation emerged through his experiences as a student in Heidelberg and Vienna and as a revolutionary in his native Hungary. The influence of Hegel, together with idealism and utopianism, characterized his early thinking, and although he was steadfastly opposed to the social democratic and opportunistic currents of the early 1920s, Lukács acknowledged that his work tended to view Marxism exclusively as a theory of society and not as a theory of nature. For this reason he overlooked labor as an interacting concept between society and nature. "What I failed to realize, however, was that in the absence of a basis in real praxis, in labour as its original form and model, the over-extension of the concept of praxis would lead to its opposite: a relapse into idealistic contemplation" (Lukács 1971: xviii). Lukács lamented that his work placed the concept of totality at the center, thereby diminishing the significance of economics. This was a Hegelian "distortion" but nevertheless helped to counter revisionist efforts to cast Marxism as science. The revival of the Hegelian tradition also provoked interest within bourgeois philosophy. These considerations exemplify the confusion not only in Lukács's thought but in the writings of others attracted to the Hegelian-Marxist theory.

Lucien Goldmann (1977) in his comparison of the thought of Lukács and Martin Heidegger established Lukács as the representative figure of the break with positivism and the Kantian influence that had prevailed during the second half of the nineteenth century and until 1910. In Heidelberg, Kantian philosophers came into contact with social scientists such as Weber, and at the neighboring university in Freiburg there emerged a new philosophical current of phenomenology under Edmund Husserl. Lukács, of course, became a prominent name in these developments.

> It was at the beginning of this century, around two German universities, Heidelberg and Freiburg, and within what is usually called "the south-west German philosophical school," that a change was effected which was to prove the source of the principal European philosophical currents of the first half of the twentieth century. This change was to take two directions: on the one hand, the birth of phenomenology and, from it, existentialism, and on the other hand, via phenomenology and existentialism, the birth of dialectical Marxism, with Lukács and the Lukácsian school.
> [Goldmann 1977: 1–2]

The thought of Lukács influenced the Frankfurt school of philosophers (Slater 1977), which in turn generated an impact on some of the early leaders of Austro-Marxism (Bottomore 1978).

From Lukács many lines of thought appear. The Frankfurt school carried on in the struggle against positivism. Michael Harrington in *The Twilight of Capitalism* (1976) identified during the Second World War two tendencies opposed to the "scientific" ideals of nazism under Hitler. Theodor Adorno, Max Horkheimer, and Herbert Marcuse represented one tendency. Adorno and Horkheimer in *Dialectic of the Enlightenment* (1944) argued that the Nazi regime, in its arbitrary engineering of the destiny of individuals, reflected practices of the Enlightenment. Marcuse in *Reason and Revolution* (1941) argued that fascism is a totalitarian form of capitalism. Franz Neumann represented a second tendency. In *Behemoth* (1958) he argued that Nazi Germany was under the control of capitalists and run according to their interests and priorities.

The concern of the critical theorists with positivism set in motion a debate after 1961 within German social scientific and philosophical circles. A detailed exposition of this debate, together with essays representing divergent perspectives, was organized by Adorno (1976). One of the participants in the ongoing dispute is Jürgen Habermas who is one of Germany's most outstanding political theorists (McCarthy 1978).

Habermas represents the younger generation of the Frankfurt philosophers. According to Anthony Giddens, Habermas pursued two lines of thought developed by the older generation of Frankfurt scholars: the relation between theory and critique and the developments of Western capitalism. His attention to Marx incorporated the Hegelian influences, critiqued orthodox Marxism, and offered perspectives distinguishable from the positions of Adorno, Horkheimer, and Marcuse. Habermas offered a reappraisal of Marx's understanding of capitalist development, prompting Giddens to comment,

> His reappraisal of Marx, in respect of the latter's analysis of liberal capitalism at least, seems to me to be both too revisionist and not revisionist enough. Not revisionist enough, because he accepts too readily that Marx's account was valid in the 19th century; Habermas' portrayal of competitive capitalism is a rather orthodox one in this regard. Too revisionist, because he writes off too completely the relevance of some central Marxian ideas today. [Giddens 1977: 212]

Tony Flood (1977–1978) referred to the claim of Habermas that Marx showed that the class struggle takes the form of ideological delusion, a novel notion that suggests that class struggle is not recognizable by capitalists and workers alike. Habermas also called for a reconstruction of the manifestations of the consciousness of classes as well as for a revision of theory so as to avoid a mechanistic treatment of the relationship of base to superstructure. These reviews emphasize the significant contributions of Habermas to critical theory.

Critical theory has influenced other perspectives of state and class. Alan Wolfe (1974) tied the Hegelian-Marxist tradition to some aspects of structuralism and focused on alienated politics in an attempt to set forth a new theory. Claus Offe, a student of the critical school under Habermas, rejected both instrumentalism and structuralism as theories that fail to deal with the mechanisms within the state that shape its class character. Offe focused on specific mechanisms such as ideology and repression. Julian Hochfeld (1967), a Polish sociologist, examined consciousness in relation to class interests. His conceptualization parallels the ideal typing in Max Weber rather than the notion of consciousness in Lukács, a position one critic described as dogmatic (Rich 1976).

Statism and Class Struggle

Esping-Andersen, Friedland, and Wright (1976) elaborated on the interconnections among class struggle, state structures, and state policies. They examined ways in which the class struggle shapes the structure of the state and the ways in which the structure of the state shapes the class struggle. They also looked at how the policies of the state shape and are shaped by demands raised in the class struggle. Specifically, they drew upon theory implicit in the work of Claus Offe and James O'Connor.

Offe examined the structure of authority in liberal capitalist societies and argued that political institutions should be analyzed in class terms. First, the bourgeoisie uses its ideology to align state policy with its own interests in foreign affairs, finance, and social areas. Second, action of the state is limited to maintaining public order through the military, courts, and police, thus creating conditions for private capital accumulation. In the advanced or late capitalist society, however, "an all-pervasive system of mechanisms for state intervention has been established" (Offe 1972b: 80). In contrast to liberal capitalist societies in which the bourgeois state limits authority, late capitalist societies are regulated and sustained by permanent political intervention. Thus the state may assume responsibility for managing crises in the economy. Offe contended that the establishment of a "welfare" state implies support of the lower classes, but in fact it allows corporate business to derive far greater benefits (1972a). At the same time the state remains independent of direct class controls. Esping-Andersen et al. believed that Offe's conception of autonomy and state intervention into crisis situations "leads him to ignore the extent to which classes are differentially able to shape the state machinery and voice specific demands for state action" (1976: 191).

James O'Connor's *The Fiscal Crisis of the State* (1973) deals with the relation of the internal structure of the state to contradictions in the accumulation process. He also analyzed the relationship between the class struggle and the internal structure. In particular, he looked at how the class struggle limits the state's ability to rationalize capitalism and how state structures serve as barriers to the challenge of the working class.

The theory implicit in Offe and O'Connor led Esping-Andersen et al. to four propositions as to how state structures are shaped by class struggle. First, they saw state structures as the outcome of class struggle, not simply as mechanisms conceived and maintained for the reproduction of capital and the repression of the working class. Second, these structures mediate, on the one hand, demands to the state from the ruling class and, on the other, state policies that constrain the class struggle. Third, the capitalist class shapes these structures with the objective of limiting the state to intervention compatible with the needs of capital accumulation and of politically neutralizing the demands of the working class. Fourth, these structures are inevitably contradictory and never totally neutralize the class struggle and incorporate the working class into an apolitical state.

Esping-Andersen et al. also examined how the forms and direction of the class struggle are shaped by the state. They began with a typology of the political class struggle, which incorporates aspects of the production process and circulation between commodities. They also considered the "class content," "transformations," and "contradictions" of the political class struggle.

In a critical response to Esping-Andersen et al., the Capitol Kapitalistate Group (1977) reaffirmed the significance of according the class struggle a central place in the historical process that shapes the state. However, they found fault with the methodology, especially the typology, used by Esping-Andersen et al.: "While thought provoking, their typology appears to be static and undialectical, reproducing some of the methodological shortcomings of bourgeois social science." Despite this reservation Esping-Andersen et al. "pioneered the integration of class struggle into the analysis of the state" (1977: 209). Clearly effort in this direction is needed in an attempt to transcend the various schools of theory on state and class and to find both a useful theory and a useful analysis.

The Issues of a Class Analysis

Pluralism continues to influence comparative study. Western specialists of comparative politics ignore approaches shaped by Marxist theory and methodology, and the field stagnates in the face of the exciting and innovative contributions of rival disciplines. Fortunately, we can turn to Miliband, Wolfe, and a handful of other political scientists who are interested in questions of state and class. We find various lines of thought, debate, and a plethora of unresolved issues. As a way of summarizing some of the divergent trends that run through the present chapter, issues of class analysis are identified and discussed: (1) the role of the state and the ruling class, (2) the class categories of analysis, (3) the levels of conceptualization of class, (4) the relationship of base and superstructure, (5) the implications of precapitalist and capitalist social formations.

The Role of State and Ruling Class

Primitive forms of state were organized along lines of kinship rather than of class. Prior to such primitive forms, societies were organized communally and collectively to deal with order and conflict. Modern forms of the state developed in response to the social division of labor into classes, those who produce goods and services and those who manage and profit from the production. The prevalent contemporary form of the state evolved from a period of usury and primitive accumulation of merchant capital to an era of expanding money capital in which the state increasingly serves progressive capital accumulation and the capitalist mode of production. The absolutist state replaced the feudal state as the monarchies of Europe consolidated their rule over the nobles. The bourgeois state evolved from the absolutist state as the emerging bourgeois class seized power and the state institutions.

What then are the principal activities of the bourgeois state? Mandel classified these activities into three categories: provision of conditions of production not guaranteed by the ruling class; repression of any threat to the prevailing mode of production through the use of army, police, judiciary system, and prison; and cohesion of the exploited classes to ensure their acceptance of the ruling ideology. Szymanski (1978) identified ways in which the state stimulates the process of capital accumulation: providing a labor force for corporations, facilitating commerce, stimulating consumption, repressing cyclical tendencies in the economy, subsidizing individual corporations, allowing corporations to regulate their own activities, and providing economic and military assistance to enhance corporate foreign activities.

Given this description of the bourgeois state, the central theoretical issue then revolves around the relationship of the state to the ruling class. In *The Communist Manifesto,* Marx and Engels referred to the "executive" of the state as a committee that manages the affairs of the bourgeoisie. Lenin wrote of the army and the police as "instruments" of the state. Perry Anderson essentially analyzed the absolutist state in an instrumentalist context. Ernest Mandel argued that the hierarchical organization as well as its total structure determines the state's role as an instrument of bourgeois rule. He agreed with Ralph Miliband that in Great Britain advancement to state executive positions is determined not so much by professional competence as by conformity to the norms of bourgeois conduct. Domhoff, of course, believed a similar pattern exists in the United States. These views have been questioned by structuralists such as Althusser and Poulantzas, who suggested that the state functions independently of class forces in order to protect the interests of the bourgeois capitalist class.

These contrasting perspectives reflect the experience of advanced industrial societies, but what of underdeveloped societies that display precapitalist forms? The question is complex and deserving of elaboration elsewhere, but it may suffice to note the findings of some observers.

Horowitz and Trimberger (1976), for example, examined the state in Latin America as a means for transcending the dependency model, which overlooks national differences. They examined the relationship of the state apparatus to the class structure of Latin American societies and concluded that capitalism, and ultimately socialism, can advance only when the state breaks down class barriers to industrialization or creates an independent entrepreneurial class. In the face of constraints upon external expansion, the state must turn inward to mobilize capital; the state must become centralized, efficient, and autonomous. State autonomy requires that bureaucrats not be from the ruling classes nor be controlled by a parliamentary or party apparatus; the military bureaucracy fulfills such a role in a state, which necessarily will be authoritarian. Horowitz and Trimberger distinguished their model from the structuralist position of Poulantzas, then they outlined three patterns: state-initiated national capitalist development, organized by military and civil bureaucrats who gain power through revolution from above; state-initiated dependent capitalist development, under the control of a coalition of military and civil bureaucrats who have broken the power of the landed bourgeoisie; and state-directed socialist development, led by military bureaucrats who seize power through mass revolution, destroy the landed bourgeoisie and national bourgeoisie, and seize foreign investments.

The role of the state in Africa and Asia apparently differs from that in Latin America. Colin Leys (1976) assessed the work of Hamza Alavi on Pakistan and Bangladesh and of John Saul on Tanzania. Both analyzed postcolonial society. Alavi believed that the postcolonial state inherits a strong military and administrative base whose origins are rooted in the metropole. During colonial times the task of this state is to control all internal classes. After independence, the state wins the support of at least one of those classes, and thus it becomes "overdeveloped" in relation to its previous status. This overdeveloped state appropriates a large share of the economic surplus and allocates it to bureaucratically directed developmental activity. In relating Alavi's propositions to Africa, Saul noted the absence of strong internal classes. He argued that the state's independence is due to a balance between internal and external class forces, so the state is likely to be dependent on strong external classes. If the state is strong, the absence of internal classes may make it more powerful. Saul believed that the state bureaucracy is likely to be a new type of class, which appropriates and controls productive resources by regulating them or acquiring private capital. Alternatively, the state bureaucracy may be exposed to contradictory forces as national, working-class, and peasant-class interests confront domestic and foreign capital. Saul used this latter position in his analysis of Tanzania. Leys criticized this stance, arguing that the notion of a "bureaucratic bourgeoisie" as a ruling class is nebulous: "the contradictions of the situation are obscured by this lumping together of different elements in the state apparatus" (1976: 48).

Class Categories of Analysis

The unique conditions of each society largely determine which classes can be analyzed. Social scientists who employ stratification analysis refer to a classification of upper, middle, and lower classes. The identification of such classes usually relates to such criteria as income, status, and education, and the categories of class are used in isolation one from another. Thus stratification analysis tends to be static, focused at any particular time on position within a system of hierarchical levels rather than on a theory of change. An analysis of ruling elites or power elites looks to a small, cohesive, and relatively closed elite that controls decisions of importance and defends its interests in maintaining the status quo. Both elite and stratification analyses are differentiated from the Marxist analysis of class, which assumes that at least two classes stand in dialectical opposition to each other, that conflict is likely to be the outcome between contradictory interests. Marx offered no explicit definition of class but analyzed the structure of classes in terms of each society's mode of production. Marx analyzed society in terms of a dominant or ruling class and a subordinate class. Thus, the feudal lords and serfs were the two major classes in feudal Europe; slave owners and slaves, in the United States prior to the Civil War; and capitalists and workers, in contemporary capitalist society. Class analysis, however, also refers to related classes as well as to elements within classes. At issue is a recognition of Marx's methodology as a basis for class analysis. Otherwise the student may be misguided by pointless endeavors to formulate new theories of class. To facilitate an understanding of contrasting situations, we now turn to various attempts to identify classes within a Marxist methodology.

In *The Communist Manifesto,* Marx and Engels emphasized two principal classes under capitalism—one that lives by owning; the other, by working. In the last chapter of volume three of *Capital,* Marx alluded to the three great classes of landowners, capitalists, and wage laborers, but in the *Eighteenth Brumaire,* he analyzed French politics of the midnineteenth century in terms of shifting class alignments, the monarchy being divided by the Legitimists, bolstered by large landed property, and the Orleanists, supported by high finance, large-scale industry, and commerce. Ultimately a bourgeois republic came to power, supported by an aristocracy of finance, industrial bourgeoisie, middle class, petty bourgeoisie, army, and lumpenproletariat. Repressed were the proletariat and their opposing interests. Marx's multiple use of classes reflected the emerging class struggles of an era in which feudalism and absolute monarchical rule were succumbing to bourgeois class forces, which emerged in the mercantile and industrial forms of capitalism.

The consolidation of capitalism during the twentieth century makes the task of a class analysis exceedingly complex. Although in the industrial nations like the United States classes are more clearly delineated in a mode of advanced monopoly capitalism and multinational enterprise, in the underdeveloped nations foreign capital and technology intrude upon conditions usually characterized as precapitalist. Thus, Szymanski focused on four classes in the United States: the capitalist class, which owns the means of production; the petty bourgeoisie of professionals, small merchants, independent farmers, and artisans; the working class of industrial, rural, and white-collar laborers; and the lumpenproletariat of people who live by means of welfare or crime (1978: 26).

In an analysis of classes in Latin America, however, it is not unusual to find reference to old oligarchies and new groups of petty bourgeoisie and white-collar workers, the urban industrial proletariat. Often an imperialist or international bourgeoisie, tied to foreign interests, is contrasted to a dependent or national bourgeoisie. Such is the case of Aníbal Quijano's *Nationalism and Capitalism in Peru* (1971). Quijano concentrated on a dominant class of landholding bourgeoisie and industrial bourgeoisie, and he referred to upper and middle levels within each segment.

In Africa and areas recently liberated from colonial rule, a capitalist mode of production may be scarcely evident, as was the case in Guinea-Bissau, once a Portuguese possession. Although Portuguese monopolists operated in the colony, no industrialization implanted itself. A small indigenous colonial bureaucracy and a small class of foreign merchants, along with a minuscule urban labor force, constituted the major classes when the nation achieved independence in 1975. Relatively undeveloped, independent Guinea-Bissau was led by petty bourgeois revolutionaries and supported by a mass of subsistence-farming peasants. The basis of their revolutionary organization stemmed from the horizontal and communalistic structures of the Balantu tribe. The Balantus traditionally had resisted Portuguese colonialism and had quarreled with the rival Fula tribes. The Fulas were traders who carried their enterprise over a long distance and in protection of their interests tended to ally with the Portuguese during colonial times. Basil Davidson, in *Let Freedom Come: Africa in Modern History* (1978), labeled such activity a "lineage mode," comprising elements of a capitalist mode yet lacking the force to build fully capitalist formations. Gail Omvedt (1973) also contributed to class theory in colonial situations with her classification and assessment of such classes as an industrial bourgeoisie (small, often nonexistent because of the dominance of foreign monopoly capital); commercial bourgeoisie (a dominant force in urban areas and merged with the rural class of rentier landlords); intelligentsia (Western-educated and often in positions of the colonial bureaucracy); petty bourgeoisie (a subelite of clerks, lower-level teachers, and traders who often became leaders of the national liberation movements); traditional aristocracy (nobles, rulers, and chieftains who cooperated with colonial administrators); rentier landlords (the ruling class on the land); peasantry; and industrial working class.

The present discussion is intended only to guide the student toward establishing categories for class analysis and at the same time to reveal some misconceptions that may arise in such a task. Among some sources on Marx's use of class, see Ossowski (1963), Hodges (1959), and Stolzman and Gamberg (1973–1974), and see Hazelrigg (1972) and Zeitlin (1974), who moved toward a Marxist view in rebutting bourgeois conceptions of class.

Levels of Conceptualization of Class

Dos Santos (1970) argued that Marx intended to analyze the concept of class on several interdependent levels and that this approach is consistent with the dialectical method. Marx situated the first of these levels in an analysis of the mode of production. When this mode and its relations of production are based on private property, then social classes engage in struggle as a result of their antagonistic and contradictory relations. Although this level of analysis tends toward abstraction in its emphasis on theoretical categories, Dos Santos believed that it arises from "practice" and "the concrete relations in which men live in the reality of history" (1970: 176). A second level emphasized an analysis of social structure in which the analysis will be descriptive and concrete, examining specific forms of relations among the components of the mode of production; for example, social forms that are antagonistic to the ruling formation so that there is a struggle between ruling and ruled classes in opposing modes of production such as feudalism and capitalism. A third level relates to social situations, in particular, social stratification or hierarchization of individuals in society according to class as well as to differences in income, profession, politics, and so on. "On this level important problems arise concerning contradictions between *class* interests of a class and its immediate interests; contradictions between its class interests and its historical origins; between its mentality as conditioned by the existing structure, the values of social stratification, race relations, etc., and the class interests that are the condition of its possibilities for class action" (Dos Santos 1970: 179). A fourth level looks at the crises and deep changes that occur in the cycles of capitalism. Dos Santos observed that the prolonged capitalist development leads to tendencies to deny capitalist crises. Mass consumption also obscures class relations since "empiricists substitute mass society for class society" (180). In identifying these different perceptions, Marx, according to Dos Santos, established "a structured system of planes of abstraction ranging from the most concrete to the most abstract and from the most abstract to the most concrete" (180). In dealing with the concrete, Marxism must define general laws in complex terms; the abstract must relate to social reality but not as formal theory, which stresses empirical observation and allows for absolutes, codification, and ideal types.

Relationship of Base and Superstructure

The emphasis that Marxists give the economic base in the analysis of class must not overshadow a concern with ideological implications of class as related to the superstructure. (The essays in Bloomfield 1977 shed light on this issue.) Bourgeois conceptions of state, bureaucracy, and party, for example, may result in some of the misplaced emphasis on elite position that runs through the instrumentalist school, or they may result in the rigid categories of structure and institution that reveal the shortcomings of the structuralist school. Likewise, attention to ideology and consciousness, central concerns of the critical school, must not outweigh analysis of mode of production, forces of production, and the like. A dialectical assessment is demanded.

The elements of class consciousness and ideology are of crucial importance in Marxist politics. Class consciousness refers to the consciousness that members of

a class have of their own interests. Under capitalism, these interests would be defined by the possession or lack of possession of property and privilege. It may be
that a class manifests a false consciousness, believing that its interests are of universal and classless character. Thus, ideology implies the attempt by a class to give
ideal form to a class interest, and this, according to Marx, is a false representation
of reality. Deliberate deception also might be employed in defense of a class interest. Recognition and understanding of deception or false consciousness by an exploited class, for instance, the urban workers, may lead to a revolutionary struggle
for the exploited class's liberation, the overthrow of capitalism. But revolutionary
consciousness may be a highly subjective phenomenon and cannot be described
simply by given formulas and categories. At issue, then, is a need to recognize the
subtle implications of class analysis and to combine and synthesize the various
approaches, thereby avoiding some of the pitfalls of past investigation.

Implications of Precapitalist and
Capitalist Social Formations

In the previous chapter, I alluded to the debate over the various interpretations of
dual society in Latin America. The widely accepted view assumes that the area is
feudal, a remnant of times in Spain and Portugal when the conquest and settle-
ment of Latin America took place and the Iberian monarchies imposed a feudal
aristocracy and system. The development of capitalism in the countryside was
impeded, but commercial contact in urban areas allowed for development in the
cities. Consequently, there emerged two societies, one rural, feudal, and backward, and the other urban, capitalist, and advanced. This view has been defended
on the Left by critics who have contended that Latin American societies have always been feudal in character and continue today as closed, traditional, resistant
to change, and unintegrated into a market economy; that is, those societies remain clearly precapitalist in mode. But, it is argued, a bourgeois-democratic revolution is imminent, which will usher in capitalism and break down the feudal
stagnation. That position has been challenged by those on the Left who claim that
the area has been capitalist from its conception when it was incorporated into the
world market of the colonial period. Capitalism, however, has promoted the present backwardness and underdevelopment of the area, and only a struggle by the
masses against the bourgeoisie and imperialism will lead to socialism and a break
with dependent capitalism. At issue is an emphasis on production, on the one
hand, and on market or exchange, on the other.

Such diverse interpretations challenge theoretical understandings of the role of
classes in the transition of feudalism to capitalism and of capitalism to socialism.
Proponents of the view that precapitalist economic formations prevail in a given
society may emphasize the role of the feudal class elements while looking to an
emerging national bourgeoisie in the promotion of progressive capitalism in a
backward society. Opponents of this view would argue that rural and urban in-

dustrial interests determine the class character of the ruling class and that a national bourgeoisie cannot assume a progressive role in the face of imperialist capital.

This discussion has concerned economies other than those of industrial capitalist countries, but the debate over the transition from feudalism to capitalism has its origins in diverse understandings of the European experience. Marx elaborated on precapitalist economic formations, and Eric Hobsbawm (1965), the English historian, brought this material together with his own introduction. The English economic historian Maurice Dobb presented an overview in *Studies in the Development of Capitalism* (1946), and Paul Sweezy, Dobb, and others debated questions about the transition in the ensuing decade (edited by Rodney Hilton, 1976). Perry Anderson's *Passages from Antiquity to Feudalism* (1974) attempts to move from a theoretical stance to a historical interpretation of the various social formations that characterized the feudal mode of production in the medieval epoch of Western Europe. His sequel, *Lineages of the Absolutist State* (1974), deals with the transition of feudalism to capitalism. Immanuel Wallerstein's *The Modern World-System* (1974) also sheds light on this controversial topic, as does Barry Hindess and Paul Q. Hirst's *Pre-Capitalist Modes of Production* (1975).

Several debates are evident in this literature. The first centers on the origins of capitalism, whether in the rise of commercial life as early as the twelfth century or the beginnings of manufacturing and wage labor since the sixteenth century. The second addresses the question of how capitalism belatedly reached the less advanced nations of the Third World in the face of imperialism and foreign capitalist powers. A third controversy involves the extent to which all advanced industrial and less developed nations participate in worldwide capitalist production and markets. A fourth concern is the traditional antagonism between ruling capitalist classes and the working classes and the extent to which they seek conciliation and understandings in their particular interests, the role of the state in shaping consensus, and so on. Finally, despite past doubts about socialism and socialist experiences, there will continue to be discussion on how to achieve a transition to socialism, on the reformist and revolutionary activity involved in such a process, and on the implications for central planning, market economy, and collective and individual autonomy.

References

Adorno, Theodor W. (ed.). 1976. *Positivist Dispute in German Ideology.* Translated by Glyn Adey and David Frisby. London: Heinemann. Collection of essays that deal with issues relating to positivism and critical theory that have divided German philosophers during the twentieth century. Includes an introduction by David Frisby and essays by Adorno, Jürgen Habermas, and Karl Popper.

Althusser, Louis. 1970. *For Marx.* Translated by Ben Brewster. New York: Vintage Books. One of the more popular of the author's works in English. Essays deal with the criticism of Marxist humanism.

————. 1971. "Ideology and Ideological State Apparatuses (Notes Towards an Investigation)." In Althusser, *Lenin and Philosophy and Other Essays*, 121–173. London: New Left Books. Outlines the structure of state in terms of repressive and ideological apparatuses that serve the interests of the ruling class.

Bachrach, Peter, and Morton Baratz. 1962. "The Two Faces of Power." *American Political Science Review* 57 (December), 947–952. Argues for a look at the "nondecision" and attacks pluralist and decision-making studies of power.

Bahro, Rudolf. 1984. *From Red to Green*. London: Verso. A plea for egalitarianism and collective resolution of societal problems. Anticapitalist perspective in favor of a socialist outcome.

Bailey, Norman A. 1968. "Toward a Praxeological Theory of Conflict." *Orbis* 11 (Winter), 1081–1112. An exhaustive review of the literature on conflict with attention to Polish thought on praxeology.

Barbalet, J. M. 1974. "Political Science, the State, and Marx." *Politics* 9 (May), 69–73. A review of Poulantzas (1973).

Bloomfield, Jon (ed.). 1977. *Class, Hegemony, and Party*. London: Lawrence and Wishart. Papers from the Communist University of London. Includes pieces by Stuart Hall, "Rethinking the 'Base-and-Superstructure' Metaphor," 43–72; and Barry Hindess, "The Concept of Class in Marxist Theory and Marxist Politics," 95–107.

Bottomore, T. B. 1964. *Elites and Society*. Middlesex, England: Penguin Books. A useful synthesis of various conceptions of elite within Marxist and non-Marxist theories.

————. 1978. *Austro-Marxism*. Texts translated and edited by T. B. Bottomore and Patrick Goode with an introduction by Bottomore. Oxford: Clarendon Press. Essays by Otto Bauer, Max Adler, Rudolf Hilferding, Karl Renner, and Wilhelm Hausenstein who were the leading Austro-Marxists. Although there were connections with the Frankfurt school, the Austro-Marxists moved in a different direction, away from critical questions and metaphysical orientations toward the development of Marxism as an empirical social science.

Bowles, Samuel, and Herbert Gintis. 1986. *Democracy and Capitalism: Property, Community, and the Contradictions of Modern Social Thought*. New York: Basic Books. Sets forth a theory of postliberalism in a search for space between liberal and Marxist thought.

Braverman, Harry. 1974. *Labor and Monopoly Capital: The Degradation of Work in the Twentieth Century*. New York: Monthly Review Press. A seminal treatment of labor in the era of monopoly capital. Sets forth conceptualization and examples in clear and comprehensive ways.

Bridges, Amy Beth. 1974. "Nicos Poulantzas and the Marxist Theory of the State." *Politics and Society* 4 (Winter), 161–190. A detailed and devastating review of Poulantzas (1973).

Burawoy, Michael. 1989. "Marxism Without Micro-Foundations." *Socialist Review* 14 (Summer), 53–86. With a response by Adam Przeworski, "Class, Production and Politics: A Reply to Burawoy," 87–111. A critique of the work of Przeworski that shows how analytical Marxists have purged Marxism of its dogmatic elements by introducing the clear and rigorous thinking of analytical philosophy and the logico-deductive models of neoclassical economics.

Burris, Val. 1987. "Class Structure and Political Ideology." *Insurgent Sociologist* 14 (Summer), 5–46. Focuses on the class position of salaried intermediaries and their role in the class struggle. Examines the question of specifying the boundaries between the intermediate class and the working class and their alignment with the bourgeoisie or proletariat.

_____ (ed.). 1988. "New Directions in Class Analysis." *Critical Sociology* 15 (Spring), 57–66. Critique of Erik Olin Wright's *Classes* (1985). Part of a symposium on Wright, including other critiques by Arthur Stinchcombe, "Education, Exploitation, and Class Consciousness," 67–71; Peter F. Meiksins, "A Critique of Wright's Theory of Contradictory Class Locations," 73–82; Johanna Brenner, "Work Relations and the Formation of Class Consciousness," pp. 83–89; and a rejoinder by Wright in his "Exploitation, Identity, and Class Structure: A Reply to My Critics," 91–110.

Capitol Kapitalistate Group. 1977. "Typology and Class Struggle: Critical Notes on 'Modes of Class Struggle and the Capitalist State.'" *Kapitalistate* 6 (Fall), 209–215. Critical review of Esping-Andersen and others (1976).

Carchedi, Guglielmo. 1975. "On the Economic Identification of the New Middle Class." *Economy and Society* 4 (February), 1–86. An early elaboration of the meaning of the new middle class.

Chilcote, Edward B., and Ronald H. Chilcote. 1992. "The Crisis of Marxism: An Appraisal of New Directions." *Rethinking Marxism* 5 (Summer), 84–106. Review and assessment of two moments in the return to Marx: Althusser in the 1960s and 1970s; and post-Marxism, analytical Marxism, and the new structuralism in the 1980s and 1990s.

Cohen, G. A. 1978. *Karl Marx's Theory of History: A Defense*. Princeton: Princeton University Press. A major theoretical analysis of Marx by a prominent historian.

Cohen, Jean L. 1982. *Class and Civil Society: The Limits on Marxian Critical Theory*. Amherst: University of Massachusetts Press. Critical of the thought of Marx and his followers, the author sets out to lay the framework for "a post-Marxist critical stratification theory able to come to grips with the diversity and innovations of contemporary capitalist society without ignoring the Marxian achievement" (2).

Cornforth, Maurice. 1963. *The Theory of Knowledge*. New York: International Publishers. A Marxist synthesis of the nature of mind and body in relation to thinking, language, and logic; of the development of ideas from abstractions to ideological illusions and science; of truth and freedom. Especially important for understanding ideology and consciousness and false consciousness and their impact on bourgeois society.

Cunningham, Frank. 1975–1976. "Pluralism and Class Struggle." *Science and Society* 39 (Winter), 385–416. Contrasts pluralist analysis to Marxist analysis, with a preference for the latter.

Dahl, Robert A. 1958. "A Critique of the Ruling-Elite Model." *American Political Science Review* 52 (June), 463–469. Attacks ruling-elite methodology and defends pluralism.

_____. 1961. *Who Governs? Democracy and Power in an American City*. New Haven: Yale University Press. A community study of New Haven, which emphasizes the pluralist basis of power politics.

_____. 1971. *Polyarchy, Participation, and Opposition*. New Haven: Yale University Press. A focus on polyarchies, generally Western states in which autonomy and pluralism are evident.

_____. 1978. "Pluralism Revisited." *Comparative Politics* 10 (January), 191–203. A restatement of earlier perspectives on pluralism. Here Dahl attempts to combine liberal and Marxist views of imperialism.

Dahrendorf, Ralf. 1959. *Class and Class Conflict in Industrial Society*. Stanford: Stanford University Press. Synthesizes Marx's theory of class and criticizes it in relation to later theory and experience.

Domhoff, G. William. 1970. *The Higher Circles: The Governing Class in America*. New York:

Vintage Books. Utilizing his power-structure methods, Domhoff analyzes the results of his research on the governing class of the United States.

_____. 1976. "I Am Not an 'Instrumentalist': A Reply to 'Modes of Class Struggle and the Capitalist State' and Other *Kapitalistate* Critics." *Kapitalistate* 4–5 (Summer), 221–224. Argues that his work does not follow instrumentalist thought, that it is Marxist in conception.

_____. 1978. *Who Really Rules? New Haven and Community Power Reexamined*. New Brunswick, New Jersey: Transaction Books. Using a methodology different than that of Dahl (1961), Domhoff presents a new analysis and understanding of that city's power structure.

_____ (ed.). 1975. "New Directions in Power Structure Research." *Insurgent Sociologist* 5 (Spring), 1–264. Full issue. Includes studies of various state agencies, socioeconomic connections of government decision makers, mapping power structures, and critiques of power-structure research. Domhoff edited a follow-up issue, "Power Structure Research II," *Insurgent Sociologist* 9 (Winter 1980), 1–142.

Domhoff, G. William, and Hoyt B. Ballard (eds.). 1968. *C. Wright Mills and the Power Elite*. Boston: Beacon Press. A collection of essays critical of Mills's thought, including liberal, radical, and highbrow critics and a response by Mills himself.

Dos Santos, Theotônio. 1970. "The Concept of Social Classes." *Science and Society* 34 (Summer), 166–193. Demonstrates that the concept of social class was not initially formulated by Marx. Shows that Marx did not give systematic treatment to class and reviews criticisms by Georges Gurvitch and Stanislaw Ossowski. Finally, identifies five levels that Marx used to deal with class analysis: mode of production, social structure, social situation, cycles, and class consciousness.

Ehrenreich, Barbara, and John Ehrenreich. 1977. "The Professional-Managerial Class." *Radical America* 11 (March-April), 7–31. An important analysis of the middle class.

Elliott, Gregory. 1987. *Althusser: The Detour of Theory*. London: Verso. A first-rate critical assessment of Althusser, his life and thought.

Elster, Jon. 1985. *Making Sense of Marx*. Cambridge: Cambridge University Press. A comprehensive and complex overview of the thought of Marx. Discounts the theory of value and declining rate of profits; shows weaknesses and inconsistencies in Marx; argues that the basic problem is that much in Marx is teleological and cannot be demonstrated through quantitative and precise analysis. He believes, however, that Marx's contributions are substantial, and he offers revisions in order to make Marxist thought more useful and coherent.

Esping-Andersen, Gosta, Roger Friedland, and Erik Olin Wright. 1976. "Modes of Class Struggle and the Capitalist State." *Kapitalistate* 4–5 (Summer), 186–220. Review of current approaches to a theory of the capitalist state. Critically reviewed by the Capitol Kapitalistate Group (1977).

Flood, Tony. 1977–1978. "Jürgen Habermas's Critique of Marxism." *Science and Society* 41 (Winter), 448–464. A sympathetic review of Habermas's efforts to place Marx within critical theory.

Frankel, Boris. 1987. *The Post-Industrial Utopians*. Madison: University of Wisconsin Press. The author sets out to bridge the intellectual gap between the traditional Left and proponents of alternative social movements. He concludes that the utopian postindustrial theorists advocate a more tolerant, pluralistic, and democratic future, yet are oblivious to the crises and issues of the contemporary world.

Freiburg, J. W. 1973. "Sociology and the Ruling Class." *Insurgent Sociologist* 3 (Summer), 12–26. Examines Western bourgeois thought and Eastern European socialist thought on the question of ruling class and notes common interests.

Frentzel-Zagórska, Janina, and Krzysztof Zaagórski. 1989. "East European Intellectuals on the Road of Dissent: The Old Prophecy of a New Class Re-examined." *Politics and Society* 17 (March), 89–113. The authors discount theories of a "new intellectual class" coming to power in state socialist societies and conclude that in Eastern Europe there is no third road between Soviet-type statism and market capitalism.

Friedman, Jonathan. 1974. "Marxism, Structuralism, and Vulgar Materialism." *Man* 9 (September), 444–469. Besides its attack on vulgar and mechanical materialism, this article examines the structuralist Marxist model.

Giddens, Anthony. 1973. *The Class Structure of the Advanced Societies.* London: Hutchinson University Library. A detailed analysis of past and current uses of class. Examines Marxian and Weberian interpretations as well as theories by Ralf Dahrendorf, Raymond Aron, and others. Reassesses a theory of class and discusses the prospects for a class society.

_____. 1977. "Review Essay: Habermas's Social and Political Theory." *American Journal of Sociology* 83 (July), 198–212. Useful review of Habermas's major works in English.

Girardin, Jean-Claude. 1974. "On the Marxist Theory of the State." *Politics and Society* 4 (Winter), 193–223. Critical assessment of the French structuralist approach to a theory of the state along with other perspectives.

Godelier, Maurice. 1973. "Structure and Contradiction in Capital." In Robin Blackburn (ed.), *Ideology in Social Science,* chap. 15, 334–368. New York: Vintage Books. Identifies elements of structuralism that appear in Marx and Lévi-Strauss.

Gold, David A., Clarence Y.H. Lo, and Erik Olin Wright. 1975. "Recent Developments in Marxist Theories of the Capitalist State." *Monthly Review* 27 (October), 29–43 and (November), 36–51. Comprehensive review of various approaches to the study of the capitalist state.

Goldmann, Lucien. 1977. *Lukács and Heidegger: Towards a New Philosophy.* Translated by William Q. Boelhower. London: Routledge and Kegan Paul. Attempts to portray similarities and differences between Heidegger's existentialism and Lukács's Marxism. Includes a glossary of terms and concepts related to their critical perspectives.

Gorz, André. 1980. *Farewell to the Working Class.* London: Pluto Press. Questions assumptions about the role of the working class in the formation of socialist society, suggests that the importance of heavy industry in society is declining, and turns attention to groups based on gender, race, age, and community.

Gramsci, Antonio. 1971. *Selections from the Prison Notebooks of Antonio Gramsci.* Edited and translated by Quintin Hoare and Geoffrey Nowell Smith. London: Lawrence and Wishart. Especially useful are the selections on state and civil society.

Hazelrigg, Lawrence E. 1972. "Class, Property, and Authority: Dahrendorf's Critique of Marx's Theory of Class." *Social Forces* 50 (June), 473–487. Exposes Dahrendorf's critique of Marx's class theory and concludes with support for Marx.

Hilton, Rodney (ed.). 1976. *The Transition from Feudalism to Capitalism.* London: New Left Books. Collection of articles published during the 1950s and 1960s that reflect a debate among Sweezy, Dobb, and others concerning the transition from feudalism to capitalism.

Hobsbawm, Eric J. 1965. "Introduction." In Karl Marx, *Pre-Capitalist Economic Formations.* Translated by Jack Cohen. New York: International Publishers. A useful overview of

Marx's treatment of precapitalist formations, which introduces a segment from the *Grundrisse*.

Hochfeld, Julian. 1967. "The Concept of Class Interest." *Polish Sociological Bulletin* 16 (2), 5–14. An orthodox Marxist perspective of class and class interest as related to consciousness.

Hodges, Donald Clark. 1959. "The Role of Classes in Historical Materialism." *Science and Society* 23 (Winter), 16–26. Explores Marx's basic proposition that "the division into classes lies at the root of historical modes of production and at the heart of historical materialism."

Hopkins, Terence K. 1977. "Notes on Class Analysis and the World-System." *Review* 1 (Summer), 67–72. Elaboration of how class analysis may be used in Wallerstein's conception of world system.

Horowitz, Irving Louis, and Ellen Kay Trimberger. 1976. "State Power and Military Nationalism in Latin America." *Comparative Politics* 8 (January), 223–244. Assessment of the role of the state in Latin America in light of approaches toward achieving autonomous development.

Jessop, Bob. 1985. *Nicos Poulantzas: Marxist Theory and Political Strategy*. London: Macmillan. A sympathetic, in-depth, and critical examination of Poulantzas's thought.

Johnson, Dale. 1978. "Strategic Implications of Recent Social Class Theory." *Insurgent Sociologist* 8 (Winter), 40–44. Acknowledges advances in structuralist theory of state and class but remains critical of its static implications.

Keleman, Paul. 1976. "Towards a Marxist Critique of Structuralist Anthropology." *Sociological Review* 24 (November), 869–875. A critique of some of the ideas in the early writings of structuralist Lévi-Strauss.

Laclau, Ernesto. 1975. "The Specificity of the Political: Around the Poulantzas-Miliband Debate." *Economy and Society* 5 (February), 87–110. Reprinted in Laclau, *Politics and Ideology in Marxist Theory*. London: New Left Books. A critique of Poulantzas (1973) and an assessment of Miliband (1973).

Laclau, Ernesto, and Chantal Mouffe. 1985. *Hegemony and Socialist Strategy: Towards a Radical Democratic Politics*. London: Verso. Sets forth a post-Marxist position, favoring political parties and social movements rather than the working class, in the search for a politics of change.

Leys, Colin. 1976. "The 'Overdeveloped' Post-Colonial State: A Re-evaluation." *Review of African Political Economy* 5 (January-April), 39–48. Critique of writings on the postcolonial state in Africa, including the work of Hamza Alavi and John Saul.

Lockwood, David. 1958. *The Blackcoated Worker: A Study in Class Consciousness*. London: George Allen and Unwin. An empirical study of consciousness in clerical and manual workers, based on data relating to occupation and mobility, position in the division of labor, and status.

Lukács, Georg. 1971. *History and Class Consciousness: Studies in Marxist Dialectics*. Translated by Rodney Livingstone. London: Merlin Press. A seminal work that establishes, along with Marx's early writings, a basis for critical theory of class and class consciousness.

McCarthy, Thomas. 1978. *The Critical Theory of Jürgen Habermas*. Cambridge: M.I.T. Press. Detailed analysis of Habermas divided into five sections: on theory and practice in our scientific civilization; knowledge and human interests; toward a methodology of critical theory; foundations—a theory of communication; and legitimation problems in advanced capitalism. A biobibliographic study.

McClosky, Herbert. 1964. "Consensus and Ideology in American Politics." *American Political Science Review* 58 (June), 361–382. Defense of the thesis that U.S. politics is characterized by consensus.

McNall, Scott G., Rhonda F. Levine, and Rick Fantasia (eds.). 1991. *Bringing Class Back In: Contemporary and Historical Perspectives*. Boulder, Colorado: Westview Press. An anthology of articles on social class, with an appeal to focus on questions of class in the social sciences. Sections on class structure; class formation; class power, conflict, and struggle; and culture, ideology, and consciousness. They argue that "class has an objective and subjective component, is a process, is defined in opposition to other class processes, and is historically contingent" (4).

Masters, Marick F., and John D. Robertson. 1988. "Class Compromises in Industrial Democracies." *American Political Science Review* 82 (December), 1183–1201. An effort to integrate class conflict into the broader concept of democratic stability. Concludes that economics is the root of class compromise and conflict; politics is relevant to the extent that parties assent to state involvement; and the institutionalization of class relations leads not only to state intervention but to mitigation of class conflict.

Miliband, Ralph. 1969. *The State in Capitalist Society: An Analysis of the Western System of Power*. New York: Basic Books. An "instrumentalist" approach to the state and class by a leading British Marxist.

———. 1973. "Poulantzas and the Capitalist State." *New Left Review* 82 (November-December), 83–92. A review of Poulantzas's structuralist theory.

Mollenkopf, John. 1975. "Theories of the State and Power Structure Research." *Insurgent Sociologist* 3 (Summer), 245–264. Critique of the instrumentalist and structuralist schools. Attempts to transcend those schools by proposing a research agenda for future study.

Mosca, Gaetano. 1939. *The Ruling Class: Elementi di Scienza Politica*. Edited and revised with an introduction by Arthur Livingston, translated by Hannah D. Kahn. New York: McGraw-Hill Book Co.

Navarro, Vicente. 1991. "Class and Race: Life and Death Situations." *Monthly Review* 43 (September 1991), 1–13. Argues that class as a category is obscured in statistical analysis by emphasis on race, gender, and region and the myth that most Americans are middle class.

Offe, Claus. 1972a. "Advanced Capitalism and the Welfare State." *Politics and Society* 2, no. 4 (Summer), 479–488. Examines the contradictions of the welfare state under advanced capitalism.

———. 1972b. "Political Authority and Class Structures—An Analysis of Late Capitalist Societies." *International Journal of Sociology* 2 (Spring), 73–108. Looks at the tendency of states to intervene in late capitalist societies and emphasizes analysis in terms of class.

Omvedt, Gail. 1973. "Towards a Theory of Colonialism." *Insurgent Sociologist* 3 (Spring), 1–24. An analysis of various classes in colonial society.

Ossowski, Stanislaw. 1963. *Class Structure in the Social Consciousness*. Translated by Sheila Patterson. London: Routledge and Kegan Paul. A critical overview of historical and contemporary conceptions of class by a Polish scholar.

Parenti, Michael. 1970. "Power and Pluralism: A View from the Bottom." *Journal of Politics* 32 (August), 501–530. Examines pluralist and antipluralist views to questions of power.

Pareto, Vilfredo. 1966. *Sociological Writings*. Selected and introduced by S. E. Finer, translated by Derick Mirfin. New York: Frederick A. Praeger. Selections from Pareto, *Treatise on General Sociology*, with a useful introduction to the thought of Pareto.

Parkin, Frank. 1971. *Class Inequality and Political Order: Social Stratification in Capitalist and Communist Societies.* New York: Praeger Publishers. Critique of neo-Weberian approaches to stratification and an examination of ideas relating to the nature of social class in capitalist and communist societies.

Polsby, Nelson W. 1963. *Community Power and Political Theory.* New Haven: Yale University Press. A critical and systematic look at previous community studies and a plea for the pluralist alternative.

Poster, Mark. 1974. "Althusser on History Without Man." *Political Theory* 2 (November), 393–409. A useful overview of the central ideas in Althusser's thought.

Poulantzas, Nicos. 1969. "The Problem of the Capitalist State." *New Left Review* 58 (November-December), 67–78. A review of Miliband (1969).

_____. 1973. *Political Power and Social Classes.* London: New Left Books and Sheed and Ward. The author introduces his structuralist theory on state and classes.

_____. 1976a. "The Capitalist State: A Reply to Miliband and Laclau." *New Left Review* 95 (January-February), 63–83. Criticism and self-criticism, taking into account the concerns of Miliband and Laclau in earlier reviews of Poulantzas's work.

_____. 1976b. *The Crisis of the Dictatorships: Portugal, Greece, Spain.* London: NLB. Comparative study of the transitions from dictatorship to democratic rule in Spain, Portugal, and Greece.

_____. 1977. "The New Petty Bourgeoisie." In Alan Hunt (ed.), *Class and Class Structure,* 113–124. London: Lawrence and Wishart. Elaboration of the author's theory on the middle class, which he calls the new petty bourgeoisie.

_____. 1978. *State, Power, and Socialism.* London: NLB. The last book of this author and a clear statement of state and class with attention to class and social movements.

Prewitt, Kenneth, and Alan Stone. 1973. *The Ruling Elite: Elite Theory, Power, and American Democracy.* New York: Harper and Row. A systematic review of perspectives on elite theory, with attention to the debate between those advocating the power-elite thesis and those in favor of the pluralist thesis.

Resnick, Stephen, and Richard D. Wolff. 1982. "Classes in Marxian Theory." *Review of Radical Political Economics* 13 (Winter), 1–18. An attempt to transcend the two-class approach evident in orthodox Marxist work.

Rich, Harvey. 1976. "Marxism as Dogma, Ideology, and Theory in Contemporary Political Sociology." *Canadian Journal of Political Science* 9 (December), 654–667. Examination of three contemporary applications of Marxism to political sociology: the dogmatic application by Julian Hochfeld of Marxist categories to contemporary class structures; the extension of Marxist theory of the state to contemporary bourgeois democracies by Ralph Miliband; and the empirical assessment of working-class polarization in advanced countries by Michael Mann.

Roemer, John. 1988. *Free to Lose.* Cambridge: Harvard University Press. A digest of his previous work, with attention to exploitation in property relations. He relates class to wealth and exploitation and argues that wealth and domination, but not exploitation, contribute to class struggle.

_____. 1989. "Visions of Capitalism and Socialism." *Socialist Review* 19 (July-August), 93–100. In this brief analysis, Roemer argues his thesis that exploitation is the consequence of unequal distribution of property rights. A focus on property rights rather than on the relations of domination at the point of production leads to understanding of exploitation.

Rose, Arnold M. 1967. *The Power Structure: Political Process in American Society.* London: Oxford University Press. Critical of previous definitions of power. The author argues for a pluralistic conception of power in his examination of U.S. politics.

Sitton, John F. 1990. "Citizens and Classes: Political Isolation and Class Formation." *Critical Sociology* 17 (Summer), 3–33. Examines various theoretical positions of classical and current theorists on the question of whether the development of democracy under capitalism will serve as an advance for the organization of workers to pursue their own class objectives. Looks at how capitalist democracy disrupts the working class in the views of Gramsci, Lukács, Poulantzas, Przeworski, and Katznelson.

Slater, Phil. 1977. *Origin and Significance of the Frankfurt School: A Marxist Perspective.* London: Routledge and Kegan Paul. A detailed study of the origins and evolution of the Frankfurt school and its major participants.

Stolzman, James, and Herbert Gamberg. 1973–1974. "Marxist Analysis Versus Stratification Analysis as General Approaches to Social Inequality." *Berkeley Journal of Sociology* 18, 105–125. Argues that a comprehension of Marx's approach to class must include an understanding of the theory of surplus value and of the processes of capital accumulation.

Sweezy, Paul. 1991. "Class Societies: The Soviet Union and the United States." *Monthly Review* 43 (December), 1–17. Two interviews with this well-known American economist who urges a class analysis as a means of understanding rapidly changing conditions in the two countries.

Szymanski, Albert. 1978. *The Capitalist State and the Politics of Class.* Cambridge, Massachusetts: Winthrop Publishers. A useful text on the state and class, with emphasis on a Marxist approach and the experience of the United States.

Therborn, Goran. 1976. "What Does the Ruling Class Do When It Rules? Some Different Approaches to the Study of Power in Society." *Insurgent Sociologist* 6 (Spring), 1–16. Critical appraisal of major approaches to the study of class and power. Affirms that Marx conceptualizes classes in terms of relations of production, not market and the relations of circulation.

Wacquant, Löic J.D. 1991. "Making Class: the Middle Class(es) in Social Theory and Social Structure." In Scott G. McNall, Rhonda F. Levine, and Rick Fantasia (eds.), *Bringing Class Back In*, 39–64. Boulder, Colorado: Westview Press. A useful critical overview of approaches to the middle class in Marxist and non-Marxist analysis.

Wallerstein, Immanuel. 1975. "Class-Formation in the Capitalist World-Economy." *Politics and Society* 5 (3), 367–375. Within a triad of world system (core, semiperiphery, and periphery), assesses the significance of classes and ethnonations.

Wolfe, Alan. 1974. "New Directions in the Marxist Theory of Politics." *Politics and Society* 4 (Winter), 131–160. A review of efforts to formulate a theory of the state. Especially significant is the emphasis on the role of the state as a theme in contemporary political science.

Wood, Ellen Meiksins. 1989. "Rational-Choice Marxism: Is the Game Worth the Candle?" *New Left Review* 177 (September-October), 41–88. Followed by a reply by Alan Carling, "In Defence of Rational Choice: A Reply to Ellen Meiksins Wood," 97–109. A systematic critique of rational-choice Marxism. Observes that the attempt of this approach to reestablish rigor in Marxism has led to a general repudiation of Marxism in theory and practice.

Wright, Erik Olin. 1976. "Class Boundaries in Advanced Capitalist Societies." *New Left Review* 98 (July-August), 3–44. A detailed and critical appraisal of Poulantzas's *Classes in Contemporary Capitalism.*

_____. 1978. *Class, Crisis, and the State*. London: NLB. The author's first book on social classes, including his thesis on contradictory locations of class.

_____. 1985. *Classes*. London: NLB. Deals with criticism of his earlier formulation of contradictory locations within class relations (1978), then examines his new formulation with emphasis on exploitation. The second part of the book offers empirical data and attempts to demonstrate the validity of his conceptualization. Burris (1988) and others provide a critique of this work.

_____. 1991. "The Conceptual Status of Class Structure in Class Analysis." In Scott G. McNall, Rhonda F. Levine, and Rick Fantasia (eds.), *Bringing Class Back In*, 17–37. Boulder, Colorado: Westview Press. Distinguishes between macro and micro approaches to class and justifies his micro approach as a basis for building analytical power in concrete analysis. Elaborates on his own commitment to a Marxian conception of class and compares and contrasts the Marxian and Weberian conceptions.

Zeitlin, Maurice. 1974. "Corporate Ownership and Control: The Large Corporation and the Capitalist Class." *American Journal of Sociology* 79 (March), 1073–1119. Critique of various theories on ownership and control of large corporations in an attempt to suggest an approach for research on the dominant class in the United States.

PART FOUR

Conclusion

9

Political Economy
and a Reconstitution
of Comparative Politics
and Political Science

This book initially argues that comparative politics embraces all questions of politics and that the study of politics cannot be isolated from social and economic questions. The mainstream literature of comparative politics, however, often ignores these propositions, yet it enhances and perpetuates the ethnocentric and static paradigm that originated in nineteenth-century positivism and now pervades contemporary Western social science. I have summarized the content of this literature by reference to theories of system and state, development and underdevelopment, culture, and class and have synthesized the major criticisms of these theories. This critique exposes the weaknesses and contradictions of the mainstream literature and paradigm and identifies the attempts of scholars to move comparative politics toward alternative approaches. In their search for an alternative, these scholars inevitably have turned to Marx and to questions of political economy. Marx's critique of political economy drew on methodology alien to bourgeois social science but in turn established a counterparadigm that influenced generations of future scholarship.

In this concluding chapter I focus on political economy and summarize the discussion of the earlier chapters by reference to major thinkers and ideas. First, I review some definitions of political economy and identify a problem central to it, and then I explore several possibilities for transcending that problem. Second, I examine the epistemological origins and strains that have shaped the intellectual traditions of political economy from classical to modern times, in particular, with a focus on Marx's assessment of those efforts. Last, I call for a new synthesis of political economy, suggesting lines of inquiry that may be pursued in the study of comparative and international political economy and identifying the major thinkers who shape our focus on political economic themes today. An attempt is made to distinguish between non-Marxist and Marxist thought so that academics and their students clearly perceive the methodologies and values upon which their investigations are based.

Toward a Marxist Understanding of Political Economy

Webster's Third New International Dictionary simply defines political economy as a "social science dealing with the interrelationship of political and economic processes." Economists usually stress the economic ramifications of political economy. Mandel, for example, dated political economy to "the development of a society based on petty commodity production" (1968: 2:692). Marx's major work, *Capital,* is subtitled "A Critique of Political Economy" and emphasizes commodities, money, surplus value, and accumulation of capital. In his preface to *A Contribution to the Critique of Political Economy,* Marx began with such terms as capital, landed property, and wage labor (1904: 9). In his introduction, Marx focused on "all material production by individuals as determined by society" (265), and he indicted his predecessors Adam Smith and Pierre Joseph Proudhon, among others, for basing their conceptions of political economy upon illusions of an eighteenth-century society of free competition in which the individual appears liberated from the constraints of nature. Marx reminded us that this notion of individual freedom evolved with the breakup of feudal forms of society and, since the sixteenth century, with the creation of new forces of production. By the eighteenth century, bourgeois society had implanted itself. It was a period in which the view of the isolated individual prevailed, yet was one in which the interrelationships of individual and society had reached such a high level that the individual could develop only in society, not in isolation from it. Against this illusion of individualism, personified in Daniel Defoe's *Robinson Crusoe,* Marx set his critique of the early bourgeois conceptions of political economy. The work of Adam Smith tended to perpetuate this bourgeois conception, influencing David Ricardo whose theory of value served the utopian socialists such as Robert Owen in England and Pierre Joseph Proudhon in France. Marx's discovery of Ricardo's thought led him to a reassessment, critique, and a new understanding of political economy.

If economics has dominated the theories of political economy, what about politics? Webster's dictionary identifies political economy in the eighteenth century as a field of government concerned with directing policies toward the enhancement of government and community wealth. The dictionary adds that in the nineteenth century political economy was a social science related to economics but primarily concerned with government rather than commercial or personal economics. Curiously, no great tradition of political economy seems to have established itself in the discipline of government or political science, and only recently has it come in vogue. During the early decades of the twentieth century, the work of political scientists tended to be more descriptive than theoretical and focused on formal legal and governmental institutions. The work of the midtwentieth century followed in this tradition but also turned attention to informal institutions and processes and to problems often limited in scope and significance. The contemporary revival of interest in political economy is more the consequence of efforts by radical economists and sociologists than of efforts by political scientists.

As late as 1970 the *International Encyclopedia of the Social Sciences* conspicuously neglected to include an article on political economy, and David Easton, writing on political science, failed to mention political economy. Easton described political science as a discipline in search of an identity, and he acknowledged the discipline's debt to Marx for differentiating between state and society. "In part, political science could emerge as a discipline separate from the other social sciences because of the impetus Marx had given to the idea of the difference between state and society, an idea virtually unheard of before his time" (Easton 1968: 295). In his critique of Hegel, Marx examined the emergence of the state in modern times. The separation between civil society and the state, he argued, was a modern phenomenon reinforced by capitalism. Although Easton credited Marx with this insight, Easton himself influenced and set in motion the movement in political science to discard the state as a concept, replacing it with political system. The Marxist understanding of state had also been denuded of its significance by the attention of German positivist political scientists who emphasized the legal and constitutional aspects of the state and influenced the early U.S. political scientists.

In his political and economic studies, Marx discovered this conception of the state. Early in the 1840s, embarrassed by his ignorance on economic questions, Marx shifted his attention from jurisprudence to material interests. "I was led by my studies to the conclusion that legal relations as well as forms of state could neither be understood by themselves, nor explained by the so-called general progress of the human mind, but that they are rooted in the material conditions of life" (Marx 1904: 11). In 1845 and 1846 Marx and Engels related their conception of the state to the productive base of society through successive periods of history. They examined the interests of the individual, the individual family, and the communal interests of all individuals. Division of labor and private property tend to promote contradictions between individual and community interests so that the latter takes on an independent form as the state separates from the real interests of individual and community. In showing this separation of state from society, Marx and Engels argued that we should not look for categories in every period of history; that would be idealistic. Instead we must be able to explain the formation of ideas from material practice; we should examine the whole or the totality of interrelationships between material production and the state along with its forms of consciousness, religion, and the like.

This conception of history depends on our ability to expound the real process of production, starting out from the material production of life itself, and to comprehend
the form of intercourse connected with this and created by this mode of production
... , as the basis of all history; and to show it in its action as State, to explain all the
different theoretical products and forms of consciousness, religion, philosophy, ethics, etc, etc. and trace their origins and growth from that basis; by which means, of
course, the whole thing can be depicted in its totality. [Marx and Engels 1970: 58]

Marx and Engels are quoted to show that in this early period they had worked
out a conception of base and superstructure that Marx later delineated in 1859
(Marx 1904: 11–13). Accordingly, the base or economic structure of society becomes the real foundation on which people enter into essential relations over
which they exercise little control. In contrast, the legal and political superstructure is a reflection of that base, and changes in the economic foundation bring
about transformations in the superstructure. The famous passage in the preface
to *A Contribution to the Critique of Political Economy,* in which this conception of
base and superstructure is depicted, has been attacked as determinist, dogmatic,
and static. Admittedly Marx's synthesis of his own perspective appears to reduce
societal relationships to a dichotomy of categories and to simplistic formulations.
Yet one also finds in this passage the essential concepts of Marxism as well as a departure point for comprehending the relationship of politics and economics. We
turn to these concepts below, but the dubious academic and student should also
read Marx's writings extensively in order to capture the depth and insight that his
orientation to political economy has provided us.

Although a focus on political economy may help to bridge the gap that today
divides politics from economics, the problem of the separation of politics into
comparative and international fields should be addressed. Traditionally, comparative politics looked at the role of government and the state, but in the late 1950s
specialists in the field determined that the concept of political system should replace that of state. Influenced by Easton, Gabriel Almond and others believed that
the concept of state was limited by legal and institutional meanings. As a more
neutral term, the use of system diverted attention from class society, from the relationship of different classes to the means of production and productive forces.
Today the use of system usually pertains to a nation, and comparative politics
tends toward configurative and analytical country studies. System also was employed in the study of international politics, notably by Richard Snyder and Morton Kaplan. Alongside the systems approach, the conventional historic, geopoliti-
cal, behavioral, and balanced-power or equilibrium approaches are evident in the
field of international politics. These approaches generally emphasize politics and
conspicuously overlook economic considerations. When international politics
addresses questions of imperialism or dependency, however, perspectives on political economy become possible.

Once we turn to imperialism and dependency, however, still another problem
confronts us. The First and Second Worlds are separated from a Third World and,
sometimes, even a Fourth World. Developed or advanced nations are contrasted

with developing, underdeveloped, or less developed nations. A look at capitalism on a world scale often leads to an examination of activity in nations of the industrial or modern center as well as in the backward nations of the periphery. External considerations are distinguished from internal ones, or metropolises from satellites. Rarely does synthesis adequately integrate these apparently dichotomous areas or phenomena as we succumb to segmented rather than holistic perspectives. An exception to this practice is Paul Kennedy's *The Rise and Fall of the Great Powers* (1987). Clearly there is a need to transcend these problems. A solution is possible with pedagogy, theory, method, and concept, and we briefly turn to each of these concerns.

Pedagogy

Following in the tradition of Thomas Kuhn, awareness of paradigmatic differences may lead to new directions in teaching and learning (Deol 1976). Kuhn suggested that scientific practice is guided by paradigms. A paradigm is the perspective of the world generated by the scientific community and includes beliefs and commitments to theory, methodology, method, and concept.

I have characterized the dominant mainstream paradigm of political science today. The origins of this paradigm are found in the positivist traditions that influenced many thinkers of the late nineteenth century and the behaviorists of the twentieth century. Their thought contributed to the separation of fact from value in the contemporary study of politics. The paradigm also assimilates the liberal premise that every person is entitled to hold and profess an opinion. Liberty of conscience and secularism are ideals of the paradigm and buttress the prevailing U.S. view that pluralism and consensus pervade politics. The thought of Max Weber has been influential for this view. In contrast, the effort to formulate an alternative paradigm may be traced to its historicist origins and the antipositivistic reactions to the present century. Radical alternative thought draws its assumptions primarily from Marxist thought.

Theory

Marxist thought is holistic, broadly ranged, unified, and interdisciplinary in contrast to the ahistorical, compartmentalized, and often narrow parameters of the mainstream paradigm. A recognition of these differences allows us to make some distinctions between the Marxist and bourgeois influences that have shaped the epistemological strains of political economy over the past century as well as distinctions among the major lines of inquiry that can be suggested for our proposal to combine comparative with international political economy. My use of Marxism is intended to be open and flexible since I believe that Marx himself considered Marxism to be unfinished and in a state of flux, subject to change and adjustment in accordance with reality and practical experience.

Method

Dialectics may be employed as a method in our search for a theory of Marxism. The vulgar Marxist assumption promoted by Stalinists and others that dialectics inevitably leads to scientific truth should be rejected; so also should the view of materialist Marxists who cast aside dialectics as unscientific. Marx believed that dialectics should be combined with a materialist, not an idealist, view of history.

Hegel's dialectic was idealist and mystical and was set forth rigidly as a system. Marx's dialectic was intended to be a flexible method of analysis, not a dogma or a complete and closed system. Dialectics allows for the building of theory upon new facts as well as for the interpreting of facts in relation to new theory. Dialectics does not need to be intended as a set of universal laws that solve all problems and relate to all knowledge of past and present history. There is no precise formula for dialectical inquiry, but some guidelines might be employed. For example, always look for the interconnections of problems to all of society, but avoid dealing with problems in isolation. Always approach problems in a dynamic, not a static, way by examining their origin and evolution. Always identify opposing forces, their relationship and conflict. Always explain the relation of quantitative to qualitative changes and vice versa. Always ask if one aspect may be eliminated when it has eliminated or negated an opposing aspect or if a new aspect may supersede or include an old aspect. Such guidelines, even in abstract form, may lead to questions that can be asked about everyday problems. Such guidelines serve as the foundation for a scientifically viable method, in the sense indicated by Marx, who emphasized that the study of political economy necessitates concreteness, unity of many elements, and synthesis. A category or a concept treated in isolation leads to abstraction, but the method of political economy must combine abstract definition with concrete synthesis.

> The concrete is concrete, because it is a combination of many objects with different destination, i.e. a unity of diverse elements. In our thought, it therefore appears as a process of synthesis, as a result, and not as a starting point, although it is the real starting point and, therefore, also the starting point of observation and conception … the abstract definitions lead to the reproduction of the concrete subject in the course of reasoning. [Marx 1904: 293]

Concept

If theory is Marxist, and the method is dialectical, then what concepts are useful to comparative and international political economy? Some of the essential concepts are defined in Table 9.1; these concepts, of course, should be utilized in relation to each other. Marxist methodology includes a plethora of concepts. Necessary production, for example, satisfies the basic human needs for food, drink, and so on. Surplus production evolved with inventions and new knowledge that made possible increases in the productivity of labor. Surplus production led to the division and specialization of labor. Changes in the forces of production affected rela-

TABLE 9.1
Concepts of Political Economy

Economic Base	Political Superstructure
"The sum total of these relations of production constitutes the economic structure of society—the real foundation, on which rise legal and political superstructures and to which correspond definite forms of social consciousness." (Marx 1904: 11)	

Mode of Production: the mix of productive forces and relations of production among people in society at a given time in history. Examples include primitive communism, feudalism, capitalism, and socialism.

State: the legal forms and instruments, such as police and standing army, that maintain class rule.

Forces of Production: the productive capacity, including plant and machinery, technology, and labor skill.

Class: large groups of people distinguishable from one another by relations to means of production, division of labor, share of wealth, and position. Marx identified three large classes: wage laborers, capitalists, and landowners.

Relations of Production: the division of labor that puts productive forces in motion and whose activity is related to property and ownership of means of production.

Ideology (or false consciousness): related to legal, political, religious, and philosophical forms.

Means of Production: the tools, land, buildings, and machinery with which workers produce material goods for themselves and society.

---

tions of production so that revolution and class struggle became possible at certain junctures of history. As Marx described this process,

> At a certain stage of their development, the material forces of production in society come in conflict with the existing relations of production, or—what is but a legal expression for the same thing—with the property relations within which they had been at work before. From forms of development of the forces of production these relations turn into their fetters. Then comes the period of social revolution. With the change of the economic foundation the entire immense superstructure is more or less rapidly transformed. In considering such transformations the distinction should always be made between the material transformation of the economic conditions of production which can be determined with the precision of natural science, and the legal, political, religious, aesthetic or philosophic—in short ideological forms in which men become conscious of this conflict and fight it out. ... No social order ever disappears before all the productive forces for which there is room in it have been developed; and new higher relations of production never appear before the material conditions of their existence have matured in the womb of the old society. [Marx 1904: 12]

Let me summarize my thinking to this point. First, I have advocated that inquiry be holistically and historically oriented rather than limited to segments and current affairs. I seek synthesis and overview in the search for an understanding and explanation of the problems and issues of society. Second, I believe that the study of politics should be combined with economics. Distinctions between poli-

TABLE 9.2
Phases in the Theory of Political Economy

Petty commodityism
Mercantilism
Classical liberalism
Utopian socialism
Marxism
Marginalism and neoclassicalism
Keynesianism
Post-Keynesianism
Neo-Marxism

tics and economics as well as between the fields of comparative and international politics in political science often lead to confusion and a distortion of reality. Theoretical and conceptual difficulties also arise with such dichotomous terms as center and periphery, metropolis and satellite. I suggest the use of dialectics as a method in the hope that dynamic and integrated analysis will ensue. Third, contrasting methodologies are identifiable in the study of political economy—orthodox and radical methodologies, which generate sharply different questions and explanations. I argue for a distinction between Marxist and non-Marxist criteria in order to perceive the differences between those methodologies. I eschew dogmatic and inflexible interpretations and acknowledge the failure of much of the scholarly work to clarify concepts and theory. I note a tendency to rely on fuzzy notions of politics and economics as well as on impressionistic observations and descriptions. Thus, I see Marxism as a methodology rather than an ideology and as such hope to diffuse some of the polarization that the term evokes. At the same time, I believe that academics and students can legitimately pursue inquiry along Marxist as well as non-Marxist lines. Thus I now turn to a discussion of the epistemological origins and strains of political economy in an effort to show the differences between those two lines of inquiry.

Origins and Evolution of Political Economy

The origins and evolution of political economy are identifiable in historical phases as portrayed in Table 9.2, and this discussion draws from various sources. E. K. Hunt (1972) offered a very general but comprehensive overview, which is especially useful to beginning students. Paresh Chattopadhyay (1974) reviewed varying interpretations of political economy from its earliest usage to the present. Daniel R. Fusfeld (1966) traced the evolution of economic thought in a similar fashion, but in more depth and detail. Although Robert L. Heilbroner (1961) examined the lives, times, and ideas of specific economic thinkers, including Smith,

Ricardo, Marx, Veblen, and Keynes, Ronald L. Meek (1956) focused on studies on the labor theory of value as the foundation for understanding political economy. He began with Aquinas, briefly reviewed the contributions of mercantilist writers, and then emphasized the thought of Smith, Ricardo, and Marx. Meek also examined the critics of Marxist political economy, a concern that pervades Nikolai Bukharin's (1927) treatment of the theory of value. Among all these writers, Ernest Mandel (1968: 2, chap. 18:690–730) has provided a comprehensive interpretation and summary of developments in political economy from ancient times until today. All these works emphasize the theoretical, conceptual, and methodological differences between bourgeois and Marxist political economy. A recognition of these differences may assist us in turning to past thought in an effort to constitute a contemporary understanding of political economy.

The following outline is necessarily sketchy, but it is intended to be a general overview of the major thinkers, trends, and influences that have shaped the conceptions of political economy. In short, the following remarks serve as a guide to the past in order to facilitate those seeking a contemporary understanding of political economy. Mandel (1968: 2:692) dated the origin of political economy to petty commodity production. Once commodity production responds to market and money appears, then fluctuations in prices occur, some producers fall into debt, and primitive communal relations begin to dissolve. The major thinkers and ideas that shaped a theory of political economy from ancient to modern times are identified below.

Theorists of the Ancient and Middle Ages

Petty commodity production seems to have first emerged in ancient China and Greece. Mang-Tsze in China and Plato and Aristotle in Greece attempted to analyze the instability that accompanied petty commodity production and to find ways to overcome it on behalf of the communal society. They recognized the impact of the division of labor on commodity production and were able to distinguish between use value and exchange value. Aristotle in particular identified this dual concept of commodity. Mang-Tsze believed that agricultural labor was the source of value, and Plato came close to offering "a real theory of labor value" (Mandel 1968: 2:694). The expansion of petty commodity production in the Middle Ages stimulated the scholastic theologians Albert Magnus and Thomas Aquinas to set forth the "canonist approach to the value problem" (Meek 1956: 12). Aquinas sought to find a "just" price, thereby justifying the merchant's profit and defending the established order. In the face of international trade and money, this medieval concept of just price lost its significance. Duns Scotus, another scholastic thinker, worked with a theory of exchange value based on labor, and Abd-al-Rahman-Ibn-Khaldun, an Islamic philosopher, elaborated a historical-materialist view of history (Mandel 1968: 2:697).

The Mercantilists

Between the fourteenth and seventeenth centuries, great advances in political economy were not evident. The principal concern was the nature of wealth in an impersonal system of markets. The transformation of Europe from feudalism to a profit-oriented market economy of buyers and sellers was marked by a period that witnessed the discovery and conquest of new geographical areas, new flows of capital to and from the New World, and the rise of monarchs and merchants who promoted nationalism, undermined local barriers to commerce, and benefited from foreign trade and the erosion of the power of the old order of church and nobility.

Mercantilist writings of the period pragmatically analyzed how nations produce wealth. They assumed that regulation and control were necessary in order to constrain the selfish individualism that would lead to less wealth. Their attention was to a credit balance of payments, a favorable trade balance, manufacturing, and fertile soil. The early mercantilists described economic life in terms of a circulation of commodities, and writers in the late seventeenth and eighteenth centuries addressed questions about the social surplus product that became evident with the growth in manufacturing and technology in agriculture. Two strains of political economy appeared, according to Mandel. One, the British school, was represented by William Petty (*Political Arithmetic*, 1631), who concentrated his analysis on the agricultural origins of surplus value. Petty wrote about rent, not profit, while the mercantilists in general encountered difficulty in reconciling the relationship of labor and land. The French Physiocratic school, represented by Pierre Boisguillebert (*Détail de la France*, 1695), constituted the other strain. Boisguillebert emphasized agricultural labor as the only source of value. François Quesnay (*Economic Table*, 1758), a leading Physiocrat, argued against the mercantilist assumption that wealth springs from trade and industry and placed emphasis on the surplus produced in agriculture. He advocated that taxes be paid by the landowners, not the small farmers, merchants, and manufacturers who were considered to be productive. Although he did not consider industrial capital as significant and instead emphasized communal profit, Nicholas Barbon (*A Discourse of Trade*, 1690) related the value of a commodity to the cost of making goods. Meek believed Barbon represents a transition from mercantilism to the classical approach of Adam Smith and others.

The Classical Liberals

The English thinkers Dudley North (*Discourses Upon Trade*, 1691) and John Locke contributed to the economic liberalism of the classical theory developed by Smith (Fusfeld 1966). North criticized the nationalistic policies of mercantilism and advocated free trade. Locke tied labor to private property and wealth, arguing that production is the consequence of individual effort to satisfy human needs and that the worker should be able to use or consume his or her own product. Liberals believed that private property should be protected and that the production of wealth was based on the incentive to work that the right to property instilled in the individual. They agreed that individual initiative must be free of mercantilist constraints.

Adam Smith consolidated these ideas into classical political economy. In his *Inquiry into the Nature and Causes of the Wealth of Nations* (1776), he brought together the major themes of commodity, capital and value, simple and complex labor. He was the first to formulate a labor theory of value "which reduces the value of commodities to the amounts of labour contained in them" (Mandel 1968: 2:701–702). Smith identified laws of the market that explain the drive of individual self-interest in a competitive milieu and how this results in goods desired by society according to demand and the price it is willing to pay. Individualism signified order, not chaos, in the market economy as Smith envisaged a competitive market equilibrium.

David Ricardo in *Principles of Political Economy and Taxation* (1817) was both a disciple and critic of Smith, and he offered refinements to political economy. Ricardo advocated the accumulation of capital as the basis for economic expansion. He believed that restrictions on private investment should be eliminated and that governments should not intervene in the economy. He applied these principles to the international political economy, arguing that a division of labor and free trade policies would benefit all nations. Thus, he related Smith's ideas of orderly growth and market equilibrium to the international economic system. He also noted the conflict between the interests of landlords and capitalists—the interests of the landlord were opposed to the community, the interests of the capitalist were favorable to it. Engels reflected on the importance of Ricardo's work, especially its influence on socialist interpretations of political economy.

> In so far as modern socialism, no matter of what tendency, starts out from bourgeois political economy, it almost exclusively links itself to the Ricardian theory of value. The two propositions which Ricardo proclaimed in 1817 right at the beginning of his *Principles*, (1) that the value of any commodity is purely and solely determined by the quantity of labour required for its production, and (2) that the product of the entire social labour is divided among the three classes: landowners (rent), capitalists (profit) and workers (wages), had ever since 1821 been utilized in England for socialist conclusions, and in part with such sharpness and decisiveness that this literature, which has now almost disappeared, and which to a large extent was first rediscovered by Marx, remained unsurpassed until the appearance of *Capital*. [Preface to Marx 1955: 6]

Among other classical liberals were Thomas R. Malthus (*Principles of Political Economy*, 1820) and Jeremy Bentham (*Introduction to the Principles of Morals and Legislation*, 1789). Malthus contributed a theory of population to political economy, arguing that population reproduces faster than food production so that unless population growth were checked, the masses would face starvation and death.

Thus government should not aid the poor, for such action drains wealth and income from the higher echelons of society. Bentham viewed man's selfishness as natural and desirable but believed that individual and public interests should coincide. Government action was acceptable if not in response to the narrow interests of special groups, and individuals should be allowed freedom within a framework of moral and legal constraint.

The Utopian Socialists

Through the insights of Ricardo into labor and production and the gloomy prognosis of Malthus, there evolved a group of utopian socialists—romantic nineteenth-century protesters of capitalism in its most devastating form. Robert Owen struggled for labor reforms, including a shorter working day and the ending of child labor. He believed that with a change in conditions a paradise could be established, and he promoted village cooperatives as his utopian scheme, then turned to the organization of the English working classes. Count Claude Henri de Rouvroy de Saint-Simon, an aristocrat later relegated to conditions of poverty, believed that the workers deserved the highest rewards of society; the idlers, the least. He argued for the reorganization of society. Heilbroner included John Stuart Mill among the utopians. Mill manifested socialist leanings in his *Principles of Political Economy* (1848) in which he retraced the path of Smith and Ricardo but placed emphasis on production rather than on distribution. Proudhon, another utopian socialist, was a critic of the orthodox economics of his time. Critics, including Marx, easily exposed the weaknesses of utopian socialism, yet Harrington reminded us that although the utopians' ideas were viewed as but "an immature first step, a prelude, rather than as something of enduring value," we must not forget that the movement provided "the first serious definition of socialism as communitarian, moral, feminist, committed to the transformation of work" (1992: 41).

Marx

Marx transcended the theory of the utopian socialists as well as the classical liberal thinkers. He worked out a theory of surplus value as well as a synthesis that allowed for an explanation of class struggle. He developed theories on the prices of production and the tendency of the rate of profit to fall. He set forth basic laws of development: "Through his working out of a theory of the reproduction of capital and of national income, and through his adumbration of a theory of crises, he simultaneously achieved a first practical synthesis of micro-economic and macro-economic ideas" (Mandel 1968: 2:705). Marx's early work attacked the utopian socialists (Marx 1955), and his later work concentrated on all his predecessors, but in particular on the classical liberal economists Ricardo and Smith (Marx 1904, 1967, and 1973). For example, in *The Poverty of Philosophy* Marx exposed the "metaphysics" of Proudhon's political economy, and he argued against the use of "fixed, immutable eternal categories." Instead, one should examine "the historical movement of production relations," not their theoretical expression as categories nor as spontaneous or abstract ideas. In addition, he insisted that the production relations of every society form a whole; the parts cannot be separated from the whole so that one can explain society in terms of all relations simultaneously coexisting and supporting one another (Marx 1955: 91–110).

The Marginalist Neoclassicists

The threat of socialism led to the formation of the marginalist theory of value and neoclassical political economy. The popularization of Ricardo's thought, the impact of the utopian socialists, and the influence of Marx as well as Engels led not only to a bourgeois onslaught on Marxism but to efforts to bring about the demise of the labor theory of value, which had evolved through Smith, Ricardo, and the classical thinkers. The neoclassicists attempted to be rigorous, detailed, and abstract in the tradition of microeconomists. Various neoclassical schools opposed Marxism, including the historicist school in Germany, represented by Wilhelm Roscher, Eduard Hildebrandt, Gustav Schmoller, Karl Bücher, and others; the Austrian school of Karl Menger, Eugen von Böhm-Bawerk, and Friedrich von Wieser; the British school of William Stanley Jevons; and the Swiss school of Léon Walras. Bukharin systematically examined the ideas and thought of these schools, in particular focusing on Böhm-Bawerk. The neoclassicists emphasize equilibrium and so are often criticized for not accounting for the disturbances that affect equilibrium; their framework is static, not dynamic, it does not deal with structural crises, nor does it relate capitalism to imperialism.

The Keynesians

These problems led some economists, including Schumpeter, to study periodical crises. After the great depression, John Maynard Keynes in his *General Theory of Employment, Interest, and Money* (1936) moved political economy from an apologetic stance on capitalism to a pragmatic one. Rather than justify capitalism in theory, it was now essential to preserve it in practice by mitigating the extent of periodical fluctuations. One of Keynes's followers, Paul Samuelson, and others have followed in this macroeconomic tradition to the present period.

The Post-Keynesians

The post-Keynesians have provided "a positive statement of methodology, ideology and content" and are "united not just because of their critical attitude to neoclassical economics, but more importantly because of their attempt to provide an alternative paradigm to orthodox economics" (Arestis 1990: 223). Post-Keynesianism emphasizes realism with attention to the relevance of real economic problems. It builds on "realistic abstractions" rather than on "imaginary models." It stresses explanation rather than prediction. It focuses on history and institutions: "institutional structure and industrial organization … are continuously evolving and influencing the historical development of economies" (227). Among the basic premises of this school are that a free market economic process is fundamentally unstable; production rather than exchange is at the base of analysis; and disequilibrium and change over time rather than equilibrium and stability are essential. Post-Keynesianism draws its intellectual inspiration from Keynes and M. Kalecki. Four principal approaches are identifiable: first, that which gives attention to uncertainty and money-wages in capital accumulation and is influenced by the ideas of Marshall; second, that which looks at effective demand failures from a social class perspective and is influenced by Kalecki and Marx and includes the contributions of Joan Robinson and her followers; third, that which looks at and explains long-period levels of income and employment and is influenced by Straffian contributions; and, fourth, that which is linked to the institutionalist tradition of Veblen (Arestis 1990).

The Neo-Marxists

Although bourgeois economics remained dominant in the United States and much of Europe, followers of Marx carried on in a Marxist tradition. Engels edited and published the second and third volumes of Marx's *Capital,* followed by Kautsky's editing of Marx's *History of Economic Doctrines.* Thereafter, Kautsky's treatment of capitalism in agriculture, Rudolf Hilferding's *Das Finanzkapital* (1910), Rosa Luxemburg's *Accumulation of Capital* (1913), and Lenin's *Imperialism: The Last Phase of Capitalism* (1917) were efforts to expand upon Marx's earlier work.

The Stalinist period dampened interest in Marxist theories of political economy, but after about 1960 there was a revival of interest, promoted by the work of Paul Baran, Leo Huberman, and Paul Sweezy along with the writings and teachings of hundreds of other Marxists throughout the United States and other parts of the world.

Guidelines for the Study of Political Economy

The examination of epistemology, theory, method, and concept suggests a dichotomy between bourgeois and Marxist political economy. As long as contrasting

form in the nineteenth and twentieth centuries. Two views of the new imperialism prevailed. One, the radical or Marxist view, argued that imperialism was a reflection of an expanding capitalism, necessitated by the contradictions of the capitalist mode of production; the other, the liberal or non-Marxist view, argued that the inequities of the capitalist system could be readily adjusted.

The thought of Hobson, Kautsky, and Schumpeter contributed to a liberal view of imperialism. J. A. Hobson believed that underconsumption is the cause of imperialism and that with an increase in domestic consumption in his home country, Great Britain, there would be no drive to expand into foreign markets. Karl Kautsky, a leading Marxist of his time whose view tended toward liberalism, felt that the class conflicts of capitalism would diminish through peaceful processes, that the interests of the capitalist class as a whole would conflict with a minority of powerful capitalists who relied on military means to support their expansionist efforts. Joseph Schumpeter emphasized that imperialism is a precapitalist phenomenon and will disappear in a rational and progressive era of capitalism.

Representative of the Marxist view of imperialism would be the thought of Luxemburg, Bukharin, Lenin, Baran and Sweezy, and Magdoff. Rosa Luxemburg elaborated a theory of imperialism that explained continuous capital accumulation and, in particular, examined the penetration of capital into primitive economies. Nikolai Bukharin, a leading Bolshevik theoretician at the time of the Russian revolution, attacked Luxemburg's theory as "voluntaristic" and modeled after Hobson. Bukharin drew his theory from Rudolf Hilferding's notion of finance capital and offered a clear and detailed exposition of imperialism as an advanced stage of capitalism, while criticizing interpretations related to race and conquest. V. I. Lenin acknowledged the influence of Hobson and Hilferding upon the theory of imperialism. He understood imperialism to be the highest stage of capitalism, and he studied the rapid concentration of production in large industrial monopolies as well as the growing influence of large banks in the powerful monopolies. Paul Baran and Paul Sweezy referred specifically to Hilferding, Luxemburg, and Lenin in their formulation of a Marxist theory of imperialism. They suggested that such a theory explains relations within the capitalist world, clarifies the development of social and economic conditions in capitalist countries, and analyzes the unequal relations between advanced and underdeveloped nations. In particular they focused on the generation of capital surplus and its disposal. They turned analysis from competitive capitalism to monopoly and oligopoly and assessed the role of the giant corporations and their managers. Harry Magdoff traced the patterns of U.S. foreign policy and its impact on the international expansion of U.S. business. He aggregated data and information to show the coincidence of the military and political presence of the United States overseas, the dominant position of U.S. capital in the multinationals, and the dominance of multinational banking; he examined patterns of U.S. aid and trade as well as the ever-expanding U.S. "empire."

Efforts to promote a theory of dependency have emanated from both non-Marxist and Marxist understandings of imperialism. Raúl Prebisch and the ECLA school of economists argued that Latin America should set high tariff barriers and establish national industries to substitute for the increasing demand for foreign products; import-substitution policies would bring local control over the economy and stimulate national development. Osvaldo Sunkel and Celso Furtado elaborated a deeper understanding of dependency in this anti-imperialist, non-Marxist tradition. Pablo González Casanova's notion of internal colonialism followed a somewhat similar line, and the poles-of-development conceptions of François Perroux should also be considered. Another tradition of dependency stems from Marxism. Lenin wrote of dependency in his work on imperialism. Trotsky influenced Silvio Frondizi and other Latin Americans to write about dependency after the Second World War. Rebelling against the orthodoxy and dogmatism of Stalinism, Theotônio Dos Santos and fellow Brazilian Ruy Mauro Marini attempted to assimilate dependency into their Marxist theory of capitalism and Leninist theory of imperialism. In this way an analysis of imperialism could be combined with a class analysis of international conditions in the underdeveloped world. At the same time, Fernando Henrique Cardoso and some Marxists advocating dependency believed that modern capitalism and imperialism differ from Lenin's earlier conception.

All of these theories assume an anti-imperialist stance, yet they are distinguishable along Marxist and non-Marxist lines. This distinction is important because many social scientists incorporate dependency into their view that the diffusion of capital and technology from the industrial to the backward nations will inevitably bring about development. Consequently, confusion and contradiction pervade much of the writing on dependency. Let us now turn to a brief discussion of the non-Marxist and Marxist theories of dependency.

The non-Marxist theories are based on several positions. One position advocates turning inward to development by promoting national autonomy through state control and planning of the political economy under the direction of the petty-bourgeois intelligentsia and the industrial bourgeoisie. Under the modernizing state the bourgeoisie will become a progressive influence and support national interests as capitalist development diffuses itself into rural areas and as economic and political policies restrict the influence of foreign interests. A dual society, one advanced and modern and the other backward and feudal, characterizes the developing nations, which in turn represent a primary producing periphery whose resources tend to be appropriated by the industrial center. Furtado developed this position by examining inequalities in Brazil throughout historical periods and tracing the shift of major economic activity and production from the Northeast to the Center-South region where São Paulo is located. He believed that the state should intervene to rectify this imbalance and to move capitalist development along its future course. Sunkel argued that the transformation of existing structures is necessary for autonomous growth and that planning and control can bring about structural changes to eliminate underdevelopment and make capitalist development possible. Following another non-Marxist position, González Casanova alluded to internal colonialism, in which the center-peripheral conditions of colonialism are found internally within nations. Monopoly and dependency create deformation and decapitalization of the national economy and promote backwardness. He believed that a national solution is possible as marginal peoples are assimilated into society through the formation of a national bourgeoisie, which itself can resist the intrusions of monopoly capitalism and capitalist exploitation.

A third position, somewhat similar to internal colonialism and promoted by Perroux, identifies centers of natural resources where concentrated growth and markets can develop. Thus, capital and technology can be diffused to undeveloped centers that have a potential for industrialization. Cardoso contended with the idea that capitalism promotes underdevelopment, arguing that development can occur within dependent societies. He believed that dependent capitalist development becomes a new form of monopolistic expansion in the peripheral nations. New trends in international capitalism result in increased interdependence in production activities at the international level and in a modification in the patterns of dependence that limit developmental policy in the peripheral countries. He agreed that international capitalism has gained a disproportionate influence over industry in the peripheral areas, but he found misleading the assumption that there is a lack of growth in dependent economies because of imperialism. Cardoso believed that his approach updates theory established by Marx and Lenin, and he considered his understanding of dependency to be flexible in the face of orthodox and dogmatic Marxist conceptions.

Other writings on dependency fall more clearly into a Marxist framework. Baran and Sweezy are representative of independent Marxist thinkers whose ideas have influenced some *dependentistas,* but they have attempted to update Lenin and are sometimes criticized for not following a "pure" line. Marini's notion of subimperialism considers Brazilian capitalism as superexploitative, with a rapid accumulation of capital benefiting the owners of the means of production. Brazilian expansion and penetration into foreign markets have been based on the ability of the bourgeoisie to compete abroad. André Gunder Frank provided another facet of dependency theory with his emphasis on commercial monopoly as the means whereby national and regional metropolises exploit and appropriate surplus from the economic satellites. Thus capitalism on a world scale is viewed as promoting developing metropolises at the expense of underdeveloping and dependent satellites. Dos Santos took exception to Frank's emphasis on surplus extraction as the principal cause of underdevelopment and instead was concerned with the formation of internal structure conditioned by the international relationships of dependency. He stressed that the cause for the new dependency that emerged after the Second World War was massive investments by multinationals.

Criticisms of dependency theory abound. The non-Marxist theories are attacked for the emphasis on interdependence, implying that mutual cooperation between capitalist center and developing periphery might benefit both sides. Internal colonialism emphasizes internal forms and the role of a national bourgeoisie without taking into account the force of international capital and markets.

Other theories overlook the role of class struggle—a criticism that applies to most of the Marxist theories as well. Critics accuse Frank of failing to relate analysis of capitalism to modes of production; González Casanova is attacked for conferring on dependency a "nationalist" character; Dos Santos is charged with confusing worldwide expansion of capitalism with economic growth in the periphery; and Cardoso is indicted for mixing Marxist and bourgeois concepts.

One must conclude that to date no unified theory of dependency exists, and it may be that dependency can be utilized only to enhance a theory of imperialism. Indeed critics doubt that dependency is compatible with Marxist theory. Yet, even though the search for a unified theory of dependency may prove unproductive, it is clear that such a theory must be grounded in historical reality and should address such conceptualization as historical materialism and class struggle.

Comparative Political Economy and Theories of State and Class

Although recognizing that the central concerns of international political economy are imperialism and dependency, I also briefly review the complementary concerns of comparative political economy, namely state and class. As with theories of imperialism and dependency, distinctions can be made between bourgeois and Marxist theories of state and class.

Bourgeois theory might return to the formal-legal studies of James Bryce and Woodrow Wilson, among others of the early twentieth century. Or perhaps it might turn to the structural-functional categories of Gabriel Almond, to the rational-choice approach of Robert Bates (1988), or to Peter Katzenstein's analysis of industrial policy in *Small States in World Markets* (1985). The prevailing bourgeois conception, however, sees the state as a political marketplace through which filter the demands and interests of competing groups and individuals. Two views prevail. On the one hand, neutral state agencies mediate conflict that emanates from party and group competition. On the other, agencies of the state function as bases of political power; competition among these agencies for funding determines their relationship to parties and interest groups. These views reflect the liberal, non-Marxist tradition of U.S. social science. They may also be applicable to some socialist states, for example the workers' control once practiced in Yugoslavia or the proliferation of organizational life that emerged in Czechoslovakia during the spring of 1968. Eurocommunism in France and Italy exhibited strains of pluralism, and "socialist pluralism" was a manifestation of leftist groups in the aftermath of the Portuguese coup of 1974. Robert Dahl, once the leading liberal proponent of pluralism, drew attention to these bourgeois and socialist perspectives of the pluralist state and incorporated social class trends, cleavages, and conflict into a theory of organizational pluralism. In the 1970s and 1980s social democratic and socialist governments emerged in Spain, Portugal, Greece, France, and elsewhere in Western Europe. Pluralism pervaded the thinking of these regimes, as it also did after the fall in 1989 of commandist-statist regimes in Eastern Europe where the prevailing cohesion broke apart among the disparate nationalities and ethnic groupings.

Marx never fully developed a theory of state and class, nor did he elaborate a systematic theory of politics. Ralph Miliband noted that "a Marxist politics has to be constructed or reconstructed from the mass of variegated and fragmented material which forms the corpus of Marxism" (1977: 2). Miliband referred to A. Gramsci during his years in an Italian prison and Leon Trotsky during his years in exile as two writers who sustained a Marxist commentary on the role of the state through a period of Stalinism and fascism. Searching for a Marxist politics, Miliband reminded us that (1) textual priority should be given to Marx and Engels, then to others who followed in their tradition; (2) review will reveal different and sometimes contradictory Marxist interpretations; (3) the separation of politics from economics is an ideological distortion—politics is an integral part of political economy; and (4) the emphasis of many Marxists on the economic base has led to economic determinism and to the neglect of the superstructure, but Marx and Engels rejected mechanistic and deterministic explanations. As to the primacy of economics,

> the notion of "primacy" constitutes an important and illuminating guideline, not an analytical straitjacket. The ways in which that "primacy" determines and conditions political and other forms remain to be discovered, and must be treated in each case as specific, circumstantial, and contingent; and this also leaves open for assessment the ways in which political forms and processes in turn affect, determine, condition, and shape the economic realm, as of course they do and as they are acknowledged to do by Marxists, beginning with Marx. [Miliband 1977: 8–9]

The construction of a Marxist politics and theory of state and class necessitates initially an examination of the thought of Hegel, Marx, Engels, and Lenin. Marx critiqued Hegel's doctrine of the state, accepting that a fundamental contradiction exists between the state and the civil society of citizens but insisting that forms of the state be separated from an ideal or abstract conception and instead be rooted in the material conditions of life. Whereas in ancient Greece and during medieval times there was a sense of unity between the people and the state and between private and public interests, under capitalism, Marx argued, there is a separation of state from civil society, and an estrangement develops between public and private life. In addition, the civil society fragments into private interests competing against one another as the state legitimizes the pursuit of particular interests through private property. Private property promotes inequality and disunity among the people. One solution to this would be a return to a people's democracy, not a bourgeois democracy. In *The Origin of the Family, Private Property, and the State*, Engels summed up Marx's early writing on the state and class and also showed the significance of economic considerations. In *State and Revolution* (1932), Lenin drew on the theory of state elaborated by Marx and Engels. He insisted that the state does not reconcile class conflict but ensures the oppression of one class by another. Furthermore, he argued that state power must be destroyed through violent revolution, that compromise and reformist solutions do not resolve class antagonisms. He saw the police and standing army as "instruments" of state power. The proletariat struggles against the state until bourgeois democracy becomes proletarian democracy, the existence of classes is no longer necessary, and the state disappears altogether.

Marx, Engels, and Lenin emphasized a theory of state premised on the impact of capitalism. This focus stimulated work in the journal *Kapitalistate: Working Papers on the Capitalist State.* Three traditions seem to have caught the attention of contemporary scholars who are concerned with state and class. One tradition, known as instrumentalism and prevalent in the United States, emanated from community studies that identified power along the lines of position and reputation. This perspective is enhanced by Lenin's reference to instruments of state power and by Marx and Engels's concern expressed in *The Communist Manifesto* that the executive of the state "is but a committee for managing the affairs of the whole bourgeoisie" (Marx 1974: 69). Thus the state is the instrument of the ruling or dominant class. Instrumentalism focuses on the class that rules and the ties and mechanisms that link ruling-class instruments and state policies. Instrumentalism has been criticized for its failure to transcend the pluralist emphasis on social and political groupings rather than on classes tied to the means of production. The instrumentalist perspective of state has been advanced by G. William Domhoff and Ralph Miliband.

A second tradition revolves around the structuralist view of the state and is found in the writings of French Marxists. Nicos Poulantzas elaborated a political side of this structuralism by arguing that the bourgeoisie is unable as a class to dominate the state, that the state itself organizes and unifies the interest of that class. An economic side of structuralism is exemplified by Baran and Sweezy, who stressed the activity of the state in resolving economic contradictions and averting crises related to monopoly capitalism. Critics of structuralism argue that it cannot explain class action arising from class consciousness, that analysis tends to be static and tied to inputs and outputs rather than to class activity.

A third tradition, rooted in the critical perspectives of Hegel and Marx and carried on by Herbert Marcuse and others of the Frankfurt school, attempts to expose the mystification of the state and its ideology and false consciousness. This "critical" perspective sometimes is seen as abstract and unrelated to concrete politics and state activity. Beyond these three perspectives, Claus Offe and Esping-Andersen, Friedland, and Wright have suggested a focus on political class struggle—on the internal structures of the state and how these structures shape the class struggle. They examined the relationship of class struggle and state policies.

Marx and Engels distinguished state from society in order to clarify the interrelationship of political and economic life. They defined politics in terms of the power of the state, the superstructure that represents bourgeois society and reflects the economic needs of the class controlling production. Has a Marxist paradigm established itself? In *The Twilight of Capitalism* Michael Harrington responded in the affirmative.

> Even though it shares insights with, and has influenced, the various social sciences, it is distinctive and cohesive both as a method and in the results it facilitates. ... It poses the right questions about the contemporary world; it suggests some profound ways of seeking out the answers; and it is therefore relevant to the theory and practice of the twenty-first century. [1976: 184]

Harrington traced the crusade against Marxism that has been waged by U.S. academic disciplines during the past half century. The Marxist paradigm, he argued, integrates the separate analyses of the social science disciplines. He made clear, however, that the Marxist paradigm does not consist of some preconceived Marxist model of society. To the contrary, it offers important methodological themes. It is critical, even of its own concepts and terminology. It is rigorously scientific, yet it makes no pretense of being free of values but is aware of biases and ideologies that permeate social science; the values of Marxism link to politics favoring the working class rather than the ruling bourgeoisie. The Marxist paradigm also does not prescribe any particular solution for the ills of capitalist society— whether that society be democratic planning by the majority or bureaucratic and exploitative collectivism. Further, the Marxist paradigm looks for contradictions in society; it offers a complex theory of social classes, and it distinguishes possibilities, symptoms, and causes in an analysis of crisis and changing technology.

This revision of my original work on the search for a paradigm in political science and comparative politics brings us to the study of political economy, the point of departure for a sequel entitled *Comparative Political Economy: The Unending Search for New Paradigms* (forthcoming). The sequel elaborates on some themes emanating from this book as well as different themes that are fundamental to theory and inquiry in comparative political economy. An initial concern is with theories of transitions, with focus on essential issues such as the agrarian question and the transition from feudalism and precapitalism to capitalism and all the paths in that direction; capitalist development and capital accumulation, and relations of capitalist production; and impact of capitalism on socialism, the weaknesses of socialist experiences, the prospects for renovation, and the socialist transition. Second, I turn to theories of class, with attention to the origins and evolution of class analysis since the nineteenth century; twentieth-century formulations of class; and alternatives during the 1990s. Third, I examine theories of the state, tracing the origins and evolution of the state in the thought of Hegel, Marx, Engels, Lenin, Gramsci, Poulantzas, and other contemporary thinkers. Fourth, I look at theories of imperialism, elaborating on nineteenth-century influences and the evolution of ideas in the twentieth century since Hobson, Bukharin, Lenin, Kautsky, Schumpeter, and current writers; the links between theories of imperialism and development are identified in an attempt to reconceptualize contemporary debate in a traditional context. Fifth, I elaborate on theories of democracy, stressing formal and representative, indirect forms in contrast with direct informal and participatory forms; the thought of liberal, postliberal, social democratic, and radical democratic socialist theorists is examined. Finally, these theoretical themes are analyzed in the context of comparative historical work in an attempt to combine and compare historical examples and case studies. Issues drawn from understanding the international capitalist system, comparative revolutionary experiences, difficulties of the socialist transition, and so on allow for unveiling of the theoretical and methodological implications of this work.

The present generation of political scientists wrestles with the question of what is political and what is political science. Although a few acknowledge the contributions of Marx to this question, most tend to steer clear of the onus of Marxism, preferring instead to distinguish politics from economics and to avoid issues of state, power, class, and class struggle. It is to be hoped that such issues will be meaningfully addressed through attention to political economy.

The pursuit of political economy suggests provocative and controversial possibilities. Marx considered political economy as essentially an ideology, and he attempted to transcend ideology by questioning bourgeois political economy. Mandel suggested that such questions will eventually allow political economy to wither away together with the categories it seeks to explain. The result will be the evolution of a new science:

> What is certain is that, by virtue of the questions it will seek to answer, it will have little in common with past and present economic theory, with bourgeois political economy, or with the Marxist criticism of it. Marxist economists can claim the honour of being the first category of men of learning to work consciously towards the abolition of their own profession. [Mandel 1968: 2:730]

References

Arestis, Philip. 1990. "Post-Keynesianism: A New Approach to Economics." *Review of Social Economy* 48 (Fall), 222–246. An effort to identify major characteristics of the post-Keynesian school and their implications. Argues that this school "represents a positive statement of methodology, ideology and content" (223). Acknowledges that a coherent post-Keynesian paradigm has yet to be established. He delves into methodology and the main theoretical framework of this school. Suggests that this thought emphasizes realism and is based on concrete situations and historical experiences.

Bates, Robert (ed.). 1988. *Toward a Political Economy of Development: A Rational-Choice Perspective*. Berkeley: University of California Press. A collection of original essays with emphasis on a rational-choice approach to development.

Brenner, Robert. 1977. "The Origins of Capitalist Development: A Critique of Neo-Smithian Marxism." *New Left Review* 104 (July-August), 25–92. A detailed critique of André Gunder Frank, Paul Sweezy, and Immanuel Wallerstein, which traces the roots of their theory to Adam Smith.

Bukharin, Nikolai I. 1927. *The Economic Theory of the Leisure Class*. London: Martin Lawrence Limited. Originally written in 1914, this work contains a useful introduction that reviews bourgeois political economy since Marx, as well as a first chapter that distinguishes methodological foundations of bourgeois and Marxist theory.

Chattopadhyay, Paresh. 1974. "Political Economy: What's in a Name?" *Monthly Review* 25 (April), 23–33. A historical overview of various interpretations and understandings of political economy, from its origins to the present.

Deol, D. 1976. *Liberalism and Marxism: An Introduction to the Study of Contemporary Politics.* Delhi: Sterling Publishers. Elementary but useful synthesis of contrasting methodologies in political science.

Easton, David. 1968. "Political Science." In *International Encyclopedia of the Social Sciences,* 12: 282–297. Edited by David L. Sills. New York: Macmillan Company and Free Press. Review of the struggle to establish political science as a discipline. Demonstrates the importance of Marx's conception of the state, yet argues that current inquiry has transcended concepts such as state, with recent attention to the political system.

Foley, Duncan K. 1986. *Understanding "Capital."* Cambridge: Harvard University Press. Accompanies the three volumes of Marx's *Capital* as a device for understanding its content and revealing how people can understand and transform their lives.

Fusfeld, Daniel R. 1966. *The Age of the Economist: The Development of Modern Economic Thought.* Glenview, Illinois: Scott, Foresman and Co. Overview that sharply distinguishes positions of Marxists from bourgeois economists. Looks at various periods of political economic thought from the rise of market economy to central economic planning. Includes chapters on Smith, Ricardo, Marx.

Gilpin, Robert. 1987. *The Political Economy of International Relations.* With the assistance of Jean M. Gilpin. Princeton: Princeton University Press. A major overview and synthesis of international political economy.

Harrington, Michael. 1976. *The Twilight of Capitalism.* New York: Simon & Schuster. Chapter 7 outlines eight methodological themes that constitute the Marxist paradigm that the author favors.

_____. 1992. *Socialism: Past and Present.* New York: Penguin and Mentor. A synthesis of the interesting ideas of a passionate and influential socialist, written in his dying days.

Heilbroner, Robert L. 1961. *The Worldly Philosophers: The Lives, Times, and Ideas of the Great Economic Thinkers.* New York: Simon & Schuster. An overview of economic thinking with attention to the work and thought of Smith, Malthus, and Ricardo, the utopian socialists, and Marx, Veblen, and Keynes.

Hunt, E. K. 1972. *Property and Prophets: The Evolution of Economic Institutions and Ideologies.* New York: Harper and Row. A general statement and overview, from a Marxist perspective, of economic developments from precapitalist Europe to contemporary corporate and liberal capitalism.

Ito, Makoto. 1988. *The Basic Theory of Capitalism: The Forms and Substance of the Capitalist Economy.* Totowa, New Jersey: Barnes and Noble Books. Sets forth Marx's economic method in line with the Japanese school of Marxism and the work of Kozo Uno. In his review of this work, John Bellamy Foster (*Monthly Review* 40, January 1990, 51–55) suggested that Ito overcomes problems that emerge in criticism of Uno's emphasis on stage theory as reflected in Hilferding's *Finance Capital* and Lenin's *Imperialism,* especially the role of stage theory and the need to link theory and history.

Mandel, Ernest. 1968. *Marxist Economic Theory.* Translated by Brian Pearce. New York: Monthly Review Press. 2 vols. Chapter 18 synthesizes trends of political economy and provides an excellent critical overview.

_____. 1975. *Late Capitalism.* Translated by Joris De Bres. London: New Left Books. An overview of capitalism during the past hundred years with attention to late capitalism, evident since the Second World War.

Marx, Karl. 1904. *A Contribution to the Critique of Political Economy.* Translated from the second German edition by N. I. Stoke. Calcutta: Bharati Libaray. Translation of an edition published in 1897 by Karl Kautsky. Includes the famous preface and two chapters on capital, which deal with commodities and money, as well as an appendix consisting of the introduction to the *Critique of Political Economy.*

————. 1955. *The Poverty of Philosophy: Answer to the "Philosophy of Poverty" by M. Proudhon.* Moscow: Progress Publishers. An early Marxist critique of utopian socialist and idealist metaphysical interpretations of political economy.

————. 1967. *Capital: A Critique of Political Economy.* Edited by Frederick Engels. New York: International Publishers. 3 vols.

————. 1973. *Grundrisse: Foundations of the Critique of Political Economy.* Translated with a foreword by Martin Nicolaus. New York: Vintage Books.

————. 1974. *The Revolutions of 1848.* Edited with an introduction by David Fernbach. New York: Vintage Books.

Marx, Karl, and Frederick Engels. 1970. *The German Ideology.* Edited with introduction by C. J. Arthur. New York: International Publishers. The authors show the relationship between material base and ideology as a manifestation of the state in its separation from the whole society.

Meek, Ronald L. 1956. *The Labour Theory of Value.* London: Lawrence and Wishart. An excellent critical overview of labor theory, which examines theories prior to Adam Smith, the theories of Smith, Ricardo, and Marx, and critiques of Marxian theory.

Miliband, Ralph. 1977. *Marxism and Politics.* Oxford: Oxford University Press. An attempt to summarize the politics of Marxism or the Marxist approach to politics through a synthesis of the ideas in Marx, Engels, and Lenin.

Zarembka, Paul (ed.). 1977–1990. *Research in Political Economy.* Greenwich, Connecticut: JAI Press. Twelve volumes of essays on a broad range of topics related to political economy.

Appendix 1: Notes on
Comparative Terminology

The following notes are intended as a guide, both for me and to the reader, so that this book can be read with some common understanding. It is not my intention, however, to delineate in an exhaustive manner the meaning of each term. Nor does the identification of the terms below imply that I necessarily employ them in my own teaching and research. They are mentioned frequently in political science and in social science in general, and they are often used indiscriminately and without definition. Thus I hope to provide the reader with a basis for understanding and, through the references, show how more precise definitions can be found for terms that abound in the mainstream of political science.

Theory and Inquiry

Many years ago Samuel Beer and Adam Ulam outlined the steps in comparative inquiry, and the steps involved description, classification, explanation, and confirmation. Roy Macridis has also proposed a procedure. First, the collection and description of facts are drawn from some classificatory scheme. Second, the uniformities and differences are identified and described. Third, tentative hypotheses about the interrelationships in the political process are formulated. Fourth, these tentative hypotheses are verified through rigorous empirical observation. Fifth, the acceptable findings are set forth.

A reformulation of the steps and procedures suggested by these specialists suggests, first, that comparative inquiry integrates with theory and, second, that theory relates to description, analysis, and synthesis. *Theory* involves viewing and thinking; theory generates insight. Loosely conceived theory comprises sets of systematically related generalizations. More specifically, theory is a coherent body of generalizations and principles associated with the practice of a field of inquiry. These generalizations and principles might be hypothetical and conceptual. *Description* is a statement about the parts or relations of something and may involve classification, identification, and specification. *Analysis* is the separation or breaking up of the whole into its fundamental parts and subjecting them to detailed qualitative or quantitative examination; analysis may involve clarification and explication. *Synthesis* is the combining of the parts into a whole, of diverse ideas and forces into a coherent or cohesive complex.

These are aspects of theory and inquiry generally understood by the investigator of comparative politics. However, there are divergent lines of thinking in the field. Those people who are influenced by Max Weber, for instance, tend to stress the notion of ideal types or situations. The ideal is projected as a possibility that might be realized through time. The ideal often is based on a particular example or experience that a society might emulate. For example, U.S. democracy often is recognized as an idealized political type that, given time, might be realized by a less developed society. Such a notion suggests a unilinear and an evolutionary pattern of change through which societies evolve, and when it is discovered that backward societies may not be permitted to advance, it is possible that the ideal becomes confused with reality.

In contrast, Marxists might relate theory not to ideal types but to real situations, and they would combine theory with practice in a process called praxis. Marxists would see changes in society as the consequence of a dialectical and historical interplay of social forces in relation to production. Real historical changes would be explained theoretically in terms of synthesis as the dialectical outcome of thesis and antithesis.

Aspects of Theory

The example of divergent thinking just given justifies the need to elucidate further on theory. The literature tends to discuss theory in general terms, and definitions are likely to reflect the preferences of individual authors. Therefore, in order that the reader may reach an understanding of theory and its usefulness in inquiry, I turn now to a discussion of the following aspects of theory.

Concepts
Generalizations, propositions, and hypotheses
Types and levels
Approaches
Models and paradigms

Concepts

Comparative politics, indeed political science itself, suffers from ambiguity and imprecision of concepts. Conceptualization should be clear and well formulated, devoid of ambiguity and a multiplicity of different meanings, which may obfuscate connotation. Conceptualization must be realized prior to description and classification, prior to measurement and statistical application, and prior to testing of theory.

Concepts are ideas or thoughts expressed in differing ways. For example, Sartori (1984) suggested three levels of conceptualization: universal, general, and configurative. Universal conceptualizations are useful in cross-area comparisons and global theory. General conceptualizations are useful in intra-area comparisons and middle-range theory. Configurative conceptualizations are useful in country-by-country study and narrow-gauge theory. Some concepts are observable within a real world situation in which details and complexities can be identified. Other concepts are general abstractions, less dependent on a particular case but related to people, places, and events.

Comparative politics makes use of basic concepts in theory building. Concepts may be worked into definitional schema, classificatory arrangements, or systematic orderings that accompany a particular theoretical approach. Measurement and evaluation procedures may come into play. The resulting data and information are then subject to either qualitative or quantitative analysis. Qualitative analysis relates to generality and sometimes imprecision, and quantitative analysis relates to specificity and exactness, criteria often exaggerated in an age of technological advances.

Comparative politics tends to combine qualitative and quantitative techniques of research. Variables are measurements of concepts that have quantitative or qualitative attributes. Numerical values, such as age or size, can be utilized with quantitative variables, whereas nonnumerical values are employed with qualitative variables. Variables also may be dependent or independent. Dependent variables depend on at least one other variable, and independent variables are completely autonomous from other variables. Although these definitions may assist the reader in understanding the terminology of comparative politics, a word of caution is in order. Sophisticated techniques are not an escape from questions of substantive theory. However precisely defined, conceptualization undoubtedly will suffer in comparative investigation. Differing language connotations from culture to culture may pose a problem.

Generalizations, Propositions, and Hypotheses

The terms generalizations, propositions, and hypotheses are often used interchangeably, although different connotations and nuances of language may be associated with each term. Certainly there is no widespread consensus as to meaning of many terms, but the discussion that follows attempts clarification. Qualitative analysts usually stress the term generalizations, and quantitative analysts may employ the term hypotheses; propositions may be the concern of either type of analysis. A *generalization* is a general statement of uniformities and regularities. It is the simplest form of explanation. Knowledge of subject matter is essential to the capacity to generalize. Meehan (1965: 91–92) identified three forms of generalizations. The first is a universal generalization (all of one thing is the same as another); in some cases a universal generalization is a law, for it has withstood intensive testing. The second form is a probabilistic generalization (a percentage of one thing is equal to another); a probabilistic generalization frequently is referred to as a *proposition.* The third form is a tendency generalization (one thing tends to be another); a tendency generalization is expressed in tentative and conjectural terms and is thus a *hypothesis,* which may be true but not yet tested. Thus laws are universal, propositions are probabilistic, and hypotheses are tentative.

Generalizations, propositions, and hypotheses are especially useful in sciences such as chemistry and physics, which rely upon precise measurement and complex and detailed classifications. Classifications depend upon uniformities and similarities. However, political science finds its explanations of human behavior limited if only uniformities and similarities are noted. Human behavior is usually unpredictable. Thus diversity and dissimilar patterns of behavior become important in the study of politics. The demand for the study of patterns of dissimilarity as well as irregularity, echoed by Roy Macridis and other specialists in comparative politics over the past two decades, has caused skepticism about the application of science to politics.

Types and Levels

Two types of explanatory reasoning are prominent in theory. *Induction* is the process of inferring a generalization from a pattern of specific observations, whereas *deduction* is the process of determining that if a universal generalization is true, then a lesser generalization can be true. In comparative politics, induced generalizations and propositions are suspect, because they may be viewed as deterministic or deemed to be correct and true when in fact conclusive evidence may be lacking or deviant cases to disprove them may exist. Since political science has few, if any, universal generalizations or laws, then deductive explanation is unlikely to have much impact on the discipline. Given this fact, Meehan assumed that probabilistic explanations will be utilized. That is, explanation is set forth that suggests it is probable that something will occur. Instead of reaching the certain conclusions anticipated in deductive reasoning, conclusions might be stated with uncertainty and in relative terms (for example, "usually" replaces "always").

These reservations are not held by social scientists who accept that the logic of deductive explanation in natural science is compatible with that in social science. Their defense of deductive explanation is widespread. Thus such terms as "scientific method" and "rules of science" pervade the most prestigious theoretical literature. For Meehan, deductive explanation has become "an albatross around the neck of the social scientists," a charge elaborated in an essay by John G. Gunnell (1969).

The debate over deductive and inductive explanation is not new to science. For centuries scientists and philosophers have exposed the misconceptions that have emanated from both forms of explanation. During the latter half of the nineteenth century, Frederick Engels, in his *Anti-Dühring* and *Dialectics of Nature,* decried the one-sided arguments in favor of deduction *or* induction and argued instead that they belong together, that they supplement each other.

Earlier in discussing concepts, three levels of theory were identified: *global, middle-range,* and *narrow-gauge* levels. Global or grand theory seeks universal conceptualizations; the efforts to establish such theory for comparative politics have been largely discredited because of generality, vagueness, and abstraction. Narrow-gauge theory has suffered from overemphasis with technique rather than substance; often sensitive issues of politics are obscured by limiting the scope of inquiry to small problems and to easily manageable data. This concern with scope allows for a dichotomization of theory into two broad categories. Among the social sciences global theory is known as *macro theory* and narrow-gauge theory may be called *micro theory.* In between these extremes is the middle-range theory preferred by most practitioners of comparative politics today. This level emphasizes the study of institutions (structures) and their activities (functions).

Approaches

Three approaches to the study of politics were summarized by Apter and Andrain (1968). First, there is the *normative approach,* which in comparative politics usually implies the evolution of constitutional democracy as a central manifestation of modernization. Especially attractive to political scientists interested in the history of political ideas and the sociology of knowledge, the normative approach represents a traditional tendency, dating to times before philosophy was divorced from politics. This approach looks to the cultural values in society that are considered desirable. It also examines norms in the form of rules or rights and obligations that tell us how values are to be realized. Normative analysts attempt to transcend their crude empirical observations of events by seeking higher meaning as they relate their own values to those of the society they observe. Normative analysts use the whole society as their unit of analysis, and they sometimes assume that change in society is the consequence of a dialectical conflict between opposing values and ideas. Marxists, for example, might see such conflict among contending social classes in society. Many U.S. political scientists, in contrast, tend to assume that democracy and modernization are premised on shared rather than divisive values, and they look for compromise, bargaining, and consensus as the components of a democratic society.

Second, there is the *structural approach.* Apter and Andrain distinguished among five emphases: (1) legal and formal, usually administrative, institutions, which were the concern of specialists studying the nature of empires and colonies prior to the Second World War; (2) neo-institutional structures, such as a civil service and political parties, which are given attention along with legal structures and constitutions; (3) groups, including formal ones such as political parties, church, and army and informal ones such as trade unions, business groups, and farmers' groups; (4) structures and functions that constitute a system of related parts; and (5) structures in the form of groups and classes, which neo-Marxists analyze in terms of their economic interests. Structural analysts tend to examine issues of system maintenance and stability. Whole societies or nations, macro units, are studied, and assumptions about development range from an emphasis on separation of powers among the legal governmental institutions, on the one hand, to the struggle between economic classes, on the other.

Third, there is the *behavioral approach,* influenced by psychology. Behaviorism focuses on a variety of problems related to the learning and socialization process, motivations, perceptions, and attitudes toward authority and other considerations. The unit of analysis is the individual and the small group. Apter and Andrain identified behavioral assumptions as those that relate to individual optimism that change is desirable and possible and that development is the consequence of peoples' needs for achievement.

The distinctions among these approaches help to identify the multiplicity of research tendencies employed in the study of comparative politics. The mainstream of comparative politics has tended to utilize the structural or structural-functional approach, labeling it middle range in theoretical orientation. More recently there has been a tendency to pursue narrow, micro orientations through the behavioral approach. Disillusionment with the failure of behaviorism to deal with the issues and problems of society and with the tendency of structuralism to deal with segments of systems without relating them to the whole society has led many professionals to emphasize the normative approach. On the one hand, there are those who continue to stress the values and norms of democratic society as evidenced by the Anglo-American experience. On the other, there are serious, more radical, attempts to criticize such interpretations as static and not very useful. The chapters in this book identify and distinguish between such understandings of politics and attempt to transcend the three approaches suggested by Apter and Andrain.

Models and Paradigms

I have already referred to the use of definitional schema, classificatory arrangements, and systematic orderings, which are useful in the search for theory. These terms might also be described as *taxonomies* or *frameworks. Typologies* divide and order information and facts along the lines of classifications, taxonomies, and frameworks, but they do so in somewhat precise, even subtle, ways so as to allow a utilization of quantitative techniques. The use of *models* in the study of comparative politics has broader implications. Models construct, bring disparate parts together, and demonstrate relationships. Models tend to simplify representations of the real world. They can facilitate understanding, but they do not explain. They help comparative specialists bring order to the mass of information available to students of comparative politics. Models, like typologies and classifications, are limited, however. They are mental constructions, not theories, although they are often distorted to signify theoretical advancement.

A *paradigm* is a scientific community's perspective of the world, its set of beliefs and commitments—conceptual, theoretical, methodological, instrumental. A paradigm guides the scientific community's selection of problems, evaluation of data, and advocacy of theory. In Chapter 3 the existence of paradigms in comparative politics is elaborated on, and two principal paradigms that have influenced comparative politics during the past century are identified.

Methods and Inquiry

Methods involve techniques and are the procedures of inquiry. Methods may be qualitative or quantitative. Lijphart (1971: 683) suggested that the comparative method is basically simple: "a method of discovering empirical relationships among variables, not a method of measurement." The comparative method, then, involves qualitative, not quantitative, analysis. The comparative method in this sense is a broad, general method, not a narrow, specialized technique.

This understanding of the comparative method recognizes that efforts to formulate solid theory and methods in the study of comparative politics have not always been successful. Lines of comparison have been drawn, but rigorous study has been limited by the complexities of comparative investigation. Ambitious comparative schemes have assimilated information from many nations, but the results have been largely descriptive. Data banks have gathered together statistics from throughout the world, but the data may not be reliable. These problems reflect the experience of most investigators of comparative politics. Warwick and Osherson (1973) outlined some of these problems in their treatment of the comparative research method and technique, and Ward and others (1964) set forth a manual of recommendations, which should be helpful to the study of politics abroad, especially in the Third World. Sidney Verba (1967) looked at single-nation and global comparative studies and urged students to adopt a disciplined, narrow focus, but Merritt and Rokkan (1966) were more optimistic in their attempt to identify methods in the use of quantitative data in cross-national research. Finally, Heinz Eulau (1962) argued that the narrow research of North American investigators might contribute to new understandings of comparative analysis and method.

Lijphart argued persuasively for an identification of the comparative method, yet other methods are available and indeed are utilized by specialists of comparative politics. These other methods are the experimental, statistical, linguistic, and case methods.

The comparative method involves the analysis of a small number of cases. According to Lijphart, it may be the most promising approach because of the time, energy, and financial resources demanded by analysis of many cases. Attention to a few cases also allows for depth rather than superficiality in analysis.

The experimental method utilizes an experimental group and a control group and studies the comparisons. Only the experimental group is exposed to a stimulus, and the other group is isolated. Meehan elaborated on one form of experimental technique, used in some branches of psychology. It involves the treatment of a single complex system within which behavior is observed in relation to various stimuli and the results are recorded and measured. The system is structured like a box in which stimuli serve as the inputs and behaviors represent the outputs and a feedback relationship exists between both elements. A psychiatrist might think of a human being as the box and accordingly study stimuli and behavior. As is noted in Chapter 5, this conception of system has been adapted to David Easton's study of politics. However, the experimental method is rarely used in political science research, largely because politics is difficult to control.

The statistical method is an "approximation" of the experimental method and is facilitated by the use of modern computers. "It entails the conceptual (mathematical) manipulation of empirically observed data—which cannot be manipulated situationally as in experimental design—in order to discover controlled relationships among variables" (Lijphart 1971: 684). The evaluation of competing explanations is achieved through statistical control, but in comparative investigation data are often inadequate due to lack of information and limited resources. However, decisions that affect the lives of people may be made on the basis of statistical studies. Thus, it is important to know something about statistics, to be able to identify obvious misuses of statistics in political life and in the economy—a plea inherent in the very useful applications of statistics for social change identified by Horowitz and Ferleger (1980).

The study of politics is muddled by fussy terminology, and a meticulous study of nomenclature and syntax is overdue. A clarification of meanings might eliminate ambiguous language and allow utilization of the linguistic method. The linguistic method employs procedures for identifying, recording, and measuring recurrent patterns in written and spoken communications. Recently the linguistic method has been combined with the statistical method and the use of computers.

The case-study method is closely associated with the comparative method, and certainly it is useful to other methods as well, as elaborated by Harry Eckstein (1975). Lijphart believed that the case-study method can contribute to theory building in political science. He identified six types of case studies: (1) atheoretical traditional or single-country studies of no theoretical value; (2) interpretative studies that use theoretical generalizations but relate to a specific case and do not contribute to theory building; (3) hypothesis-generating studies of a number of cases; (4) theory-confirming and (5) theory-infirming studies of single cases within a framework of established generalizations; and (6) studies of single cases that deviate from established generalizations.

All of these methods employ a variety of sources of information. Among these sources are elite and voting data, mass opinion, aggregative figures, historical data, and content findings of documents and speeches. The comparative study of politics utilizes quantitative techniques in the analysis and synthesis of such information.

In his examination of trends since about 1970, David Collier (1991) reminded us of Harold Lasswell's affirmation that the scientific method is undeniably "comparative." Collier suggested that despite innovations in research designs and statistical techniques, the value of quantitative and statistical approaches today is more in doubt than in the past, and that qualitative research of few cases is more useful in comparative research. Illustrative of this preference are Charles Ragin's (1987) holistic approach to case studies and causal patterns, and the comparative framework suggested by Skocpol and Somers (1980) in their contribution to comparative historical analysis.

Conclusion

This discussion has emphasized the traditional terminology of comparative politics and social science. Many of these terms, however, are applicable both to the mainstream and the alternative lines of thought that are delineated throughout the chapters in this book. In particular, the concluding chapter focuses on political economy and offers definitions of Marxist terminology. Major schools of political economy are identified, and Marxist theory, method, and concepts are described. An earlier chapter on Marx and Weber may also be helpful. And elsewhere I have discussed the implications of analytical Marxism (Chapter 8).

Michael Harrington in his *Twilight of Capitalism* observed that there are many Marxisms, believing that Marx interpreted things in different ways throughout an illustrative and prolific career of writing about the contradictions of capitalism. Thus the students of Marxism need not adhere to rigid formulations. The fact is, however, that the revision of some of Marx's theory has led to confusion, and the result is not unlike the indiscriminate use of terminology that pervades bourgeois social science.

It is likely that the reader may desire to delve more deeply into the meaning of the terminology of Marxism. The intimidated yet curious reader might initially benefit from a brief look at the depiction by Rius, the Mexican cartoonist, in *Marx for Beginners* (1976), which includes a short dictionary of terms. Leo Huberman and Paul M. Sweezy in their *Introduction to Socialism* (1968) also provide access to an understanding of Marxism in the chapter on "The ABC of Socialism." In addition, Ralph Miliband's *Marxism and Politics* stresses a discussion of class and class conflict through strategies of reform and revolution. Ernest Mandel's *From Class Society to Communism: An Introduction to Marxism* (1977) is a comprehensive yet simply written work, which gives clear answers to basic questions and identifies the major theoretical issues. Mandel's work attempts to describe social inequality and social struggle throughout history, to examine the state and ruling classes, to trace development from petty commodity production to the capitalist mode of production, and to explain the impact of monopoly capitalism and the world imperialist system.

References

Apter, David E., and Charles Andrain. 1968. "Comparative Government: Developing New Nations." In Marian D. Irish (ed.), *Political Science: Advance of the Discipline*, 82–126. Englewood Cliffs, New Jersey: Prentice-Hall. Reprint from *Journal of Politics* 30 (May 1968). Identification of six trends in the study of new nations in relation to three approaches: normative, structural, and behavioral.

Burrowes, Robert. 1970. "Multiple Time-Series Analysis of Nation-Level Data." *Comparative Political Studies* 2 (January), 419–442. Argues for the use of longitudinal techniques to test the strength of relationships among variables. Builds a case for longitudinal study of one or a small number of nations, long neglected by comparative political analysts.

Collier, David. 1991. "New Perspectives on the Comparative Method." In Dankwart A. Rustow and Kenneth Paul Erickson (eds.), *Comparative Political Dynamics: Global Research Perspectives*, 7–31. New York: HarperCollins. A useful view of past work on comparative method, with attention to Lijphart (1971), and a syntheses of innovations in recent years.

Eckstein, Harry. 1975. "Case Studies and Theory in Political Science." In Fred Greenstein and Nelson W. Polsby (eds.), *Handbook of Political Science*, vol. 7. Reading, Massachusetts: Addison-Wesley. Reviews the method of case study and refines a typology of how case studies relate to broader comparison and theory testing.

Eulau, Heinz. 1962. "Comparative Political Analysis: A Methodological Note." *Midwest Journal of Political Science* 6 (November), 397–407. Argues that Americanists can contribute to an understanding of comparative analysis and method by relating their research to that of those working in comparative politics. Eulau supports his view by drawing upon experiences in research on state legislatures and offers methodological observations on comparative analysis.

Gunnell, John G. 1969. "Deduction, Explanation, and Social Scientific Inquiry." *American Political Science Review* 63 (December), 1233–1246. A detailed critique of deductive explanation that has become the basis for most work in social science. Calls for a reexamination of the idea that "there is logical symmetry between explanations in the natural and social sciences" and urges an investigation into "the logical and epistemological foundations of these two enterprises."

Horowitz, Lucy, and Lou Ferleger. 1980. *Statistics for Social Change*. Boston: South End Press. A popular and easy-to-use text on how to apply statistics to the study of problems and change in society.

Lijphart, Arend. 1971. "Comparative Politics and the Comparative Method." *American Political Science Review* 65 (September), 682–693. Differentiates the comparative method from the experimental, statistical, and case-study methods. Comparative method is "a method of discovering empirical relationships among variables, not as a method of measurement." Comparative method is not a technique. The author examines strengths and weaknesses of the comparative method.

Meehan, Eugene J. 1965. *The Theory and Method of Political Analysis*. Homewood, Illinois: Dorsey Press. Examines major questions about science, explanation, epistemology, method and technique, and values with critical judgments that are especially useful for comparative politics.

Merritt, Richard L., and Stein Rokkan (eds.). 1966. *Comparing Nations: The Use of Quantitative Data in Cross-National Research*. New Haven: Yale University Press. Critical discussion of recent efforts to quantify data across many nations.

Ragin, Charles. 1987. *The Comparative Method: Moving Beyond Qualitative and Quantitative Strategies.* Berkeley: University of California Press. Looks at causal patterns within a holistic approach to case-oriented research.

Sartori, Giovanni (ed.). 1984. *Social Science Concepts: A Systematic Analysis.* Beverly Hills, California: Sage Publications. Effort to build a common, consistent, and comprehensible set of social scientific concepts, following the guidelines and method suggested by Sartori in his introductory discussion.

Skocpol, Theda, and Margaret Somers. 1980. "The Uses of Comparative History in Macrosocial Inquiry." *Comparative Studies in Society and History* 22 (April), 174–197. Examines the objectives of comparison of case studies, with attention to three approaches: systematic study among cases in order to test hypotheses; examination of cases through a model or set of concepts; and contrast of two or more cases to show their differences.

Verba, Sidney. 1967. "Some Dilemmas in Comparative Research." *World Politics* 20 (October), 111–127. Assessment of single-nation and global comparative studies in which the author urges students of macropolitics to focus on an intermediate goal of "a disciplined configurative approach."

Ward, Robert E., et al. 1964. *Studying Politics Abroad: Field Research in the Developing Areas.* Boston: Little, Brown and Co. Essays on field research techniques, design, and setting especially relevant to the Third World.

Warwick, Donald P., and Samuel Osherson (eds.). 1973. *Comparative Research Methods.* Englewood Cliffs, New Jersey: Prentice-Hall. Essays on problems of comparative research with attention to the random probe, linguistic comparability, unusual conditions, and participant observation, as well as sampling, measurement, and interviewing.

Appendix 2:
The General Literature
of Comparative Politics
Since 1980

A prolific and varied literature inundates the field of comparative politics. The following discussion provides a brief overview of fundamental works that may be useful, not only to scholars and specialists with particular interests but to teachers and students who must contend with comparative politics in their classes. My review purposely limits itself to the important literature since about 1980 and therefore incorporates only limited reference to material identified in the survey of literature that appeared in the original edition. I mention trends in the earlier period only to reflect on developments since 1980, and I follow a similar pattern by examining the evolution of comparative literature, general overviews, cross-national studies, comparative series, area and country studies, and comparative periodicals. Where I cite a work by author and title in the text, the work is well known and easily accessible or it has been identified and annotated elsewhere in the text or can be found through the index. I encourage readers to return to the survey of the first edition for an overview and historiography of comparative politics from about 1945 to 1980.

Appraisals of the Field

A generation ago Harry Eckstein provided an overview of the field from the time of the Greek political philosophers; there have also been useful reviews through the American Political Science Association and at various conferences. The May 1968 conference at New York University served to launch the quarterly journal *Comparative Politics*, and twenty years later a commemorative conference at New York University provided a reassessment and an important anthology of papers edited by Dankwart Rustow and Kenneth Erickson (1991). The emphasis in James Bill and Robert Hardgrave, Jr., *Comparative Politics: The Quest for Theory* (1981) complements my own work on comparative theory but is presented at a more introductory level. J. C. Johari, *Comparative Political Theory* (1987), has also focused on comparative theory of the state, ideology, law, and other themes. In his edited anthology *New Directions in Comparative Politics*, Howard Wiarda provides a rather pessimistic view of the "crisis" in the field, a position also underscored by an essay by Sidney Verba: "Despite the large number of new and innovative studies, there is too little work that leads to cumulative knowledge" (Verba, in Wiarda 1985: 35). With emphasis on rational-choice models and aggregate data, Russell Dalton (1991) remains more enthusiastic in his survey of the field. Recent reassessments also include efforts at identifying the historiography of the discipline, with much of the work especially relevant to comparative politics; for example, see David Easton and John Gunnell, with Luigi Graziano, *The Development of Political Science: A Comparative Survey* (1991), with emphasis on U.S. experience and attention to Western Europe as a basis for comparison with other areas, including China and Africa; and the forthcoming anthology of essays by John Dryzek, James Farr, and Stephen Leonard, *Political Science and Its History: Research Programs and Political Traditions.*

For important and useful overviews and assessments of related disciplines, see on anthropology, Marvin Harris, *The Rise of Anthropological Theory* (1968) and *Cultural Materialism: The Struggle for a Science of Culture* (1979); on economics, Richard D. Wolff and Stephen A. Resnick, *Economics: Marxian Versus Neoclassical* (1987); and on sociology, Peter Knapp and Alan J. Spector, *Crisis and Change: Basic Questions of Marxist Sociology* (1991), and Howard J. Sherman and James L. Wood, *Sociology: Traditional and Radical Perspectives* (1979).

Texts

Much of the introductory text material now is published by HarperCollins, including *Comparative Politics: A Theoretical Framework* by Gabriel A. Almond, G. Bingham Powell, Jr., and Robert J. Mundt (1993), which uses the familiar approach to comparative politics (systems, structures, and functions) and is a condensation of their earlier texts; *Comparative Politics Today,* edited by Almond and Powell (5th ed., 1992), which treats comparative concepts and countries; *Introduction to Comparative Government,* edited by Michael Curtis (3d ed., 1993), which contains essays on nine countries; *Introduction to Comparative Politics: Regimes and Change* by the late Roy C. Macridis and Steven L. Burg (1991); *Comparative Political Dynamics,* a collection of eighteen timely topical essays edited by Rustow and Erickson (1991); and *Comparative Politics: Diverse States in an Interdependent World* by David Roth, Paul V. Warwick, and David Paul (1989), which deals with general comparisons rather than detailed descriptions of politics within countries.

Charles F. Andrain, *Foundations of Comparative Politics: A Policy Perspective* (1983), offers an emphasis on policy analysis within a historical setting and attention to the political setting and political system in nine countries. James F. Barnes,

Marshall Carter, and Max J. Skidmore organized an introductory text, *The World of Politics: A Concise Introduction* (1984), and James N. Danziger's *Understanding the Political World* (1991), is an imaginative and useful approach to concepts and comparative analysis. See also Alex Dragnich, Lawrence Graham, Jorgen Rasmussen, and Taketsugu Tsurutani, *Politics and Government* (1982), an introductory text focused on ten countries. Dan N. Jacobs, David P. Conradt, B. Guy Peters, and William Safran in *Comparative Politics: An Introduction to the Politics of the United Kingdom, France, Germany, and the Soviet Union* (1983) focus on power in four nations with a concluding chapter on political ideologies, political leadership and elites, revolutions, and comparative public policy. Other texts include Mark Kesselman and Joel Krieger and others, *European Politics in Transition* (1992), a volume of innovative essays; Thomas M. Magstadt, *Nations and Governments* (1991), a regional comparative approach; John D. Nagle, *Introduction to Comparative Politics: Political System Performance in Three Worlds* (1992), with attention to advanced liberal democracies, communist systems, and developing nations in terms of economic development, social equality, personal liberty, and quality of life; Martin C. Needler, *The Concepts of Comparative Politics* (1991), an elementary treatment of some essential terminology; and W. Philips Shively, *Power and Choice* (1987), a rational-choice approach to concepts with case examples. Another introductory text by Harmon Zeigler, *The Political Community: A Comparative Introduction to Political Systems and Society* (1990), looks at comparative political systems from a perspective of democracy, authoritarianism, and totalitarianism.

Readers

Two readers are noteworthy: the traditional text of Macridis and Brown, eds. (1990), the seventh edition of a four-part collection of readings on comparative regimes, institutions and processes, and development and revolution; and the more interesting collection of readings on trends, methodologies, and alternative paradigms by Cantori and Ziegler, Jr., eds. (1988).

Comparative Series

In contrast with the earlier years, only a few commercial publishers remain committed to series of volumes specifically oriented toward college class use. Interestingly, a number of university presses sponsor series relevant to comparative politics. Under the editorship of Peter Lange, for example, Cambridge University Press publishes the "Cambridge Studies in Comparative Politics," which is aimed at "comparative research that seeks to explain important cross-national domestic political phenomena." Cambridge also publishes the important "Studies in Marxism and Social Theory," edited by G. A. Cohen, Jon Elster, and John Roemer. The "California Series on Social Choice and Political Economy," edited by Brian Barry,

Robert H. Bates, and Samuel L. Popkin and published by the University of California Press, emphasizes monographs based on rational-choice theory and includes a theoretical overview by Bates (1988), regional studies on Africa by Bates, and country studies on France by William Brustein and on Nicaragua by Forrest D. Colburn. Among the commercial series, the well-known traditional comparative politics and country studies organized by Gabriel Almond is now available through HarperCollins and includes volumes by Lucian W. Pye on China (4th ed., 1991); Bradley M. Richardson and Scott C. Flanagan on Japan (1984); Russell J. Dalton on Germany (2d ed., 1993); Howard J. Wiarda on Spain and Portugal (1993); Henry W. Ehrmann and Martin A. Schain on France (5th ed., 1992); Richard Rose on England (5th ed., 1989); and James A. Bill and Robert Springborg on the Middle East (3d ed., 1990). Westview Press publishes a number of series relevant to comparative politics, including one called "New Directions in Comparative Politics," edited by Peter H. Merkl and Haruhiro Fukui; another titled "Dilemmas in World Politics," edited by George A. López; another on political cultures, edited by Aaron Wildavsky; another on interventions, edited by Stephen Eric Broner; and a number of volumes on gender studies, for example *Unequal Burden* (1992) by Lourdes Benería and Shelley Feldman. During the late 1980s, Sage Publications published several useful volumes on comparative politics, some of them including reprinted material dating to earlier themes by Gabriel Almond (1990) and Lawrence Mayer (1989) on the state of the discipline. Additionally, Sage issued David Apter, *Rethinking Development* (1987), and Alvin So, *Social Change and Development* (1990). South End Press publishes radical and policy-oriented studies on ecology, feminism, and gender issues along with critical overviews of situations in Latin America, the Middle East, and other areas. New Left Books publishes in cloth and also as Verso in paperback important volumes on politics and theory as well as individual country studies: for example, Boris Kagarlitsky, *The Year the Walls Came Down: 1989, A Soviet Chronicle* (1989), and Colin Mooers, *The Making of Bourgeois Europe* (1990). The annual edition of *Comparative Politics,* published by the Dushkin Publishing Group, comprises reprinted material from newspapers, academic journals, and other sources, with attention to Western democracies, the communist world, and the Third World. In 1991 Zed Press, in conjunction with the United Nations Non-Governmental Liaison Service, launched a "Women and World Development Series" with works such as Jeanne Vickers, *Women and the World Economic Crisis* (1991), and Annabel Rodda, *Women and the Environment* (1991), to complement an illustrious line of books on Third World women, including many works on the role of women in particular country situations.

Cross-National Studies

Two types of studies have appeared, one limited to the selection of variables common to a large number of countries with the reporting and analysis of data related to those variables; and the other oriented to comparison of historical case studies.

Systematic annual collection of data on European nations has led to a plethora of studies. Examples include Russell Dalton's study (1988) of public opinion in the United States, Great Britain, West Germany, and France; Ronald Inglehart's study (1977) of cultural values in Western Europe; and the work of Sidney Verba, Norman H. Nie, and Jae-on Kim (1978), a survey of attitudes on political participation in seven nations (Austria, India, Japan, Netherlands, Nigeria, United States, and Yugoslavia). See also Mancur Olson (1982) for an overview of the rise and decline of powerful states; see Ames (1987) on bureaucracies and public policies in seventeen Latin American nations.

Historical comparisons, in contrast, follow in the tradition of Barrington Moore, Jr., *Social Origins of Dictatorship and Democracy* (1966); Theda Skocpol, *States and Social Relations* (1979); or Charles Tilly, *From Mobilization to Revolution* (1978). Some important examples of historical comparisons of many countries, with a focus on power, include Reinhard Bendix (1978), a look at the authority of kings in Japan, Russia, imperial Germany and Prussia, and England and the consequences for and reactions of the people; Ben Crow and Mary Thorpe (1988), an analysis of production and producers in the Third World; John A. Hall (1985) on powers and liberties in agrarian civilizations (China, India, and Islam) and in the modern world (Europe, the United States, the former Soviet Union, and the Third World); Paul Kennedy (1987) in a study of the rise and decline of imperial powers; Michael Mann (1986) on European power in its ideological, economic, military, and political forms; Dieter Senghaas (1985), the analysis of development theories in European history; Immanuel Wallerstein (1974, 1980), in a reinterpretation of the origins and evolution of capitalism in Europe; Eric R. Wolf (1982), an overview of European peasantry, workers, and minorities; and Peter Worsley (1984), a synthesis of culture, peasantry, working class, ethnicity, and nationalism in the Third World. Comprehensive studies of theories of nationalism and European influences are Ernest Gellner (1983) and Anthony Smith (1983). David McNally (1988) provides a reinterpretation of political economy theory based on the agrarian capitalist experience in England and France. For other important comparative treatments of Europe, based on theories and models but illustrated with case studies, see the edited collection by Suzanne Berger (1983), the important comparisons in Peter Katzenstein (1984 and 1985), the interesting focus on scandal in Andrei Markovits and Mark Silverstein (1988), and Charles Tilly (1975).

Thematic Comparisons

Some of the important comparative work around the specialized subject areas emphasized in this book has been discussed in various chapters, but a brief summary of selected and especially significant and useful references follows.

On state theory the standard syntheses are Bob Jessop, *The Capitalist State* (1982) and *State Theory* (1990); Martin Carnoy, *The State and Political Theory* (1984); and John Holloway and Sol Picciotto, *State and Capital: A Marxist Debate* examination of the revolutionary origins in England, France, the United States, China, India, and Japan.

Nagle, John D. 1992. *Introduction to Comparative Politics: Political System Performance in Three Worlds.* Chicago: Nelson-Hall Publishers. 3d ed. 2d ed., 1989; 1st ed., 1985. An introductory text that focuses on advanced liberal democracies, communist systems, and developing nations in terms of economic development, social equality, personal liberty, and quality of life.

Needler, Martin C. 1991. *The Concepts of Comparative Politics.* New York: Praeger. Offers a rudimentary conceptualization of a series of concepts such as revolution, dictatorship, legitimacy, political development, political culture, social class, and political institutions and presents examples and illustrations from different country experiences.

O'Connor, James. 1987. *The Meaning of Crisis: A Theoretical Introduction.* London: Blackwell. Assesses the important Marxist, neo-Marxist, and post-Marxist explanations of the modern crisis, with attention to market theory, value theory, and social-psychological theory.

O'Donnell, Guillermo, Philippe C. Schmitter, and Laurence Whitehead (eds.). 1986. *Transitions from Authoritarian Rule.* Baltimore: Johns Hopkins University Press. Published in cloth as a single volume and in paperback as a series of volumes with the main title *Prospects for Democracy* and different subtitles: *Southern Europe; Latin America; Comparative Perspectives;* and *Tentative Conclusions About Uncertain Democracies.* Papers originally commissioned for a conference sponsored by the Woodrow Wilson International Center for Scholars between 1979 and 1981.

Olson, Mancur. 1982. *Rise and Decline of Nations: Economic Growth, Stagflation, and Social Rigidities.* New Haven: Yale University Press. An important comparative study based on aggregate data and analysis of many situations.

Pridham, Geoffrey (ed.). 1984. *The New Mediterranean Democracies: Regime Transition in Spain, Greece, and Portugal.* London: Frank Cass. Comparative studies of the transition from dictatorship to representative democracy.

Przeworski, Adam. 1985. *Capitalism and Social Democracy.* New York: Cambridge University Press. A critical assessment of social democracy in capitalist systems, theoretically oriented but accompanied by data and examples.

Rustow, Dankwart A., and Kenneth Paul Erickson (eds.). 1991. *Comparative Political Dynamics: Global Research Perspectives.* New York: HarperCollins Publishers. An introduction and conclusion by the editors with sixteen essays: David Collier, Howard Wiarda, and S. N. Eisenstadt on comparative method and models; Ronald Chilcote, David Becker, and Edmond Keller on state, class, and dependency; Terry Karl, Metin Heper, and Henry Bienen and Jeffrey Herbst on democracy; Michel Oksenberg and Bruce Dickson, Blaus von Beyme, Nikki Keddie, and Susan Eckstein on reform and revolution; and Douglas Ashford, Jack Hayward, and T. J. Pempel on policy in industrial states.

Scott, James C. 1985. *Weapons of the Weak: Everyday Forms of Peasant Rebellion.* New Haven: Yale University Press. A major study of peasant resistance to dominant rule and to capitalism; significant for comparative investigation.

Senghaas, Dieter. 1985. *The European Experience: A Historical Critique of Development Theory.* Dover, New Hampshire: Berg Publishers. Critically examines various theories of development in European history: autocentric and export-led development through capitalism, peripheral capitalism, and socialism.

Shively, W. Phillips. 1987. *Power and Choice: An Introduction to Political Science.* New York: Random House. An introductory text that sees politics as the use of power or public choice. The author prefers a behavioral approach but includes emphasis on policy and institutions. A topical rather than country-by-country approach, with brief case examples at the end of each chapter.

Skinner, Quentin (ed.). 1985. *The Return of Grand Theory in the Human Sciences.* Cambridge: Cambridge University Press. Skinner argues in the introduction that with the flourishing of Marxism and other trends there has been a revival in grand theory. This anthology of essays focuses on eight thinkers, including Foucault, Kuhn, Althusser, and Lévi-Strauss.

Skocpol, Theda. 1979. *States and Social Relations: A Comparative Analysis of France, Russia, and China.* Cambridge: Cambridge University Press. A comparative study of social revolutions that examines alternative theory, causes of social revolutions, and the outcomes of social revolutions in three countries.

Smith, Anthony D. 1983. *Theories of Nationalism.* New York: Holmes and Meier Publishers. An overview and critique of theories of nationalism, including relevant comparative politics literature. Early chapters explore theories of nationalism as related to modernization, anticolonialism, and industrialization; later chapters identify definitions, typologies, and varieties of nationalism.

Sternberg, David. 1981. *How to Complete and Survive a Doctoral Dissertation.* New York: St. Martin's Press. A useful guide for doctoral students that identifies obstacles in graduate work and how to overcome them and move on to a professional career with a Ph.D. in hand.

Stewart, William S. 1988. *Understanding Politics: The Cultures of Societies and the Structures of Governments.* Novato, California: Chandler and Sharp Publishers. Culture becomes a foundation to examine governmental structure through Tory corporatism, oligarchy, classical liberalism, radical liberalism, democratic socialism, Leninist socialism, and fascist corporatism.

Stokes, Geoff. 1990. "Towards the Good and Rational Life: Method and Value in the Crisis of Political Theory." *International Political Science Review* 11 (1), 45–57. Argues that the legacy of positivism has limited the scope of political theory and that "political theorists will need to engage in systematic critique informed by a conception of the good life."

Tilly, Charles (ed.). 1975. *The Formation of National States in Europe.* Princeton: Princeton University Press. A collection of essays on the origins and evolution of nation-states.

———. 1978. *From Mobilization to Revolution.* Reading, Massachusetts: Addison-Wesley Publishing. An imaginative study of collective action, based on examples and data of European and American experience. Examines competing theories of collective action; presents a set of concepts and models for analysis; focuses on conflict, repression, and struggles for power; looks at specific forms of collective action; turns to violence; and assesses rebellions and revolutions.

Verba, Sidney, Norman H. Nie, and Jae-on Kim. 1978. *Participation and Political Equality: A Seven-Nation Comparison.* New York: Cambridge University Press. Chicago: Chicago University Press. Replicates some portions of the earlier *Civic Culture* study but extends it with new questions focused on citizen involvement in political life in Austria, India, Nigeria, Japan, Netherlands, Yugoslavia, and the United States.

Wallerstein, Immanuel. 1974, 1980, and 1989. *The Modern World-System.* Vol. 1: *Capitalist Agriculture and the Origins of the European World-Economy in the Sixteenth Century.* Vol. 2: *Mercantilism and the Consolidation of the European World-Economy, 1600–1750.* Vol. 3: *The Second Era of the Great Expansion of the Capitalist World-Economy, 1730–1840s.* San